Alzheimer Disease

SOURCEBOOK

Sixth Edition

Health Reference Series

Sixth Edition

Alzheimer Disease

SOURCEBOOK

Basic Consumer Health Information about Alzheimer Disease and Other Forms of Dementia, Including Mild Cognitive Impairment, Corticobasal Degeneration, Dementia with Lewy Bodies, and Vascular Dementia, Dementia Caused by Infections, and Other Health Conditions That Cause Dementia

Along with Information about Recent Research on the Diagnosis and Prevention of Alzheimer Disease and Genetic Testing, Tips for Maintaining Cognitive Functioning, Strategies for Long-Term Planning, Advice for Caregivers, a Glossary of Related Terms, and Directories of Resources for Additional Help and Information

OMNIGRAPHICS

615 Griswold, Ste. 901, Detroit, MI 48226

Bibliographic Note

Because this page cannot legibly accommodate all the copyright notices, the Bibliographic Note portion of the Preface constitutes an extension of the copyright notice.

* * *

Omnigraphics, Inc.

Editorial Services provided by Omnigraphics, Inc., a division of Relevant Information, LLC

Keith Jones, *Managing Editor*

* * *

Copyright © 2016 Relevant Information, LLC

ISBN 978-0-7808-1470-7

E-ISBN 978-0-7808-1469-1

Library of Congress Cataloging-in-Publication Data

Names: Omnigraphics, Inc.

Title: Alzheimer disease sourcebook : basic consumer health information about alzheimer disease and other forms of dementia, including mild cognitive impairment, corticobasal degeneration, dementia with lewy bodies, frontotemporal dementia, huntington disease, parkinson disease, and vascular dementia; along with information about recent research on the diagnosis and prevention of alzheimer disease and genetic testing, tips for maintaining cognitive functioning, strategies for long-term planning, advice for caregivers, a glossary of related terms, and directories of resources for additional help and information.

Description: Sixth edition. | Detroit, MI : Omnigraphics, Inc., [2016] | Includes bibliographical references and index.

Identifiers: LCCN 2016002343 (print) | LCCN 2016003085 (ebook) | ISBN 9780780814707 (hardcover: alk. paper) | ISBN 9780780814691 (ebook)

Subjects: LCSH: Alzheimer's disease--Popular works. | Dementia--Popular works.

Classification: LCC RC523.2 .A45 2016 (print) | LCC RC523.2 (ebook) | DDC 616.8/31--dc23

LC record available at http://lccn.loc.gov/2016002343

Table of Contents

Part IV: Recognizing, Diagnosing, and Treating Symptoms of Alzheimer Disease and Dementias

Part V: Living with Alzheimer Disease and Dementias

Part VI: Caregiver Concerns

Part VII: Additional Help and Information

Preface

About This Book

More than 5.3 million Americans experience the progressive, incurable, fatal brain disorder known as Alzheimer disease (AD). AD, which accounts for between 50% and 80% of all cases of dementia, destroys brain cells, causes memory loss and confusion, and worsens over time until patients eventually lose the ability to work, walk, and communicate. Each year, Americans spend $216 billion caring for people with AD. In addition, 17.9 million unpaid caregivers—mostly family members and loved ones—offer assistance to AD patients.

Alzheimer Disease Sourcebook, Sixth Edition, provides updated information about causes, symptoms, and stages of AD and other forms of dementia, including mild cognitive impairment, corticobasal degeneration, dementia with Lewy bodies, frontotemporal dementia, Huntington disease, Parkinson disease, and dementia caused by infections. It discusses the structure of the brain, how it changes with age, and the cognitive decline and degeneration that occur in dementia. Facts about genetic testing, cognitive and behavioral symptoms, AD clinical trials, and recent research efforts are also included, along with information about legal, financial, and medical planning and coping strategies for caregivers. The book concludes with a glossary of related terms and directories of resources.

How to Use This Book

This book is divided into parts and chapters. Parts focus on broad areas of interest. Chapters are devoted to single topics within a part.

Part I: Facts about the Brain and Cognitive Decline provides information about healthy brain function and examines changes in cognitive functions and memory that occur during the typical aging process. Facts about the types, symptoms, causes, risk factors, and prevalence of dementia—a brain disorder that significantly impairs intellectual functions—are also included.

Part II: Alzheimer Disease (AD): The Most Common Type of Dementia discusses Alzheimer disease (AD), an irreversible and progressive brain disease and identifies the signs, symptoms, and diagnostic stages of this disorder. Information about the role that genetics, brain injuries, weight, and substance abuse play in the development of AD is also presented, along with facts about younger-onset AD, a form of the disease that affects people under the age of 65. It also discusses the factors that influence AD risk, such as alcohol and nicotine.

Part III: Other Dementia Disorders identifies types, signs, and symptoms of dementia other than AD, including mild cognitive impairment, corticobasal degeneration, dementia with Lewy bodies, frontotemporal disorders, Huntington disease, Parkinson disease, and vascular dementia. It details various causes of dementia, such as AIDS, cancer, delirium, and other diseases.

Part IV: Recognizing, Diagnosing, and Treating Symptoms of Alzheimer Disease and Dementias explains neurocognitive and imaging tools used to assess and diagnose dementia, such as positron emission tomography, single photon emission computed tomography, magnetic resonance imaging, and biomarker testing. Interventions used to manage AD and other dementias, such as medications for cognitive and behavioral changes, are identified, and information about participating in AD clinical trials and studies is included. An explanation of recent developments in AD research is also provided.

Part V: Living with Alzheimer Disease and Dementias describes strategies for maintaining health and wellness after a dementia diagnosis. Patients and caregivers will find information about nutrition, exercises, and dental care for dementia patients, tips on telling someone about the diagnosis, strategies for slowing the rate of cognitive decline, and advice on pain, sleep problems, and sexuality in people with dementia.Alternative medicine therapies for cognitive functions are also discussed. Information about Medicare and financial, legal, and health care planning is included.

Part VI: Caregiver Concerns offers advice to those who care for people with AD or dementia. Strategies for coping with challenging behaviors, communicating, and planning daily activities for someone with dementia are discussed, along with tips on creating a safe environment at home. Caregivers struggling to control frustration and cope with fatigue will find information about respite, home health, and nursing home care, as well as suggestions on evaluating difficult health decisions near the end of life.

Part VII: Additional Help and Information provides a glossary of terms related to AD and dementia and a directory of organizations that provide health information about AD and dementia. A list of the Alzheimer Disease Resource Centers across the United States is also included.

Bibliographic Note

This volume contains documents and excerpts from publications issued by the following U.S. government agencies: Administration for Community Living (ACL); Administration on Aging (AOA); Centers for Disease Control and Prevention (CDC); Centers for Medicare and Medicaid Services (CMS); National Cancer Institute (NCI); National Center for Complementary and Integrative Health (NCCIH); National Institute of Biomedical Imaging and Bioengineering (NIBIB); National Institute of Diabetes and Digestive and Kidney Diseases (NIDDK); National Institute of Neurological Disorders and Stroke (NINDS); National Institute on Aging (NIA); National Institute on Alcohol Abuse and Alcoholism (NIAAA); National Institutes of Health (NIH); Office of the Surgeon General; U.S. Department of Health and Human Services (HHS); and U.S. Department of Veterans Affairs (VA).

About the Health Reference Series

The *Health Reference Series* is designed to provide basic medical information for patients, families, caregivers, and the general public. Each volume takes a particular topic and provides comprehensive coverage. This is especially important for people who may be dealing with a newly diagnosed disease or a chronic disorder in themselves or in a family member. People looking for preventive guidance, information about disease warning signs, medical statistics, and risk factors for health problems will also find answers to their questions in the *Health Reference Series*. The *Series*, however, is not intended to serve as a tool for diagnosing illness, in prescribing treatments, or as a substitute for the physician/patient relationship. All people concerned about medical symptoms or the possibility of disease are encouraged to seek professional care from an appropriate health care provider.

A Note about Spelling and Style

Health Reference Series editors use *Stedman's Medical Dictionary* as an authority for questions related to the spelling of medical terms and the *Chicago Manual of Style* for questions related to grammatical structures, punctuation, and other editorial concerns. Consistent adherence is not always possible, however, because the individual volumes within the *Series* include many documents from a wide variety of different producers, and the editor's primary goal is to present material from each source as accurately as is possible. This sometimes means that information in different chapters or sections may follow other guidelines and alternate spelling authorities.

Medical Review

Omnigraphics contracts with a team of qualified, senior medical professionals who serve as medical consultants for the *Health Reference Series*. As necessary, medical consultants review reprinted and originally written material for currency and accuracy. Citations including the phrase, "Reviewed (month, year)" indicate material reviewed by this team. Medical consultation services are provided to the *Health Reference Series* editors by:

Dr. Vijayalakshmi, MBBS, DGO, MD
Dr. Senthil Selvan, MBBS, DCH, MD

Our Advisory Board

We would like to thank the following board members for providing initial guidance on the development of this series:

- Dr. Lynda Baker, Associate Professor of Library and Information Science, Wayne State University, Detroit, MI

- Nancy Bulgarelli, William Beaumont Hospital Library, Royal Oak, MI

- Karen Imarisio, Bloomfield Township Public Library, Bloomfield Township, MI

- Karen Morgan, Mardigian Library, University of Michigan-Dearborn, Dearborn, MI

- Rosemary Orlando, St. Clair Shores Public Library, St. Clair Shores, MI

Health Reference Series *Update Policy*

The inaugural book in the *Health Reference Series* was the first edition of *Cancer Sourcebook* published in 1989. Since then, the *Series* has been enthusiastically received by librarians and in the medical community. In order to maintain the standard of providing high-quality health information for the layperson the editorial staff at Omnigraphics felt it was necessary to implement a policy of updating volumes when warranted.

Medical researchers have been making tremendous strides, and it is the purpose of the *Health Reference Series* to stay current with the most recent advances. Each decision to update a volume is made on an individual basis. Some of the considerations include how much new information is available and the feedback we receive from people who use the books. If there is a topic you would like to see added to the update list, or an area of medical concern you feel has not been adequately addressed, please write to:

Managing Editor
Health Reference Series
Omnigraphics, Inc.
615 Griswold, Ste. 901
Detroit, MI 48226

Part One

Facts about the Brain and Cognitive Decline

Chapter 1

Basics of a Healthy Brain

Introduction

The brain is the most complex part of the human body. This three-pound organ is the seat of intelligence, interpreter of the senses, initiator of body movement, and controller of behavior. Lying in its bony shell and washed by protective fluid, the brain is the source of all the qualities that define our humanity. The brain is the crown jewel of the human body.

For centuries, scientists and philosophers have been fascinated by the brain, but until recently they viewed the brain as nearly incomprehensible. Now, however, the brain is beginning to relinquish its secrets. Scientists have learned more about the brain in the last 10 years than in all previous centuries because of the accelerating pace of research in neurological and behavioral science and the development of new research techniques. As a result, Congress named the 1990s the *Decade of the Brain*. At the forefront of research on the brain and other elements of the nervous system is the National Institute of Neurological Disorders and Stroke (NINDS), which conducts and supports scientific studies in the United States and around the world.

Architecture of the Brain

The brain is like a committee of experts. All the parts of the brain work together, but each part has its own special properties. The brain

Text in this chapter is excerpted from "Brain Basics: Know Your Brain," National Institute of Neurological Disorders and Stroke (NINDS), April 17, 2015.

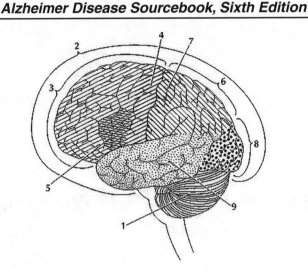

Figure 1.1. *Human Brain*

can be divided into three basic units: the **forebrain**, the **midbrain**, and the **hindbrain.**

The hindbrain includes the upper part of the spinal cord, the brain stem, and a wrinkled ball of tissue called the **cerebellum (1)**. The hindbrain controls the body's vital functions such as respiration and heart rate. The cerebellum coordinates movement and is involved in learned rote movements. When you play the piano or hit a tennis ball you are activating the cerebellum. The uppermost part of the brainstem is the midbrain, which controls some reflex actions and is part of the circuit involved in the control of eye movements and other voluntary movements. The forebrain is the largest and most highly developed part of the human brain: it consists primarily of the **cerebrum (2)** and the structures hidden beneath it.

When people see pictures of the brain it is usually the cerebrum that they notice. The cerebrum sits at the top most part of the brain and is the source of intellectual activities. It holds your memories, allows you to plan, enables you to imagine and think. It allows you to recognize friends, read books, and play games.

The cerebrum is split into two halves (hemispheres) by a deep fissure. Despite the split, the two cerebral hemispheres communicate with each other through a thick tract of nerve fibers that lies at the base of this fissure. Although the two hemispheres seem to be mirror images of each other, they are different. For instance, the ability to form words seems to lie primarily in the left hemisphere, while the right hemisphere seems to control many abstract reasoning skills.

For some as-yet-unknown reason, nearly all of the signals from the brain to the body and vice-versa crossover on their way to and from the brain. This means that the right cerebral hemisphere primarily controls the left side of the body and the left hemisphere primarily controls the right side. When one side of the brain is damaged, the opposite side of the body is affected. For example, a stroke in the right hemisphere of the brain can leave the left arm and leg paralyzed.

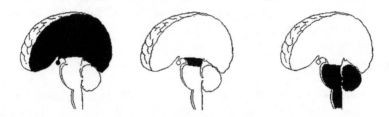

Figure 1.2. *Forebrain, Midbrain, and Hindbrain*

Geography of Thought

Each cerebral hemisphere can be divided into sections, or lobes, each of which specializes in different functions. To understand each lobe and its specialty we will take a tour of the cerebral hemispheres, starting with the two **frontal lobes** (**3**), which lie directly behind the forehead. When you plan a schedule, imagine the future, or use reasoned arguments, these two lobes do much of the work. One of the ways the frontal lobes seem to do these things is by acting as short-term storage sites, allowing one idea to be kept in mind while other ideas are considered. In the rearmost portion of each frontal lobe is a **motor area** (**4**), which helps control voluntary movement. A nearby place on the left frontal lobe called **Broca's area** (**5**) allows thoughts to be transformed into words.

When you enjoy a good meal—the taste, aroma, and texture of the food—two sections behind the frontal lobes called the **parietal lobes** (**6**) are at work. The forward parts of these lobes, just behind the motor areas, are the primary **sensory areas** (**7**). These areas receive information about temperature, taste, touch, and movement from the rest of the body. Reading and arithmetic are also functions in the repertoire of each parietal lobe.

As you look at the words and pictures on this page, two areas at the back of the brain are at work. These lobes, called the **occipital**

lobes (8), process images from the eyes and link that information with images stored in memory. Damage to the occipital lobes can cause blindness.

The last lobes on our tour of the cerebral hemispheres are the **temporal lobes (9)**, which lie in front of the visual areas and nest under the parietal and frontal lobes. Whether you appreciate symphonies or rock music, your brain responds through the activity of these lobes. At the top of each temporal lobe is an area responsible for receiving information from the ears. The underside of each temporal lobe plays a crucial role in forming and retrieving memories, including those associated with music. Other parts of this lobe seem to integrate memories and sensations of taste, sound, sight, and touch.

Cerebral Cortex

Coating the surface of the cerebrum and the cerebellum is a vital layer of tissue the thickness of a stack of two or three dimes. It is called the cortex, from the Latin word for bark. Most of the actual information processing in the brain takes place in the cerebral cortex. When people talk about "gray matter" in the brain they are talking about this thin rind. The cortex is gray because nerves in this area lack the insulation that makes most other parts of the brain appear to be white. The folds in the brain add to its surface area and therefore increase the amount of gray matter and the quantity of information that can be processed.

Inner Brain

Deep within the brain, hidden from view, lie structures that are the gatekeepers between the spinal cord and the cerebral hemispheres. These structures not only determine our emotional state, they also modify our perceptions and responses depending on that state, and allow us to initiate movements that you make without thinking about them. Like the lobes in the cerebral hemispheres, the structures described below come in pairs: each is duplicated in the opposite half of the brain.

The **hypothalamus (10)**, about the size of a pearl, directs a multitude of important functions. It wakes you up in the morning, and gets the adrenaline flowing during a test or job interview. The hypothalamus is also an important emotional center, controlling the molecules that make you feel exhilarated, angry, or unhappy. Near the hypothalamus lies the **thalamus (11)**, a major clearinghouse for information going to and from the spinal cord and the cerebrum.

An arching tract of nerve cells leads from the hypothalamus and the thalamus to the **hippocampus (12)**. This tiny nub acts as a memory indexer—sending memories out to the appropriate part of the cerebral hemisphere for long-term storage and retrieving them when necessary. The **basal ganglia** are clusters of nerve cells surrounding the thalamus. They are responsible for initiating and integrating movements. Parkinson disease, which results in tremors, rigidity, and a stiff, shuffling walk, is a disease of nerve cells that lead into the basal ganglia.

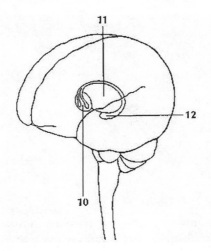

Figure 1.3. *Inner Brain*

Making Connections

The brain and the rest of the nervous system are composed of many different types of cells, but the primary functional unit is a cell called the neuron. All sensations, movements, thoughts, memories, and feelings are the result of signals that pass through neurons. Neurons consist of three parts. The **cell body (13)** contains the nucleus, where most of the molecules that the neuron needs to survive and function are manufactured. **Dendrites (14)** extend out from the cell body like the branches of a tree and receive messages from other nerve cells. Signals then pass from the dendrites through the cell body and may travel away from the cell body down an **axon (15)** to another neuron, a muscle cell, or cells in some other organ. The neuron is usually surrounded by many support cells. Some types of cells wrap around the axon to form an insulating **sheath (16)**. This sheath can include a fatty molecule called myelin, which provides insulation for the axon and helps nerve signals travel faster and farther. Axons may be very short, such as those that carry signals from one cell in the cortex to another cell less than a hair's width away. Or axons may be very long, such as those that carry messages from the brain all the way down the spinal cord.

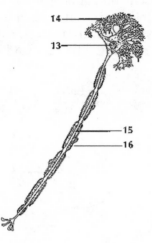

Figure 1.4. *Neuron*

Scientists have learned a great deal about neurons by studying the synapse—the place where a signal passes from the neuron to another cell. When the signal reaches the end of the axon it stimulates the release of tiny **sacs (17)**. These sacs release chemicals known as **neurotransmitters (18)** into the **synapse (19)**. The neurotransmitters cross the synapse and attach to **receptors (20)** on the neighboring

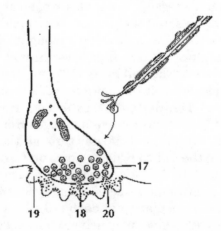

Figure 1.5. *Synapse*

cell. These receptors can change the properties of the receiving cell. If the receiving cell is also a neuron, the signal can continue the transmission to the next cell.

Some Key Neurotransmitters at Work

Acetylcholine is called an *excitatory neurotransmitter* because it generally makes cells more excitable. It governs muscle contractions and causes glands to secrete hormones. Alzheimer disease, which initially affects memory formation, is associated with a shortage of acetylcholine.

GABA (gamma-aminobutyric acid) is called an inhibitory neurotransmitter because it tends to make cells less excitable. It helps control muscle activity and is an important part of the visual system. Drugs that increase GABA levels in the brain are used to treat epileptic seizures and tremors in patients with Huntington disease.

Serotonin is a neurotransmitter that constricts blood vessels and brings on sleep. It is also involved in temperature regulation. Dopamine is an inhibitory neurotransmitter involved in mood and the control of complex movements. The loss of dopamine activity in some portions of the brain leads to the muscular rigidity of Parkinson disease. Many medications used to treat behavioral disorders work by modifying the action of dopamine in the brain.

Neurological Disorders

When the brain is healthy it functions quickly and automatically. But when problems occur, the results can be devastating. Some 50 million people in this country—one in five—suffer from damage to the nervous system. The NINDS supports research on more than 600 neurological diseases. Some of the major types of disorders include: neurogenetic diseases (such as Huntington disease and muscular dystrophy), developmental disorders (such as cerebral palsy), degenerative diseases of adult life (such as Parkinson disease and Alzheimer disease), metabolic diseases (such as Gaucher disease), cerebrovascular diseases (such as stroke and vascular dementia), trauma (such as spinal cord and head injury), convulsive disorders (such as epilepsy), infectious diseases (such as AIDS dementia), and brain tumors.

Chapter 2

The Changing Brain in Healthy Aging

In the past several decades, investigators have learned much about what happens in the brain when people have a neurodegenerative disease such as Parkinson disease, AD, or other dementias. Their findings also have revealed much about what happens during healthy aging. Researchers are investigating a number of changes related to healthy aging in hopes of learning more about this process so they can fill gaps in our knowledge about the early stages of AD.

As a person gets older, changes occur in all parts of the body, including the brain:

- Certain parts of the brain shrink, especially the prefrontal cortex (an area at the front of the frontal lobe) and the hippocampus. Both areas are important to learning, memory, planning, and other complex mental activities.

- Changes in neurons and neurotransmitters affect communication between neurons. In certain brain regions, communication between neurons can be reduced because white matter (myelin-covered axons) is degraded or lost.

Text in this chapter is excerpted from "Alzheimer's Disease: Unraveling the Mystery," National Institute on Aging (NIA), January 22, 2015.

- Changes in the brain's blood vessels occur. Blood flow can be reduced because arteries narrow and less growth of new capillaries occurs.

- In some people, structures called plaques and tangles develop outside of and inside neurons, respectively, although in much smaller amounts than in AD.

- Damage by **free radicals** increases (free radicals are a kind of molecule that reacts easily with other molecules).

- Inflammation increases (inflammation is the complex process that occurs when the body responds to an injury, disease, or abnormal situation).

What effects does aging have on mental function in healthy older people?

Some people may notice a modest decline in their ability to learn new things and retrieve information, such as remembering names. They may perform worse on complex tasks of attention, learning, and memory than would a younger person. However, if given enough time to perform the task, the scores of healthy people in their 70s and 80s are often similar to those of young adults. In fact, as they age, adults often improve in other cognitive areas, such as vocabulary and other forms of verbal knowledge.

It also appears that additional brain regions can be activated in older adults during cognitive tasks, such as taking a memory test. Researchers do not fully understand why this happens, but one idea is that the brain engages mechanisms to compensate for difficulties that certain regions may be having. For example, the brain may recruit alternate brain networks in order to perform a task. These findings have led many scientists to believe that major declines in mental abilities are not inevitable as people age. Growing evidence of the adaptive (what scientists call "plastic") capabilities of the older brain provide hope that people may be able to do things to sustain good brain function as they age. A variety of interacting factors, such as lifestyle, overall health, environment, and genetics also may play a role.

Another question that scientists are asking is why some people remain cognitively healthy as they get older while others develop cognitive impairment or dementia. The concept of "cognitive reserve" may provide some insights. Cognitive reserve refers to the brain's ability to operate effectively even when some function is disrupted. It also refers to the amount of damage that the brain can sustain before changes in cognition are evident. People vary in the cognitive reserve they have, and this variability may be because of differences in genetics, education, occupation, lifestyle, leisure activities, or other life experiences. These factors could provide a certain amount of tolerance and ability to adapt to change and damage that occurs during aging. At some point, depending on a person's cognitive reserve and unique mix of genetics, environment, and life experiences, the balance may tip in favor of a disease process that will ultimately lead to dementia. For another person, with a different reserve and a different mix of genetics, environment, and life experiences, the balance may result in no apparent decline in cognitive function with age.

Scientists are increasingly interested in the influence of all these factors on brain health, and studies are revealing some clues about actions people can take that may help preserve healthy brain aging. Fortunately, these actions also benefit a person's overall health. They include:

- Controlling risk factors for chronic disease, such as heart disease and diabetes (for example, keeping blood cholesterol and blood pressure at healthy levels and maintaining a healthy weight)

- Enjoying regular exercise and physical activity

- Eating a healthy diet that includes plenty of vegetables and fruits

- Engaging in intellectually stimulating activities and maintaining close social ties with family, friends, and community

Chapter 3

Understanding Memory Loss

Introduction

We've all forgotten a name, where we put our keys, or if we locked the front door. It's normal to forget things once in awhile. However, forgetting how to make change, use the telephone, or find your way home may be signs of a more serious memory problem.

Differences between Mild Forgetfulness and More Serious Memory Problems

What Is Mild Forgetfulness?

It is true that some of us get more forgetful as we age. It may take longer to learn new things, remember certain words, or find our glasses. These changes are often signs of mild forgetfulness, not serious memory problems.

See your doctor if you're worried about your forgetfulness. Tell him or her about your concerns. Be sure to make a follow-up appointment to check your memory in the next 6 months to a year. If you think you might forget, ask a family member, friend, or the doctor's office to remind you.

Text in this chapter is excerpted from "Understanding Memory Loss," National Institute on Aging (NIA), October 2015.

What Can I Do about Mild Forgetfulness?

You can do many things to help keep your memory sharp and stay alert.

Here are some ways to help your memory:

- Learn a new skill.
- Volunteer in your community, at a school, or at your place of worship.
- Spend time with friends and family.
- Use memory tools such as big calendars, to-do lists, and notes to yourself.
- Put your wallet or purse, keys, and glasses in the same place each day.
- Get lots of rest.
- Exercise and eat well.
- Don't drink a lot of alcohol.
- Get help if you feel depressed for weeks at a time

What Is a Serious Memory Problem?

Serious memory problems make it hard to do everyday things. For example, you may find it hard to drive, shop, or even talk with a friend. Signs of serious memory problems may include:

- asking the same questions over and over again
- getting lost in places you know well
- not being able to follow directions
- becoming more confused about time, people, and places
- not taking care of yourself—eating poorly, not bathing, or being unsafe

What Can I Do about Serious Memory Problems?

See your doctor if you are having any of the problems listed above. It's important to find out what might be causing a serious memory problem. Once you know the cause, you can get the right treatment.

Serious Memory Problems—Causes and Treatments

Many things can cause serious memory problems, such as blood clots, depression, and **Alzheimer disease**. Read below to learn more about causes and treatments of serious memory problems.

Medical Conditions

Certain medical conditions can cause serious memory problems. These problems should go away once you get treatment. Some medical conditions that may cause memory problems are:

- bad reaction to certain medicines
- depression
- not eating enough healthy foods, or too few vitamins and minerals in your body
- drinking too much alcohol
- blood clots or tumors in the brain
- head injury, such as a concussion from a fall or accident
- thyroid, kidney, or liver problems

Treatment for Medical Conditions

These medical conditions are serious. See your doctor for treatment.

Emotional Problems

Some emotional problems in older people can cause serious memory problems. Feeling sad, lonely, worried, or bored can cause you to be confused and forgetful.

Treatment for emotional problems

- You may need to see a doctor or counselor for treatment. Once you get help, your memory problems should get better.
- Being active, spending more time with family and friends, and learning new skills also can help you feel better and improve your memory.

Mild Cognitive Impairment

As some people grow older, they have more memory problems than other people their age. This condition is called **mild cognitive**

17

impairment, or MCI. People with MCI can take care of themselves and do their normal activities. MCI memory problems may include:

- losing things often

- forgetting to go to events or appointments

- having more trouble coming up with words than other people of the same age

Your doctor can do thinking, memory, and language tests to see if you have MCI. He or she also may suggest that you see a specialist for more tests. Because MCI may be an early sign of Alzheimer disease, it's really important to see your doctor or specialist every 6 to 12 months.

Treatment for MCI

- At this time, there is no proven treatment for MCI. Your doctor can check to see if you have any changes in your memory or thinking skills over time.

- You may want to try to keep your memory sharp.

Alzheimer Disease

Alzheimer disease causes serious memory problems. The signs of Alzheimer disease begin slowly and get worse over time. This is because changes in the brain cause large numbers of brain cells to die.

It may look like simple forgetfulness at first, but over time, people with Alzheimer disease have trouble thinking clearly. They find it hard to do everyday things like shopping, driving, and cooking. As the illness gets worse, people with Alzheimer disease may need someone to take care of all their needs at home or in a nursing home. These needs may include feeding, bathing, and dressing.

Treatment for Alzheimer disease

- Taking certain medicines can help a person in the early or middle stages of Alzheimer disease. These medicines can keep symptoms, such as memory loss, from getting worse for a time. The medicines can have side effects and may not work for everyone. Talk with your doctor about side effects or other concerns you may have.

- Other medicines can help if you are worried, depressed, or having problems sleeping.

Vascular Dementia

Many people have never heard of **vascular dementia**. Like Alzheimer disease, it is a medical condition that causes serious memory problems. Unlike Alzheimer disease, signs of vascular dementia may appear suddenly. This is because the memory loss and confusion are caused by strokes or changes in the blood supply to the brain. If the strokes stop, you may get better or stay the same for a long time. If you have more strokes, you may get worse.

Treatment for vascular dementia

You can take steps to lower your chances of having more strokes. These steps include:

- Control your high blood pressure.

- Treat your high cholesterol.

- Take care of your diabetes.

- Stop smoking.

Help for Serious Memory Problems

What Can I Do If I'm Worried about My Memory?

See your doctor. If your doctor thinks your memory problems are serious, you may need to have a complete health check-up. The doctor will review your medicines and may test your blood and urine. You also may need to take tests that check your memory, problem solving, counting, and language skills.

In addition, the doctor may suggest a **brain scan**. Pictures from the scan can show normal and problem areas in the brain. Once the doctor finds out what is causing your memory problems, ask about the best treatment for you.

What Can Family Members Do to Help?

If your family member or friend has a serious memory problem, you can help the person live as normal a life as possible. You can help the person stay active, go places, and keep up everyday routines. You can remind the person of the time of day, where he or she lives, and what is happening at home and in the world. You also can help the person remember to take medicine or visit the doctor.

19

Some families use the following things to help with memory problems:

- big calendars to highlight important dates and events
- lists of the plans for each day
- notes about safety in the home
- written directions for using common household items (most people with Alzheimer disease can still read)

Chapter 4

Dementia and Its Types

Introduction

Alzheimer disease (AD) is the most common form of dementia in those over the age of 65. As many as 5 million Americans age 65 and older may have AD, and that number is expected to double for every 5-year interval beyond age 65. But AD is only one of many dementia disorders; an estimated 20 to 40 percent of people with dementia have some other form of the disorder. Among all people with dementia, many are believed to have a mixed type of dementia that can involve more than one of the disorders.

Age is the primary risk factor for developing dementia. For that reason, the number of people living with dementia could double in the next 40 years with an increase in the number of Americans who are age 65 or older—from 40 million today to more than 88 million in 2050. Regardless of the form of dementia, the personal, economic, and societal demands can be devastating.

Research over the past 30 years has helped us learn more about dementia—possible causes, who is at risk, and how it develops and affects the brain. This work offers the hope of better drugs and treatments for these disorders.

Text in this chapter is excerpted from "The Dementias, Hope through Research," National Institute of Neurological Disorders and Stroke (NINDS), November 2, 2015.

Basics of Dementia

Dementia is the loss of cognitive functioning, which means the loss of the ability to think, remember, or reason, as well as behavioral abilities, to such an extent that it interferes with a person's daily life and activities. Signs and symptoms of dementia result when once-healthy neurons (nerve cells) in the brain stop working, lose connections with other brain cells, and die. While everyone loses some neurons as they age, people with dementia experience far greater loss.

Researchers are still trying to understand the underlying disease processes involved in the disorders. Scientists have some theories about mechanisms that may lead to different forms of dementias, but more research is needed to better understand if and how these mechanisms contribute to the development of dementia.

While dementia is more common with advanced age (as many as half of all people age 85 or older may have some form of dementia), it is not a normal part of aging. Many people live into their 90s and beyond without any signs of dementia.

Memory loss, though common, is not the only sign of dementia. For a person to be considered to have dementia, he or she must meet the following criteria:

- Two or more core mental functions must be impaired. These functions include memory, language skills, visual perception, and the ability to focus and pay attention. These also include cognitive skills such as the ability to reason and solve problems.

- The loss of brain function is severe enough that a person cannot do normal, everyday tasks.

In addition, some people with dementia cannot control their emotions. Their personalities may change. They can have delusions, which are strong beliefs without proof, such as the idea that someone is stealing from them. They also may hallucinate, seeing or otherwise experiencing things that are not real.

Types of Dementia

Various disorders and factors contribute to the development of dementia. Neurodegenerative disorders such as AD, frontotemporal disorders, and Lewy body dementia result in a progressive and irreversible loss of neurons and brain functions. Currently, there are no cures for these progressive neurodegenerative disorders.

However, other types of dementia can be halted or even reversed with treatment. Normal pressure hydrocephalus, for example, often resolves when excess cerebrospinal fluid in the brain is drained via a shunt and rerouted elsewhere in the body. Cerebral vasculitis responds to aggressive treatment with immunosuppressive drugs. In rare cases, treatable infectious disorders can cause dementia. Some drugs, vitamin deficiencies, alcohol abuse, depression, and brain tumors can cause neurological deficits that resemble dementia. Most of these causes respond to treatment.

Some types of dementia disorders are described below.

Tauopathies

In some dementias, a protein called tau clumps together inside nerve cells in the brain, causing the cells to stop functioning properly and die. Disorders that are associated with an accumulation of tau are called tauopathies.

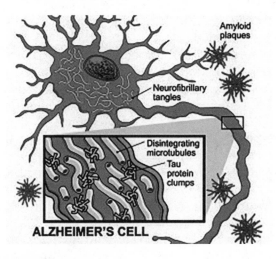

Figure 4.1. *Tauopathies*

In AD, the tau protein becomes twisted and aggregates to form bundles, called neurofibrillary tangles, inside the neurons. Abnormal clumps (plaques) of another protein, called amyloid, are prominent in spaces between brain cells and are a hallmark of the disease. Both plaques and tangles are thought to contribute to reduced function and nerve-cell death in AD, but scientists do not fully understand this relationship. It is not clear, for example, if the plaques and tangles cause the disorder, or if their presence flags some other process that leads to neuronal death in AD.

23

Other types of tauopathies include the following disorders:

Corticobasal degeneration (CBD) is a progressive neurological disorder characterized by nerve-cell loss and atrophy (shrinkage) of specific areas of the brain, including the cerebral cortex and the basal ganglia. The disorder tends to progress gradually, with the onset of early symptoms around age 60. At first, one side of the body is affected more than the other side, but as the disease progresses both sides become impaired. An individual may have difficulty using one hand, or one's hand may develop an abnormal position.

Other signs and symptoms may include memory loss; trouble making familiar, focused movements (apraxia) such as brushing one's teeth; involuntary muscular jerks (myoclonus) and involuntary muscle contractions (dystonia); alien limb, in which the person feels as though a limb is being controlled by a force other than oneself; muscle rigidity (resistance to imposed movement); postural instability; and difficulty swallowing (dysphagia). People with CBD also may have visual-spatial problems that make it difficult to interpret visual information, such as the distance between objects.

There is no cure for CBD. Supportive therapies are available to reduce the burden of certain symptoms. For example, botulinum toxin can help control muscle contractions. Speech therapy and physical therapy may help one learn how to cope with daily activities.

Frontotemporal disorders (FTD) are caused by a family of brain diseases that primarily affect the frontal and temporal lobes of the brain; they account for up to 10 percent of all dementia cases. Some, but not all, forms of FTD are considered tauopathies. In some cases, FTD is associated with mutations in the gene for tau (MAPT), and tau aggregates are present. However, other forms of FTD are associated with aggregates of the protein TDP-43, a mutated protein found among people with a type of ALS that is inherited. Mutations in a protein called progranulin may also play a role in some TDP43-opathies.

In FTD, changes to nerve cells in the brain's frontal lobes affect the ability to reason and make decisions, prioritize and multitask, act appropriately, and control movement. Some people decline rapidly over 2 to 3 years, while others show only minimal changes for many years. People can live with frontotemporal disorders for 2 to 10 years, sometimes longer, but it is difficult to predict the time course for an affected individual. In some cases, FTD is associated with progressive neuromuscular weakness otherwise known as amyotrophic lateral sclerosis (ALS, or Lou Gehrig's disease). The signs and symptoms may vary greatly among individuals as different parts of the brain are affected. No treatment that can cure or reverse FTD is currently available.

Clinically, FTD is classified into two main types of syndromes:

- Behavioral variant frontotemporal dementia
- Primary progressive aphasia (PPA)

Other types of FTDs include:

- Frontotemporal dementia with parkinsonism linked to chromosome 17 (FTDP-17)
- Pick's disease

Progressive supranuclear palsy (PSP) is a rare brain disorder that damages the upper brain stem, including the substantia nigra (a movement control center in the midbrain). This region also is affected in Parkinson disease, which may explain an overlap in motor symptoms shared by these disorders. Eye movements are especially affected, causing slow and then limited mobility of the eye. The most common early signs and symptoms include loss of balance, unexplained falls, general body stiffness, apathy, and depression. A person with this type of dementia may suddenly laugh or cry very easily (known as pseudobulbar affect). As the disorder progresses, people develop blurred vision and a characteristic vacant stare that involves loss of facial expression. Speech usually becomes slurred, and swallowing solid foods or liquids becomes difficult. PSP gets progressively worse, but people can live a decade or more after the onset of symptoms. Dextromethorphan, a common ingredient in cough medicine, has been approved for the treatment of pseudobulbar affect.

Argyrophilic grain disease is a common, late-onset degenerative disease characterized by tau deposits called argyrophilic grains in brain regions involved in memory and emotion. The disease's signs and symptoms are indistinguishable from late-onset AD. Confirmation of the diagnosis can be made only at autopsy.

Synucleinopathies

In these brain disorders, a protein called alpha-synuclein accumulates inside neurons. Although it is not fully understood what role this protein plays, changes in the protein and/or its function have been linked to Parkinson disease and other disorders.

One type of synucleinopathy, **Lewy body dementia**, involves protein aggregates called Lewy bodies, balloon-like structures that form inside of nerve cells. The initial symptoms may vary, but over time, people with these disorders develop very similar cognitive, behavioral, physical, and sleep-related symptoms. Lewy body dementia is one of the most common causes of dementia, after Alzheimer disease and vascular disease. Types of Lewy body dementia include:

- *Dementia with Lewy bodies (DLB),* One of the more common forms of progressive dementia. Symptoms such as difficulty sleeping, loss of smell, and visual hallucinations often precede movement and other problems by as long as 10 years, which consequently results in DLB going unrecognized or misdiagnosed as a psychiatric disorder until its later stages. Neurons in the substantia nigra that produce dopamine die or become impaired, and the brain's outer layer (cortex) degenerates. Many neurons that remain contain Lewy bodies.

- *Parkinson disease dementia (PDD),* A clinical diagnosis related to DLB that can occur in people with Parkinson disease. PDD may affect memory, social judgment, language, or reasoning. Autopsy studies show that people with PDD often have amyloid plaques and tau tangles similar to those found in people with AD, though it is not understood what these similarities mean. A majority of people with Parkinson disease develop dementia, but the time from the onset of movement symptoms to the onset of dementia symptoms varies greatly from person to person.

Vascular Dementia and Vascular Cognitive Impairment

Vascular dementia and vascular cognitive impairment (VCI) are caused by injuries to the vessels supplying blood to the brain. These disorders can be caused by brain damage from multiple strokes or any injury to the small vessels carrying blood to the brain. Dementia risk can be significant even when individuals have suffered only small strokes. Vascular dementia and VCI arise as a result of risk factors that similarly increase the risk for cerebrovascular disease (stroke), including atrial fibrillation, hypertension, diabetes, and high cholesterol. Vascular dementia also has been associated with a condition called amyloid angiopathy, in which amyloid plaques accumulate in the blood-vessel walls, causing them to break down and rupture. Symptoms of vascular dementia and VCI can begin suddenly and progress or subside during one's lifetime.

Some types of vascular dementia include:

- Cerebral autosomal dominant arteriopathy with subcortical infarcts and leukoencephalopathy (CADASIL).

- Multi-infarct dementia.

- Subcortical vascular dementia, also called Binswanger's disease.

Mixed Dementia

Autopsy studies looking at the brains of people who had dementia suggest that a majority of those age 80 and older probably had "mixed dementia," caused by both AD-related neurodegenerative processes and vascular disease-related processes. In fact, some studies indicate that mixed vascular-degenerative dementia is the most common cause of dementia in the elderly. In a person with mixed dementia, it may not be clear exactly how many of a person's symptoms are due to AD or another type of dementia. In one study, approximately 40 percent of people who were thought to have AD were found after autopsy to also have some form of cerebrovascular disease. Several studies have found that many of the major risk factors for vascular disease also may be risk factors for AD.

Researchers are still working to understand how underlying disease processes in mixed dementia influence each other. It is not clear, for example, if symptoms are likely to be worse when a person has brain changes reflecting multiple types of dementia. Nor do we know if a person with multiple dementias can benefit from treating one type, for example, when a person with AD controls high blood pressure and other vascular disease risk factors.

Chapter 5

Dementia: Causes and Risk Factors

Conditions That Cause Dementia

Doctors have identified many other conditions that can cause dementia or dementia-like symptoms.

Brain Diseases

Creutzfeldt-Jakob disease (CJD). A rare brain disorder that affects about one in every million people worldwide each year, CJD belongs to a family of diseases known as the transmissible spongiform encephalopathies, or TSEs. Spongiform refers to the fact that the brain becomes filled with microscopic swellings that give the appearance of holes, like a sponge. CJD and other TSEs are believed to be caused by infectious proteins called prions that become misfolded. Scientists believe that the presence of misfolded prions can trigger normal proteins to misfold as well, causing a chain reaction. These abnormal prion proteins tend to clump together, which is believed to be related to the brain damage.

Symptoms usually begin after age 60, and most people die within a year of onset. In most cases, CJD occurs in people who have no known

Text in this chapter is excerpted from "The Dementias, Hope Through Research," National Institute of Neurological Disorders and Stroke (NINDS), November 2, 2015.

risk factors for the disease; however, an estimated 5 to 10 percent of cases in the United States are associated with genetic mutations. In addition, a type of CJD, called variant CJD (vCJD), has been found in Great Britain and several other European countries. vCJD has been observed to affect people who are younger than those with other forms of CJD and is believed to be caused by eating beef from cattle infected with a TSE called bovine spongiform encephalopathy, more commonly known as "mad cow disease." Inherited forms of CJD include:

- *Fatal familial insomnia.* This prion disease causes a part of the brain involved in sleep to slowly degenerate. People with the disease have trouble sleeping and may show signs of poor reflexes and hallucinations.

- *Gerstmann-Straussler-Scheinker disease.* Symptoms include a loss of coordination (ataxia) and dementia that begin when people are 50 to 60 years old.

Huntington disease. This hereditary disorder is caused by a faulty gene for a protein called huntingtin. Symptoms begin around age 30 or 40 years and include abnormal and uncontrollable movements called chorea, as well as gait changes and lack of coordination. Huntington disease may affect a person's judgment, memory, and other cognitive functions. As the disease progresses, these cognitive problems worsen, and motor difficulties lead to complete loss of ability for self-care. Children of people with Huntington have a 50 percent chance of having the disorder.

Secondary dementias. These dementias occur in people with disorders that damage brain tissue. Such disorders may include multiple sclerosis; meningitis; encephalitis; and Wilson's disease, in which excessive amounts of copper build up to cause brain damage. In rare cases, people with brain tumors may develop dementia because of damage to their brain circuits or a buildup of pressure inside the skull. Symptoms may include changes in personality, psychotic episodes, or problems with speech, language, thinking, and memory.

Head Injury

Chronic traumatic encephalopathy, initially known as dementia pugilistica, is caused by repeated traumatic brain injury (TBI), such as in boxers or in people who suffered multiple concussions while playing a contact sport. People with this condition often develop poor coordination, slurred speech, and other symptoms similar to those seen in Parkinson disease, along with dementia, 20 years or more after the TBI events. This form of dementia also is characterized by brain atrophy and widespread deposits of tau aggregates. In some individuals, even just 5 to 10 years beyond the TBI events, behavioral and mood changes may occur. Dementia may not yet be present and the brain may not have atrophied, but small focal deposits of tau are seen in the brain at autopsy.

Subdural hematoma, or bleeding between the brain's surface and its outer covering (the dura), is common in the elderly after a fall. Subdural hematomas can cause dementia-like symptoms and changes in mental function. With treatment, some symptoms can be reversed.

Reversible Dementias

Many conditions that cause dementia can be reversed with the appropriate treatment.

- Cerebral vasculitis, an inflammation and necrosis (tissue death) of blood vessel walls, can cause a form of dementia that may resolve when the person is treated with immune suppressants.

- Some studies have shown that people with depression are at increased risk of developing dementia. Severe depression can cause dementia and can be treated.

- Infections can cause confusion or delirium due to related fever or other side effects associated with the body's response to a foreign entity.

- Metabolic disorders of the nervous system, such as mitochondrial disorders, leukodystrophies, and lysosomal storage diseases, can lead to dementia.

- Metabolic problems and endocrine abnormalities such as thyroid problems, low blood sugar levels (called hypoglycemia), and low or high levels of sodium or calcium also may also cause dementia.

- Normal pressure hydrocephalus is an abnormal buildup of cerebro-spinal fluid in the brain. Elderly individuals with the condition usually have trouble with walking and bladder control before onset of dementia. Normal pressure hydrocephalus can be treated or even reversed by implanting a shunt system to divert fluid from the brain.

- Nutritional deficiencies of vitamin B1 (thiamine), caused by chronic alcoholism, and vitamin B12 deficiencies can be reversed with treatment.

- Paraneoplastic syndromes (a group of symptoms that may develop when substances released by some cancer cells disrupt the normal function of surrounding cells and tissue) can cause symptoms that resemble dementia. Such symptoms generally occur in people with cancer when the body's immune response to the cancer also ends up targeting proteins in the central nervous system. In many cases, the neurologic condition occurs before the cancer is detected. Circulating antibodies against brain proteins are common in both neurologic and cancer conditions.

- Side effects of medications or drug combinations may cause dementias that arise quickly or develop slowly over time.

Environmental Factors

Environmental factors may play a role in the development of certain types of dementia. This relationship is complex, however, since a person may carry genetic mutations that influence his or her response to environmental factors. Examples of environmental factors include:

Anoxia. Anoxia and a related condition, hypoxia, are terms often used to describe a state in which there is a curtailed supply of oxygen to an organ's tissues. Anoxia and hypoxia can lead to the loss of neurons and diffuse brain injury. Characteristics of the resulting dementia include confusion, personality changes, hallucinations, or memory loss. This type of dementia commonly occurs in people who survive cardiac arrest.

Poisoning. Exposure to lead, mercury, other heavy metals, or poisonous substances can lead to symptoms of dementia. These symptoms may or may not resolve after treatment, depending on how severely the brain is damaged.

Substance abuse. People who have abused substances such as alcohol and recreational drugs sometimes display signs of dementia even after the substance abuse has stopped. This condition is known as substance-induced persisting dementia.

Infectious Disease

HIV-associated dementia (HAD) can occur in people who are positive for the human immunodeficiency virus, the virus that causes AIDS. HAD damages the brain's white matter and leads to a type of dementia associated with memory problems, social withdrawal, and trouble concentrating. People with HAD may develop movement problems as well. The incidence of HAD has dropped dramatically with the availability of effective antiviral therapies for managing the underlying HIV infection.

Risk Factors for Dementia

The following risk factors can increase a person's chance of developing one or more kinds of dementia. Some of these factors can be modified, while others cannot.

- **Age.** The risk goes up with advanced age.

- **Alcohol use.** Most studies suggest that drinking large amounts of alcohol increases the risk of dementia, while drinking a moderate amount may be protective.

- **Atherosclerosis.** The accumulation of fats and cholesterol in the lining of arteries, coupled with an inflammatory process that leads to a thickening of the vessel walls (known as atherosclerosis), can hinder blood from getting to the brain, which can lead to stroke or another brain injury. For example, high levels of low-density lipoprotein (LDL, or "bad" cholesterol) can raise the risk for vascular dementia. High LDL levels also have been linked to AD.

- **Diabetes.** People with diabetes appear to have a higher risk for dementia, although the evidence for this association is modest. Poorly controlled diabetes, however, is a well-proven risk factor for stroke and cardiovascular disease-related events, which in turn increase the risk for vascular dementia.

- **Down syndrome**. Many people with Down syndrome develop early-onset AD, with signs of dementia by the time they reach middle age.

- **Genetics.** One's likelihood of developing a genetically linked form of dementia increases when more than one family member has the disorder. But in some cases, such as with CADASIL, having just one parent who carries a mutation increases the risk of inheriting the condition. In other instances, genetic mutations may underlie dementias in specific populations. For example, a mutation of the gene TREM2 has been found to be common among people with a form of very early onset frontotemporal dementia that runs in Turkish families.

- **Hypertension.** High blood pressure has been linked to cognitive decline, stroke, and types of dementia that affect the white matter regions of the brain.

- **Mental illness.** Depression has been associated with mild mental impairment and cognitive function decline.

- **Smoking.** Smokers are prone to diseases that slow or stop blood from getting to the brain.

Chapter 6

Mortality Rate and Global Burden of Dementia

Statistics on Dementia Prevalence and Mortality

Quick Stats: Death Rates from Dementia among Persons Aged ≥75 Years, by Sex and Age Group—United States, 2000–2013

During 2000–2013, death rates for dementia per 100,000 population increased for both men and women among persons aged 75–84 years and ≥85 years. Among persons aged 75–84 years, the rate increased 21% for men and 31% for women. Among persons aged ≥85 years, the rate increased 32% for men and 36% for women. Among persons aged ≥85 years, death rates were higher for women than men throughout the period, with death rates 25% higher among women than men in 2013 (4,077.4 versus 3,261.6 per 100,000 population).

Burden of Dementia

The cause of most dementia is unknown, but the final stages of this disease usually means a loss of memory, reasoning, speech, and other cognitive functions. The risk of dementia increases sharply with

This chapter includes excerpts from "Morbidity and Mortality Weekly Report (MMWR)," Centers for Disease Control and Prevention (CDC), May 29, 2015; and text from "The Burden of Dementia," National Institute on Aging (NIA), January 22, 2015.

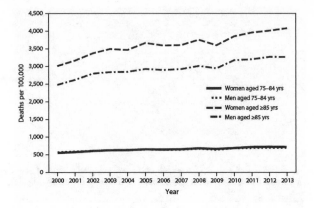

Figure 6.1. *Death Rates from Dementia—United States – 2000–2013*

age and, unless new strategies for prevention and management are developed, this syndrome is expected to place growing demands on health and long-term care providers as the world's population ages. Dementia prevalence estimates vary considerably internationally, in part because diagnoses and reporting systems are not standardized. The disease is not easy to diagnose, especially in its early stages. The memory problems, misunderstandings, and behavior common in the early and intermediate stages are often attributed to normal effects of aging, accepted as personality traits, or simply ignored. Many cases remain undiagnosed even in the intermediate, more serious stages. A cross-national assessment conducted by the Organization for Economic Cooperation and Development (OECD) estimated that dementia affected about 10 million people in OECD member countries around 2000, just under 7 percent of people aged 65 or older.

Alzheimer disease (AD) is the most common form of dementia and accounted for between two-fifths and four-fifths of all dementia cases cited in the OECD report. More recent analyses have estimated the worldwide number of people living with AD/dementia at between 27 million and 36 million. The prevalence of AD and other dementias is very low at younger ages, then nearly doubles with every five years of age after age 65. In the OECD review, for example, dementia affected fewer than 3 percent of those aged 65 to 69, but almost 30 percent of those aged 85 to 89. More than one-half of women aged 90 or older had dementia in France and Germany, as did about 40 percent in the United States, and just under 30 percent in Spain.

The projected costs of caring for the growing numbers of people with dementia are daunting. The 2010 World Alzheimer Report by

Alzheimer Disease International estimates that the total worldwide cost of dementia exceeded U.S. $600 billion in 2010, including informal care provided by family and others, social care provided by community care professionals, and direct costs of medical care. Family members often play a key caregiving role, especially in the initial stages of what is typically a slow decline. Ten years ago, U.S. researchers estimated that the annual cost of informal caregiving for dementia in the United States was U.S. $18 billion.

The complexity of the disease and the wide variety of living arrangements can be difficult for people and families dealing with dementia, and countries must cope with the mounting financial and social impact. The challenge is even greater in the less developed world, where an estimated two-thirds or more of dementia sufferers live but where few coping resources are available. Projections by Alzheimer Disease International suggest that 115 million people worldwide will be living with AD/dementia in 2050, with a markedly increasing proportion of this total in less developed countries (Figure 6.2). Global efforts are underway to understand and find cures or ways of preventing such age-related diseases as Alzheimer.

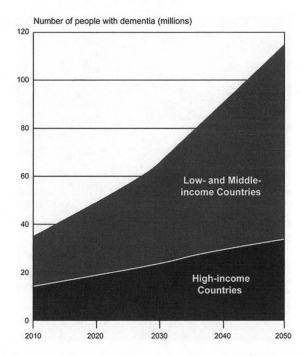

Figure 6.2. *Projected Growth of Numbers of People with Dementia in High-income Countries and Low- and Middle-income Countries: 2010–2050*

Chapter 7

National Plan to Address Alzheimer Disease and Related Dementias

National Alzheimer Project Act

On January 4, 2011, President Barack Obama signed into law the National Alzheimer Project Act (NAPA), requiring the Secretary of the U.S. Department of Health and Human Services (HHS) to establish the National Alzheimer Project to:

- Create and maintain an integrated National Plan to overcome (AD).

- Coordinate Alzheimer disease research and services across all federal agencies.

- Accelerate the development of treatments that would prevent, halt, or reverse the course of Alzheimer disease.

- Improve early diagnosis and coordination of care and treatment of Alzheimer disease.

Text in this chapter is excerpted from "National Plan to Address Alzheimer's Disease: 2015 Update," U.S. Department of Health and Human Services (HHS), 2015.

- Decrease disparities in Alzheimer disease for ethnic and racial minority populations that are at higher risk for Alzheimer disease.

- Coordinate with international bodies to fight Alzheimer disease globally.

The law also establishes the Advisory Council on Alzheimer Research, Care, and Services (Advisory Council) and requires the Secretary of HHS, in collaboration with the Advisory Council, to create and maintain a National Plan to overcome Alzheimer disease and related dementias (ADRD).

NAPA offers a historic opportunity to address the many challenges facing people with Alzheimer disease and their families. Given the great demographic shifts that will occur over the next 30 years, including the doubling of the population of older adults, the success of this effort is of great importance to people with ADRD and their family members, public policy makers, and health and social service providers.

Alzheimer Disease and Related Dementias

Alzheimer disease is an irreversible, progressive brain disease that affects as many as 5.1 million Americans. It slowly destroys brain function, leading to cognitive decline (e.g., memory loss, language difficulty, poor executive function), behavioral and psychiatric disorders (e.g., depression, delusions, agitation), and declines in functional status (e.g., ability to engage in activities of daily living (ADLs) and self-care). In 1906, Dr. Alois Alzheimer first documented the disease when he identified changes in the brain tissue of a woman who had memory loss, language problems, and unpredictable behavior. Her brain tissue included abnormal clumps (amyloidal plaques) and tangled bundles of fibers (neurofibrillary tangles). Brain plaques and tangles, in addition to the loss of connections between neurons, are the main features of AD.

In addition to Alzheimer disease, this National Plan addresses related dementias, consistent with the approach Congress used in NAPA. Related dementias include frontotemporal dementia (FTD), Lewy body, mixed, and vascular dementias. It is often difficult to distinguish between ADRD in terms of clinical presentation and diagnosis. Some of the basic neurodegenerative processes have common pathways.

People with dementia and their families face similar challenges in finding appropriate and necessary medical and supportive care.

As such, many of the actions described in this plan are designed to address these conditions collectively.

The first symptom of Alzheimer disease, and sometimes ADRD, is often memory impairment. However, in ADRD, behavioral, visual, sleep disruption or motor symptoms can often be the presenting symptoms. As the disease progresses, memory can decline, and other functions like language skills and decision making become more difficult. Personality and behavior changes often occur. Over time, a person with the disease may no longer recognize family and friends. Eventually, persons who survive with AD and ADRD are completely reliant on others for assistance with even the most basic ADLs, such as eating.

In more than 90% of people with ADRD, symptoms do not appear until after age 60, and the incidence of the disease increases with age. The causes of ADRD are not completely understood, but researchers believe they include a combination of genetic, environmental, and lifestyle factors. The importance of any one of these factors in increasing or decreasing the risk of developing Alzheimer disease may differ from person to person. In rare cases, known as early or younger-onset AD, people develop symptoms of AD in their 30s, 40s, or 50s. A significant number of people with Down syndrome develop dementia in their 50s, often placing increased burden on their families and caregivers.

ADRD is a major public health issue and will increasingly affect the health and well-being of the population. Unless the disease can be effectively treated or prevented, the number of Americans with Alzheimer disease will increase significantly in the next two decades. The number of people age 65 and older in the United States is expected to grow from an estimated 47.8 million in 2015 to 74.1 million in 2030. The prevalence of people with ADRD doubles for every 5-year interval beyond age 65. Without a preventative treatment or cure, the significant growth in the population over age 85 that is estimated to occur between 2015 and 2030 (from 6.3 million to 9.1 million) suggests a substantial increase in the number of people with AD.

The disease places enormous emotional, physical, and financial stress on individuals who have it and their family members. Unpaid caregivers, such as family members and friends, provide the majority of care for people with ADRD in the community. Unpaid caregivers often do not identify themselves as such; they are a wife, daughter, husband, parent, son, or friend helping a person whom they care about. However, the intensive support required for a person with ADRD can negatively impact the caregiver's emotional and physical health and well-being, and their ability to work. Unpaid caregivers often report symptoms of depression and anxiety, and they have poorer health outcomes than their peers who do not provide such care.

Dementia care costs are significant and often a burden to families providing unpaid care. Recent estimates from one nationally representative study found that paid and unpaid care costs of caring for people older than age 70 with dementia in the United States in 2010 were between $159 billion and $215 billion. These figures include direct medical expenditures, costs for long-term services and supports (LTSS) including institutional and community care, and the two different estimates of the value of unpaid care provided by family members and friends. These costs could rise dramatically with the increase in the numbers of older adults in coming decades. Care costs per person with dementia in 2010 ranged from $41,000 to $56,000 depending on how unpaid care costs were estimated. These national dementia care costs are comparable to, if not greater than, those for heart disease and cancer.

Caring for people with the disease also strains health and long-term care systems. Individuals with ADRD use a disproportionate amount of health care resources; for instance, they are hospitalized 2-3 times as often as people the same age who do not have the disease. Similarly, while people living in nursing homes are a small percentage of the older population, nearly half (48%) of nursing home residents have ADRD. As the number of people with ADRD grows over the next two decades, this disease will place a major strain on these care systems as well as on Medicare and Medicaid, the major funders of this care. Although Medicaid, a program for eligible low income Americans, covers long-term care services (custodial care), Medicare does not.

Challenges

This National Plan is designed to address the major challenges presented by Alzheimer disease:

1. While research on ADRD has made steady progress, there are no pharmacological or other interventions to definitively prevent, treat, or cure the disease.

2. While HHS and other groups have taken steps to develop quality measures to assess dementia care and to improve the training of the health and long-term care workforce—both paid and unpaid caregivers—there is room for improvement.

3. Family members and other unpaid caregivers, who take on the responsibility of caring for a loved one with ADRD, need

services and support. The majority of people with ADRD live in the community, where their families provide most of their care. The toll of caregiving can have major implications for caregivers and families as well as population health, with about one-third of caregivers reporting symptoms of depression.

4. Stigmas and misconceptions associated with ADRD are widespread and profoundly impact the care provided to and the isolation felt by people with ADRD and their families.

5. Public and private sector progress is significant, but should be coordinated and tracked. In addition, data to track the incidence, prevalence, trajectory and costs of ADRD are limited.

Framework and Guiding Principles

The enactment of NAPA creates an opportunity to focus the Nation's attention on the challenges of ADRD. In consultation with stakeholders both inside and outside of the Federal Government, this National Plan represents the blueprint for achieving the vision of a nation free of ADRD.

Central to and guiding the National Plan are the people most intimately impacted by ADRD—those who have the disease and their families and other caregivers. Individuals with ADRD and their caregivers receive assistance from both the clinical health care system and long-term care including home and community-based services (HCBS), legal services, and other social services. Both the clinical care and community/support environments need better tools to serve people with ADRD and their unpaid caregivers. Ongoing and future research seeks to identify interventions to assist clinicians, supportive service providers, HCBS providers, persons with ADRD, and caregivers. All of these efforts must occur in the context of improved awareness of the disease and its impacts and the opportunities for improvement. The plan aims to address these key needs. HHS is committed to tracking and coordinating the implementation of NAPA and making improvements aimed at achieving its ambitious vision.

The National Plan is also guided by three principles:

1. Optimize Existing Resources, and Improve and Coordinate Ongoing Activities. The first step in developing the National Plan was to set up a federal interagency working group and conduct an inventory of all federal activities involving Alzheimer disease.

In creating the plan, HHS and its partners sought to leverage these resources and activities, improve coordination, and reduce duplication of efforts to better meet the challenges of ADRD. The activities included in the inventory comprise ongoing work and new opportunities created by the Affordable Care Act. The federal working group process continues to improve coordination and awareness throughout the Federal Government and set in motion commitments for further collaboration. Further, this process has allowed for identification of non-AD-specific programs and resources that may be leveraged to advance AD care.

2. Support Public-Private Partnerships. The scope of the problem of ADRD is so great that partnerships with a multitude of public and private stakeholders will be essential to making progress. This National Plan begins the partnership process by identifying areas of need and opportunity. The plan relies on the Advisory Council in particular to identify key areas where public-private partnerships can improve outcomes.

3. Transform the Way We Approach ADRD. The National Plan recognizes that this undertaking that will require large-scale, coordinated efforts across the public and private sectors. With principles 1 and 2 above, as well as the ambitious vision that the Federal Government is committing to through this plan, HHS and its federal partners seek to take the first of many transformative actions that will be needed to address this disease. Through an ongoing dialogue with the Advisory Council, the Federal Government is identifying the most promising areas for progress and marshalling resources from both within and outside the government to act on these opportunities.

Goals as Building Blocks for Transformation

Achieving the vision of eliminating the burden of ADRD starts with concrete goals. Below are the five that form the foundation of this National Plan:

1. Prevent and Effectively Treat Alzheimer Disease by 2025.

2. Enhance Care Quality and Efficiency.

3. Expand Supports for People with Alzheimer Disease and their Families.

4. Enhance Public Awareness and Engagement.

5. Track Progress and Drive Improvement.

2015 Update to the National Plan

The activities outlined in this National Plan vary in scope and impact, and include: (1) immediate actions that the Federal Government has taken and will take; (2) actions toward the goals that can be initiated by the Federal Government or its public and private partners in the near term; and (3) longer-range activities that will require numerous actions to achieve. This is a national plan and not a federal plan. Active engagement of public and private sector stakeholders is needed to achieve these national goals. In the case of many of the long-range activities, the path forward will be contingent upon resources, scientific progress, and focused collaborations across many partners. Over time, HHS will work with the Advisory Council and stakeholders to incorporate and update additional transformative actions.

Goal 1: Prevent and Effectively Treat Alzheimer Disease by 2025

Research continues to expand our understanding of the causes of, treatments for, and prevention of Alzheimer disease. This goal seeks to develop effective prevention and treatment modalities by 2025. Ongoing research and clinical inquiry can inform our ability to delay onset of AD, minimize its symptoms, and delay its progression. Under this goal, HHS will prioritize and accelerate the pace of scientific research and ensure that as evidence-based solutions are identified they are quickly translated, put into practice, and brought to scale so that individuals with AD can benefit from increases in scientific knowledge. HHS will identify interim milestones and set ambitious deadlines for achieving these milestones in order to meet this goal.

In 2014/2015, Goal 1 of the National Plan moved forward with expanded and innovative research initiatives, with a focus on intensified translational studies in target identification and drug discovery, and the start of major new trials to test therapies as early as possible in the disease process. Investigator-initiated research remains the mainstay of National Institutes of Health (NIH)-funded efforts to learn more about ADRD, including studies to uncover their molecular, cellular and genetic causes.

At the same time, the national conversation to regularly re-examine and update research priorities included more diverse voices, beyond the research community and advocates to directly engaging people with ADRD and clinicians. All these efforts were supported with enhanced collaboration among governments and with the private sector to leverage research opportunities and further accelerate the pace of progress.

The NIH is supporting research across many diverse topics in ADRD. The section below offers several examples of recent progress; however the NIH will continue to invest in high-priority research areas, as identified through the 2012 and 2015 Alzheimer Disease Research Summits, the 2013 Alzheimer Disease-Related Dementias, and the 2013 Advancing Treatment for Alzheimer Disease in Individuals with Down Syndrome, among other strategic planning efforts.

These efforts, as well as other research plans and activities in ADRD, will be considered as the NIH develops an annual bypass budget estimate for the President and Congress, as mandated in Section 230, Division G of the Consolidated and Further Continuing Appropriations Act, 2015. Per the Act's language, the Secretary of HHS, as well as the Advisory Council, may review and comment on, but not alter, the NIH bypass budget submission. Each annual bypass budget will be estimated based on the NIH components of the most recent update to the National Plan. This process will include activities relevant to Goal 1, as well as other Goals outlined in the National Plan.

Goal 2: Enhance Care Quality and Efficiency

Providing all people with ADRD with the highest-quality care in the most efficient manner requires a multi-tiered approach. High-quality care requires an adequate supply of culturally-competent professionals with appropriate skills, ranging from direct care workers to community health and social workers, to HCBS providers, to primary care providers and specialists. High-quality care should be provided from the point of diagnosis onward in settings including doctor's offices, hospitals, people's homes and nursing homes. Person-centered quality should be measured accurately and inter-operably across all settings of care, coupled with quality improvement tools. Further, care should address the complex care needs that persons with ADRD have due to the physical, cognitive, emotional, and behavioral symptoms of the disease and any co-occurring chronic conditions. High-quality and efficient care depends on: (1) smooth transitions between care settings; (2) coordination among health care and LTSS providers; and (3) dementia-capable health care and LTSS.

Goal 3: Expand Supports for People with Alzheimer Disease and Their Families

People with Alzheimer disease and their families need supports that go beyond the care provided in formal settings such as doctor's offices, hospitals, or nursing homes. Families and other informal caregivers play a central role. Supporting people with AD and their families and caregivers requires giving them the tools that they need, helping to plan for future needs, and ensuring that safety and dignity are maintained. Under this goal, the Federal Government and partners will undertake strategies and actions that will support people with the disease and their families and caregivers.

Goal 4: Enhance Public Awareness and Engagement

Most of the public is aware of Alzheimer disease; more than 85% of people surveyed can identify the disease and its symptoms. AD is also one of the most feared health conditions. Yet there are widespread and significant public misperceptions about diagnosis and clinical management. These issues can lead to delayed diagnosis, and to people with the disease and their caregivers feeling isolated and stigmatized. Enhancing public awareness and engagement is an essential goal because it forms the basis for advancing the subsequent goals of the National Plan. A better understanding of AD will help engage stakeholders who can help address the challenges faced by people with the disease and their families. These stakeholders include a range of groups such as health care providers who care for people with AD and their caregivers, employers whose employees request flexibility to care for a loved one with the disease, groups whose members are caregivers, and broader aging organizations. The strategies and actions under this goal are designed to educate these and other groups about the disease.

Goal 5: Improve Data to Track Progress

The Federal Government is committed to better understanding ADRD and its impact on individuals, families, the health and long-term care systems, and society as a whole. Data and surveillance efforts are paramount to tracking the burden of Alzheimer disease on individual and population health, and will be used to identify and monitor trends in risk factors associated with ADRD, and assist with understanding health disparities among populations such as racial and ethnic minorities. HHS will make efforts to expand and enhance data infrastructure and make data easily accessible to federal agencies and other researchers. This data infrastructure will help HHS in its multi-level monitoring and evaluation of progress on the National Plan.

Part Two

Alzheimer Disease (AD): The Most Common Type of Dementia

Chapter 8

Facts about Alzheimer Disease

Alzheimer disease (AD) is an irreversible, progressive brain disorder that slowly destroys memory and thinking skills and, eventually, the ability to carry out the simplest tasks. In most people with Alzheimer, symptoms first appear in their mid-60s. Estimates vary, but experts suggest that more than 5 million Americans may have Alzheimer.

Alzheimer disease is currently ranked as the sixth leading cause of death in the United States, but recent estimates indicate that the disorder may rank third, just behind heart disease and cancer, as a cause of death for older people.

AD is the most common cause of dementia among older adults. Dementia is the loss of cognitive functioning—thinking, remembering, and reasoning—and behavioral abilities to such an extent that it interferes with a person's daily life and activities. Dementia ranges in severity from the mildest stage, when it is just beginning to affect a person's functioning, to the most severe stage, when the person must depend completely on others for basic activities of daily living.

The causes of dementia can vary, depending on the types of brain changes that may be taking place. Other dementias include Lewy body dementia, frontotemporal disorders, and vascular dementia. It is

Text in this chapter is excerpted from "Alzheimer's Disease: Fact Sheet," National Institute on Aging (NIA), May 2015.

common for people to have mixed dementia—a combination of two or more disorders, at least one of which is dementia. For example, some people have both Alzheimer disease and vascular dementia.

Alzheimer disease is named after Dr. Alois Alzheimer. In 1906, Dr. Alzheimer noticed changes in the brain tissue of a woman who had died of an unusual mental illness. Her symptoms included memory loss, language problems, and unpredictable behavior. After she died, he examined her brain and found many abnormal clumps (now called amyloid plaques) and tangled bundles of fibers (now called neurofibrillary, or tau, tangles).

These plaques and tangles in the brain are still considered some of the main features of Alzheimer disease. Another feature is the loss of connections between nerve cells (neurons) in the brain. Neurons transmit messages between different parts of the brain, and from the brain to muscles and organs in the body.

Changes in the Brain

Scientists continue to unravel the complex brain changes involved in the onset and progression of Alzheimer disease. It seems likely that damage to the brain starts a decade or more before memory and other cognitive problems appear. During this preclinical stage of Alzheimer disease, people seem to be symptom-free, but toxic changes are taking place in the brain. Abnormal deposits of proteins form amyloid plaques

Healthy Brain   **Severe Alzheimer's**

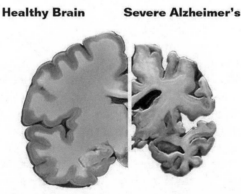

Figure 8.1. *Healthy Brain vs Severe AD*

Cross sections of the brain show atrophy, or shrinking, of brain tissue caused by Alzheimer disease.

and tau tangles throughout the brain, and once-healthy neurons stop functioning, lose connections with other neurons, and die.

The damage initially appears to take place in the hippocampus, the part of the brain essential in forming memories. As more neurons die, additional parts of the brain are affected, and they begin to shrink. By the final stage of AD, damage is widespread, and brain volume has shrunk significantly.

Signs and Symptoms

Memory problems are typically one of the first signs of cognitive impairment related to Alzheimer disease. Some people with memory problems have a condition called mild cognitive impairment (MCI). In MCI, people have more memory problems than normal for their age, but their symptoms do not interfere with their everyday lives. Movement difficulties and problems with the sense of smell have also been linked to MCI. Older people with MCI are at greater risk for developing AD, but not all of them do. Some may even go back to normal cognition.

The first symptoms of AD vary from person to person. For many, decline in non-memory aspects of cognition, such as word-finding, vision/spatial issues, and impaired reasoning or judgment, may signal the very early stages of Alzheimer disease. Researchers are studying biomarkers (biological signs of disease found in brain images, cerebrospinal fluid, and blood) to see if they can detect early changes in the brains of people with MCI and in cognitively normal people who may be at greater risk for AD. Studies indicate that such early detection may be possible, but more research is needed before these techniques can be relied upon to diagnose Alzheimer disease in everyday medical practice.

Mild Alzheimer Disease

As Alzheimer disease progresses, people experience greater memory loss and other cognitive difficulties. Problems can include wandering and getting lost, trouble handling money and paying bills, repeating questions, taking longer to complete normal daily tasks, and personality and behavior changes. People are often diagnosed at this stage.

Moderate Alzheimer Disease

In this stage, damage occurs in areas of the brain that control language, reasoning, sensory processing, and conscious thought. Memory loss and confusion grow worse, and people begin to have problems recognizing family and friends. They may be unable to learn new things, carry out multi step tasks such as getting dressed, or cope with new situations. In addition, people at this stage may have hallucinations, delusions, and paranoia and may behave impulsively.

Severe Alzheimer Disease

Ultimately, plaques and tangles spread throughout the brain, and brain tissue shrinks significantly. People with severe AD cannot communicate and are completely dependent on others for their care. Near the end, the person may be in bed most or all of the time as the body shuts down.

What Causes AD?

Scientists don't yet fully understand what causes Alzheimer disease in most people. In people with early-onset Alzheimer, a genetic mutation is usually the cause. Late-onset Alzheimer arises from a complex series of brain changes that occur over decades. The causes probably include a combination of genetic, environmental, and lifestyle factors. The importance of any one of these factors in increasing or decreasing the risk of developing AD may differ from person to person.

The Basics of AD

Scientists are conducting studies to learn more about plaques, tangles, and other biological features of Alzheimer disease. Advances in brain imaging techniques allow researchers to see the development and spread of abnormal amyloid and tau proteins in the living brain, as well as changes in brain structure and function. Scientists are also exploring the very earliest steps in the disease process by studying changes in the brain and body fluids that can be detected years before AD symptoms appear. Findings from these studies will help in understanding the causes of AD and make diagnosis easier.

One of the great mysteries of Alzheimer disease is why it largely strikes older adults. Research on normal brain aging is shedding light on this question. For example, scientists are learning how age-related changes in the brain may harm neurons and contribute to AD damage. These age-related changes include atrophy (shrinking) of certain parts of the brain, inflammation, production of unstable molecules called free radicals, and mitochondrial dysfunction (a breakdown of energy production within a cell).

Genetics

Most people with AD have the late-onset form of the disease, in which symptoms become apparent in their mid-60s. The apolipoprotein E (APOE) gene is involved in late-onset Alzheimer. This gene has several forms. One of them, APOE ε4, increases a person's risk of developing the disease and is also associated with an earlier age of disease onset. However, carrying the APOE4 form of the gene does not mean that a person will definitely develop Alzheimer disease, and some people with no APOE ε4 may also develop the disease.

Also, scientists have identified a number of regions of interest in the genome (an organism's complete set of DNA) that may increase a person's risk for late-onset Alzheimer to varying degrees.

Early-onset Alzheimer disease occurs in people age 30 to 60 and represents less than 5 percent of all people with AD. Most cases are caused by an inherited change in one of three genes, resulting in a type known as early-onset familial Alzheimer disease, or FAD. For others, the disease appears to develop without any specific, known cause, much as it does for people with late-onset disease.

Most people with Down syndrome develop AD. This may be because people with Down syndrome have an extra copy of chromosome 21, which contains the gene that generates harmful amyloid.

Health, Environmental, and Lifestyle Factors

Research suggests that a host of factors beyond genetics may play a role in the development and course of Alzheimer disease. There is a great deal of interest, for example, in the relationship between cognitive decline and vascular conditions such as heart disease, stroke, and high blood pressure, as well as metabolic conditions such as diabetes and obesity. Ongoing research will help us understand whether and how reducing risk factors for these conditions may also reduce the risk of AD.

A nutritious diet, physical activity, social engagement, and mentally stimulating pursuits have all been associated with helping people stay healthy as they age. These factors might also help reduce the risk of cognitive decline and Alzheimer disease. Clinical trials are testing some of these possibilities.

Diagnosis of Alzheimer Disease

Doctors use several methods and tools to help determine whether a person who is having memory problems has "possible Alzheimer dementia" (dementia may be due to another cause) or "probable Alzheimer dementia" (no other cause for dementia can be found).

To diagnose AD, doctors may:

- Ask the person and a family member or friend questions about overall health, past medical problems, ability to carry out daily activities, and changes in behavior and personality

- Conduct tests of memory, problem solving, attention, counting, and language

- Carry out standard medical tests, such as blood and urine tests, to identify other possible causes of the problem

- Perform brain scans, such as computed tomography (CT), magnetic resonance imaging (MRI), or positron emission tomography (PET), to rule out other possible causes for symptoms.

These tests may be repeated to give doctors information about how the person's memory and other cognitive functions are changing over time.

Alzheimer disease can be definitively diagnosed only after death, by linking clinical measures with an examination of brain tissue in an autopsy.

People with memory and thinking concerns should talk to their doctor to find out whether their symptoms are due to AD or another cause, such as stroke, tumor, Parkinson disease, sleep disturbances, side effects of medication, an infection, or a non-Alzheimer dementia. Some of these conditions may be treatable and possibly reversible.

If the diagnosis is AD, beginning treatment early in the disease process may help preserve daily functioning for some time, even though the underlying disease process cannot be stopped or reversed. An early diagnosis also helps families plan for the future. They can take care of financial and legal matters, address potential safety issues, learn about living arrangements, and develop support networks.

In addition, an early diagnosis gives people greater opportunities to participate in clinical trials that are testing possible new treatments for Alzheimer disease or other research studies.

Treatment of Alzheimer Disease

Alzheimer disease is complex, and it is unlikely that any one drug or other intervention will successfully treat it. Current approaches focus on helping people maintain mental function, manage behavioral symptoms, and slow or delay the symptoms of disease. Researchers hope to develop therapies targeting specific genetic, molecular, and cellular mechanisms so that the actual underlying cause of the disease can be stopped or prevented.

Maintaining Mental Function

Several medications are approved by the U.S. Food and Drug Administration (FDA) to treat symptoms of AD. Donepezil (Aricept®), rivastigmine (Exelon®), and galantamine (Razadyne®) are used to treat mild to moderate Alzheimer (donepezil can be used for severe Alzheimer as well). Memantine (Namenda®) is used to treat moderate to severe Alzheimer. These drugs work by regulating neurotransmitters, the brain chemicals that transmit messages between neurons. They may help maintain thinking, memory, and communication skills, and help with certain behavioral problems. However, these drugs don't change the underlying disease process. They are effective for some but not all people and may help only for a limited time.

Managing Behavior

Common behavioral symptoms of AD include sleeplessness, wandering, agitation, anxiety, and aggression. Scientists are learning why these symptoms occur and are studying new treatments—drug and nondrug—to manage them. Research has shown that treating behavioral symptoms can make people with AD more comfortable and makes things easier for caregivers.

Looking for New Treatments

Alzheimer disease research has developed to a point where scientists can look beyond treating symptoms to think about addressing underlying disease processes. In ongoing clinical trials, scientists are developing and testing several possible interventions, including immunization therapy, drug therapies, cognitive training, physical activity, and treatments used for cardiovascular disease and diabetes.

Support for Families and Caregivers

Caring for a person with Alzheimer disease can have high physical, emotional, and financial costs. The demands of day-to-day care, changes in family roles, and decisions about placement in a care facility can be difficult. There are several evidence-based approaches and programs that can help, and researchers are continuing to look for new and better ways to support caregivers.

Becoming well-informed about the disease is one important strategy. Programs that teach families about the various stages of AD and about ways to deal with difficult behaviors and other caregiving challenges can help.

Good coping skills, a strong support network, and respite care are other ways that help caregivers handle the stress of caring for a loved one with Alzheimer disease. For example, staying physically active provides physical and emotional benefits.

Some caregivers have found that joining a support group is a critical lifeline. These support groups allow caregivers to find respite, express concerns, share experiences, get tips, and receive emotional comfort. Many organizations sponsor in-person and online support groups, including groups for people with early-stage Alzheimer and their families.

Chapter 9

What Happens to the Brain in Alzheimer Disease?

The healthy human brain contains tens of billions of neurons, specialized cells that process and transmit information via electrical and chemical signals. Most neurons have three basic components: a cell body, multiple dendrites, and an axon. The cell body contains the nucleus, which houses the genetic blueprint that directs and regulates the cell's activities. Dendrites are branched-like structures that radiate from the cell body and collect information from other neurons. The axon is a cable-like structure that extends from the other end of the cell body and transmits messages to other neurons.

The function and survival of neurons depend on several key biological processes:

- **Communication.** When a neuron receives signals from other neurons, it generates an electrical charge that travels down the length of the neuron's axon to a specialized structure called the synapse, where the axon comes into close contact with the dendrites of another neuron. At the synapse, chemicals called neurotransmitters are released and move across a microscopic gap to one of the dendrites of another neuron. There, each

This chapter includes excerpts from "A Primer on Alzheimer's Disease and the Brain," National Institute on Aging (NIA), December 21, 2012; and text from "Untangling Alzheimer's Biology," National Institute on Aging (NIA), February 15, 2014.

neurotransmitter molecule binds to a specific receptor molecule, like a key fitting into a lock, and triggers chemical or electrical signals within the dendrite that either stimulate or inhibit the next neuron's activity. Each neuron's axon can make connections with the dendrites of many other neurons, and each dendrite can receive connections from many axons. In fact, scientists estimate that in this brain cell communications network, one neuron may have as many as 7,000 synaptic connections with other neurons.

- **Metabolism.** This term encompasses all chemical reactions that take place in a cell to support its survival and function. These reactions require chemical energy in the form of oxygen and glucose, which is supplied by blood circulating through the brain. The brain has one of the richest blood supplies of any organ and consumes up to 20 percent of the energy used by the human body—more than any other organ.

- **Repair, remodeling, and regeneration.** Unlike many cells in the body, which are relatively short-lived, neurons have evolved to live a long time—more than 100 years in humans. As a result, neurons must constantly maintain and repair themselves. Neurons also continuously remodel their synaptic connections depending on how much stimulation they receive from other neurons. Neurons may strengthen or weaken synaptic connections, or even break down connections with one group of neurons and reestablish connections with a different group of neurons. In addition, a number of brain regions continue to generate new neurons, even in adults. Remodeling of synaptic connections and the generation of new neurons are thought to be important for learning, memory, and possibly brain repair.

Neurons are the cells responsible for transmitting messages between different parts of the brain, and from the brain to the muscles and organs of the body. However, the brain contains other cell types as well. In fact, glial cells are by far the most numerous cells in the brain, outnumbering neurons by at least 10 to 1. Glial cells (of which there are several varieties) surround neurons and play critical roles in supporting neuronal function. For example, glial cells help protect neurons from physical and chemical damage and are responsible for clearing foreign substances and cellular debris from the brain. To carry out these functions, glial cells often act in collaboration with blood vessel cells, which in the brain have specialized features not found in blood vessels elsewhere in the body. Together, glial and blood vessel cells regulate the delicate chemical balance within the brain to ensure optimal neuronal function.

How Does Alzheimer Disease (AD) Affect the Brain?

While the brain may shrink to some degree in healthy aging, it does not lose neurons in large numbers. In Alzheimer disease, however, damage is widespread as many neurons stop functioning, lose connections with other neurons, and die. AD disrupts processes vital to neurons and their networks, including communication, metabolism, and repair.

At first, the disease typically destroys neurons and their connections in parts of the brain involved in memory, including the entorhinal cortex and the hippocampus. It later affects areas in the cerebral cortex responsible for language, reasoning, and social behavior. Eventually, many other areas of the brain are damaged, and a person with AD becomes helpless and unresponsive to the outside world.

What Are the Main Characteristics of the Brain with Alzheimer Disease?

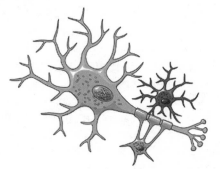

Figure 9.1. *Healthy Neuron*

Many changes take place in the brain of a person with Alzheimer disease. Some of these changes can be observed in brain tissue under the microscope after death. The three abnormalities most evident in the brains of people who have died with the disease are:

- **Amyloid plaques.** Found in the spaces between neurons, plaques consist predominantly of abnormal deposits of a protein fragment called beta-amyloid. Beta-amyloid is formed from the breakdown of a larger protein called amyloid precursor protein. Beta-amyloid comes in several different molecular forms. One of these, beta-amyloid 42, has a strong tendency to clump together.

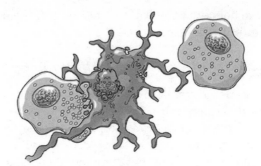

Figure 9.2. *Dying Neuron*

When produced in excess, beta-amyloid 42 accumulates into plaques. Scientists used to think that amyloid plaques were the primary cause of the damage to neurons seen in AD. Now, however, many think that unclumped forms of beta-amyloid, seen earlier in the plaque formation process, may be the major culprits. Scientists have not yet determined if plaques are a cause or a byproduct of Alzheimer disease.

- **Neurofibrillary tangles.** Found inside neurons, neurofibrillary tangles are abnormal clumps of a protein called tau. Healthy neurons are internally supported in part by structures called microtubules, which help guide nutrients and molecules from the cell body to the axon and dendrites. Researchers believe that tau normally binds to and stabilizes microtubules. In Alzheimer disease, however, tau undergoes abnormal chemical changes that cause it to detach from microtubules and stick to other tau molecules, forming threads that eventually clump together to form tangles. The tangles disrupt the microtubule network and create blocks in the neuron's transport system. Abnormal tau may also cause blocks in synaptic signaling. As with beta-amyloid, some scientists think that other, smaller forms of abnormal tau may cause the most damage to neurons.

- **Loss of neuronal connections and cell death.** In Alzheimer disease, the synaptic connections between certain groups of neurons stop functioning and begin to degenerate. This degeneration may be due to the abnormal deposits of beta-amyloid and tau. When neurons lose their connections, they cannot function properly and eventually die. As neuronal injury and death spread through the brain, connections between networks of neurons break down, and affected regions begin to shrink in a process called brain atrophy. By the final stage of AD, damage is widespread, and brain tissue has shrunk significantly.

Amyloid plaques, neurofibrillary tangles, synaptic loss, and cell death are the most striking features of the AD brain when it is viewed under the microscope after death. However, scientists are now realizing that many other cellular changes occur in the brain during the Alzheimer disease process. For example, glial cells show abnormalities, as certain populations of glial cells begin to swell up and divide to produce more glial cells.

The AD brain also shows signs of inflammation, a tissue response to cellular injury. In addition, brain blood vessel cells as well as brain neurons show signs of degeneration. Some of these other cellular changes likely occur in response to neuronal malfunction, and many of them could contribute to neuronal malfunction.

What Causes Alzheimer Disease?

In some rare cases, people develop AD in their late 30s, 40s, or 50s. This form of the disease, called early-onset dominantly inherited Alzheimer disease, always runs in families and is caused by a mutation in one of three genes that a person has inherited from a parent. A National Institute on Aging (NIA)-funded clinical study is underway to identify the sequence of brain changes in this form of early-onset Alzheimer, even before symptoms appear.

More than 90 percent of AD cases occur in people age 60 and older. The development and progression of this late-onset form of the disease are very similar to what is seen in the early-onset form. The causes of late-onset Alzheimer are not yet known, but they are believed to include a combination of genetic, environmental, and lifestyle factors. The importance of any one of these factors in increasing or decreasing the risk of developing AD differs from person to person—even between twins.

Much basic research in Alzheimer disease has focused on genes that cause early-onset disease and on how mutations in these genes disrupt cellular function and lead to the disorder. Scientists hope that what they learn about early-onset Alzheimer disease can be applied to the late-onset form of the disease.

Perhaps the greatest mystery is why Alzheimer disease largely strikes people of advanced age. The single best-known risk factor for Alzheimer is age, and studies show that the prevalence of the disease dramatically increases after age 70. Research on how the brain changes normally as people age will help explain Alzheimer prevalence in older adults. Other risk factors for Alzheimer may include cardiovascular disease, diabetes, depression, and certain lifestyle factors such as being physically inactive.

Untangling Alzheimer Biology

Alzheimer disease and related dementias are complex disorders. Research points to the abnormal accumulation of beta-amyloid, tau, and other toxic proteins in the brain as key players in the loss of communication between neurons and the eventual damage and death of once-healthy brain cells. Beyond these obvious hallmarks of Alzheimer disease, scientists are examining a wide range of brain functions and factors that may also play a role. Research conducted in 2013 offered several new insights into the cellular and molecular changes that occur in Alzheimer disease. Understanding these underlying mechanisms and disease pathways—and how they interact with one another in disease onset and progression—may help identify valid targets for interventions.

Increased Beta-Amyloid Production in Familial Alzheimer Disease

Researchers have long believed that people with the familial, early-onset form of Alzheimer disease produce too much beta-amyloid 42, an especially toxic type of beta-amyloid protein. Researchers studied 11 volunteers, most of them in their 40s and carriers of the presenilin gene mutation associated with early-onset Alzheimer, and 12 of their siblings who do not carry the gene. By injecting the volunteers with a tracer that labels beta-amyloid 42, the researchers could monitor its production and clearance.

The investigators found that volunteers with presenilin mutations produced about 20 percent more beta-amyloid 42 than their mutation-free siblings. The mutation carriers also cleared less of the toxic protein, as evidenced by lower amounts detected in their cerebrospinal fluid—a finding that suggested more beta-amyloid 42 was forming amyloid plaques in the brain.

Unexplained Mechanisms of Late-Life Cognitive Decline

Much of the cognitive decline seen in late life may not be caused by any of the known mechanisms associated with the three most common disorders found in older people with dementia: Alzheimer disease,

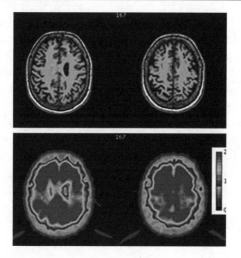

Figure 9.3. *Amyloid Deposition in Brain*

cerebrovascular disease, and Lewy body disease. Scientists studied post-mortem brain samples from 856 donors who underwent annual cognitive tests for up to 18 years before their deaths at the average age of 88. The researchers scored each brain for levels of amyloid plaque, neurofibrillary tangles, Lewy bodies, and tissue damaged by large and small strokes.

They found that the volunteers whose brains showed higher levels of any of these pathologies after death had also experienced faster trajectories of cognitive decline. However, these three disorders combined accounted for only 41 percent of the variations in cognitive decline in the volunteers. This finding suggests that disease pathways other than those we know are associated with Alzheimer disease, cerebrovascular disease, and Lewy body disease may be responsible for more than half of the age-related cognitive decline in this group. More research is needed to identify the pathways involved in cognitive decline and the unknown mechanisms that contribute to the onset and progression of mild cognitive impairment.

Abnormal TDP-43 Protein and Cognitive Decline

Abnormal intracellular clumps of the transactive response DNA-binding protein 43 (TDP-43) are a hallmark of frontotemporal dementia and amyotrophic lateral sclerosis, but they can also be found in the brain cells of older people who are not diagnosed with these diseases. Researchers found that the presence of TDP-43 pathology in the brains of older people is associated with faster cognitive decline. The researchers conducted post-mortem analyses of the brains of 130 volunteers in the Religious Orders Study. Each volunteer was cognitively tested annually for 10 years prior to death, and about 40 percent of the group developed dementia.

The researchers found TDP-43 pathology in the brains of almost half of the participants. This pathology accounted for nearly as much of the cognitive decline in this group as did AD pathology. This study suggests that TDP-43 pathology is one of the major neurodegenerative changes associated with late-life cognitive decline and dementia.

Possible Role of Brain Blood-Vessel Cells in Alzheimer Disease

A study in mice showed how a breakdown in the brain's blood vessels may influence Alzheimer disease. Pericytes are cells that surround the outside of blood vessels. Found in the blood-brain barrier, they help transport nutrients and waste molecules between the blood and the fluid that surrounds brain cells. The loss of pericytes may be key to whether increased beta-amyloid leads to tangles and loss of neurons, according to a study.

To study how pericytes influence AD, the researchers crossbred two mouse models. One model had an amyloid precursor protein (APP) gene mutation and accumulated beta-amyloid in the brain as it aged. The second had a mutation in the gene for platelet-derived growth factor receptor-beta receptor that resulted in fewer pericytes, decreased blood flow, and damage to the blood-brain barrier.

Crossbreeding the two mouse strains slightly worsened existing problems with learning and memory. The mice also developed more beta-amyloid deposits, extensive neurofibrillary tangles, and loss of neurons in the hippocampus and cerebral cortex—brain regions typically affected in human Alzheimer disease. This finding suggests that the loss of pericytes may play a role in AD. Further experiments suggested that pericytes help transport beta-amyloid out of the brain and into the blood, and that pericyte degeneration may slow beta-amyloid clearance. Pericytes and other blood-brain cells may be a new therapeutic target for treating AD.

Chapter 10

Signs and Symptoms of Alzheimer Disease

About Alzheimer Disease: Symptoms

The course of Alzheimer disease (AD) is not the same in every person, but symptoms seem to develop over the same general stages. In most people with AD, symptoms first appear in their mid-60s.

Scientists know that AD progresses on a spectrum with three stages—an early, preclinical stage with no symptoms; a middle stage of mild cognitive impairment (MCI); and a final stage of Alzheimer dementia. At this time, doctors cannot predict with any certainty which people with MCI will or will not develop AD.

Early Signs and Symptoms

The first symptoms of AD vary from person to person. Memory problems are typically one of the first signs of cognitive impairment related to Alzheimer disease. For many, decline in non-memory aspects of cognition, such as word-finding, vision/spatial issues, and impaired

This chapter includes excerpts from "About Alzheimer's Disease: Symptoms," National Institute on Aging (NIA), June 8, 2015; text from "Understanding Alzheimer's Disease," National Institute on Aging (NIA), October 2015; and text from "Alzheimer's Symptoms," U.S. Department of Health and Human Services (HHS), May 16, 2012.

reasoning or judgment, may signal the very early stages of Alzheimer disease.

Mild Alzheimer Disease

As the disease progresses, people experience greater memory loss and other cognitive difficulties. Problems can include:

- wandering and getting lost
- trouble handling money and paying bills
- repeating questions
- taking longer to complete normal daily tasks
- losing things or misplacing them in odd places
- personality and behavior changes

Alzheimer disease is often diagnosed at this stage.

Moderate Alzheimer Disease

In this stage, damage occurs in areas of the brain that control language, reasoning, sensory processing, and conscious thought. Symptoms may include:

- increased memory loss and confusion
- problems recognizing family and friends
- inability to learn new things
- difficulty carrying out multi step tasks such as getting dressed
- problems coping with new situations
- hallucinations, delusions, and paranoia
- impulsive behavior

Severe Alzheimer Disease

People with severe AD cannot communicate and are completely dependent on others for their care. Near the end, the person may be in bed most or all of the time as the body shuts down. Their symptoms often include:

- inability to communicate
- weight loss

- seizures
- skin infections
- difficulty swallowing
- groaning, moaning, or grunting
- increased sleeping
- lack of control of bowel and bladder

Mild Cognitive Impairment

Some older people have a condition called mild cognitive impairment, or MCI. It can be an early sign of Alzheimer. But, not everyone with MCI will develop Alzheimer disease. People with MCI can still take care of themselves and do their normal activities. MCI memory problems may include:

- losing things often
- forgetting to go to events or appointments
- having more trouble coming up with words than other people of the same age.

If you have MCI, it's important to see your doctor or specialist every 6 to 12 months. Ask him or her to check for changes in your memory and thinking.

Differences between Alzheimer Disease and Normal Aging

Use the chart below to help you understand the differences between Alzheimer disease and the normal signs of aging.

Table 10.1. Differences between Alzheimer Disease and Normal Aging

Alzheimer Disease	Normal Aging
Making poor judgments and decisions a lot of the time	Making a bad decision once in a while
Problems taking care of monthly bills	Missing a monthly payment
Losing track of the date or time of year	Forgetting which day it is and remembering it later
Trouble having a conversation	Sometimes forgetting which word to use
Misplacing things often and being unable to find them	Losing things from time to time

What Other Diseases Have Similar Symptoms?

Memory loss or confusion can be caused by other problems, too. Sometimes these same symptoms are caused by an easily treatable issue, such as reaction to a medicine taken for a different health problem, or even a vitamin deficiency. It's important to get the right diagnosis so treatment can target the right problem.

Who Is Most at Risk for Developing Alzheimer?

Age is the best-known risk factor for AD. The older you get, the greater your chance of developing AD. Genetics may play a role as well. In rare families, certain genes may cause the disease. For most people who develop the disease later in life, some genes may increase your risk, but do not cause the disease.

Some studies suggest that the rate of AD is higher in certain racial or ethnic groups, such as African Americans, and scientists are exploring possible explanations.

- People with specific medical histories are at greater risk of AD, including people with: Down Syndrome and other intellectual and developmental disorders

- Repeated concussions (falls, sports injuries, and car accidents are common causes of concussions and TBI)

- Traumatic brain injury (TBI and mild TBI)

Being at higher risk for Alzheimer disease does not necessarily mean that you will develop the disease. Scientists continue to explore factors that may increase your chances of having AD and, equally important, what may protect people from developing the disease.

Chapter 11

Clinical Stages of Alzheimer Disease

Preclinical Alzheimer Disease

Alzheimer disease (AD) begins deep in the brain, in the entorhinal cortex, a brain region that is near the hippocampus and has direct connections to it. Healthy neurons in this region begin to work less efficiently, lose their ability to communicate, and ultimately die. This process gradually spreads to the hippocampus, the brain region that plays a major role in learning and is involved in converting short-term memories to long-term memories. Affected regions begin to atrophy. Ventricles, the fluid-filled spaces inside the brain, begin to enlarge as the process continues.

Scientists believe that these brain changes begin 10 to 20 years before any clinically detectable signs or symptoms of forgetfulness appear. That's why they are increasingly interested in the very early stages of the disease process. They hope to learn more about what happens in the brain that sets a person on the path to developing AD. By knowing more about the early stages, they also hope to be able to develop drugs or other treatments that will slow or stop the disease process before significant impairment occurs.

Text in this chapter is excerpted from "Alzheimer's Disease: Unraveling the Mystery," National Institute on Aging (NIA), January 22, 2015.

Pittsburgh Compound B (PiB)

Imagine being able to see deep inside the brain tissue of a living person. If you could do that, you could find out whether the AD process was happening many years before symptoms were evident. This knowledge could have a profound impact on improving early diagnosis, monitoring disease progression, and tracking response to treatment.

Scientists have stepped closer to this possibility with the development of a radiolabeled compound called Pittsburgh Compound B (PiB). PiB binds to beta-amyloid plaques in the brain, and it can be imaged using PET scans. Initial studies showed that people with AD take up more PiB in their brains than do cognitively healthy older people. Since then, scientists have found high levels of PiB in some cognitively healthy people, suggesting that the damage from beta-amyloid may already be underway. The next step will be to follow these cognitively healthy people who have high PiB levels to see whether they do, in fact, develop AD over time.

Very Early Signs and Symptoms

At some point, the damage occurring in the brain begins to show itself in very early clinical signs and symptoms. Much research is being done to identify these early changes, which may be useful in predicting dementia or AD. An important part of this research effort is the development of increasingly sophisticated neuroimaging techniques and the use of biomarkers. Biomarkers are indicators, such as changes in sensory abilities, or substances that appear in body fluids, such as blood, cerebrospinal fluid, or urine. Biomarkers can indicate exposure to a substance, the presence of a disease, or the progression over time of a disease. For example, high blood cholesterol is a biomarker for risk of heart disease. Such tools are critical to helping scientists detect and understand the very early signs and symptoms of AD.

Mild Cognitive Impairment

As some people grow older, they develop memory problems greater than those expected for their age. But they do not experience the personality changes or other problems that are characteristic of AD. These people may have a condition called mild cognitive impairment (MCI). MCI has several subtypes. The type most associated with memory loss is called amnestic MCI. People with MCI are a critically important group for research because a much higher percentage of them go on to develop AD than do people without these memory problems.

About 8 of every 10 people who fit the definition of amnestic MCI go on to develop AD within 7 years. In contrast, 1 to 3 percent of people older than 65 who have normal cognition will develop AD in any one year.

However, researchers are not yet able to say definitively why some people with amnestic MCI do not progress to AD, nor can they say who will or will not go on to develop AD. This raises pressing questions, such as: In cases when MCI progresses to AD, what was happening in the brain that made that transition possible? Can MCI be prevented or its progress to AD delayed?

Scientists also have found that genetic factors may play a role in MCI, as they do in AD. And, they have found that different brain regions appear to be activated during certain mental activities in cognitively healthy people and those with MCI. These changes appear to be related to the early stages of cognitive impairment.

Other Signs of Early AD Development

As scientists have sharpened their focus on the early stages of AD, they have begun to see hints of other changes that may signal a developing disease process. For example, in the Religious Orders Study, a large AD research effort that involves older nuns, priests, and religious brothers, investigators have explored whether changes in older adults' ability to move about and use their bodies might be a sign of early AD. The researchers found that participants with MCI had more movement difficulties than the cognitively healthy participants but less than those with AD. Moreover, those with MCI who had lots of trouble moving their legs and feet were more than twice as likely to develop AD as those with good lower body function.

It is not yet clear why people with MCI might have these motor function problems, but the scientists who conducted the study speculate that they may be a sign that damage to blood vessels in the brain or damage from AD is accumulating in areas of the brain responsible for motor function. If further research shows that some people with MCI do have motor function problems in addition to memory problems, the degree of difficulty, especially with walking, may help identify those at risk of progressing to AD.

Other scientists have focused on changes in sensory abilities as possible indicators of early cognitive problems. For example, in one study they found associations between a decline in the ability to detect odors and cognitive problems or dementia.

These findings are tentative, but they are promising because they suggest that, some day, it may be possible to develop ways to improve early detection of MCI or AD. These tools also will help scientists answer questions about causes and very early development of AD, track changes in brain and cognitive function over time, and ultimately track a person's response to treatment for AD.

Mild AD

As AD spreads through the brain, the number of plaques and tangles grows, shrinkage progresses, and more and more of the cerebral cortex is affected. Memory loss continues and changes in other cognitive abilities begin to emerge. The clinical diagnosis of AD is usually made during this stage. Signs of mild AD can include:

- Memory loss
- Confusion about the location of familiar places (getting lost begins to occur)
- Taking longer than before to accomplish normal daily tasks
- Trouble handling money and paying bills
- Poor judgment leading to bad decisions
- Loss of spontaneity and sense of initiative
- Mood and personality changes, increased anxiety and/or aggression

In mild AD, a person may seem to be healthy but is actually having more and more trouble making sense of the world around him or her. The realization that something is wrong often comes gradually to the person and his or her family. Accepting these signs as something other than normal and deciding to go for diagnostic tests can be a big hurdle for people and families. Once this hurdle is overcome, many families are relieved to know what is causing the problems. They also can take comfort in the fact that despite a diagnosis of MCI or early AD, a person can still make meaningful contributions to his or her family and to society for a time.

Moderate AD

By this stage, AD damage has spread to the areas of the cerebral cortex that control language, reasoning, sensory processing, and conscious thought. Affected regions continue to shrink, ventricles enlarge, and signs and symptoms of the disease become more pronounced and widespread. Behavioral problems, such as wandering and agitation, can occur. More intensive supervision and care become necessary, which can be difficult for many spouses and families. The symptoms of this stage can include:

- Increasing memory loss and confusion

- Shortened attention span

- Inappropriate outbursts of anger

- Problems recognizing friends and family members

- Difficulty with language and problems with reading, writing, and working with numbers

- Difficulty organizing thoughts and thinking logically

- Inability to learn new things or to cope with new or unexpected situations

- Restlessness, agitation, anxiety, tearfulness, wandering—especially in the late afternoon or at night

- Repetitive statements or movement, occasional muscle twitches

- Hallucinations, delusions, suspiciousness or paranoia, irritability

- Loss of impulse control (shown through undressing at inappropriate times or places or vulgar language)

- An inability to carry out activities that involve multiple steps in sequence, such as dressing, making a pot of coffee, or setting the table

Behavior is the result of complex brain processes, all of which take place in a fraction of a second in the healthy brain. In AD, many of those processes are disturbed, and these disrupted communications between neurons are the basis for many distressing or inappropriate behaviors. For example, a person may angrily refuse to take a bath or get dressed because he does not understand what his caregiver has asked him to do. If he does understand, he may not remember how to do it. The anger can be a mask for his confusion and anxiety. Or, a person with AD may constantly follow her husband or caregiver and fret when the person is out of sight. To a person who cannot remember the past or anticipate the future, the world can be strange and frightening. Sticking close to a trusted and familiar caregiver may be the only thing that makes sense and provides security.

Severe AD

In the last stage of AD, plaques and tangles are widespread throughout the brain, most areas of the brain have shrunk further, and ventricles have enlarged even more. People with AD cannot recognize family and loved ones or communicate in any way. They are completely dependent on others for care. Other symptoms can include:

- Weight loss
- Seizures
- Skin infections
- Difficulty swallowing
- Groaning, moaning, or grunting
- Increased sleeping
- Lack of bladder and bowel control

Near the end, the person may be in bed much or all of the time. The most frequent cause of death for people with AD is aspiration pneumonia. This type of pneumonia develops when a person is not able to swallow properly and takes food or liquids into the lungs instead of air.

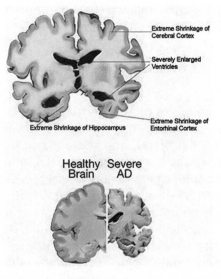

Figure 11.1. *Healthy Brain vs Severe AD*

Chapter 12

Genetics of
Alzheimer Disease

Chapter Contents

Section 12.1

Early-Onset and Late-Onset Alzheimer Disease

Text in this section is excerpted from "Alzheimer's Disease Genetics," National Institute on Aging (NIA), August 2015.

Scientists believe that many factors influence when Alzheimer disease (AD) begins and how it progresses. The more they study this devastating disease, the more they realize that genes play an important role. Research conducted and funded by the National Institute on Aging (NIA) at the National Institutes of Health (NIH) and others is advancing our understanding of Alzheimer disease genetics.

Genetics of Disease

Some diseases are caused by a genetic mutation, or permanent change in one or more specific genes. If a person inherits from a parent a genetic mutation that causes a certain disease, then he or she will usually get the disease. Sickle cell anemia, cystic fibrosis, and early-onset familial Alzheimer disease are examples of inherited genetic disorders.

In other diseases, a genetic variant may occur. A single gene can have many variants. Sometimes, this difference in a gene can cause a disease directly. More often, a variant plays a role in increasing or decreasing a person's risk of developing a disease or condition. When a genetic variant increases disease risk but does not directly cause a disease, it is called a genetic risk factor.

Identifying genetic variants may help researchers find the most effective ways to treat or prevent diseases such as Alzheimer in an individual. This approach, called precision medicine, takes into account individual variability in genes, environment, and lifestyle for each person.

Types of Alzheimer Disease

Alzheimer disease is an irreversible, progressive brain disease. It is characterized by the development of amyloid plaques and neurofibrillary, or tau, tangles; the loss of connections between nerve cells (neurons) in the brain; and the death of these nerve cells. There are two types of Alzheimer—early-onset and late-onset. Both types have a genetic component.

1. Early-Onset Alzheimer Disease

Early-onset Alzheimer disease occurs in people age 30 to 60 and represents less than 5 percent of all people with AD. Most cases are caused by an inherited change in one of three genes, resulting in a type known as early-onset familial Alzheimer disease, or FAD. For others, the disease appears to develop without any specific, known cause.

A child whose biological mother or father carries a genetic mutation for early-onset FAD has a 50/50 chance of inheriting that mutation. If the mutation is in fact inherited, the child has a very strong probability of developing early-onset FAD.

Early-onset FAD is caused by any one of a number of different single-gene mutations on chromosomes 21, 14, and 1. Each of these mutations causes abnormal proteins to be formed. Mutations on chromosome 21 cause the formation of abnormal amyloid precursor protein (APP). A mutation on chromosome 14 causes abnormal presenilin 1 to be made, and a mutation on chromosome 1 leads to abnormal presenilin 2.

Each of these mutations plays a role in the breakdown of APP, a protein whose precise function is not yet fully understood. This breakdown is part of a process that generates harmful forms of amyloid plaques, a hallmark of Alzheimer disease.

Critical research findings about early-onset Alzheimer have helped identify key steps in the formation of brain abnormalities typical of the more common late-onset form of AD. Genetics studies have helped explain why the disease develops in people at various ages.

NIA-supported scientists are continuing research into early-onset disease through the Dominantly Inherited Alzheimer Network (DIAN), an international partnership to study families with early-onset FAD. By observing the Alzheimer-related brain changes that occur in these families long before symptoms of memory loss or cognitive issues appear, scientists hope to gain insight into how and why the disease develops in both its early-and late-onset forms.

In addition, an NIA-supported clinical trial is testing the effectiveness of an amyloid-clearing drug in symptom-free volunteers at high risk of developing early-onset FAD.

2. Late-Onset Alzheimer Disease

Most people with AD have the late-onset form of the disease, in which symptoms become apparent in the mid-60s and later. The causes of late-onset Alzheimer are not yet completely understood, but they likely include a combination of genetic, environmental, and lifestyle factors that affect a person's risk for developing the disease.

Researchers have not found a specific gene that directly causes the late-onset form of the disease. However, one genetic risk factor—having one form of the apolipoprotein E (APOE) gene on chromosome 19—does increase a person's risk. APOE comes in several different forms, or alleles :

- APOE ε2 is relatively rare and may provide some protection against the disease. If Alzheimer disease occurs in a person with this allele, it usually develops later in life than it would in someone with the APOE ε4 gene.

- APOE ε3, the most common allele, is believed to play a neutral role in the disease—neither decreasing nor increasing risk.

- APOE ε4 increases risk for Alzheimer disease and is also associated with an earlier age of disease onset. A person has zero, one, or two APOE ε4 alleles. Having more APOE ε4 alleles increases the risk of developing AD.

APOE ε4 is called a risk-factor gene because it increases a person's risk of developing the disease. However, inheriting an APOE ε4 allele does not mean that a person will definitely develop AD. Some people with an APOE ε4 allele never get the disease, and others who develop AD do not have any APOE ε4 alleles.

Using a relatively new approach called genome-wide association study (GWAS), researchers have identified a number of regions of interest in the genome (an organism's complete set of DNA, including all of its genes) that may increase a person's risk for late-onset Alzheimer to varying degrees. By 2015, they had confirmed 33 regions of interest in the Alzheimer genome.

A method called whole genome sequencing determines the complete DNA sequence of a person's genome at a single time. Another method called whole exome sequencing looks at the parts of the genome that directly code for proteins. Using these two approaches, researchers can identify new genes that contribute to or protect against disease risk. Recent discoveries have led to new insights about biological pathways involved in AD and may one day lead to effective interventions.

Genetic Testing

A blood test can identify which APOE alleles a person has, but results cannot predict who will or will not develop AD disease. It is unlikely that genetic testing will ever be able to predict the disease with 100 percent accuracy, researchers believe, because too many other factors may influence its development and progression. Currently, APOE testing is used in research settings to identify study participants who may have an increased risk of developing Alzheimer. This knowledge helps scientists look for early brain changes in participants and compare the effectiveness of treatments for people with different APOE profiles. Most researchers believe that APOE testing is useful for studying Alzheimer disease risk in large groups of people but not for determining any one person's risk.

Genetic testing is used by researchers conducting clinical trials and by physicians to help diagnose early-onset Alzheimer disease. However, genetic testing is not otherwise recommended.

Epigenetics: Nature Meets Nurture

Scientists have long thought that genetic and environmental factors interact to influence a person's biological makeup, including the predisposition to different diseases. More recently, they have discovered the biological mechanisms for those interactions. The expression of genes (when particular genes are "switched" on or off) can be affected—positively and negatively—by environmental factors at any time in life. These factors include exercise, diet, chemicals, or smoking, to which an individual may be exposed, even in the womb.

Epigenetics is an emerging science focused on how and when particular genes are turned on or off. Diet and exposure to chemicals in the environment, among other factors, can alter a cell's DNA in ways that affect the activity of genes. That can make people more or less susceptible to developing a disease.

There is emerging evidence that epigenetic mechanisms contribute to Alzheimer disease. Epigenetic changes, whether protective, benign, or harmful, may help explain, for example, why one family member develops the disease and another does not. Scientists are learning more about Alzheimer-related epigenetics, with the hope of developing individualized treatments based on epigenetic markers and their function.

Section 12.2

Identifying the Genetics of Alzheimer Disease

Text in this section is excerpted from "Identifying the
Genetics of Alzheimer's Disease," National Institute on
Aging (NIA), February 15, 2014.

Age and genetics are the best-known risk factors for Alzheimer
disease. Most people with AD do not start showing symptoms until age
60 or older. However, in rare cases, people develop Alzheimer disease
(AD) much earlier, between the ages of 30 and 60. This "early-onset"
form of AD always runs in families. It is caused by a mutation in one
of three genes inherited from a parent that causes abnormal proteins
to be formed.

In early-onset Alzheimer disease, mutations on chromosome 21
cause the formation of abnormal amyloid precursor protein (APP),
a mutation on chromosome 14 causes abnormal presenilin 1 to be
made, and a mutation on chromosome 1 leads to abnormal presenilin
2. Scientists know that each of these mutations plays a role in the
cleavage of APP, a protein whose precise function is not yet known.
This breakdown is part of a process that generates harmful forms
of beta-amyloid, which lead to amyloid plaques, a hallmark of the
disease.

The more common "late-onset" form of the disease typically occurs
after age 65. While no single gene mutation is known to cause this form
of AD, evidence of a hereditary component is mounting. Environmental and lifestyle factors may also contribute to the risk of developing
late-onset Alzheimer.

The apolipoprotein E (APOE) gene is the strongest common genetic
risk factor identified to date for late-onset Alzheimer. The APOE gene,
found on chromosome 19, comes in three different forms, or alleles: ε2,
ε3, and ε4. The APOE ε2 allele is the least common form, found in 5
percent to 10 percent of people, and appears to reduce risk. The APOE
ε3 allele, the most common form, is found in 70 percent to 80 percent
of the population and appears to play a neutral role in the disease. The
APOE ε4 allele, found in 10 percent to 15 percent of the population,
increases risk for Alzheimer disease by three- to eight-fold, depending

on whether a person has one or two copies of the allele. The APOE ε4 allele is also associated with an earlier age of disease onset.

APOE ε4 is called a risk-factor gene because it increases a person's risk of developing the disease but is not the direct cause. Inheriting an APOE ε4 allele does not mean that a person will definitely develop AD. Some people with an APOE ε4 allele never get the disease, and many who develop AD do not have any APOE ε4 alleles.

Technology, Collaboration Key to Genetic Advances

Researchers are working collaboratively on genome-wide association studies (GWAS) to identify other genes that may influence Alzheimer disease. Technological advances have enabled them to detect subtle gene variants involved in this complex disorder by scanning thousands of DNA samples from people with Alzheimer disease and from unaffected individuals. By identifying genetic factors that may confer risk or protection, we gain insights into the molecular mechanisms and disease pathways that influence disease onset and progression.

Until 2009, APOE ε4 was the only known genetic risk factor for AD, but now GWAS researchers have detected and confirmed a growing list of others: PICALM, CLU, CR1, BIN1, MS4A, CD2AP, EPHA1, ABCA7, SORL1, and TREM2. In 2013, this list expanded to include another 11 genes, described below.

Scientists are using other techniques as well. Whole genome sequencing, which identified the TREM2 gene, captures genetic variations in an entire complement of a person's DNA. Researchers are also looking for genes that protect against the disease. In 2013, they identified one such protective gene, a variant of the APP gene, described below. These discoveries are helping to uncover the cellular pathways involved in AD and could lead to new avenues for therapeutic approaches.

New Gene Variants Associated with Risk of Alzheimer Disease

In the largest GWAS of Alzheimer disease to date, the International Genomic Alzheimer Project (IGAP) identified 11 new genes that contribute to risk of late-onset Alzheimer disease. The IGAP, a collaboration among four consortia in the United States and Europe, found the new genes by analyzing DNA sequence data from more than 74,000 older volunteers with and without Alzheimer disease from 15 countries.

The newly discovered genes (HLA-DRB5/HLA0DRB1, PTK2B, SLC24A4-0 RING3, DSG2, INPP5D, MEF2C, NME8, ZCWPW 1, CELF1, FERMT2, and CASS4) strengthened evidence about the involvement in Alzheimer disease of certain biological pathways, including amyloid metabolism and immune responses. The results also pointed to new candidate pathways, including pathways involved in microglial function and cellular protein degradation.

This GWAS study brought to light not only 11 new Alzheimer disease risk genes, but also another 13 DNA sequence variants that merited further analysis. Researchers at Washington University School of Medicine in St. Louis, the Alzheimer disease Genetics Consortium, the European Alzheimer disease Initiative, and others followed up on one of these, a sequence variation lying near the triggering receptor expressed on myeloid cells 2 (TREM2) gene that appears to protect against Alzheimer disease. This sequence variant turned out to lie not in the gene for TREM2, but in a nearby gene, the TREM-like 2 (TREML2) gene. As with TREM2, TREML2 is expressed by microglia but seems to have effects opposing those of TREM2—it reduces inflammation rather than promoting it. This study emphasizes the importance of deeper analysis of GWAS "hits" associated with Alzheimer disease and supports the idea that changes in microglial gene function can impact disease risk.

Disrupted Microglial Gene Function

To better understand which biological processes go awry in Alzheimer disease, researchers at the Icahn School of Medicine at Mount Sinai, New York City, looked for networks of genes whose normal pattern of activation is disrupted in the brains of people with the disease. (Activated genes are those from which protein is actively being made; different sets of genes are activated in different tissues.) The researchers compared the activation patterns of almost 40,000 different genes in brain tissue samples at autopsy from 376 participants with late-onset Alzheimer disease and 173 with normal cognition.

They identified gene networks that are disturbed in the brain regions most damaged by Alzheimer disease. The most strongly affected network contained genes responsible for controlling the brain's immune system, in particular the function of microglia—cells that help maintain brain health by removing cellular debris and infectious agents. Activation of many of these genes is controlled by a master regulatory gene called TYROBP. Because TYROBP is also involved in the clearing of beta-amyloid by microglia, it may be a promising therapeutic target.

Microglial Gene Triples Alzheimer Risk

Alzheimer geneticists discovered rare mutations in the TREM2 gene that appear to increase Alzheimer disease risk as much as three-fold. Scientists had previously found that both copies of the TREM2 gene are mutated in some cases of frontotemporal dementia. To learn if mutations in just one copy of the gene might be associated with Alzheimer disease, the scientists, from a number of academic institutions and NIA, analyzed thousands of DNA sequences from people with and without AD.

They identified a set of TREM2 mutations that occurred at much higher frequencies in people with Alzheimer disease than in controls. Unlike APOE ε4, the TREM2 mutations are very rare in the general population. Nonetheless, the discovery of these mutations sheds new light on the biology of AD.

Finding Genes Involved in Tau Pathology

Alzheimer disease GWAS studies typically look for DNA sequence variations that occur more frequently in people with cognitive symptoms of the disease and then compare them with the DNA of cognitively normal volunteers. A research team from the Alzheimer Disease Genetics Consortium and the Alzheimer Disease Neuroimaging Initiative (ADNI), led by scientists at the Washington University School of Medicine, St. Louis, took a different approach. They looked for sequence variations associated with two protein biomarkers of the disease: elevated levels of tau and phosphorylated tau (ptau) in the cerebrospinal fluid (CSF).

The researchers studied DNA samples from almost 1,300 participants, about half of whom had Alzheimer disease and the rest of whom were cognitively healthy. Four sets of DNA sequence variations were associated with increased CSF tau and ptau levels. Two of these variations lay within genes already associated with Alzheimer disease, APOE and TREM. The third variant lay in a region of chromosome 3 that contains several genes involved in development of synapses. The fourth lay in a gene called GLI3 that has been implicated in diabetes. These new genetic discoveries could improve our understanding of how abnormal tau contributes to Alzheimer disease and point to possible new drugs that might target tau pathology.

85

Microglial Function and the CD33 Gene

Microglia help maintain brain health by scavenging and digesting cellular debris, including beta-amyloid plaque. Previous GWAS have indicated a link between Alzheimer disease and variations in the DNA sequences of certain microglial genes, but it has been unclear how those microglial genes might influence pathology. Studies from researchers at Massachusetts General Hospital, Boston, and a group from ADNI, Brigham and Women's Hospital, Boston, and Rush University, Chicago, now suggest that one of these genes, CD33, regulates the ability of microglia to clear beta-amyloid from the brain.

The Massachusetts General researchers found that microglia in the brains of Alzheimer disease patients produce higher levels of CD33 protein than do microglia in the brains of people with normal cognition and that microglia in mouse models of Alzheimer lacking the CD33 gene proved better at engulfing and digesting beta-amyloid. They also found that in human brains, a CD33 gene variant that protects against Alzheimer disease reduced both CD33 production and beta-amyloid levels in human brains.

The other group of researchers found, conversely, that a variant of the CD33 gene that increases Alzheimer disease risk was associated with increased levels of both CD33 protein and brain beta-amyloid. These studies show that CD33 gene variants can either increase or decrease levels of CD33 protein in the brain, and that CD33 protein inhibits the ability of microglia to clear beta-amyloid. Therefore, the CD33 gene may prove a viable therapeutic target.

Alzheimer Risk Gene and the Oldest-Old

The ε4 allele of the APOE gene, the most established genetic risk factor for late-onset Alzheimer disease, appears to have less impact on risk of cognitive decline in people over age 90 than in younger people. University of California, Irvine, researchers evaluated cognition every 6 months for an average of 2.3 years in 904 volunteers age 90 years and older in The 90+ Study. In this group of the "oldest-old," carriers of the APOE ε4 allele did not develop dementia or die at higher rates than did non carriers. This finding suggests that the known risk associated with this gene may be age dependent and that the gene may not play a role in dementia and mortality at very old ages.

Section 12.3

Genetic Risks in Minority Populations

Text in this section is excerpted from "Health
Disparities and Alzheimer's Disease," National Institute on
Aging (NIA), February 15, 2014.

Health Disparities and Alzheimer Disease

Studies and surveys suggest that certain racial, ethnic, and
socio-economic groups may be at greater risk than others for cognitive decline and dementia. There may also be gender differences in
risk for cognitive decline. Understanding these differences is critical
to developing appropriate risk assessments and diagnostic tools and
providing the most effective interventions to prevent and treat Alzheimer disease (AD) for everyone.

African-American Gene Linked to Alzheimer Risk

A variant of a gene involved in cholesterol and lipid metabolism,
ABCA7, appears to be a stronger risk factor for late-onset Alzheimer disease in African Americans than in non-Hispanic whites of
European ancestry. In the largest genome-wide association study conducted to date in African Americans, the Alzheimer Disease Genetics
Con-sortium and Columbia University Medical Center, New York
City, researchers analyzed genetic data from 5,896 participants age
60 or older, of whom 1,968 had Alzheimer disease and the rest were
cognitively normal.

The gene variants associated with increased Alzheimer disease
risk in African Americans matched variants previously identified as
risk factors in white Americans of European ancestry. However, the
ABCA7 gene variant almost doubled the risk of Alzheimer disease in
African Americans, whereas variants in the same gene increased risk
by only 10 to 20 percent in whites.

The risk from the ABCA7 gene variant was as strong in African
Americans as that from the apolipoprotein E ε4 (APOE ε4) allele, the
most important known genetic risk factor for late-onset Alzheimer
in whites. Although preliminary, these findings suggest that the two

87

racial groups may have different genetic risk profiles for the most common form of Alzheimer dementia.

Risk Factors for Cognitive Decline among Mexican Americans

Known risk factors for mild cognitive impairment (MCI) in non-His-panic populations may not be predictive of MCI among Mexican Americans. Researchers at the University of North Texas Science Center, Fort Worth, analyzed data from 1,006 non-Hispanic and 626 Hispanic participants aged 50 or older in two studies of cognitive aging. They found that both groups had similar rates of MCI incidence and that age was the greatest risk factor. However, on average Mexican Americans developed cognitive loss when 10 years younger than the non-Hispanic group. In addition, unlike the non-Hispanic group, higher levels of education did not protect against MCI, and diabetes did not confer greater risk for MCI in the Mexican-American volunteers. These findings indicate the need to better understand the factors that may influence MCI in this fast-growing segment of the U.S. population.

Researchers at the University of California, San Francisco, studied the impact of diabetes on risk of dementia and cognitive impairment without dementia (CIND) among older Mexican Americans. Their study included more than 1,600 participants age 60 to 98 from the Sacramento Area Latino Study on Aging. The volunteers, all dementia-free at the start of the study, were followed with annual blood sugar measurements and cognitive tests for up to 10 years. Participants with diabetes had a twofold increased risk of developing dementia/CIND, but whether treated or untreated, Mexican Americans with diabetes were at increased risk. Given the high burden of diabetes among Mexican Americans, future rates of dementia in this population might be reduced by efforts to prevent diabetes onset.

Gender, Genetics May Influence Treatment Responses

Preliminary studies show that insulin delivered via a nasal spray might be a safe and effective treatment for memory loss associated with MCI and Alzheimer disease, and major clinical trials to test such a drug are underway. However, one study from the University of Washington School of Medicine, Seattle, suggests that patient responses to this treatment could vary with gender and APOE ε4 genotype. The study involved 104 older volunteers with MCI or Alzheimer disease who were randomly assigned to receive a daily dose of 20 International

Units (IU) of insulin, 40 IU of insulin, or a placebo during 4 months. Both men and women showed improvement on a memory test when taking 20 IU of insulin, but only men showed improvement with the 40 IU dose. For the 40 IU dose, APOE ε4-negative men improved, APOE ε4-negative women worsened, and APOE ε4-positive participants remained cognitively stable. These findings will inform future research investigating the use of insulin nasal spray as a treatment for Alzheimer.

Chapter 13

Health Conditions Linked to Alzheimer Disease

Chapter Contents

91

Section 13.1

Down Syndrome and Alzheimer Disease

Text in this section is excerpted from "Alzheimer's Disease
in People with Down Syndrome," National Institute on
Aging (NIA), November 2015.

The Connection between Down Syndrome and Alzheimer Disease

Many, but not all, people with Down syndrome develop Alzheimer disease when they get older. Alzheimer disease is an irreversible, progressive brain disorder that slowly destroys memory and thinking skills and, eventually, the ability to carry out simple tasks.

Alzheimer disease (AD) is the most common cause of dementia among older adults. Dementia is the loss of cognitive functioning—thinking, remembering, and reasoning—and behavioral abilities to such an extent that it interferes with a person's daily life and activities.

People with Down syndrome are born with an extra copy of chromosome 21, which carries the APP gene. This gene produces a specific protein called amyloid precursor protein (APP). Too much APP protein leads to a buildup of protein clumps called beta-amyloid plaques in the brain. By age 40, almost all people with Down syndrome have these plaques, along with other protein deposits, called tau tangles, which cause problems with how brain cells function and increase the risk of developing Alzheimer dementia.

However, not all people with these brain plaques will develop the symptoms of Alzheimer disease. Estimates suggest that 50 percent or more of people with Down syndrome will develop dementia due to Alzheimer disease as they age, many now into their 70s.

Symptoms of Alzheimer Disease

Many people with Down syndrome begin to show symptoms of Alzheimer disease in their 50s or 60s. But, like in all people with Alzheimer, changes in the brain that lead to these symptoms are thought to begin at least 10 years earlier. These brain changes include the buildup of plaques and tangles, the loss of connections between

92

nerve cells, the death of nerve cells, and the shrinking of brain tissue (called atrophy).

The risk for Alzheimer disease increases with age, so it's important to watch for certain changes in behavior, such as:

- increased confusion

- short-term memory problems (for example, asking the same questions over and over)

- reduction in or loss of ability to do everyday activities

Other possible symptoms of Alzheimer dementia are:

- seizures that begin in adulthood

- problems with coordination and walking

- reduced ability to pay attention

- behavior and personality changes, such as wandering and being less social

- decreased fine motor control

- difficulty finding one's way around familiar areas

If you notice any of these changes, see a healthcare provider to find out more. Keep in mind, though, that not all dementia symptoms are caused by Alzheimer disease. Other conditions, such as medication side effects, depression, and kidney, thyroid, and liver problems, can also cause dementia symptoms. Some of these conditions can be treated and reversed.

Currently, Alzheimer disease has no cure, and no medications have been approved to treat Alzheimer in people with Down syndrome.

Down Syndrome and Alzheimer Research

Alzheimer disease can last several years, and symptoms usually get worse over time. Scientists are working hard to understand why some people with Down syndrome develop dementia while others do not. They want to know how Alzheimer disease begins and progresses, so they can develop drugs or other treatments that can stop, delay, or even prevent the disease process.

Research in this area includes:

- basic studies to improve our understanding of the genetic and biological causes of brain abnormalities that lead to Alzheimer disease

- observational research to measure cognitive changes in people over time

- studies of biomarkers (biological signs of disease), brain scans, and other tests that may help diagnose Alzheimer disease—even before symptoms appear—and show brain changes as people with Down syndrome age

- clinical trials to test treatments for dementia in adults with Down syndrome. Clinical trials are best the way to find out if a treatment is safe and effective in people.

Section 13.2

Obesity May Raise Risk of Alzheimer Disease and Dementia

This section includes excerpts from "Adults Obese or Overweight at Midlife May Be at Risk for Earlier Onset of Alzheimer's Disease," National Institute on Aging (NIA), September 1, 2015; and text from "Translating Knowledge into Promising Treatments," National Institute on Aging (NIA), February 15, 2014.

Adults Obese or Overweight at Midlife May Be at Risk for Earlier Onset of Alzheimer Disease

Being obese or overweight in middle age has been linked to increased risk of dementia. To learn more, researchers at the National Institute on Aging, part of the NIH, further explored the relationship between weight at midlife and Alzheimer disease (AD) among volunteers participating in the Baltimore Longitudinal Study of Aging (BLSA), one of the longest running studies of human aging in North America. They found that being obese or overweight at midlife—as measured by body mass index (BMI) at age 50—may predict earlier age of onset of the devastating neurodegenerative disorder.

Cognitively healthy at the start of the nearly 14-year study, each of the 1,394 BLSA participants received cognitive testing every one to two years; 142 volunteers eventually developed Alzheimer disease. The investigators found:

- Each unit increase in BMI at age 50 accelerated onset by nearly 7 months in those who developed Alzheimer disease.

- Higher midlife BMI was associated with greater levels of neurofibrillary tangles—a hallmark of the disease—in the brains of 191 volunteers, including those who did not develop Alzheimer disease.

- Among 75 cognitively healthy volunteers who had brain imaging to detect amyloid, a protein whose fragments make up the brain plaques that are a hallmark of Alzheimer disease, those with higher midlife BMI had more amyloid deposits in the precuneus, a brain region that often shows the earliest signs of Alzheimer disease-related changes.

More study is needed to determine the relationship behind BMI at midlife and Alzheimer disease onset. The findings suggest, however, that maintaining a healthy BMI at midlife might be considered as one way to delay the onset of Alzheimer disease.

Are Brain Glucose Transport Systems a Viable Target?

As people age, the brain gradually shifts from relying on glucose as an energy source to alternative fuel sources, such as fatty acids and ketone bodies. To better understand what causes this shift, researchers at the University of Southern California, Los Angeles, used positron emission tomography imaging to study changes in brain glucose metabolism during menopause in normal female mice and Alzheimer disease model female mice. In both types of mice, the earliest change was a significant decline in glucose uptake in the brain that occurred just prior to the transition to menopause. This study suggests potential new targets and treatment windows for preventing age- and Alzheimer disease-related declines in brain glucose metabolism.

Calorie Reduction May Improve Brain Health

Previous studies suggest that reducing calorie consumption can extend lifespan and help prevent age-related cognitive decline. A study in aging mice led by researchers at the Cold Spring Harbor Laboratory, NY, suggests that caloric restriction benefits cognition by slowing age-related declines in neurogenesis. Starting at 6 months of age, mice were fed either a standard diet (in which they had free access to food) or a nutritious but calorie-restricted diet (60 percent of the free-access diet).

A year later, female mice on the calorie-restricted diet showed significantly more proliferating neuronal precursor cells in the hippocampus (a structure important for learning and memory) than did female mice fed the standard diet. In contrast, caloric restriction had no effect on neurogenesis in male mice. This study points to enhanced neurogenesis as a mechanism whereby caloric restriction may benefit cognitive function, and it suggests that the effect may be gender-dependent.

Section 13.3

Type 2 Diabetes and Alzheimer Disease Risk

Text in this section is excerpted from "Diabetes, Dementia, and Alzheimer's Disease," National Institute of Diabetes and Digestive and Kidney Diseases (NIDDK), August 16, 2012.

Diabetes and Dementia: Untangling the Web—Dr. Suzanne Craft, University of Washington School of Medicine

Dr. Suzanne Craft is Professor of Psychiatry and Behavioral Sciences at the University of Washington; she is also Associate Director of the Geriatric Research, Education, and Clinical Center, and Director of the Memory Disorders Clinic, at the VA Puget Sound Medical Center. With support from the NIH, the VA, and other sources, Dr. Craft has focused her research program on neuroendocrine abnormalities in the development and expression of Alzheimer Disease (AD). AD is an irreversible, progressive brain disease that slowly destroys memory and thinking skills, and eventually even the ability to carry out the simplest tasks. AD is the most common cause of dementia among older people, and prevalence increases exponentially with age. While estimates vary, experts suggest that several million Americans may have AD. Dr. Craft noted epidemiological studies finding that insulin resistance, hyperinsulinemia, and impaired glucose tolerance (IGT)/type 2 diabetes are associated with increased risk for cognitive impairment and AD; these observations are consistent with evidence showing that insulin normally plays a positive role in brain function and cognition. As a result, Dr. Craft and other researchers are investigating biological mechanisms that could be responsible for the increased risk for diminished brain function associated with prediabetes and diabetes.

The brain's primary energy source is the sugar glucose. Through imaging studies of people with preclinical AD, Dr. Craft and colleagues have observed patterns of impaired glucose metabolism in the brain that can be detected well before clinical onset of the disease. Conversely, they have observed that patterns virtually identical to the AD risk patterns can be found in cognitively normal people with prediabetes and type 2 diabetes, a resemblance that increases with increasing levels of insulin resistance.

Delving into the potential molecular mechanisms linking development of cognitive impairment with dysfunctional glucose metabolism in the brain, Dr. Craft and her colleagues examined the interplay between insulin, insulin resistance, and beta amyloid, also called A-— the key component of the "senile plaques" that are a hallmark of AD. Dr. Craft pointed out that evidence now indicates that the formation of these insoluble peptide plaques may actually be a defense mechanism to deal with a greater threat—smaller complexes of A molecules called oligomers. A oligomers are soluble, synaptotoxic (damaging to inter-neuron signaling), cause neuronal loss, and ultimately lead to cognitive impairment. In the brain, insulin helps to regulate A levels (and hence levels of the oligomers).

Experiments revealed a reciprocal relationship between insulin and A oligomers: treating laboratory-grown neurons with insulin could protect them from A oligomer induced-synapotoxicity, but treating neurons with oligomers alone caused insulin receptors to move away from synaptic surfaces (dendritic membranes)—likely reducing insulin signaling and contributing to insulin resistance in the brain. Moreover, experiments in non-human primates showed that administering A oligomers directly into the brain induced a chemical change in a protein called IRS-1 that, in other tissues, is characteristic of insulin resistance—further suggesting that A oligomers play a role in insulin resistance in the brain.

Dr. Craft and her colleagues have also examined the effect of insulin resistance in the rest of the body on A levels in the brain. Experiments in animal models of AD showed that inducing insulin resistance and hyperinsulinemia increased the burden of A in the brain. In humans, Dr. Craft and her colleagues found through an experimental diet intervention study that 4 weeks of a diet high in saturated fat and with a high glycemic index not only had a negative impact on metabolism—increasing insulin resistance and LDL cholesterol—but also significantly increased markers of AD pathology (including A) and oxidative injury detectable in the cerebrospinal fluid, a proxy for the brain. In comparison, a diet with the same caloric value but low in saturated fat and with a low glycemic index had beneficial effects on these markers. Interestingly, these results may help explain the epidemiological observations that greater saturated fat intake in mid-life increases age-related cognitive impairment and AD risk, while lower-fat diets richer in beneficial fats and complex carbohydrates decrease risk. In another set of clinical experiments, the research team found that artificially inducing hyperinsulinemia in the absence of insulin resistance induced increases in A and markers of inflammation in cerebrospinal fluid, indicating that not all of the observed indications of AD-related pathology are the direct result of insulin resistance or elevated blood glucose: hyperinsulinemia may itself play a disease promoting-role. Some data suggest that older age may make people more vulnerable to these effects.

Diabetes and insulin resistance may also increase or augment AD risk through effects on vascular function. Deposition of Aβ in cerebral vasculature has been observed in mouse models. In mice genetically engineered to be vulnerable to AD and diabetes, the deposition is greater than in AD alone, and increases with age. When Dr. Craft and colleagues compared the amount of plaques and protein "tangles" (another AD marker) present in specimens from the brains of deceased persons who had had both dementia and diabetes, to that present in brain specimens of deceased persons who had only dementia, only diabetes, or neither, the results were surprising—plaques and tangles were highest in persons with dementia alone, not in persons with both dementia and diabetes. However, those with both diseases had a significantly greater prevalence of microvascular lesions in their brain specimens. The significance of this finding is not yet known—the lesions are too small to be causing problems on their own, but could be markers of some greater vascular pathology important to AD.

As Dr. Craft noted, their finding that amyloid pathology was not greatest in brains of people who died with both dementia and diabetes was quite intriguing. One possible explanation was that diabetes treatment affects amyloid plaque levels. However, Dr. Craft and her colleagues found that specimens from persons with dementia plus untreated diabetes displayed a similar plaque burden to that seen in dementia alone, while diabetes treatment with insulin (with or without additional oral medication) yielded a lower number of plaques, at a level closer to that seen in persons with diabetes alone (treated or untreated) or neither disease—suggesting that diabetes treatment (primarily insulin) might have a mediating effect on plaques. Similar results were seen for tangles. In contrast, however, the treated-diabetes group had the highest counts of microvascular lesions. Together, these data suggest the provocative notion that dementia in individuals with untreated diabetes is likely to show the classic pathological hallmarks of AD, while microvascular lesions are more commonly characteristic of dementia in those with treated diabetes. The data also suggest that researchers investigating the links between diabetes and dementia should consider the potential effects of diabetes treatment.

Dr. Craft noted findings from her lab and others of a reduction in insulin transport across the "blood-brain barrier" in people with AD, leading to reduced insulin signaling in the brain. These observations that increasing brain insulin levels might potentially be therapeutically beneficial in AD, and/or help prevent progression of dementia. Intranasal administration of insulin is one potentially effective route. In a mouse model of diabetes, intranasal insulin administration significantly reduced the exacerbated brain atrophy that occurs in these mice as they age. Dr. Craft and colleagues are seeking to extend these findings through clinical research—the Study of Nasal Insulin to Fight Forgetfulness (SNIFF) to test whether intranasal administration can normalize brain insulin levels and improve memory and cognition in people with AD. In one recent study, adults with mild cognitive impairment or mild AD received either daily intranasal insulin at one of two different dosing levels or a placebo over the course of 4 months. The research team found that the lower dose of insulin was best for memory, but participants receiving either dosing level of nasal insulin fared better than those receiving placebo on other measures of cognition. Live imaging studies showed improvements in glucose metabolism, including in areas known to be important to AD pathology, in participants who received intranasal insulin. On the basis of these encouraging results, a larger, longer, multi-site trial is slated to begin in the fall of 2012.

In another approach, Dr. Craft and colleagues are testing the therapeutic potential of improving insulin sensitivity in AD, rather than providing additional insulin. Studies of lifestyle approaches (exercise) have shown promise for improving cognitive function and/or AD biomarkers, setting the stage for another study beginning in fall 2012. Other laboratories are testing the pharmacologic approach, using insulin-sensitizing drugs that may improve insulin signaling in the brain.

Chapter 14

Traumatic Brain Injury, Alzheimer Disease, and Dementia

What Is a Traumatic Brain Injury (TBI)?

A Traumatic Brain Injury (TBI) occurs when physical, external forces impact the brain either from a penetrating object or a bump, blow, or jolt to the head. Not all blows or jolts to the head result in a TBI. For the ones that do, TBIs can range from mild (a brief change in mental status or consciousness) to severe (an extended period of unconsciousness or amnesia after the injury). There are two broad types of head injuries: penetrating and nonpenetrating.

Penetrating TBI (also known as open TBI) occurs when the skull is pierced by an object (for example, a bullet, shrapnel, bone fragment, or by a weapon such as hammer, knife, or baseball bat). With this injury, the object enters the brain tissue.

Non-penetrating TBI (also known as *closed head injury or blunt TBI*) is caused by an external force that produces movement of the brain within the skull. Causes include falls, motor vehicle crashes,

This chapter includes excerpts from "Traumatic Brain Injury: Hope through Research," National Institute of Neurological Disorders and Stroke (NINDS), January 7, 2016; and text from "Traumatic Brain Injury Increases Dementia Risk," U.S. Department of Veterans Affairs (VA), July 20, 2011. Reviewed February 2016.

sports injuries, or being struck by an object. Blast injury due to explosions is a focus of intense study but how it causes brain injury is not fully known.

Some accidents such as explosions, natural disasters, or other extreme events can cause both penetrating and nonpenetrating TBI in the same person.

What Are the Signs and Symptoms of TBI?

The effects of TBI can range from severe and permanent disability to more subtle functional and cognitive difficulties that often go undetected during initial evaluation. These problems may emerge days later. Headache, dizziness, confusion, and fatigue tend to start immediately after an injury, but resolve over time. Emotional symptoms such as frustration and irritability tend to develop later on during the recovery period. Many of the signs and symptoms can be easily missed as people may appear healthy even though they act or feel different. Many of the symptoms overlap with other conditions, such as depression or sleep disorders. If any of the following symptoms appear suddenly or worsen over time following a TBI, especially within the first 24 hours after the injury, people should see a medical professional on an emergency basis.

People should seek immediate medical attention if they experience any of the following symptoms:

- loss of or change in consciousness anywhere from a few seconds to a few hours

- decreased level of consciousness, i.e., hard to awaken

- convulsions or seizures

- unequal dilation in the pupils of the eyes or double vision

- clear fluids draining from the nose or ears

- nausea and vomiting

- new neurologic deficit, i.e., slurred speech; weakness of arms, legs, or face; loss of balance

Other common symptoms that should be monitored include:

- mild to profound confusion or disorientation

- problems remembering, concentrating, or making decisions

- headache

- light-headedness, dizziness, vertigo, or loss of balance or coordination

- sensory problems, such as blurred vision, seeing stars, ringing in the ears, bad taste in the mouth

- sensitivity to light or sound

- mood changes or swings, agitation (feeling sad or angry for no reason), combativeness, or other unusual behavior

- feelings of depression or anxiety

- fatigue or drowsiness; a lack of energy or motivation

- changes in sleep patterns (e.g., sleeping a lot more or having difficulty falling or staying asleep); inability to wake up from sleep

In some cases, repeated blows to the head can cause *chronic traumatic encephalopathy* (CTE) – a progressive neurological disorder associated with a variety of symptoms, including cognition and communication problems, motor disorders, problems with impulse control and depression, confusion, and irritability. CTE occurs in those with extraordinary exposure to multiple blows to the head and as a delayed consequence after many years. Studies of retired boxers have shown that repeated blows to the head can cause a number of issues, including memory problems, tremors, and lack of coordination and dementia. Recent studies have demonstrated rare cases of CTE in other sports with repetitive mild head impacts (e.g., soccer, wrestling, football, and rugby). A single, severe TBI also may lead to a disorder called *post-traumatic dementia* (PTD), which may be progressive and share some features with CTE. Studies assessing patterns among large populations of people with TBI indicate that moderate or severe TBI in early or mid-life may be associated with increased risk of dementia later in life.

Evidence suggests that genetics play a role in how quickly and completely a person recovers from a TBI. For example, researchers have found that apolipoprotein E ε4 (ApoE4)—a genetic variant associated with higher risks for Alzheimer disease—is associated with worse health outcomes following a TBI. Much work remains to be done to understand how genetic factors, as well as how specific types of head injuries in particular locations, affect recovery processes. It is hoped that this research will lead to new treatment strategies and improved outcomes for people with TBI.

What Are the Leading Causes of TBI?

According to data from the Centers for Disease Control and Prevention (CDC), falls are the most common cause of TBIs and occur most frequently among the youngest and oldest age groups. From 2006 to 2010 alone, falls caused more than half (55 percent) of TBIs among children aged 14 and younger. Among Americans age 65 and older, falls accounted for more than two-thirds (81 percent) of all reported TBIs.

TBIs caused by blast trauma from roadside bombs became a common injury to service members in recent military conflicts. From 2000 to 2014 more than 320,000 military service personnel sustained TBIs, though these injuries were not all conflict related. The majority of these TBIs were classified as mild head injuries and due to similar causes as those that occur in civilians.

Adults age 65 and older are at greatest risk for being hospitalized and dying from a TBI, most likely from a fall. TBI-related deaths in children aged 4 years and younger are most likely the result of assault. In young adults aged 15 to 24 years, motor vehicle accidents are the most likely cause. In every age group, serious TBI rates are higher for men than for women. Men are more likely to be hospitalized and are nearly three times more likely to die from a TBI than women.

What Are the Potential Effects of TBI?

The severity of a TBI may range from "mild," i.e., a brief change in mental status or consciousness, to "severe," i.e., an extended period of unconsciousness or amnesia after the injury.

TBI can cause a wide range of functional short- or long-term changes affecting thinking, sensation, language, or emotions. TBI can also cause epilepsy and increase the risk for conditions such as Alzheimer disease, Parkinson disease, and other brain disorders that become more prevalent with age.

About 75% of TBIs that occur each year are concussions or other forms of mild TBI.

Repeated mild TBIs occurring over an extended period of time (i.e., months, years) can result in cumulative neurological and cognitive deficits. Repeated mild TBIs occurring within a short period of time (i.e., hours, days, or weeks) can be catastrophic or fatal.

Traumatic Brain Injury Increases AD Risk

Patients diagnosed with traumatic brain injury (TBI) had over twice the risk of developing dementia within seven years after diagnosis compared to those without TBI, in a study of more than 280,000 older veterans conducted by researchers at the San Francisco VA Medical Center and the University of California, San Francisco.

"This finding is important because TBI is so common," said senior investigator Kristine Yaffe, MD, chief of geriatric psychiatry at SFVAMC and professor of psychiatry, neurology and epidemiology at UCSF. She noted that about 1.7 million Americans are diagnosed with TBI each year.

The study authors analyzed the medical records of 281,540 veterans age 55 or older who received care through the VA from 1997 to 2000 and did not have a prior history of dementia. They found that 15 percent of veterans who received a diagnosis of TBI developed dementia by 2007, compared with 7 percent of those not diagnosed with TBI. Even after controlling for factors such as age, medical history and cardiovascular health, the authors found that a TBI diagnosis still doubled the risk of dementia.

Lead author Deborah Barnes, PhD, a mental health researcher at SFVAMC, said that the study is one of the first to examine the association between dementia and different types of TBI diagnosis, including intra-cranial injuries, concussion, post-concussion syndrome and skull fracture. "It didn't matter what type of diagnosis it was – they were all associated with an elevated risk of dementia," said Barnes, also an associate professor of psychiatry at UCSF.

The authors speculated that among potential causes for the increased risk, the most plausible is that TBI is associated with diffuse axonal injury, or swelling of the axons that form connections between neurons in the brain. This swelling, explained Yaffe, is accompanied by the accumulation of proteins, including beta-amyloid, which is a hallmark of Alzheimer disease. "The loss of axons and neurons could result in earlier manifestation of Alzheimer disease symptoms," said Yaffe.

Chapter 15

Other Factors That Influence Alzheimer Disease Risk

Chapter Contents

107

Section 15.1

Alcohol Use and the Risk of Developing Alzheimer Disease

Text in this section is excerpted from "Alcohol Use and the
Risk of Developing Alzheimer's Disease," National Institute
on Alcohol Abuse and Alcoholism (NIAAA), April 1, 2002.
Reviewed February 2016.

Alzheimer disease (AD) is a degenerative brain disorder characterized by a progressive loss of memory and other detrimental cognitive
changes as well as lowered life expectancy. It is the leading cause of
dementia in the United States. Aside from the substantial personal
costs, AD is a major economic burden on health care and social services. Estimates of the number of people with AD in the United States
in 1997 ranged from 1 million to more than 4 million, and these figures
are expected to quadruple within 50 years unless effective interventions are developed. The risk of AD increases exponentially with age;
consequently, as the population ages, the importance of AD as a public
health concern grows, as does the need for research on the cause of AD
and on strategies for its prevention and treatment.

Studying factors that influence the risk of developing AD may lead
to the identification of those at high risk for developing it, strategies
for prevention or intervention, and clues to the cause of the disease.
Both genetic and environmental factors have been implicated in the
development of AD, but the cause of AD remains unknown, and no
cure or universally effective treatment has yet been developed.

Alcohol consumption is one possible risk factor for AD. Alcoholism
is associated with extensive cognitive problems, including alcoholic
dementia. Because alcohol's effects on cognition, brain disorders, and
brain chemistry share some features with AD's effects on these three
areas, it is plausible that alcohol use might also increase the risk of
developing AD. Investigating whether and to what degree alcohol use
is related to AD is made more difficult by the challenges of diagnosing and distinguishing alcoholic dementia and AD. Such studies are
important, however, because alcohol use is a common but preventable exposure, an association between alcohol and AD is biologically

plausible, and knowledge of the effect of alcohol on AD may provide clues to the cause of AD.

This section briefly reviews biological evidence suggesting that alcohol use may be associated with AD. It also focuses on the evidence from epidemiologic studies that link people's consumption of alcohol to whether they develop AD, considers the influence of tobacco use on the relationship between alcohol use and AD, and examines the epidemiologic evidence of the connection between alcohol consumption and types of cognitive impairment other than AD.

Effects of Alcohol Use on Brain Disorders and Cognition

Heavy alcohol consumption has both immediate and long-term detrimental effects on the brain and neuropsychological functioning. Heavy drinking accelerates shrinkage, or atrophy, of the brain, which in turn is a critical determinant of neurodegenerative changes and cognitive decline in aging.

Changes observed with alcohol-related brain disorders, however, may be no more than superficially similar to those seen with aging or AD. In contrast to aging and AD, alcohol's effects on the brain may be reversible. Atrophy decreases after abstinence from alcohol. A study that further investigated cerebral atrophy in alcoholics and age-matched control subjects found no significant differences in the number of nerve cells in the brain (i.e., neurons) between the two groups and that most of the loss occurred in the white matter, which consists largely of nerve fibers that connect neurons. The researchers concluded that, because neurons did not appear to be lost, disrupted functions could be restored after abstinence as neuronal connections were reestablished. This conclusion is supported by research that also showed no neuronal loss in alcoholics compared with nonalcoholics but did show significant loss of brain cells that provide support for neurons (i.e., glial cells) which, in contrast to neurons, can be regenerated. That alcoholics can show improved cognitive performance after abstinence provides additional evidence of a reversible effect. Other studies, however, have reported neuronal loss with chronic alcohol abuse, including loss of neurons (i.e., cholinergic neurons) that contain or are stimulated by a certain chemical messenger in the brain (i.e., the neurotransmitter acetylcholine). Cholinergic neurons are specifically affected in AD.

Improvement in cognitive function, or at least the lack of a progressive cognitive deficit, is one of the major factors used to determine whether a patient has alcoholic dementia rather than AD. Recent work suggesting that characteristic neuropsychological profiles exist for alcoholic dementia and AD may prove useful in distinguishing the two disorders. The diagnosis of alcoholic dementia, however, is itself somewhat controversial. Alcoholic dementia may have multiple causes. Pathological findings consistent with AD, nutritional deficiencies, trauma, and, in particular, stroke, also have been found in demented alcoholics. The difficulty in distinguishing alcoholic dementia from AD has been attributed to a shared substrate of brain damage in the two disorders. A diagnosis of alcoholic dementia may be appropriate for some demented patients who have a history of alcohol abuse, but the effects of more moderate levels of drinking on cognitive function (for anyone) are not known. Thus, despite evidence of an association between alcohol use and neuropathologic and cognitive deficits, including alcoholic dementia, it is not yet clear whether alcohol use at either heavy or more moderate levels of consumption is associated with AD.

Biological Mechanisms

Both alcohol and AD substantially affect the cholinergic system, and thus it is plausible that alcohol use could be linked to AD through their common effects on this system. Early studies of AD from the 1980s focused on the cholinergic system because it was known to play an important role in memory. Its role in AD was confirmed, and deficits in the cholinergic system, such as lower levels of acetylcholine and fewer receptors (proteins that bind to neurotransmitters), are now well established in AD. Although other neurotransmitter systems have since been implicated in AD, current treatment strategies still include repletion of cholinergic deficits.

The cholinergic system also is affected by alcohol use. Chronic alcohol use causes degeneration of cholinergic neurons. Alcohol has been shown to decrease acetylcholine levels, reducing its synthesis and release. These deficits may aggravate the reductions already present in AD. Improvement of cognitive function in alcoholics after abstention from alcohol suggests that the cognitive deficits may reflect neurochemical alterations rather than neuronal loss. Alcohol-related memory loss can be partially reversed by compounds that stimulate the cholinergic system (e.g., nicotine), illustrating the importance of the cholinergic system in alcohol's effects on memory. Alcohol-induced cholinergic receptor losses in alcoholics with AD may contribute to the clinical symptoms of dementia. Alcohol does not appear to accelerate the AD process but instead induces its effects on the cholinergic system, independent of the cholinergic deficits caused by AD. In addition, alcohol has extensive effects on neurotransmitter systems other than the cholinergic system and may also affect AD through these pathways.

Alcohol may interact with both the brain and the aging process. In rodents, for example, age-related impairments in learning and memory are aggravated by alcohol consumption. Alcohol-related brain damage appears to differ in young and old alcoholics. Although it has been suggested that alcohol abuse may accelerate aging-related changes in the brain at any age and that older adults may be more vulnerable to alcohol's effects and thus show more age-related cognitive changes, these hypotheses of premature aging have been questioned. Arendt (1993) has suggested that the degenerative changes associated with aging, chronic alcohol abuse, and AD are on a continuum and that they may be quantitatively different but not qualitatively so.

Although a link between alcohol use and AD is plausible, whether such a relationship does exist or what the characteristics of such an association would be has not yet been established. For example, alcohol might affect whether one developed AD, when one developed it, or the progression of AD once one had developed it. Observing no association between increased numbers of senile plaques (a characteristic marker of AD found in the brain) and alcohol-related receptor loss, Freund and Ballinger (1992) concluded that alcohol consumption did not appear to accelerate the AD process. Although it has been neither proven nor disproven that alcohol increases the risk of developing AD nor lowers the age at onset, this study suggests that alcohol does not appear to affect progression of the disease. This hypothesis is supported by a study that reported that past heavy alcohol consumption was not associated with progression of AD over a 1-year interval. Other researchers, however, have found past or current alcohol abuse to be a significant predictor of rate of decline in AD.

Epidemiologic Studies of Alcohol Use and Alzheimer Disease

Many studies have examined the effects of alcohol and alcoholism on cognitive function and the brain. However, relatively few epidemiologic studies have focused on whether people who drink alcohol have a greater or lesser chance of developing AD.

Epidemiologic studies of alcohol use and AD in the 1980s and early 1990s generally were based on a case-control design, which identifies people with AD (i.e., cases) and a corresponding group of people without AD (i.e., control subjects) and then investigates whether alcohol consumption differs between these two groups. Relatively quick and inexpensive, the case-control design is a standard epidemiologic approach used to identify potential risk factors and to determine whether more extensive studies are warranted.

A summary of 11 of these case-control studies showed that 9 of the studies found no significant relationship between alcohol use and AD, 1 found that alcohol use increased the risk, and 1 found that alcohol use decreased the risk of AD. Most of these studies examined drinking status of study participants (whether they consumed alcohol at a specific, usually high level) rather than using more detailed measures of amount consumed. These case-control studies, however, may not have found a significant association because they had too few subjects (often less than 100 cases) and thus lacked statistical power. This possibility was addressed in two reports from a meta-analysis that pooled the data from four individual case-control studies. However, the researchers did not find significant results for low, moderate, or high alcohol consumption even with this larger sample. Graves and colleagues (1991) conducted another meta-analysis that included a fifth study, which had used a different definition of alcohol use, but they still did not find a significant association between alcohol use and AD. Meta-analyses have increased power to detect significant associations but are still limited by the flaws of their constituent individual studies.

Subsequent case-control and cross-sectional studies also have failed to provide evidence of an association between alcohol use and AD. One case-control study that did find a significant effect reported a reduced risk of AD in men with "high" alcohol use (i.e., more than two drinks per day), taking into account smoking status, education, and the status of a genetic marker for AD (apolipoprotein E allele, a variant of a gene).

Although the weight of evidence from the studies summarized above suggests that alcohol use is not related to AD, any conclusions must take into account the methodological limitations of these types of studies. The early studies often failed to account for confounding factors; drinkers differ from nondrinkers in many characteristics such as tobacco use and educational level and it may be those characteristics that are related to the risk of AD rather than alcohol use per se.

The case-control design also has inherent limitations. One notable weakness is that it is essentially cross-sectional. Longitudinal studies collect data on alcohol use at baseline and follow study participants over time to determine if they develop AD. Because high levels of alcohol use are associated with greater mortality, drinkers may be more likely than nondrinkers to die before developing AD, so a protective association between alcohol use and AD may simply reflect selective mortality. Clearly, longitudinal studies provide a better design from which to address issues such as selective mortality.

In addition, case-control studies collect information on alcohol use after diagnosis of AD. But because the cognitive deficits character-istic of AD mean that self-reported information cannot be obtained from study participants, proxy respondents (e.g., family members) are required. A proxy's report is unlikely to correspond perfectly with the information that the study respondent would have provided. This problem is exacerbated if this source of error is not consistent across cases and controls (i.e., studies that use proxy reports for cases should also use proxy reports for controls). A methodological flaw in some of the case-control studies of AD has been the use of proxy-reported information for cases but self-reported data for controls.

Because of the methodological limitations of case-control studies, evidence from cohort studies-a stronger, longitudinal design-is usually given more weight, even though they also may have limitations (e.g., determination of AD based on clinical records rather than personal examination as per standard diagnostic criteria). Cohort studies gener-ally have found no significant effect of alcohol use on the risk of devel-oping AD, although some evidence of a protective effect of moderate wine consumption (defined as three to four glasses per day) has been reported-that is, moderate wine consumption has been associated with a decreased risk for AD.

It is reasonable to expect that the effect of alcohol use on the risk of developing AD might differ depending on the level of alcohol con-sumption studied, but this does not seem to explain the study results. The cohort studies that found no association between alcohol use and AD used a variety of measures of alcohol consumption, from drinking status, to amount of alcohol consumed, to alcohol abuse. Both studies reporting protective effects were based in France and focused on wine consumption. It is possible that a protective effect is specific to this situation-that wine rather than other types of alcohol, in the drinking pattern and context of French culture, could be protective. In the study by Leibovici and colleagues (1999), however, the decreased risk of AD with alcohol use was reversed to become a significantly increased risk when the participants' place of residence was considered (i.e., in the community or in an institution). Specifically, moderate wine consump-tion was associated with a lower risk of AD when place of residence was not considered, but with an increased risk when it was included in the analyses. In addition, the significant protective effect of moderate wine consumption reported in the French longitudinal study was based on very few cases of AD. Although overall most epidemiologic studies, regardless of the design, do not support an association between alcohol use and AD, further longitudinal studies are needed that overcome the methodological limitations of previous studies. The apparent lack of association between alcohol use and AD in epidemiological studies contrasts with alcohol's proven effects on cognition, neuropathology, and neurochemistry, and its association with dementias other than AD. If it is determined that alcohol does influence the risk of AD, then understanding the mechanism by which it exerts this effect may provide clues to causal pathways, interventions, and prevention.

Alcohol, Tobacco, and Alzheimer Disease

The effect of alcohol use on AD may be modified by other concurrent factors, such as tobacco use. Tobacco and alcohol use are related: "smokers drink and drinkers smoke". The heaviest drinkers are the most likely to smoke, and 70 percent to almost 100 percent of alcoholics in treatment programs report smoking. Conversely, a smoker is 10 times more likely than a nonsmoker to become an alcoholic.

The prevalence of concurrent alcohol and tobacco dependence suggests that alcohol and tobacco may share mechanisms that lead to dependence. These mechanisms may have a genetic basis. Tobacco and alcohol use may be related at least partially because both nicotine and alcohol affect brain nicotinic cholinergic receptors. Stimulation of these receptors is thought to contribute to the therapeutic effects of galantamine, a new treatment for AD.

Research shows that alcohol and tobacco use interact to influence the risk of certain diseases, such as cancer. Nicotine counteracts some of alcohol's negative effects on cognition, including increased reaction time, impaired time judgment, and slowing of brain wave activity. Epidemiologic studies have begun to investigate the effect of an interaction between smoking and drinking on AD. Adjusting for smoking status had little effect on the association between alcohol use and AD in the case-control study by Cupples and colleagues (2000).

However, an analysis of three case-control data sets has provided some support for the hypothesis that smoking influences the effect of alcohol use on AD. In one of the data sets, the risk of AD was significantly increased in drinkers. Study participants who smoked as well as drank, however, had a lower risk than those who only drank. The pattern in the other two data sets varied depending on whether the participants had a history of hypertension. A pattern similar to that of the first data set, but only marginally significant, was found for hypertensive subjects in a second data set, with the risk of AD for people who were both smokers and drinkers lower than the risk for those who were just smokers or just drinkers. It is not clear whether the effect of hypertension reflects a physiological interaction of hypertension with smoking, drinking, and AD. Few analyses on the interaction of tobacco and alcohol use have been published, but one study did find that the association between smoking and AD varied by the hypertensive status of study participants.

The observation that alcohol and tobacco use appear to influence each other's association with AD is consistent with evidence of a biological interaction between smoking and drinking. This observation also may be attributed, however, to the increased overall mortality of people who both smoke and drink, a possibility that can only be ruled out by longitudinal research. The apparent importance of hypertension suggests that a vascular mechanism may be involved in the interaction of alcohol and tobacco use on the risk of developing AD.

Epidemiologic Studies of Alcohol Use and Cognitive Impairment

Although epidemiologic studies do not generally support an association between alcohol consumption and AD, the lack of such a relationship could reflect methodological limitations, such as the difficulty in discriminating AD cases with a history of heavy alcohol consumption from cases of alcoholic dementia. It thus may also be useful to consider evidence from epidemiologic studies examining the association between alcohol use and cognitive outcomes other than AD. The ways in which alcohol use influences the risk of developing cognitive impairment might be similar to those by which it may affect AD, and some types of cognitive impairment themselves may increase the risk of developing AD.

Overall, the results of epidemiologic studies of alcohol use and cognitive impairment are consistent with results from studies of alcohol use and AD. Most studies, regardless of design, found no significant association between alcohol use and cognitive impairment. Those studies which did report a significant effect of alcohol use generally found that the results varied by gender, by apolipoprotein E allele status, or by vascular risk factors (e.g., cardiovascular disease and diabetes). Evidence of these subgroup effects is not yet compelling; for example, in people with the apolipoprotein E allele, alcohol use increased the risk of cognitive impairment in one study but decreased it in another.

In another study, apolipoprotein status had no effect. However, investigation of the effects of alcohol use on AD within these gender, genetic, or vascular risk subgroups may prove informative.

Does Alcohol Use Cause Alzheimer Disease?

Although an increased risk of AD with alcohol use is plausible based on biological evidence, the epidemiologic evidence does not support an association. In the few studies that report a significant association, alcohol consumption is more often found to reduce the risk of AD than to increase it. However, methodological factors could create an apparent protective effect of alcohol use on AD. Such factors include selective mortality of drinkers and diagnosing AD patients with heavy alcohol use as having alcoholic dementia rather than AD. In addition, in some studies reporting a protective effect of alcohol, proxy respondents provided information for the cases whereas self-reported information was used for controls. If proxy reports of drinking underestimate actual exposure, the alcohol use of cases (i.e., study participants with AD) would be artificially lowered compared with control subjects. The apparent association between alcohol use and a reduced risk of AD might therefore merely reflect bias in proxy reports rather than any true effect. Other recent reports of a protective effect may have been affected by sample size and the selection of confounding factors, such as community or institutional residence, included in the analyses.

Most studies, including the meta-analysis of case-control studies and individual cohort studies of AD have not found a significant association. Epidemiologic studies of alcohol use and cognitive impairment overall have come to similar conclusions, although some evidence exists for a heterogeneous effect of alcohol use on cognitive impairment across gender, genetic, or vascular subgroups.

The effect of alcohol use on the risk of AD has been explored much less extensively than the effect of other potential risk factors, such as tobacco use. The possibility of a protective effect of moderate drinking on AD, raised in a few studies, may not be compelling, but methodological issues need to be resolved before such an association can be definitively dismissed. Moderate drinking has been reported to have some beneficial vascular effects, which could possibly reduce the risk of AD. The nonsignificant association between alcohol use and risk of AD reported by most studies does not necessarily mean that alcohol has no effect. It may instead reflect a balance between the beneficial vascular effects of alcohol and its detrimental effects on the brain, and the relative weight of these two factors may differ within specific subgroups.

Limitations of Current Studies

Because AD has few established risk factors, most studies have examined alcohol use as only one possibly relevant exposure among many, necessitating superficial treatment. Future studies need to collect more detailed information about lifetime alcohol exposure because imprecision in estimating lifetime exposure may obscure associations, as may inconsistent definitions of drinking status or level of consumption. Evidence that alcohol's effects on AD might vary within subgroups also supports more extensive data collection on variables that characterize these subgroups.

One methodological challenge of both case-control and cohort studies is the separation of AD from alcoholic dementia. AD cannot be definitively diagnosed clinically but instead requires confirmation based on examination of the brain after death. Even when AD is accurately diagnosed before death, study participants still represent a heterogeneous group, differing in age at onset, duration, and genetic basis of AD. Case-control studies may introduce bias by using heavy alcohol consumption as an exclusionary criterion for AD cases but not for controls. As alcoholic dementia has not been uniformly diagnosed across epidemiologic studies, the discrimination of alcoholic dementia from AD also is problematic.

Section 15.2

Effects of Nicotine on Cognitive Function

Text in this section is excerpted from "The Health Consequences of Smoking—50 Years of Progress," Office of the Surgeon General, January 17, 2014.

Cognitive Function

Researchers have suggested that smoking may have cognition-enhancing properties, such as improvements in sustained attention, reaction time, and memory. Initial reports of improved cognitive function were based on empirical evidence from smokers; thus, these observations could reflect the mitigation of cognitive impairment from nicotine withdrawal, enhancement of smokers' cognitive function independent of nicotine's effects on withdrawal symptoms, or both. Interest in the effects of nicotine on cognition has since expanded to include healthy nonsmokers and individuals with underlying neuropsychiatric conditions accompanied by cognitive deficits. Concurrently, there is a growing awareness of the potential harms of nicotine exposure during certain vulnerable stages of brain development, such as during fetal and adolescent growth. This section reviews the evidence on the effects of nicotine on cognitive function in general (in smokers and nonsmokers), and in potentially vulnerable populations.

Cognitive Function and the Nicotinic Acetylcholine Receptor System

Underlying the purported connection between nicotine and cognitive enhancement is the role of nAChRs in attention, learning, memory, and cortical plasticity. nAChRs are receptors that normally bind endogenous neurotransmitter acetylcholine, but are also particularly responsive to nicotine. nAChRs are abundant in brain regions associated with learning and memory, including the prefrontal cortex, and in primate and rodent models, depletion of acetylcholine in the prefrontal cortex results in impaired attentional performance. β2 nAChRs are especially abundant in the brain and have a high affinity for nicotine. Recent evidence from animal studies suggests that β2 nAChRs play a critical role in regulating attention. Additional research has demonstrated that nicotine interferes with cholinergic control of β2 nAChRs in the prefrontal cortex in mice, which could result in acute impairment of attention and alterations of the prefrontal cortex network, and lead to long-term effects on attention. Mice lacking the β2 nAChR subunit demonstrate deficits in executive function.

Effects of Nicotine on Cognitive Function in Healthy Adult Smokers and Nonsmokers

In adults, the negative effects of nicotine withdrawal on cognitive function have been documented in both humans and animals, and the administration of nicotine during withdrawal mitigates cognitive impairment. In dependent smokers, abstinence from smoking is associated with reductions in working memory and sustained attention, and adverse effects on attention can be seen as early as 30 minutes after smoking the last cigarette. Nicotine withdrawal is also commonly

118

accompanied by symptoms of negative affect (anxiety and depression) and relief of this symptom may be an important element of addiction in smokers. Because negative affect and attentional control are related, the effects of smoking on these two domains could be interrelated.

Whether there are direct effects of nicotine on cognitive function (positive or negative) in non-abstinent smokers and in healthy non-smoking adults is less clear. In a recent meta-analysis of double-blind, placebo-controlled studies examining the acute effects of nicotine (administered mainly as nicotine replacement product) on cognitive function in nonsmokers and smokers abstinent for 2 hours or less, nicotine was found to result in cognitive enhancement in six of nine performance domains: fine motor, alerting attention-accuracy and response time (RT), orienting attention and RT, short-term episodic memory accuracy, and working memory RT. To separate the effects of nicotine on symptoms of withdrawal versus its direct effects, the results were stratified by smoking status. The effects on alerting attention accuracy and short-term episodic memory accuracy were significant in smokers but not in nonsmokers; effects on alerting attention RT were significant in nonsmokers but not in smokers; effects on working memory RT were significant in both smokers and nonsmokers, and in the remaining outcomes there were insufficient numbers of studies on smokers to conduct stratified analysis. Thus, nicotine may have some positive effects on cognitive performance that are unique to nonsmokers. No studies meeting the inclusion criteria for the review addressed learning or executive function.

Critical Periods of Exposure in the Nervous System

Across the lifespan, there are several developmental windows during which exposure to nicotine may have adverse consequences. In the fetus, nicotine targets neurotransmitter receptors in the brain, potentially resulting in abnormalities in cell proliferation and altering synaptic activity.

Human brain development continues far longer than was previously realized. In particular, areas involved in higher cognitive function such as the prefrontal cortex continue to develop throughout adolescence (the period during which individuals are most likely to begin smoking) and into adulthood. During this extended period of maturation, substantial neural remodeling occurs, including synaptic pruning and changes in dopaminergic input, as well as changes in gray and white matter volume. The density of projections from the amygdala to the prefrontal cortex increases, suggesting that there is substantial development of the connectivity between the emotional and cognitive areas of the brain. The cholinergic system, which matures in adolescence, plays a central role in maturation of cognitive function and reward.

Smoking during adolescence has been associated with lasting cognitive and behavioral impairments, including effects on working memory and attention, although causal relationships are difficult to establish in the presence of potential confounding factors. In addition, functional magnetic resonance imaging in humans showed that young adult smokers had reduced prefrontal cortex activation during attentional tasks when compared with nonsmoking controls. Diminished prefrontal cortex activity correlated with duration of smoking, supporting the hypothesis that smoking could have long-lasting effects on cognition.

The effects of nicotine exposure on cognitive function after adolescence and young adulthood are unknown. There are data to suggest that smoking accelerates some aspects of cognitive decline in adults, and that these effects appear to be mediated by an increased risk of respiratory and cardiovascular disease. However, in a cohort study of more than 7,000 men and women, the authors found that current male smokers and recent former smokers had a greater 10-year decline in global cognition and executive function than never smokers (with the greatest adverse effect on executive function); these differences were not explained by other health behaviors or measures, including heart disease and stroke, and measures of lung function. An analysis using pack-years as the exposure measure provided evidence of a dose-response relationship. The results of the latter study suggest that there may be mechanisms contributing to cognitive decline in addition to and independent of respiratory and cardiovascular disease; however, whether nicotine plays a role in accelerating cognitive decline is unknown.

Other Vulnerable Populations

Although the contribution of nicotine to the effects of smoking on cognitive decline is unclear, there has been a great deal of interest in applications of nicotine as a treatment for several conditions characterized by cognitive deficits, including Alzheimer disease and Parkinson disease. These disorders have underlying deficits in the cholinergic system, and it has been hypothesized that nicotine and/or nicotine analogs may be effective in attenuating symptoms or slowing disease progression. This hypothesis is further supported by research suggesting that acute administration of nicotine has cognitive-enhancing properties.

In addition, some early observational studies showed evidence for a reduced risk of Alzheimer in smokers, suggesting that components in tobacco smoke, such as nicotine, may have protective properties. A growing body of evidence now links smoking to an increased risk for Alzheimer disease rather than a reduced risk; however, research on nicotine as a treatment for this condition (and for Parkinson disease) continues.

Other disorders associated with cognitive and attentional impairment, such as schizophrenia and attention deficit hyperactivity disorder (ADHD), are characterized by a very high prevalence of smoking among those affected. It has been proposed that individuals with these disorders smoke in order to alleviate the symptoms of their disease, and a number of clinical trials using nicotine as a therapeutic agent have been conducted.

Alzheimer Disease

Alzheimer disease is a common form of dementia in which individuals experience ongoing deterioration of cognitive abilities. Although smoking is recognized as a risk factor for Alzheimer disease, acute nicotine administration has been reported to improve some Alzheimer symptoms, such as recall, visual attention, and mood. The plausibility of this effect is supported by studies of Alzheimer disease patients showing deficits in cholinergic systems and a loss of nicotinic binding sites. However, evidence from randomized trials to support improvement of Alzheimer symptoms from nicotine treatment is sparse. In a 2001 Cochrane review updated in 2010, the authors found no double-blind, placebo-controlled, randomized trials of treatment for Alzheimer disease with nicotine and concluded that there is no evidence to recommend nicotine as a treatment for Alzheimer disease.

Chapter 16

Alzheimer Disease: Facts and Figures

Chapter Contents

123

Section 16.1

Alzheimer Disease Mortality Rates

Text in this section is excerpted from "Mortality from Alzheimer's
Disease in the United States: Data for 2000 and 2010," Centers for
Disease Control and Prevention (CDC), March 19, 2013.

Key findings: Data from the National Vital Statistics System

- The age-adjusted death rate from Alzheimer disease (AD)
  increased by 39 percent from 2000 through 2010 in the
  United States.

- Alzheimer disease is the sixth leading cause of death in the
  United States and is the fifth leading cause among people aged
  65 years and over. People aged 85 years and over have a 5.4
  times greater risk of dying from Alzheimer disease than people
  aged 75–84 years.

- The risk of dying from Alzheimer disease is 26 percent higher
  among the non-Hispanic white population than among the
  non-Hispanic black population, whereas the Hispanic population has a 30 percent lower risk than the non-Hispanic white
  population.

- In 2010, among all states and the District of Columbia, 31 states
  showed death rates from Alzheimer disease that were above the
  national rate (25.1).

In 2010, Alzheimer disease was the underlying cause for a total of
83,494 deaths and was classified as a contributing cause for an additional 26,488 deaths. Mortality from Alzheimer disease has steadily
increased during the last 30 years. Alzheimer disease is the sixth
leading cause of death in the United States and the fifth leading cause
for people aged 65 years and over. An estimated 5.4 million persons
in the United States have Alzheimer disease. The cost of health care
for people with Alzheimer disease and other dementia was estimated
to be 200 billion dollars in 2012, including 140 billion dollars in costs

to Medicare and Medicaid and is expected to reach 1.1 trillion dollars in 2050.

Alzheimer disease mortality varies by age, sex, race, Hispanic origin, and geographic area. This report presents mortality data on Alzheimer disease based on data from the National Vital Statistics System from 2000 through 2010, the most recent year for which detailed data are available.

Alzheimer Disease Mortality Increased Compared with Selected Major Causes of Death.

Compared with other selected causes, Alzheimer disease has been on the rise since the last decade. For 2000 and 2010, the age-adjusted death rate for Alzheimer disease increased by 39 percent, whereas death rates for other major causes of death decreased (Figure 16.1). The largest decreases in death rates among selected major causes of death were observed for Stroke (36 percent), Heart disease (31 percent), and Cancer (32 percent).

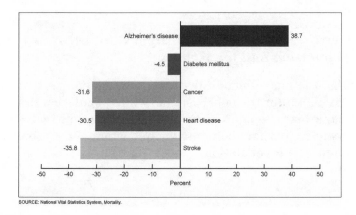

Figure 16.1. *Percent change in age-adjusted death rates for selected causes of death: United States, 2000 and 2010*

Alzheimer Disease Mortality Risk Increased Most for the Oldest Age Groups

The risk of dying from Alzheimer disease increases significantly with age. In 2010, the population aged 85 years and over was 50 times more likely to die from Alzheimer disease than the age group 65–74 years. Similarly, persons aged 85 years and over were 5 times more likely to die from Alzheimer disease than the age group 75–84 years (Figure 16.2).

125

For 2000 and 2010, age-specific death rates from Alzheimer disease for the age group 65–74 years increased 6 percent, for the age group 75–84 years the increase was 32 percent, and for the age group 85 years and over the increase was 48 percent.

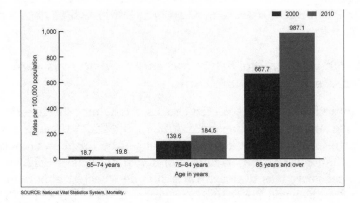

Figure 16.2. *Age-adjusted death rates for Alzheimer disease: United States, 2000 and 2010*

Alzheimer Disease Mortality Is Highest for the Non-Hispanic White Population and for Women

In 2010, the age-adjusted death rate for Alzheimer disease was 26 percent higher for the non-Hispanic white population than for the non-Hispanic black population. Similarly, the age-adjusted death rate is 43 percent higher for the non-Hispanic white population than for the Hispanic origin population (Figure 16.3).

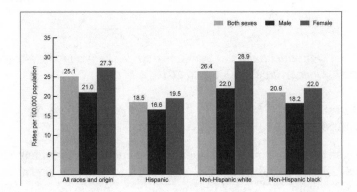

Figure 16.3. *Age-adjusted death rates for Alzheimer disease, by Hispanic origin, race for non-Hispanic population, and sex: United States, 2010*

Overall, women had a 30 percent higher risk of dying (27.3 per 100,000 population) from Alzheimer disease than men (21.0). Non-Hispanic white women had the highest mortality rate from Alzheimer disease, followed by non-Hispanic black women. Likewise, among men, the highest age-adjusted death rates were for non-Hispanic white men (22.0), followed by non–Hispanic black men (18.2). Hispanic men (16.6) and Hispanic women (19.5) had the lowest death rates for Alzheimer disease.

Alzheimer Disease Death Rates Varied Widely across the States.

The age-adjusted death rates for Alzheimer disease do not show a clear geographic pattern across the states. In 2010, the states with the highest age-adjusted death rates were Washington (43.6), Tennessee (38.5), and North Dakota (37.2). The states with the lowest age-adjusted death rates were Hawaii (10.5), New York (11.3), and Nevada (14.2). Overall, 31 states had rates above the U.S. rate (25.1), whereas 19 states and the District of Columbia had rates lower than the U.S. rate.

Section 16.2

Disparities in Prevalence, Incidence, and Diagnosis

Text in this section is excerpted from "Racial and Ethnic Disparities in Alzheimer's Disease: A Literature Review," U.S. Department of Health and Human Services (HHS), January 2, 2015.

Prevalence, Incidence, and Diagnosis

- Prevalence describes the proportion of a population with a disease at a specific point in time, while incidence describes the proportion of the population that develops a disease over a specific time period. Reported Alzheimer disease (AD) prevalence rates range from 14% to 500% higher among African Americans than among Whites. The most frequently cited estimates are that Blacks are about two times more likely than Whites to have Alzheimer disease and Hispanics are about 1.5 times more likely than Whites to have Alzheimer disease.

- Prevalence studies in New Haven, Connecticut; Copiah County, Mississippi; Houston, Texas; New York, New York; the Piedmont region of North Carolina; and East Baltimore, Maryland, have all found higher rates of dementia among ethnic minority elderly--specifically African Americans and Hispanics--compared to Whites and Asians. Among African Americans, prevalence estimates have been as high as 56%, although rates of diagnosed disease have been more in the range of 5%-16%. Prevalence rates among Hispanics have been less commonly measured, but one study estimated dementia prevalence of 8% of Caribbean Latinos in the 65-74 age group, 28% in the 75-84 age group, and 63% in those aged 85 and older. Another more recent study found that Mexican American men had significantly higher prevalence of cognitive impairment than did non-Hispanic White men.

- An analysis of 2006 Medicare claims data found that older African Americans and Hispanics were more likely than Whites to have a diagnosis of Alzheimer disease. Rates were 14% for Hispanics, 13% for African Americans, 10% for Whites, 9% for Native Americans, and 8% for Asians. The report's authors cautioned that prevalence rates based on diagnosis codes may reflect varying levels of underdiagnosis across populations. They also pointed out that the Health and Retirement Study has found that among those with cognitive impairment, 46% of Whites over age 55 had been told by a physician that they had a memory-related disease, compared to 34% of Hispanics and 34% of African Americans.

- In terms of the prevalence of cognitive impairment, the 2006 Health and Retirement Study shows a marked difference by age and race/ethnicity, as shown in Figure 15.4

- 1. Overall prevalence is about 105 per 1,000 Americans aged 55 or over. African Americans are approximately 2-3 times more likely than Whites to have cognitive impairment, and these differences are greater in the younger age groups.

Incidence estimates also suggest higher risk of Alzheimer disease among non-White populations. In a 7-year study in the Washington

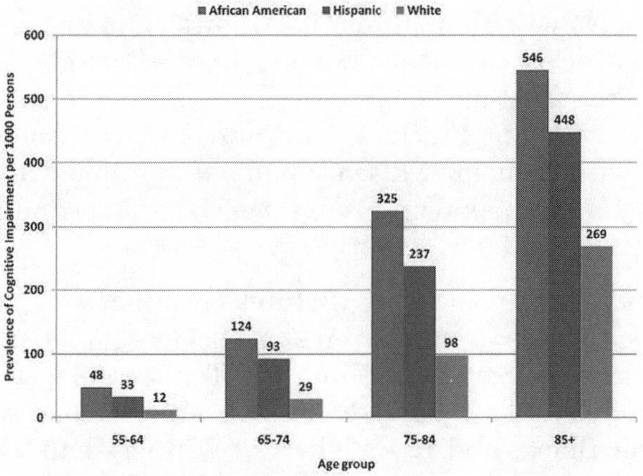

FIGURE 16.4. *Prevalence of Cognitive Impairment among Americans Aged 55 and Older (rate per 1,000 population) by Age and Race/Ethnicity, 2006 Health and Retirement Study*

Heights and Inwood communities of New York City, overall adjusted incidence rates for probable and possible Alzheimer disease (excluding vascular and other dementias) among Whites were 0.4% per person-year for ages 65-74, 2.6% for ages 75-84, and 4.2% for ages 85+. Incidence was higher among African Americans (1.7%, 4.4%, and 11.4%) and Caribbean Hispanics (1.4%, 4.4%, and 8.8%) in the same community. One recent study found that the unadjusted hazard ratio for developing dementia over 12 years was 1.44 for Black participants compared to White, but after adjusting for demographics, apolipoprotein (APOE) E4, comorbidities, lifestyle factors, and socioeconomic status, the Black-White difference was reduced to 1.09 and was no longer significant.

Health Outcomes

- Mortality and other health outcomes among people with Alzheimer disease vary by race and ethnicity. Despite a lower prevalence and incidence rate, Whites have a higher overall mortality rate from Alzheimer disease. In a recent study, Whites had dementia listed as the underlying or contributing cause of death on their death certificates more often than Blacks during 1999-2004: the age-adjusted rate per 100,000 was 647 for Whites versus 628 for Blacks. Rates were higher among Whites than

Blacks in New England, the Mid-Atlantic, and in the East and West South Central census regions. In the East and West North Central, South Atlantic, Mountain, and Pacific regions, rates were higher among Blacks than Whites. African Americans and Latinos with Alzheimer disease had a lower adjusted risk of mortality than their White counterparts. Asians and American Indians had similar mortality risk as Whites.

• In another study, Blacks and Whites born in the so-called stroke belt states (Alabama, Arkansas, Georgia, Mississippi, North Carolina, South Carolina, and Tennessee) were at higher age-adjusted and sex-adjusted risk of dementia mortality--29% higher for Blacks and 19% higher for Whites--than those born in other states, even among those who did not live in those states at death

• In a large epidemiological study aimed at identifying the prevalence of specific behaviors among patients with dementia, after adjusting for age, sex, education, income, Mini-Mental State Examination (MMSE) score, activities of daily living, and caregiver characteristics, Blacks were at increased risk (relative to Whites) of being constantly talkative, having hallucinations, expressing unreasonable anger, wandering, and waking the caregiver. Hispanics were at increased risk (relative to Whites) of having hallucinations, expressing unreasonable anger, being combative, and wandering. Whites were at increased risk of being paranoid relative to Hispanics. Older African Americans with Alzheimer disease consistently describe themselves as more impaired, with greater need for health services, than Whites--despite a lack of measured differences in the number of recent sick days, number of reported chronic conditions, cognitive status, and mortality. Whether this difference is a result of unmeasured comorbidities or different types of comorbidities, cultural differences in the perception and description of cognitive disability, or some other factor, is not known.

Participation in Clinical Trials

• Minorities are underrepresented in clinical trials and other research studies. Some researchers attribute this underrepresentation to a higher level of comorbidity among minorities (disqualifying them from participating), as well as language requirements (many clinical trials require English fluency). Others believe that past abuses, such as the Tuskegee Syphilis Study, have soured the relationship between researchers and racial/ ethnic minorities.

• A 2006 review of the literature investigated whether the under-representation of minorities in clinical research was related to a lower consent rate, and found that the differences between racial groups were small and non-significant, with no clear directionality or patterns. The authors conclude that willingness to enroll in research studies is more a function of the characteristics of individual studies than a function of racial or ethnic attitudes as a whole. Examples of factors other than willingness to participate that may be important in determining multi-ethnic participation include the choice of study site and proximity of research locations to places where minorities live and work; recruitment disparities, such as differences in knowledge about trials and invitations to participate; language barriers; and other barriers to participation, such as child care or elder care and travel expenses.

• A qualitative study to investigate barriers to participation in clinical research among Latinos found that they often do not meet clinical trial eligibility guidelines because of underdiagnosis, since many studies require participants to have a physician diagnosis of Alzheimer disease to participate. Underdiagnosis stemmed from several factors, including a perception of Alzheimer disease-related symptoms as natural part of aging, barriers to access, and a lack of information about Alzheimer disease and available services. In addition, many caregivers may also be overburdened to the point that participating in a research study would be too onerous.

Use of Long-Term Services and Supports

• Approximately 40% of persons who died in a nursing home between 1999 and 2006 had dementia (22% with mild to moderately severe dementia and 20% with advanced dementia). Historically, disparities in access to nursing homes and other formal long-term care services contributed to the lower rates of use of such services by elderly members of minority groups, compared to elderly Whites. However, as nursing home occupancy rates have declined in most markets, and assisted living and other home and community-based options have proliferated, access to nursing home care may be less of a problem for elderly minorities. In both 1999 and 2008, rates of nursing home residency were highest among Blacks, followed by Whites, Hispanics, and Asians (Figure 16.5). Between 1999 and 2008, the absolute number of elderly Hispanics and Asians living in United States nursing homes grew by 55% and 54%, respectively, while the number of elderly Black residents increased 11%. During the same period, the number of White nursing home residents declined by 10%.

- However, on a population basis, the rates per 1,000 persons declined in all four groups (Figure 16.5). A meta-analysis of seven studies showed that minorities were 40% less likely to enter a long-term care facility than Whites in the United States. Insurance status, poverty, level of impairment (activities of daily living, instrumental activities of daily living, gait, etc.) and social support/caregiver willingness to provide care are the main determinants of institutionalization.

- Although use of nursing homes by minorities has grown in recent years, there is evidence that minorities tend to live in lower quality facilities. For example, a national study of 516,082 nursing home residents found that residents in facilities with a higher proportion of African Americans had higher odds of being hospitalized, a possible marker of poor-quality.

- A meta-analysis of seven studies found that the use of community social services did not differ by race/ethnicity after controlling for dementia severity and socioeconomic status. On the other hand, in their study of respite care provided through the Alzheimer Disease Demonstration Grants to States program, found that use patterns differed by racial and ethnic groups. For example, Blacks tended to use small amounts of care for a long period of time, while Hispanics used a lot of care for a short period of time. Moreover, in this study, respite staff working with Blacks and Hispanics found a strong sense of self-sufficiency and general distrust of government services.

- A recent systematic review of 20 studies on ethnic and racial disparities at the end of life among people with dementia found that attitudes toward end-of-life care were similar in different ethnic groups, and there was conflicting evidence on hospice usage. Artificial nutrition and other life-sustaining treatments (such as ICU care and mechanical ventilation) were more

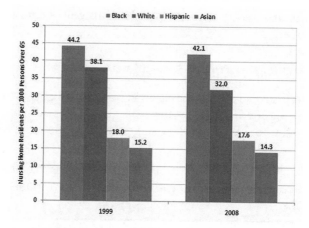

FIGURE 16.5. *Nursing Home Residents per 1,000 Over Age 65 by Race/Ethnicity, 1999 and 2008*

frequently used, and decisions to withhold treatment less common, in African Americans and Asians.

Use of Medications

Multiple studies have shown that Whites are generally more likely to be taking acetylcholinesterase inhibitors (AChEIs) and other dementia medications than are non-Whites. A meta-analysis and literature review by Cooper and colleagues (2010) that pooled the results of three studies found that African Americans were 30% less likely to be prescribed AChEIs than Whites, whereas Hispanics had a similar likelihood of prescriptions as Whites. Three other studies of the use of medications by race/ethnicity that were not included in the above meta-analysis also found that African Americans were less likely to use dementia medications. One analysis of data using the 2000-2002 Medicare Current Beneficiary Survey found the opposite: community-dwelling African American and Hispanic Medicare beneficiaries were more likely to be prescribed Aricept than were Whites. In an analysis of four state Medicaid populations, Gilligan and colleagues found significant disparities in medication (AChEIs and memantine) use between Hispanics and non-Hispanic Whites (in favor of Hispanics) in Florida, between non-Hispanic Blacks and Hispanics (in favor of Hispanics) in California and Florida, between non-Hispanic Blacks and non-Hispanic others (in favor of non-Hispanic others) in California and New York, and between Hispanics and non-Hispanic others (in favor of non-Hispanic others) in California and New York.

Health Care Expenditures

Published literature on disparities in health and long-term services and supports expenditures is very sparse. Only two peer-reviewed studies were found, one of which used data from the early 1990s, and

TABLE 16.1. Use of and Medicare Payments for Health Care Services among Medicare Beneficiaries with a Dementia Diagnosis, by Race/Ethnicity, 2006

	Overall	White	African American	Hispanic
Total mean Medicare payment per beneficiary	$15,333	$14,498	$21,044	$19,933
Mean Medicare payment for hospital care per beneficiary	$4,964	$4,563	$7,687	$6,632
Mean hospital discharges per 1,000 beneficiaries	660	632	887	731
Mean number of hospital days per beneficiary	4.2	3.9	6.4	5.2
Mean Medicare payment for physician visits per beneficiary	$1,018	$956	$1,390	$1,411
Mean number of physician visits per beneficiary	12.7	12.1	16.4	17.1
Mean Medicare payment for home health care per beneficiary	$1,118	$1,025	$1,591	$2,453
Percentage of beneficiaries with at least one home health claim	18.80%	18.20%	22.10%	25.90%
Mean Medicare payment for hospice per beneficiary	$1,732	$1,789	$1,514	$1,225
Percentage of beneficiaries with at least one hospice claim	13.70%	14.20%	11.30%	8.80%

one used Medicaid data from 2004. In the first, Blacks with vascular dementia in Tennessee had higher total expenditures than did Whites with the same diagnosis ($17,359 vs. $12,904). In the second study, Blacks had significantly higher expenditures than Whites, Hispanics, and those of other racial/ethnic backgrounds, and Hispanics and Whites had significantly higher expenditures than others

In a study funded by the Alzheimer Association, total Medicare costs were substantially (45% and 37%) higher for older African Americans and Hispanics diagnosed with Alzheimer disease than for Whites with a similar diagnosis (Table 15.1). These estimates were not adjusted, and therefore may be biased because of group-level differences in age, sex, and comorbidity burden.

Caregiving

- In a 2010 survey conducted on behalf of the Alzheimer Association, 70% of caregivers were White, 15% were African American, 12% were Hispanic, 1% were Asian American, and 2% were from other ethnic groups. Compared to caregivers of other races, African American and Hispanic caregivers were more likely to be single/never married, and more likely to have incomes less than $50,000 per year. Asian American caregivers were as likely to be male as female, in contrast to caregivers of other races, who were predominantly female. Asian American caregivers were more likely to be highly educated.

- The caregiver role is often assumed by an adult child, friend, or other family member in Black families and by an adult daughter in Hispanic families. The concept of the "primary caregiver" may not be equally applicable in all cultures; therefore, interventions that are aimed at the family, rather than just the primary caregiver, may be more culturally appropriate for these cultures. Korean and Korean American caregivers are less likely to be spouses and more likely to be another family member. The tradition in cultures with Confucian values is for the daughter-in-law of the eldest son to provide care.

- Compared with non-Hispanic Whites, Mexican American caregivers of persons with dementia report greater distress, poorer self-rated health, more somatic complaints, and increased levels of sensitivity to patient problem behaviors. Similarly, depression is more common in Hispanic family caregivers than in Whites.

- Some studies of caregiving interventions for people with dementia suggest that African Americans find some aspects of caregiving less stressful than Whites and get more emotional benefit from the experience. For example, in the Resources for Enhancing Alzheimer Caregiver Health (REACH) study, African Americans had higher scores than Whites on the Positive Aspects of Caregiving scale, and lower anxiety and fewer feelings of bother by the care recipient's behavior. The fact that caregiving is more expected in some cultures may be protective against stress. Baseline differences between groups in psychological distress may account for differences in the impact of Alzheimer disease on caregivers.

Part Three

Other Dementia Disorders

Chapter 17

Mild Cognitive Impairment

What is Mild Cognitive Impairment?

Cognitive impairment is when a person has trouble remembering, learning new things, concentrating, or making decisions that affect their everyday life. Cognitive impairment ranges from mild to severe. With mild impairment, people may begin to notice changes in cognitive functions, but still be able to do their everyday activities. Severe levels of impairment can lead to losing the ability to understand the meaning or importance of something and the ability to talk or write, resulting in the inability to live independently.

Key Facts about MCI

Cognitive impairment is not caused by any one disease or condition, nor is it limited to a specific age group. Alzheimer disease and other dementias in addition to conditions such as stroke, traumatic brain injury, and developmental disabilities, can cause cognitive impairment. A few commons signs of cognitive impairment include the following:

- Memory loss.

- Frequently asking the same question or repeating the same story over and over.

Text in this chapter is excerpted from "Cognitive Impairment: A Call for Action," Centers for Disease Control and Prevention (CDC), February 15, 2011. Reviewed February 2016.

- Not recognizing familiar people and places.

- Having trouble exercising judgment, such as knowing what to do in an emergency.

- Changes in mood or behavior.

- Vision problems.

- Difficulty planning and carrying out tasks, such as following a recipe or keeping track of monthly bills.

Risk Factors for MCI

While age is the primary risk factor for cognitive impairment, other risk factors include family history, education level, brain injury, exposure to pesticides or toxins, physical inactivity, and chronic conditions such as Parkinson disease, heart disease and stroke, and diabetes. Individuals may reduce the risk of cognitive impairment by keeping physically active and maintaining healthy cholesterol and blood sugar levels. Currently, there is no cure for cognitive impairment caused by Alzheimer disease or other related dementias. However, some causes of cognitive impairment are related to health issues that may be treatable, like medication side effects, vitamin B12 deficiency, and depression. This is why it is important to identify people who are showing signs of cognitive impairment to ensure that they are evaluated by a health care professional and receive appropriate care or treatment.

Prevalence and Economic Burden of Cognitive Impairment

More than 16 million people in the United States are living with cognitive impairment, but the impact of cognitive impairment at the state level is not well understood. In 2009, five states addressed this shortcoming by assessing the impact of cognitive impairment on their residents. This knowledge is vital to developing or maintaining effective policies and programs to address the needs of people living with cognitive impairment. The age is the greatest risk factor for cognitive impairment, and as the Baby Boomer generation passes age 65, the number of people living with cognitive impairment is expected to jump dramatically. An estimated 5.1 million Americans aged 65 years or older may currently have Alzheimer disease, the most well-known form of cognitive impairment; this number may rise to 13.2 million by 2050. Cognitive impairment is costly. People with cognitive impairment report more than three times as many hospital stays as individuals who are hospitalized for some other condition. Alzheimer disease and related dementias alone are estimated to be the third most expensive disease to treat in the United States. The average Medicaid nursing facility expenditure per state in 2010 for individuals with Alzheimer disease is estimated at $647 million, not including home- and community-based care or prescription drug costs.

The imminent growth in the number of people living with cognitive impairment will place significantly greater demands on our systems of care. There are now more than 10 million family members providing unpaid care to a person with a cognitive impairment, a memory problem or a disorder like Alzheimer disease or other dementia. In 2009 it was estimated that 12.5 billion hours of unpaid care were provided, at a value of $144 billion. Much more in-home or institutional care and unpaid assistance by family and friends will be needed in the future as the numbers of those with Alzheimer disease and other forms of cognitive impairment grow.

Why Cognitive Impairment Is an Important Issue

Americans fear losing cognitive function. We are twice as fearful of losing our mental capacity as having diminished physical ability and 60% of adults are very or somewhat worried about memory loss. Persons affected by cognitive impairment, such as adults with Alzheimer disease, veterans with traumatic brain injuries, and the families of people living with cognitive impairment, represent a significant portion of the community. Taking steps to address this issue will ultimately have a positive impact on the entire community and state. States across the country are responding to the call-for-action to improve the health and quality of life of adults living with cognitive impairment.

Chapter 18

Degenerative Neurological Disease

Chapter Contents

Section 18.1

Corticobasal Degeneration

Text in this section is excerpted from "NINDS Corticobasal
Degeneration Information Page," National Institute of Neurological
Disorders and Stroke (NINDS), February 6, 2015.

What Is Corticobasal Degeneration?

Corticobasal degeneration is a progressive neurological disorder characterized by nerve cell loss and *atrophy* (shrinkage) of multiple areas of the brain including the cerebral cortex and the basal ganglia. Corticobasal degeneration progresses gradually. Initial symptoms, which typically begin at or around age 60, may first appear on one side of the body (unilateral), but eventually affect both sides as the disease progresses. Symptoms are similar to those found in Parkinson disease, such as poor coordination, *akinesia* (an absence of movements), *rigidity* (a resistance to imposed movement), *disequilibrium* (impaired balance); and limb *dystonia* (abnormal muscle postures). Other symptoms such as cognitive and visual-spatial impairments, apraxia (loss of the ability to make familiar, purposeful movements), hesitant and halting speech, *myoclonus* (muscular jerks), and *dysphagia* (difficulty swallowing) may also occur. An individual with corticobasal degeneration eventually becomes unable to walk.

Is There Any Treatment?

There is no treatment available to slow the course of corticobasal degeneration, and the symptoms of the disease are generally resistant to therapy. Drugs used to treat Parkinson disease-type symptoms do not produce any significant or sustained improvement. Clonazepam may help the myoclonus. Occupational, physical, and speech therapy can help in managing disability.

What Is the Prognosis?

Corticobasal degeneration usually progresses slowly over the course of 6 to 8 years. Death is generally caused by pneumonia or other complications of severe debility such as sepsis or pulmonary embolism.

Section 18.2

Dementia with Lewy Bodies

Text in this section is excerpted from "Lewy Body Dementia,"
National Institutes of Health (NIH), September 2015.

Introduction

Lewy body dementia (LBD) is a complex and challenging brain disorder. It is complex because it affects many parts of the brain in ways that scientists are trying to understand more fully. It is challenging because its many possible symptoms make it hard to do everyday tasks that once came easily.

Although less known than its "cousins" Alzheimer disease and Parkinson disease, LBD is not a rare disorder. More than 1 million Americans, most of them older adults, are affected by its disabling changes in the ability to think and move.

As researchers seek better ways to treat LBD—and ultimately to find a cure—people with LBD and their families struggle day to day to get an accurate diagnosis, find the best treatment, and manage at home.

The Basics of Lewy Body Dementia

LBD is a disease associated with abnormal deposits of a protein called alpha-synuclein in the brain. These deposits, called Lewy bodies, affect chemicals in the brain whose changes, in turn, can lead to problems with thinking, movement, behavior, and mood. LBD is one of the most common causes of dementia, after Alzheimer disease and vascular disease.

Dementia is a severe loss of thinking abilities that interferes with a person's capacity to perform daily activities such as household tasks, personal care, and handling finances. Dementia has many possible causes, including stroke, brain tumor, depression, and vitamin deficiency, as well as disorders such as LBD, Parkinson, and Alzheimer.

Diagnosing LBD can be challenging for a number of reasons. Early LBD symptoms are often confused with similar symptoms found in other brain diseases like Alzheimer. Also, LBD can occur alone or along with Alzheimer or Parkinson diseases.

There are two types of LBD—*dementia with Lewy bodies* and *Parkinson disease dementia*. The earliest signs of these two diseases differ but reflect the same biological changes in the brain. Over time, people with dementia with Lewy bodies or Parkinson disease dementia may develop similar symptoms.

Who Is Affected by LBD?

LBD affects more than 1 million individuals in the United States. LBD typically begins at age 50 or older, although sometimes younger people have it. LBD appears to affect slightly more men than women.

LBD is a progressive disease, meaning symptoms start slowly and worsen over time. The disease lasts an average of 5 to 7 years from the time of diagnosis to death, but the time span can range from 2 to 20 years. How quickly symptoms develop and change varies greatly from person to person, depending on overall health, age, and severity of symptoms.

In the early stages of LBD, usually before a diagnosis is made, symptoms can be mild, and people can function fairly normally. As the disease advances, people with LBD require more and more help due to a decline in thinking and movement abilities. In the later stages of the disease, they may depend entirely on others for assistance and care.

Some LBD symptoms may respond to treatment for a period of time. Currently, there is no cure for the disease. Research is improving our understanding of this challenging condition, and advances in science may one day lead to better diagnosis, improved care, and new treatments.

Types of Lewy Body Dementia

Lewy body dementia includes two related conditions dementia with Lewy bodies and Parkinson disease dementia. The difference between them lies largely in the timing of cognitive (thinking) and movement symptoms. In dementia with Lewy bodies, cognitive symptoms are noted within a year of Parkinsonism, any condition that involves the types of movement changes, such as tremor or muscle stiffness, seen in Parkinson disease. In Parkinson disease dementia, movement symptoms are pronounced in the early stages, with cognitive symptoms developing years later.

Dementia with Lewy Bodies

People with dementia with Lewy bodies have a decline in thinking ability that may look somewhat like Alzheimer disease. But over time they also develop movement and other distinctive symptoms that suggest dementia with Lewy bodies. Symptoms that distinguish this form of dementia from others may include:

- visual hallucinations early in the course of dementia

- fluctuations in cognitive ability, attention, and alertness

- slowness of movement, difficulty walking, or rigidity (Parkinsonism)

- sensitivity to medications used to treat hallucinations

- Rapid-Eye-Movement (REM) sleep behavior disorder, in which people physically act out their dreams by yelling, flailing, punching bed partners, and falling out of bed

- more trouble with complex mental activities, such as multitasking, problem solving, and analytical thinking, than with memory

Parkinson Disease Dementia

This type of LBD starts as a movement disorder, with symptoms such as slowed movement, muscle stiffness, tremor, and a shuffling walk. These symptoms are consistent with a diagnosis of Parkinson disease. Later on, cognitive symptoms of dementia and changes in mood and behavior may arise.

Not all people with Parkinson's develop dementia, and it is difficult to predict who will. Being diagnosed with Parkinson's late in life is a risk factor for Parkinson disease dementia.

Causes and Risk Factors

The precise cause of LBD is unknown, but scientists are learning more about its biology and genetics. For example, they know that an accumulation of Lewy bodies is associated with a loss of certain neurons in the brain that produce two important neurotransmitters, chemicals that act as messengers between brain cells. One of these messengers, acetylcholine, is important for memory and learning. The other, dopamine, plays an important role in behavior, cognition, movement, motivation, sleep, and mood. Scientists are also learning

147

about risk factors for LBD. Age is considered the greatest risk factor. Most people who develop the disorder are over age 50.

Other known risk factors for LBD include the following:

- Diseases and health conditions—Certain diseases and health conditions, particularly Parkinson disease and REM sleep behavior disorder, are linked to a higher risk of LBD.

- Genetics—While having a family member with LBD may increase a person's risk, LBD is not normally considered a genetic disease. A small percentage of families with dementia with Lewy bodies has a genetic association, such as a variant of the GBA gene, but in most cases, the cause is unknown. At this time, no genetic test can accurately predict whether someone will develop LBD. Future genetic research may reveal more information about causes and risk.

- Lifestyle—No specific lifestyle factor has been proven to increase one's risk for LBD. However, some studies suggest that a healthy lifestyle—including regular exercise, mental stimulation, and a healthy diet—might reduce the chance of developing age-associated dementias.

Common Symptoms

People with LBD may not have every LBD symptom, and the severity of symptoms can vary greatly from person to person. Throughout the course of the disease, any sudden or major change in functional ability or behavior should be reported to a doctor.

The most common symptoms include changes in cognition, movement, sleep, and behavior.

Cognitive Symptoms

LBD causes changes in thinking abilities. These changes may include:

- **Dementia**—Severe loss of thinking abilities that interferes with a person's capacity to perform daily activities. Dementia is a primary symptom in LBD and usually includes trouble with visual and spatial abilities (judging distance and depth or misidentifying objects), planning, multitasking, problem solving, and reasoning. Memory problems may not be evident at first but often arise as LBD progresses. Dementia can also include changes in mood and behavior, poor judgment, loss of initiative, confusion about time and place, and difficulty with language and numbers.

- **Cognitive fluctuations**—Unpredictable changes in concentration, attention, alertness, and wakefulness from day to day and sometimes throughout the day. A person with LBD may stare into space for periods of time, seem drowsy and lethargic, or sleep for several hours during the day despite getting enough sleep the night before. His or her flow of ideas may be disorganized, unclear, or illogical at times. The person may seem better one day, then worse the next day. These cognitive fluctuations are common in LBD but are not always easy for a doctor to identify.

- **Hallucinations**—Seeing or hearing things that are not present. Visual hallucinations occur in up to 80 percent of people with LBD, often early on. They are typically realistic and detailed, such as images of children or animals. Auditory hallucinations are less common than visual ones but may also occur. Hallucinations that are not disruptive may not require treatment. However, if they are frightening or dangerous (for example, if the person attempts to fight a perceived intruder), then a doctor may prescribe medication.

Table 18.1. Main Symptoms of Lewy Body Dementia

Symptom	Dementia with Lewy Bodies	Parkinson Disease Dementia
Dementia	* Appears within a year of movement problems	* Appears later in the disease, after movement problems
Movement problems (parkinsonism)	* Appear at the same time as or after dementia	* Appear before dementia
Fluctuating cognition, attention, alertness	*	*
Visual hallucinations	*	*
REM sleep behavior disorder	‡ May develop years before other symptoms	‡ May develop years before other symptoms
Extreme sensitivity to antipsychotic medications	‡	‡

Table 18.1. Continued

Symptom	Dementia with Lewy Bodies	Parkinson Disease Dementia
Changes in personality and mood (depression, delusions, apathy)	‡	‡
Changes in autonomic (involuntary) nervous system (blood pressure, bladder and bowel control)	‡	‡

* *Primary symptom*
‡ *Common symptom*

Movement Symptoms

Some people with LBD may not experience significant movement problems for several years. Others may have them early on. At first, signs of movement problems, such as a change in handwriting, may be very mild and thus overlooked. Parkinsonism is seen early on in Parkinson disease dementia but can also develop later on in dementia with Lewy bodies. Specific signs of Parkinsonism may include:

- muscle rigidity or stiffness
- shuffling gait, slow movement, or frozen stance
- tremor or shaking, most commonly at rest
- balance problems and falls
- stooped posture
- loss of coordination
- smaller handwriting than was usual for the person
- reduced facial expression
- difficulty swallowing
- a weak voice

Sleep Disorders

Sleep disorders are common in people with LBD but are often undiagnosed. A sleep specialist can play an important role on a treatment team, helping to diagnose and treat sleep disorders. Sleep-related disorders seen in people with LBD may include:

- REM sleep behavior disorder—A condition in which a person seems to act out dreams. It may include vivid dreaming, talking in one's sleep, violent movements, or falling out of bed. Sometimes only the bed partner of the person with LBD is aware of these symptoms. REM sleep behavior disorder appears in some people years before other LBD symptoms.

- Excessive daytime sleepiness—Sleeping 2 or more hours during the day.

- Insomnia—Difficulty falling or staying asleep, or waking up too early.

- Restless leg syndrome—A condition in which a person, while resting, feels the urge to move his or her legs to stop unpleasant or unusual sensations. Walking or moving usually relieves the discomfort.

Behavioral and Mood Symptoms

Changes in behavior and mood are possible in LBD. These changes may include:

- **Depression**—A persistent feeling of sadness, inability to enjoy activities, or trouble with sleeping, eating, and other normal activities.

- **Apathy**—A lack of interest in normal daily activities or events; less social interaction.

- **Anxiety**—Intense apprehension, uncertainty, or fear about a future event or situation. A person may ask the same questions over and over or be angry or fearful when a loved one is not present.

- **Agitation**—Restlessness, as seen by pacing, hand wringing, an inability to get settled, constant repeating of words or phrases, or irritability.

- **Delusions**—Strongly held false beliefs or opinions not based on evidence. For example, a person may think his or her spouse is having an affair or that relatives long dead are still living. Another delusion that may be seen in people with LBD is Capgras syndrome, in which the person believes a relative or friend has been replaced by an imposter.

- **Paranoia**—An extreme, irrational distrust of others, such as suspicion that people are taking or hiding things

Other LBD Symptoms

People with LBD can also experience significant changes in the part of the nervous system that regulates automatic functions such as those of the heart, glands, and muscles. The person may have:

- changes in body temperature
- problems with blood pressure
- dizziness
- fainting
- frequent falls
- sensitivity to heat and cold
- sexual dysfunction
- urinary incontinence
- constipation
- a poor sense of smell

Diagnosis

It's important to know which type of LBD a person has, both to tailor treatment to particular symptoms and to understand how the disease will likely progress. Clinicians and researchers use the "1-year rule" to diagnose which form of LBD a person has. If cognitive symptoms appear within a year of movement problems, the diagnosis is dementia with Lewy bodies. If cognitive problems develop more than a year after the onset of movement problems, the diagnosis is Parkinson disease dementia.

Regardless of the initial symptoms, over time people with LBD often develop similar symptoms due to the presence of Lewy bodies in the brain. But there are some differences. For example, dementia with Lewy bodies may progress more quickly than Parkinson disease dementia.

Dementia with Lewy bodies is often hard to diagnose because its early symptoms may resemble those of Alzheimer, Parkinson disease, or a psychiatric illness. As a result, it is often misdiagnosed or missed altogether. As additional symptoms appear, it is often easier to make an accurate diagnosis.

The good news is that doctors are increasingly able to diagnose LBD earlier and more accurately as researchers identify which symptoms help distinguish it from similar disorders.

Difficult as it is, getting an accurate diagnosis of LBD early on is important so that a person:

- gets the right medical care and avoids potentially harmful treatment

- has time to plan medical care and arrange legal and financial affairs

- can build a support team to stay independent and maximize quality of life

While a diagnosis of LBD can be distressing, some people are relieved to know the reason for their troubling symptoms. It is important to allow time to adjust to the news. Talking about a diagnosis can help shift the focus toward developing a care plan.

Tests Used to Diagnose LBD

Doctors perform physical and neurological examinations and various tests to distinguish LBD from other illnesses. An evaluation may include:

- **Medical history and examination**—A review of previous and current illnesses, medications, and current symptoms and tests of movement and memory give the doctor valuable information.

- **Medical tests**—Laboratory studies can help rule out other diseases and hormonal or vitamin deficiencies that can be associated with cognitive changes.

- **Brain imaging**—Computed tomography or magnetic resonance imaging can detect brain shrinkage or structural abnormalities and help rule out other possible causes of dementia or movement symptoms.

- **Neuropsychological tests**—These tests are used to assess memory and other cognitive functions and can help identify affected brain regions.

There are no brain scans or medical tests that can definitively diagnose LBD. Currently, LBD can be diagnosed with certainty only by a brain autopsy after death.

However, researchers are studying ways to diagnose LBD more accurately in the living brain. Certain types of neuroimaging—positron emission tomography and single-photon emission computed tomography—have shown promise in detecting differences between dementia with Lewy bodies and Alzheimer disease. These methods may help diagnose certain features of the disorder, such as dopamine deficiencies. Researchers are also investigating the use of lumbar puncture (spinal tap) to measure proteins in cerebrospinal fluid that might distinguish dementia with Lewy bodies from Alzheimer disease and other brain disorders.

Medications

Several drugs and other treatments are available to treat LBD symptoms. It is important to work with a knowledgeable health professional because certain medications can make some symptoms worse. Some symptoms can improve with nondrug treatments.

Cognitive Symptoms

Some medications used to treat Alzheimer disease also may be used to treat the cognitive symptoms of LBD. These drugs, called cholinesterase inhibitors, act on a chemical in the brain that is important for memory and thinking. They may also improve behavioral symptoms.

The U.S. Food and Drug Administration (FDA) approves specific drugs for certain uses after rigorous testing and review. The FDA has approved one Alzheimer drug, rivastigmine (Exelon®), to treat cognitive symptoms in Parkinson disease dementia. This and other Alzheimer drugs can have side effects such as nausea and diarrhea.

Movement Symptoms

LBD-related movement symptoms may be treated with a Parkinson's medication called carbidopa-levodopa (Sinemet®, Parcopa®, Stalevo®). This drug can help improve functioning by making it easier to walk, get out of bed, and move around. However, it cannot stop or reverse the progress of the disease.

Side effects of this medication can include hallucinations and other psychiatric or behavioral problems. Because of this risk, physicians may recommend not treating mild movement symptoms with medication. If prescribed, carbidopa-levodopa usually begins at a low dose and is increased gradually. Other Parkinson's medications are less commonly used in people with LBD due to a higher frequency of side effects.

A surgical procedure called deep brain stimulation, which can be very effective in treating the movement symptoms of Parkinson disease, is not recommended for people with LBD because it can result in greater cognitive impairment. People with LBD may benefit from physical therapy and exercise. Talk with your doctor about what physical activities are best.

Sleep Disorders

Sleep problems may increase confusion and behavioral problems in people with LBD and add to a caregiver's burden. A physician can order a sleep study to identify any underlying sleep disorders such as sleep apnea, restless leg syndrome, and REM sleep behavior disorder.

REM sleep behavior disorder, a common LBD symptom, involves acting out one's dreams, leading to lost sleep and even injuries to sleep partners. Clonazepam (Klonopin®), a drug used to control seizures and relieve panic attacks, is often effective for the disorder at very low dosages. However, it can have side effects such as dizziness, unsteadiness, and problems with thinking. Melatonin, a naturally occurring hormone used to treat insomnia, may also offer some benefit when taken alone or with clonazepam.

Excessive daytime sleepiness is also common in LBD. If it is severe, a sleep specialist may prescribe a stimulant to help the person stay awake during the day.

Some people with LBD may have difficulty falling asleep. If trouble sleeping at night (insomnia) persists, a physician may recommend a prescription medication to promote sleep. It is important to note that treating insomnia and other sleep problems in people with LBD has not been extensively studied, and that treatments may worsen daytime sleepiness and should be used with caution.

Certain sleep problems can be addressed without medications. Increasing daytime exercise or activities and avoiding lengthy or frequent naps can promote better sleep. Avoiding alcohol, caffeine, or chocolate late in the day can help, too. Some over-the-counter medications can also affect sleep, so review all medications and supplements with a physician.

Behavioral and Mood Problems

Behavioral and mood problems in people with LBD can arise from hallucinations or delusions. They may also be a result of pain, illness, stress or anxiety, and the inability to express frustration, fear, or feeling overwhelmed. The person may resist care or lash out verbally or physically.

Caregivers must try to be patient and use a variety of strategies to handle such challenging behaviors. Some behavioral problems can be managed by making changes in the person's environment and/or treating medical conditions. Other problems may require medication.

The first step is to visit a doctor to see if a medical condition unrelated to LBD is causing the problem. Injuries, fever, urinary tract or pulmonary infections, pressure ulcers (bed sores), and constipation can worsen behavioral problems. Increased confusion can also occur.

Certain medications used to treat LBD symptoms or other diseases may also cause behavioral problems. For example, some sleep aids, pain medications, bladder control medications, and drugs used to treat LBD-related movement symptoms can cause confusion, agitation, hallucinations, and delusions. Similarly, some anti-anxiety medicines can actually increase anxiety in people with LBD. Review your medications with your doctor to determine if any changes are needed.

Not all behavioral problems are caused by illness or medication. A person's surroundings—including levels of stimulation or stress, lighting, daily routines, and relationships—can lead to behavior issues. Caregivers can alter the home environment to try to minimize anxiety and stress for the person with LBD. In general, people with LBD benefit from having simple tasks, consistent schedules, regular exercise, and adequate sleep. Large crowds or overly stimulating environments can increase confusion and anxiety.

Hallucinations and delusions are among the biggest challenges for LBD caregivers. The person with LBD may not understand or accept that the hallucinations are not real and become agitated or anxious. Caregivers can help by responding to the fears expressed instead of arguing or responding factually to comments that may not be true. By tuning in to the person's emotions, caregivers can offer empathy and concern, maintain the person's dignity, and limit further tension.

Cholinesterase inhibitors may reduce hallucinations and other psychiatric symptoms of LBD. These medications may have side effects, such as nausea, and are not always effective. However, they can be a good first choice to treat behavioral symptoms. Cholinesterase inhibitors do not affect behavior immediately, so they should be considered part of a long-term strategy.

Antidepressants can be used to treat depression and anxiety, which are common in LBD. Two types of antidepressants, called selective serotonin reuptake inhibitors and norepinephrine reuptake inhibitors, are often well tolerated by people with LBD.

In some cases, antipsychotic medications are necessary to treat LBD-related behavioral symptoms to improve both the quality of life and safety of the person with LBD and his or her caregiver. These types of medications must be used with caution because they can cause severe side effects and can worsen movement symptoms.

If antipsychotics are prescribed, it is very important to use the newer kind, called atypical antipsychotics. These medications should be used at the lowest dose possible and for the shortest time possible to control symptoms. Many LBD experts prefer quetiapine (Seroquel®) or clozapine (Clozaril®, FazaClo®) to control difficult behavioral symptoms.

Typical (or traditional) antipsychotics, such as haloperidol (Haldol®), generally should not be prescribed for people with LBD. They can cause dangerous side effects.

Warning about Antipsychotics

People with LBD may have severe reactions to or side effects from antipsychotics, medications used to treat delusions, hallucinations, or agitation. These side effects include increased confusion, worsened parkinsonism, extreme sleepiness, and low blood pressure that can result in fainting (orthostatic hypotension). Caregivers should contact the doctor if these side effects continue after a few days.

Some antipsychotics, including olanzapine (Zyprexa®) and risperidone (Risperdal®), should be avoided, if possible, because they are more likely than others to cause serious side effects.

In rare cases, a potentially deadly condition called neuroleptic malignant syndrome can occur. Symptoms of this condition include high fever, muscle rigidity, and muscle tissue breakdown that can lead to kidney failure. Report these symptoms to your doctor immediately.

Antipsychotic medications increase the risk of death in elderly people with dementia, including those with LBD. Doctors, patients, and family members must weigh the risks of antipsychotic use against the risks of physical harm and distress that may occur as a result of untreated behavioral symptoms.

Section 18.3

Frontotemporal Disorders

Text in this section is excerpted from "Frontotemporal Disorders:
Information for Patients, Families, and Caregivers," National
Institute on Aging (NIA), January 22, 2015.

The Basics of Frontotemporal Disorders

Frontotemporal disorders are the result of damage to neurons
(nerve cells) in parts of the brain called the frontal and temporal lobes.
As neurons die in the frontal and temporal regions, these lobes atrophy, or shrink. Gradually, this damage causes difficulties in thinking
and behaviors normally controlled by these parts of the brain. Many
possible symptoms can result, including unusual behaviors, emotional
problems, trouble communicating, difficulty with work, or difficulty
with walking.

A Form of Dementia

Frontotemporal disorders are forms of dementia caused by a family
of brain diseases known as frontotemporal lobar degeneration (FTLD).
Dementia is a severe loss of thinking abilities that interferes with a
person's ability to perform daily activities such as working, driving,
and preparing meals. Other brain diseases that can cause dementia
include Alzheimer disease (AD) and multiple strokes. Scientists estimate that FTLD may cause up to 10 percent of all cases of dementia
and may be about as common as Alzheimer among people younger than
age 65. Roughly 60 percent of people with FTLD are 45 to 64 years old.

People can live with frontotemporal disorders for up to 10 years,
sometimes longer, but it is difficult to predict the time course for an
individual patient. The disorders are progressive, meaning symptoms
get worse over time. In the early stages, people may have just one type
of symptom. As the disease progresses, other types of symptoms appear
as more parts of the brain are affected.

No cure or treatments that slow or stop the progression of frontotemporal disorders are available today. However, research is improving

awareness and understanding of these challenging conditions. This progress is opening doors to better diagnosis, improved care, and, eventually, new treatments.

Changes in the Brain

Frontotemporal disorders affect the frontal and temporal lobes of the brain. They can begin in the frontal lobe, the temporal lobe, or both. Initially, frontotemporal disorders leave other brain regions untouched, including those that control short-term memory.

The frontal lobes, situated above the eyes and behind the forehead both on the right and left sides of the brain, direct executive functioning. This includes planning and sequencing (thinking through which steps come first, second, third, and so on), prioritizing (doing more important activities first and less important activities last), multitasking (shifting from one activity to another as needed), and monitoring and correcting errors.

When functioning well, the frontal lobes also help manage emotional responses. They enable people to avoid inappropriate social behaviors, such as shouting loudly in a library or at a funeral. They help people make decisions that make sense for a given situation. When the frontal lobes are damaged, people may focus on insignificant details and ignore important aspects of a situation or engage in purposeless activities. The frontal lobes are also involved in language, particularly linking words to form sentences, and in motor functions, such as moving the arms, legs, and mouth.

The temporal lobes, located below and to the side of each frontal lobe on the right and left sides of the brain, contain essential areas for memory but also play a major role in language and emotions. They help people understand words, speak, read, write, and connect words with their meanings. They allow people to recognize objects and to relate appropriate emotions to objects and events. When the temporal lobes are dysfunctional, people may have difficulty recognizing emotions and responding appropriately to them.

Which lobe—and part of the lobe—is affected first determines which symptoms appear first. For example, if the disease starts in the part of the frontal lobe responsible for decision-making, then the first symptom might be trouble managing finances. If it begins in the part of the temporal lobe that connects emotions to objects, then the first symptom might be an inability to recognize potentially dangerous objects—a person might reach for a snake or plunge a hand into boiling water, for example

Section 18.4

Huntington Disease

Text in this section is excerpted from "Huntington's Disease:
Hope through Research," National Institute of Neurological
Disorders and Stroke (NINDS), April 19, 2015.

Introduction to Huntington Disease

More than 15,000 Americans have Huntington Disease (HD). At least 150,000 others have a 50 percent risk of developing the disease and thousands more of their relatives live with the possibility that they, too, might develop HD.

Until recently, scientists understood very little about HD and could only watch as the disease continued to pass from generation to generation. Families saw the disease destroy their loved ones' ability to feel, think, and move. In the last several years, scientists working with support from the National Institute of Neurological Disorders and Stroke (NINDS) have made several breakthroughs in the area of HD research. With these advances, our understanding of the disease continues to improve.

This section presents information about HD, and about current research progress, to health professionals, scientists, caregivers, and, most important, to those already too familiar with the disorder: the many families who are affected by HD.

What Causes HD?

HD results from genetically programmed degeneration of nerve cells, called *neurons*, in certain areas of the brain. This degeneration causes uncontrolled movements, loss of intellectual faculties, and emotional disturbance. Specifically affected are cells of the basal *ganglia*, structures deep within the brain that have many important functions, including coordinating movement. Within the basal ganglia, HD especially targets neurons of the *striatum*, particularly those in the caudate *nuclei* and the *pallidum*. Also affected is the brain's outer surface, or cortex, which controls thought, perception, and memory.

160

How Is HD Inherited?

HD is found in every country of the world. It is a familial disease, passed from parent to child through a *mutation* or misspelling in the normal *gene*.

A single abnormal gene, the basic biological unit of heredity, produces HD. Genes are composed of *deoxyribonucleic acid (DNA)*, a molecule shaped like a spiral ladder. Each rung of this ladder is composed of two paired chemicals called bases. There are four types of bases adenine, thymine, cytosine, and guanine—each abbreviated by the first letter of its name: A, T, C, and G. Certain bases always "pair" together, and different combinations of base pairs join to form coded messages. A gene is a long string of this DNA in various combinations of A, T, C, and G. These unique combinations determine the gene's function, much like letters join together to form words. Each person has about 30,000 genes—a billion base pairs of DNA or bits of information repeated in the nuclei of human cells—which determine individual characteristics or *traits*.

Genes are arranged in precise locations along 23 rod-like pairs of *chromosomes*. One chromosome from each pair comes from an individual's mother, the other from the father. Each half of a chromosome pair is similar to the other, except for one pair, which determines the sex of the individual. This pair has two X chromosomes in females and one X and one Y chromosome in males. The gene that produces HD lies on chromosome 4, one of the 22 non-sex-linked, or "autosomal," pairs of chromosomes, placing men and women at equal risk of acquiring the disease.

The impact of a gene depends partly on whether it is *dominant* or *recessive*. If a gene is dominant, then only one of the paired chromosomes is required to produce its called-for effect. If the gene is recessive, both parents must provide chromosomal copies for the trait to be present. HD is called an *autosomal dominant disorder* because only one copy of the defective gene, inherited from one parent, is necessary to produce the disease.

The genetic defect responsible for HD is a small sequence of DNA on chromosome 4 in which several base pairs are repeated many, many times. The normal gene has three DNA bases, composed of the sequence CAG. In people with HD, the sequence abnormally repeats itself dozens of times. Over time—and with each successive generation—the number of CAG repeats may expand further.

Each parent has two copies of every chromosome but gives only one copy to each child. Each child of an HD parent has a 50-50 chance of inheriting the HD gene. If a child does not inherit the HD gene, he or she will not develop the disease and cannot pass it to subsequent generations. A person who inherits the HD gene, and survives long enough, will sooner or later develop the disease. In some families, all the children may inherit the HD gene; in others, none do. Whether one child inherits the gene has no bearing on whether others will or will not share the same fate.

A small number of cases of HD are sporadic, that is, they occur even though there is no family history of the disorder. These cases are thought to be caused by a new genetic mutation-an alteration in the gene that occurs during sperm development and that brings the number of CAG repeats into the range that causes disease.

What Are the Major Effects of HD?

Early signs of the disease vary greatly from person to person. A common observation is that the earlier the symptoms appear, the faster the disease progresses.

Family members may first notice that the individual experiences mood swings or becomes uncharacteristically irritable, apathetic, passive, depressed, or angry. These symptoms may lessen as the disease progresses or, in some individuals, may continue and include hostile outbursts or deep bouts of depression.

HD may affect the individual's judgment, memory, and other cognitive functions. Early signs might include having trouble driving, learning new things, remembering a fact, answering a question, or making a decision. Some may even display changes in handwriting. As the disease progresses, concentration on intellectual tasks becomes increasingly difficult.

In some individuals, the disease may begin with uncontrolled movements in the fingers, feet, face, or trunk. These movements—which are signs of chorea—often intensify when the person is anxious. HD can also begin with mild clumsiness or problems with balance. Some people develop choreic movements later, after the disease has progressed. They may stumble or appear uncoordinated. Chorea often creates serious problems with walking, increasing the likelihood of falls.

The disease can reach the point where speech is slurred and vital functions, such as swallowing, eating, speaking, and especially walking, continue to decline. Some individuals cannot recognize other family members. Many, however, remain aware of their environment and are able to express emotions.

Some physicians have employed a recently developed Unified HD Rating Scale, or UHDRS, to assess the clinical features, stages, and course of HD. In general, the duration of the illness ranges from 10 to 30 years. The most common causes of death are infection (most often pneumonia), injuries related to a fall, or other complications.

At What Age Does HD Appear?

The rate of disease progression and the age at onset vary from person to person. Adult-onset HD, with its disabling, uncontrolled movements, most often begins in middle age. There are, however, other variations of HD distinguished not just by age at onset but by a distinct array of symptoms. For example, some persons develop the disease as adults, but without chorea. They may appear rigid and move very little, or not at all, a condition called *akinesia*.

Some individuals develop symptoms of HD when they are very young—before age 20. The terms "early-onset" or "juvenile" HD are often used to describe HD that appears in a young person. A common sign of HD in a younger individual is a rapid decline in school performance. Symptoms can also include subtle changes in handwriting and slight problems with movement, such as slowness, rigidity, tremor, and rapid muscular twitching, called *myoclonus*. Several of these symptoms are similar to those seen in Parkinson disease, and they differ from the chorea seen in individuals who develop the disease as adults. These young individuals are said to have "akinetic-rigid" HD or the Westphal variant of HD. People with juvenile HD may also have seizures and mental disabilities. The earlier the onset, the faster the disease seems to progress. The disease progresses most rapidly in individuals with juvenile or early-onset HD, and death often follows within 10 years.

Individuals with juvenile HD usually inherit the disease from their fathers. These individuals also tend to have the largest number of CAG repeats. The reason for this may be found in the process of sperm production. Unlike eggs, sperm are produced in the millions. Because DNA is copied millions of times during this process, there is an increased possibility for genetic mistakes to occur. To verify the link between the number of CAG repeats in the HD gene and the age at onset of symptoms, scientists studied a boy who developed HD symptoms at the age of two, one of the youngest and most severe cases ever recorded. They found that he had the largest number of CAG repeats of anyone studied so far—nearly 100. The boy's case was central to the identification of the HD gene and at the same time helped confirm that juveniles with HD have the longest segments of CAG repeats, the only proven correlation between repeat length and age at onset.

A few individuals develop HD after age 55. Diagnosis in these people can be very difficult. The symptoms of HD may be masked by other health problems, or the person may not display the severity of symptoms seen in individuals with HD of earlier onset. These individuals may also show symptoms of depression rather than anger or irritability, or they may retain sharp control over their intellectual functions, such as memory, reasoning, and problem-solving.

There is also a related disorder called *senile chorea*. Some elderly individuals display the symptoms of HD, especially choreic movements, but do not become demented, have a normal gene, and lack a family history of the disorder. Some scientists believe that a different gene mutation may account for this small number of cases, but this has not been proven.

How Is HD Diagnosed?

The great American folk singer and composer Woody Guthrie died on October 3, 1967, after suffering from HD for 13 years. He had been misdiagnosed, considered an alcoholic, and shuttled in and out of mental institutions and hospitals for years before being properly diagnosed. His case, sadly, is not extraordinary, although the diagnosis can be made easily by experienced neurologists.

A neurologist will interview the individual intensively to obtain the medical history and rule out other conditions. A tool used by physicians to diagnose HD is to take the family history, sometimes called a pedigree or genealogy. It is extremely important for family members to be candid and truthful with a doctor who is taking a family history.

The doctor will also ask about recent intellectual or emotional problems, which may be indications of HD, and will test the person's hearing, eye movements, strength, coordination, involuntary movements (chorea), sensation, reflexes, balance, movement, and mental status, and will probably order a number of laboratory tests as well.

People with HD commonly have impairments in the way the eye follows or fixes on a moving target. Abnormalities of eye movements vary from person to person and differ, depending on the stage and duration of the illness.

The discovery of the HD gene in 1993 resulted in a direct genetic test to make or confirm a diagnosis of HD in an individual who is exhibiting HD-like symptoms. Using a blood sample, the genetic test analyzes DNA for the HD mutation by counting the number of repeats

Table 18.2. Percentage of individuals having number of repeats that fall within a borderline region

No. of CAG repeats	Outcome
< 28	Normal range; individual will not develop HD
29–34	Individual will not develop HD but the next generation is at risk
35–39	Some, but not all, individuals in this range will develop HD; next generation is also at risk
> 40	Individual will develop HD

in the HD gene region. Individuals who do not have HD usually have 28 or fewer CAG repeats. Individuals with HD usually have 40 or more repeats. A small percentage of individuals, however, have a number of repeats that fall within a borderline region.

The physician may ask the individual to undergo a brain imaging test. *Computed tomography (CT)* and magnetic resonance imaging (MRI) provide excellent images of brain structures with little if any discomfort. Those with HD may show shrinkage of some parts of the brain—particularly two areas known as the caudate nuclei and *putamen*—and enlargement of fluid-filled cavities within the brain called *ventricles*. These changes do not definitely indicate HD, however, because they can also occur in other disorders. In addition, a person can have early symptoms of HD and still have a normal CT scan. When used in conjunction with a family history and record of clinical symptoms, however, CT can be an important diagnostic tool.

Another technology for brain imaging includes *positron emission tomography* (PET), which is important in HD research efforts but is not often needed for diagnosis.

What Is Presymptomatic Testing?

Presymptomatic testing is used for people who have a family history of HD but have no symptoms themselves. If either parent had HD, the person's chance would be 50-50. In the past, no laboratory test could positively identify people carrying the HD gene—or those fated to develop HD—before the onset of symptoms. That situation changed in 1983, when a team of scientists supported by the NINDS located the first genetic *marker* for HD—the initial step in developing a laboratory test for the disease.

A marker is a piece of DNA that lies near a gene and is usually inherited with it. Discovery of the first HD marker allowed scientists to locate the HD gene on chromosome 4. The marker discovery quickly led to the development of a presymptomatic test for some individuals, but this test required blood or tissue samples from both affected and unaffected family members in order to identify markers unique to that particular family. For this reason, adopted individuals, orphans, and people who had few living family members were unable to use the test.

Discovery of the HD gene has led to a less expensive, scientifically simpler, and far more accurate presymptomatic test that is applicable to the majority of at-risk people. The new test uses CAG repeat length to detect the presence of the HD mutation in blood.

There are many complicating factors that reflect the complexity of diagnosing HD. In a small number of individuals with HD—1 to 3 percent—no family history of HD can be found. Some individuals may not be aware of their genetic legacy, or a family member may conceal a genetic disorder from fear of social stigma. A parent may not want to worry children, scare them, or deter them from marrying. In other cases, a family member may die of another cause before he or she begins to show signs of HD. Sometimes, the cause of death for a relative may not be known, or the family is not aware of a relative's death. Adopted children may not know their genetic heritage, or early symptoms in an individual may be too slight to attract attention.

How Is the Presymptomatic Test Conducted?

An individual who wishes to be tested should contact the nearest testing center. (A list of such centers can be obtained from the Huntington Disease Society of America at 1-800-345-HDSA.) The testing process should include several components. Most testing programs include a neurological examination, pretest counseling, and follow up. The purpose of the neurological examination is to determine whether or not the person requesting testing is showing any clinical symptoms of HD. It is important to remember that if an individual is showing even slight symptoms of HD, he or she risks being diagnosed with the disease during the neurological examination, even before the genetic test. During pretest counseling, the individual will learn about HD, and about his or her own level of risk, about the testing procedure. The person will be told about the test's limitations, the accuracy of the test, and possible outcomes. He or she can then weigh the risks and benefits of testing and may even decide at that time against pursuing further testing.

If a person decides to be tested, a team of highly trained specialists will be involved, which may include neurologists, genetic counselors, social workers, psychiatrists, and psychologists. This team of professionals helps the at-risk person decide if testing is the right thing to do and carefully prepares the person for a negative, positive, or inconclusive test result.

Individuals who decide to continue the testing process should be accompanied to counseling sessions by a spouse, a friend, or a relative who is not at risk. Other interested family members may participate in the counseling sessions if the individual being tested so desires.

The genetic testing itself involves donating a small sample of blood that is screened in the laboratory for the presence or absence of the HD mutation. Testing may require a sample of DNA from a closely related affected relative, preferably a parent, for the purpose of confirming the diagnosis of HD in the family. This is especially important if the family history for HD is unclear or unusual in some way.

Results of the test should be given only in person and only to the individual being tested. Test results are confidential. Regardless of test results, follow up is recommended.

In order to protect the interests of minors, including confidentiality, testing is not recommended for those under the age of 18 unless there is a compelling medical reason (for example, the child is exhibiting symptoms).

Testing of a fetus (prenatal testing) presents special challenges and risks; in fact some centers do not perform genetic testing on fetuses. Because a positive test result using direct genetic testing means the at-risk parent is also a gene carrier, at-risk individuals who are considering a pregnancy are advised to seek genetic counseling prior to conception.

Some at-risk parents may wish to know the risk to their fetus but not their own. In this situation, parents may opt for prenatal testing using linked DNA markers rather than direct gene testing. In this case, testing does not look for the HD gene itself but instead indicates whether or not the fetus has inherited a chromosome 4 from the affected grandparent or from the unaffected grandparent on the side of the family with HD. If the test shows that the fetus has inherited a chromosome 4 from the affected grandparent, the parents then learn that the fetus's risk is the same as the parent (50-50), but they learn nothing new about the parent's risk. If the test shows that the fetus has inherited a chromosome 4 from the unaffected grandparent, the risk to the fetus is very low (less than 1%) in most cases.

Another option open to parents is in *vitro* fertilization with pre-implantation screening. In this procedure, embryos are screened to determine which ones carry the HD mutation. Embryos determined not to have the HD gene mutation are then implanted in the woman's uterus.

In terms of emotional and practical consequences, not only for the individual taking the test but for his or her entire family, testing is enormously complex and has been surrounded by considerable controversy. For example, people with a positive test result may risk losing health and life insurance, suffer loss of employment, and other liabilities. People undergoing testing may wish to cover the cost themselves, since coverage by an insurer may lead to loss of health insurance in the event of a positive result, although this may change in the future.

With the participation of health professionals and people from families with HD, scientists have developed testing guidelines.

How Does a Person Decide Whether to Be Tested?

The anxiety that comes from living with a 50 percent risk for HD can be overwhelming. How does a young person make important choices about long-term education, marriage, and children? How do older parents of adult children cope with their fears about children and grandchildren? How do people come to terms with the ambiguity and uncertainty of living at risk?

Some individuals choose to undergo the test out of a desire for greater certainty about their genetic status. They believe the test will enable them to make more informed decisions about the future. Others choose not to take the test. They are able to make peace with the uncertainty of being at risk, preferring to forego the emotional consequences of a positive result, as well as possible losses of insurance and employment. There is no right or wrong decision, as each choice is highly individual. The guidelines for genetic testing for HD, discussed in the previous section, were developed to help people with this life-changing choice.

Whatever the results of genetic testing, the at-risk individual and family members can expect powerful and complex emotional responses. The health and happiness of spouses, brothers and sisters, children, parents, and grandparents are affected by a positive test result, as are an individual's friends, work associates, neighbors, and others. Because receiving test results may prove to be devastating, testing guidelines call for continued counseling even after the test is complete and the results are known.

Is There a Treatment for HD?

Physicians may prescribe a number of medications to help control emotional and movement problems associated with HD. It is important to remember however, that while medicines may help keep these clinical symptoms under control, there is no treatment to stop or reverse the course of the disease.

In August 2008, the U.S. Food and Drug Administration (FDA) approved tetrabenazine to treat Huntington chorea, making it the first drug approved for use in the United States to treat the disease. Antipsychotic drugs, such as haloperidol, or other drugs, such as clonazepam, may help to alleviate choreic movements and may also be used to help control hallucinations, delusions, and violent outbursts. Antipsychotic drugs, however, are not prescribed for another form of muscle contraction associated with HD, called dystonia, and may in fact worsen the condition, causing stiffness and rigidity. These medications may also have severe side effects, including sedation, and for that reason should be used in the lowest possible doses.

For depression, physicians may prescribe fluoxetine, sertraline, nortriptyline, or other compounds. Tranquilizers can help control anxiety and lithium may be prescribed to combat pathological excitement and severe mood swings. Medications may also be needed to treat the severe obsessive-compulsive rituals of some individuals with HD.

Most drugs used to treat the symptoms of HD have side effects such as fatigue, restlessness, or hyperexcitability. Sometimes it may be difficult to tell if a particular symptom, such as apathy or incontinence, is a sign of the disease or a reaction to medication.

What Kind of Care Does the Individual with HD Need?

Although a psychologist or psychiatrist, a genetic counselor, and other specialists may be needed at different stages of the illness, usually the first step in diagnosis and in finding treatment is to see a neurologist. While the family doctor may be able to diagnose HD, and may continue to monitor the individual's status, it is better to consult with a neurologist about management of the varied symptoms.

Problems may arise when individuals try to express complex thoughts in words they can no longer pronounce intelligibly. It can be helpful to repeat words back to the person with HD so that he or she knows that some thoughts are understood. Sometimes people mistakenly assume that if individuals do not talk, they also do not understand. Never isolate individuals by not talking, and try to keep their environment as normal as possible. Speech therapy may improve the individual's ability to communicate.

It is extremely important for the person with HD to maintain physical fitness as much as his or her condition and the course of the disease allows. Individuals who exercise and keep active tend to do better than those who do not. A daily regimen of exercise can help the person feel better physically and mentally. Although their coordination may be poor, individuals should continue walking, with assistance if necessary. Those who want to walk independently should be allowed to do so as long as possible, and careful attention should be given to keeping their environment free of hard, sharp objects. This will help ensure maximal independence while minimizing the risk of injury from a fall. Individuals can also wear special padding during walks to help protect against injury from falls. Some people have found that small weights around the ankles can help stability. Wearing sturdy shoes that fit well can help too, especially shoes without laces that can be slipped on or off easily.

Impaired coordination may make it difficult for people with HD to feed themselves and to swallow. As the disease progresses, persons with HD may even choke. In helping individuals to eat, caregivers should allow plenty of time for meals. Food can be cut into small pieces, softened, or pureed to ease swallowing and prevent choking. While some foods may require the addition of thickeners, other foods may need to be thinned. Dairy products, in particular, tend to increase the secretion of mucus, which in turn increases the risk of choking. Some individuals may benefit from swallowing therapy, which is especially helpful if started before serious problems arise. Suction cups for plates, special tableware designed for people with disabilities, and plastic cups with tops can help prevent spilling. The individual's physician can offer additional advice about diet and about how to handle swallowing difficulties or gastrointestinal problems that might arise, such as incontinence or constipation.

Caregivers should pay attention to proper nutrition so that the individual with HD takes in enough calories to maintain his or her body weight. Sometimes people with HD, who may burn as many as 5,000 calories a day without gaining weight, require five meals a day to take in the necessary number of calories. Physicians may recommend vitamins or other nutritional supplements. In a long-term care institution, staff will need to assist with meals in order to ensure that the individual's special caloric and nutritional requirements are met. Some individuals and their families choose to use a feeding tube; others choose not to.

Individuals with HD are at special risk for dehydration and therefore require large quantities of fluids, especially during hot weather. Bendable straws can make drinking easier for the person. In some cases, water may have to be thickened with commercial additives to give it the consistency of syrup or honey.

Section 18.5

Parkinson Disease

Text in this section is excerpted from "Parkinson's Disease: Hope through Research," National Institute of Neurological Disorders and Stroke (NINDS), January 22, 2016.

What Is Parkinson Disease?

Parkinson disease (PD) is a degenerative disorder of the central nervous system that belongs to a group of conditions called movement disorders. It is both chronic, meaning it persists over a long period of time, and progressive, meaning its symptoms grow worse over time. As nerve cells (neurons) in parts of the brain become impaired or die, people may begin to notice problems with movement, tremor, stiffness in the limbs or the trunk of the body, or impaired balance. As these symptoms become more pronounced, people may have difficulty walking, talking, or completing other simple tasks. Not everyone with one or more of these symptoms has PD, as the symptoms appear in other diseases as well.

The precise cause of PD is unknown, although some cases of PD are hereditary and can be traced to specific genetic mutations. Most cases are sporadic—that is, the disease does not typically run in families. It is thought that PD likely results from a combination of genetic susceptibility and exposure to one or more unknown environmental factors that trigger the disease.

PD is the most common form of *Parkinsonism*, in which disorders of other causes produce features and symptoms that closely resemble Parkinson disease. While most forms of Parkinsonism have no known cause, there are cases in which the cause is known or suspected or where the symptoms result from another disorder.

No cure for PD exists today, but research is ongoing and medications or surgery can often provide substantial improvement with motor symptoms.

What Causes the Disease?

Parkinson disease occurs when nerve cells, or neurons, in the brain die or become impaired. Although many brain areas are affected, the most common symptoms result from the loss of neurons in an area near the base of the brain called the *substantia nigra*. Normally, the neurons in this area produce an important brain chemical known as *dopamine*. Dopamine is a chemical messenger responsible for transmitting signals between the substantia nigra and the next "relay station" of the brain, the *corpus striatum*, to produce smooth, purposeful movement. Loss of dopamine results in abnormal nerve firing patterns within the brain that cause impaired movement. Studies have shown that most people with Parkinson's have lost 60 to 80 percent or more of the dopamine-producing cells in the substantia nigra by the time symptoms appear, and that people with PD also have loss of the nerve endings that produce the *neurotransmitter* norepinephrine. Norepinephrine, which is closely related to dopamine, is the main chemical messenger of the sympathetic nervous system, the part of the nervous system that controls many automatic functions of the body, such as pulse and blood pressure. The loss of norepinephrine might explain several of the non-motor features seen in PD, including fatigue and abnormalities of blood pressure regulation.

The affected brain cells of people with PD contain Lewy bodies— deposits of the protein alpha-synuclein. Researchers do not yet know why Lewy bodies form or what role they play in the disease. Some research suggests that the cell's protein disposal system may fail in people with PD, causing proteins to build up to harmful levels and trigger cell death. Additional studies have found evidence that clumps of protein that develop inside brain cells of people with PD may contribute to the death of neurons. Some researchers speculate that the protein buildup in Lewy bodies is part of an unsuccessful attempt to protect the cell from the toxicity of smaller aggregates, or collections, of synuclein.

- Genetics. Scientists have identified several genetic mutations associated with PD, including the alpha-synuclein gene, and many more genes have been tentatively linked to the disorder.

172

Studying the genes responsible for inherited cases of PD can help researchers understand both inherited and sporadic cases. The same genes and proteins that are altered in inherited cases may also be altered in sporadic cases by environmental toxins or other factors. Researchers also hope that discovering genes will help identify new ways of treating PD.

- Environment. Exposure to certain toxins has caused Parkinsonian symptoms in rare circumstances (such as exposure to MPTP, an illicit drug, or in miners exposed to the metal manganese). Other still-unidentified environmental factors may also cause PD in genetically susceptible individuals.

- Mitochondria. Several lines of research suggest that mitochondria may play a role in the development of PD. Mitochondria are the energy-producing components of the cell and abnormalities in the mitochondria are major sources of free radicals—molecules that damage membranes, proteins, DNA, and other parts of the cell. This damage is often referred to as oxidative stress. Oxidative stress-related changes, including free radical damage to DNA, proteins, and fats, have been detected in the brains of individuals with PD. Some mutations that affect mitochondrial function have been identified as causes of PD.

- While mitochondrial dysfunction, oxidative stress, inflammation, toxins, and many other cellular processes may contribute to PD, the actual cause of the cell loss death in PD is still undetermined.

What Are the Symptoms of the Disease?

The four primary symptoms of PD are:

1. **Tremor**. The tremor associated with PD has a characteristic appearance. Typically, the tremor takes the form of a rhythmic back-and-forth motion at a rate of 4-6 beats per second. It may involve the thumb and forefinger and appear as a "pill rolling" tremor. Tremor often begins in a hand, although sometimes a foot or the jaw is affected first. It is most obvious when the hand is at rest or when a person is under stress. Tremor usually disappears during sleep or improves with intentional movement. It is usually the first symptom that causes people to seek medical attention.

2. **Rigidity**. Rigidity, or a resistance to movement, affects most people with PD. The muscles remain constantly tense and contracted so that the person aches or feels stiff. The rigidity becomes obvious when another person tries to move the individual's arm, which will move only in ratchet-like or short, jerky movements known as "cogwheel" rigidity.

3. **Bradykinesia**. This slowing down of spontaneous and automatic movement is particularly frustrating because it may make simple tasks difficult. The person cannot rapidly perform routine movements. Activities once performed quickly and easily—such as washing or dressing—may take much longer. There is often a decrease in facial expressions.

4. **Postural instability.** Postural instability, or impaired balance, causes affected individuals to fall easily.

PD does not affect everyone the same way, and the rate of progression and the particular symptoms differ among individuals.

PD symptoms typically begin on one side of the body. However, the disease eventually affects both sides. Even after the disease involves both sides of the body, the symptoms are often less severe on one side than on the other.

Friends or family members may be the first to notice changes in someone with early PD. They may see that the person's face lacks expression and animation (known as "masked face") or that the person moves more slowly.

Early symptoms of PD may be subtle and occur gradually. Affected people may feel mild tremors or have difficulty getting out of a chair. Activities may take longer to complete than in the past and individuals may note some stiffness in addition to slowness. They may notice that they speak too softly or that their handwriting is slow and looks cramped or small. This very early period may last a long time before the more classical and obvious motor (movement) symptoms appear.

As the disease progresses, the symptoms of Parkinson disease may begin to interfere with daily activities. Affected individuals may not be able to hold utensils steady or they may find that the shaking makes reading a newspaper difficult. People with PD often develop a so-called *parkinsonian* gait that includes a tendency to lean forward, taking small quick steps as if hurrying (called festination), and reduced swinging in one or both arms. They may have trouble initiating movement (start hesitation), and they may stop suddenly as they walk (freezing).

A number of other symptoms may accompany PD, and some can be treated with medication or physical therapy.

- *Depression.* This common disorder may appear early in the course of the disease, even before other symptoms are noticed. Some people lose their motivation and become dependent on family members. Fortunately, depression typically can be treated successfully with antidepressant medications such as amytriptyline or fluoxetine.

- *Emotional changes.* Some people with PD become fearful and insecure, while others may become irritable or uncharacteristically pessimistic.

- *Difficulty with swallowing and chewing.* Muscles used in swallowing may work less efficiently in later stages of the disease. Food and saliva may collect in the mouth and back of the throat, which can result in choking or drooling. These problems may also make it difficult to get adequate nutrition. Speech-language therapists, occupational therapists (who help people learn new ways to perform activities of daily living), and dieticians can often help with these problems.

- *Speech changes.* About half of all individuals with PD have speech difficulties that may be characterized as speaking too softly or in a monotone. Some may hesitate before speaking, slur, or speak too fast. A speech therapist may be able to help these individuals reduce some of these problems.

- *Urinary problems or constipation.* In some people with PD, bladder and bowel problems can occur due to the improper functioning of the autonomic nervous system, which is responsible for regulating smooth muscle activity. Medications can effectively treat some of these symptoms.

- *Skin problems.* In PD, the skin on the face may become oily, particularly on the forehead and at the sides of the nose. The scalp may become oily too, resulting in dandruff. In other cases, the skin can become very dry. Standard treatments for skin problems can help.

- *Sleep problems.* Sleep problems are common in PD and include difficulty staying asleep at night, restless sleep, nightmares and emotional dreams, and drowsiness or sudden sleep onset during the day. Another common problem is "REM behavior disorder," in which people act out their dreams, potentially resulting in injury to themselves or their bed partners. The medications used to treat PD may contribute to some of these sleep issues. Many of these problems respond to specific therapies.

• *Dementia or other cognitive problems.* Some people with PD may develop memory problems and slow thinking. Cognitive problems become more severe in late stages of PD, and a diagnosis of Parkinson disease dementia (PDD) may be given. Memory, social judgment, language, reasoning, or other mental skills may be affected. There is currently no way to halt PD dementia, but drugs such as rivastigmine, donepezil, or memantine may help. The medications used to treat the motor symptoms of PD may cause confusion and hallucinations.

• *Orthostatic hypotension.* Orthostatic hypotension is a sudden drop in blood pressure when a person stands up from a lying-down or seated position. This may cause dizziness, lightheadedness, and, in extreme cases, loss of balance or fainting. Studies have suggested that, in PD, this problem results from a loss of nerve endings in the sympathetic nervous system that controls heart rate, blood pressure, and other automatic functions in the body. The medications used to treat PD may also contribute to this symptom. Orthostatic hypotension may improve by increasing salt intake. Physicians treating the disorder may also reduce anti-hypertension drug dosage or by prescribing medications such as fludrocortisone.

• *Muscle cramps and dystonia.* The rigidity and lack of normal movement associated with PD often causes muscle cramps, especially in the legs and toes. Massage, stretching, and applying heat may help with these cramps. PD can also be associated with dystonia—sustained muscle contractions that cause forced or twisted positions. Dystonia in PD is often caused by fluctuations in the body's level of dopamine. Management strategies may involve adjusting medications.

• *Pain.* Many people with PD develop aching muscles and joints because of the rigidity and abnormal postures often associated with the disease. Treatment with levodopa and other dopaminergic drugs often alleviates these pains to some extent. Certain exercises may help.

• *Fatigue and loss of energy.* Many people with PD often have fatigue, especially late in the day. Fatigue may be associated with depression or sleep disorders, but it may also result from muscle stress or from overdoing activity when the person feels well. Fatigue may also result from akinesia—trouble initiating or carrying out movement. Exercise, good sleep habits, staying mentally active, and not forcing too many activities in a short time may help to alleviate fatigue.

• *Sexual dysfunction.* Because of its effects on nerve signals from the brain, PD may cause sexual dysfunction. PD-related depression or use of certain medications may also cause decreased sex drive and other problems. People should discuss these issues with their physician as they may be treatable.

Hallucinations, delusions, and other psychotic symptoms can be caused by the drugs prescribed for PD. Reducing PD medications dosages or changing medications may be necessary if hallucinations occur. If such measures are not effective, doctors sometimes prescribe drugs called atypical antipsychotics, which include clozapine and quetiapine. The typical antipsychotic drugs, which include haloperidol, worsen the motor symptoms of PD and should not be used.

What Other Diseases and Conditions Resemble Parkinson Disease?

A number of disorders can cause symptoms similar to those of PD. People with symptoms that resemble PD but that result from other causes are considered to have parkinsonism. Some of these disorders include:

• **Multiple system atrophy.** Multiple system atrophy (MSA) refers to a set of slowly progressive disorders that affect the central and autonomic nervous systems. In MSA, the protein alpha-synuclein forms harmful filament-like aggregates in the supporting cells in the brain called oligodenreoglia. MSA may have symptoms that resemble PD. It may also take a form that primarily produces poor coordination and slurred speech, or it may involve a combination of these symptoms. Other symptoms may include swallowing difficulties, male impotence, constipation, and urinary difficulties. The disorder previously called Shy-Drager syndrome refers to MSA with prominent orthostatic hypotension—a fall in blood pressure every time the person stands up. MSA with parkinsonian symptoms is sometimes referred to as MSA-P (or striatonigral degeneration), while MSA with poor coordination and slurred speech is sometimes called MSA-C (or olivopontocerebellar atrophy). Unfortunately, many of the symptoms of MSA either do not respond to PD medications or the response is minimal or short-lived.

- **Dementia with Lewy bodies.** Dementia with Lewy bodies is a neurodegenerative disorder associated with the same abnormal protein deposits (Lewy bodies) found in Parkinson disease but in widespread areas throughout the brain. Symptoms may range from primary parkinsonian symptoms such as bradykinesia, rigidity, tremor, and shuffling walk, to symptoms similar to those of Alzheimer disease (memory loss, poor judgment, and confusion). These symptoms may fluctuate, or wax and wane dramatically. Visual hallucinations are often one of the first symptoms, and individuals may suffer from other psychiatric disturbances such as delusions and depression. Cognitive problems also occur early in the course of the disease. Levodopa and other antiparkinsonian medications can help with the motor symptoms of Dementia with Lewy bodies, but they may make hallucinations and delusions worse, and affected individuals may require treatment with atypical antipsychotic medications.

- **Progressive supranuclear palsy.** Progressive supranuclear palsy (PSP) is a rare, progressive brain disorder that causes problems with control of gait and balance. The symptoms of PSP are caused by a gradual deterioration of cells in the brain stem. People often tend to fall early in the course of PSP. One of the characteristic features of the disease is an inability to move the eyes properly, which some people describe as having blurred vision. People with PSP often show alterations of mood and behavior, including depression and apathy as well as mild dementia. PSP is often misdiagnosed because some of its symptoms are much like those of PD, Alzheimer disease, and other brain disorders. PSP symptoms usually do not respond to medication, or the response is minimal and short-lasting. PSP is characterized by aggregation of a protein called tau.

- **Corticobasal degeneration.** Corticobasal degeneration (CBD) results from atrophy of multiple areas of the brain, including the cerebral cortex and the basal ganglia. Initial symptoms may first appear on one side of the body, but eventually affect both sides. Symptoms are similar to some of the features found in PD, including rigidity, impaired balance, and problems with coordination. Often there is dystonia affecting one side of the body. Other symptoms may include cognitive and visual-spatial impairments, apraxia (loss of the ability to make familiar, purposeful movements), hesitant and halting speech, myoclonus (muscular jerks), and dysphagia (difficulty swallowing). Unlike PD, CBD usually does not respond to medication. Like PSP, it is characterized by deposits of the tau protein.

Several diseases, including MSA, CBD, and PSP, are sometimes referred to as "Parkinson's-plus" diseases because they have the symptoms of PD plus additional features.

How Is Parkinson Disease Diagnosed?

There are currently no blood or laboratory tests that diagnose sporadic PD. Therefore, the diagnosis is based on medical history and a neurological examination. In some cases PD can be difficult to diagnose accurately early on in the course of the disease. Early signs and symptoms of PD may sometimes be dismissed as the effects of normal aging. Doctors may sometimes request brain scans or laboratory tests in order to rule out other disorders. However, computed tomography (CT) and magnetic resonance imaging (MRI) brain scans of people with PD usually appear normal. Since many other diseases have similar features but require different treatments, making a precise diagnosis is important so that people can receive the proper treatment.

What Is the Prognosis?

The average life expectancy of a person with PD is generally the same as for people who do not have the disease. Fortunately, there are many treatment options available for people with PD. However, in the late stages, PD may no longer respond to medications and can become associated with serious complications such as choking, pneumonia, and falls.

PD is a slowly progressive disorder. It is not possible to predict what course the disease will take for an individual person. One commonly used scale neurologists use for describing how the symptoms of PD have progressed in a patient is the Hoehn and Yahr scale.

Another commonly used scale is the Movement Disorders Society-Unified Parkinson's Disease Rating Scale (MDS-UPDRS). This four-part scale measures motor movement in PD: non-motor experiences of daily living, motor experiences of daily living, motor examination, and motor complications. Both the Hoehn and Yahr scale and the MDS-UPDRS are used to describe how individuals are faring and to help assess treatment response.

How Is the Disease Treated?

At present, there is no cure for PD, but medications or surgery can often provide improvement in the motor symptoms.

Drug Therapy

Medications for PD fall into three categories. The first category includes drugs that increase the level of dopamine in the brain. The most common drugs for PD are dopamine precursors—substances such as levodopa that cross the blood-brain barrier and are then changed into dopamine. Other drugs mimic dopamine or prevent or slow its breakdown.

The second category of PD drugs affects other neurotransmitters in the body in order to ease some of the symptoms of the disease. For example, *anticholinergic drugs* interfere with production or uptake of the neurotransmitter acetylcholine. These can be effective in reducing tremors.

The third category of drugs prescribed for PD includes medications that help control the non-motor symptoms of the disease, that is, the symptoms that don't affect movement. For example, people with PD-related depression may be prescribed antidepressants.

- Levodopa/Carbidopa. The cornerstone of therapy for PD is the drug levodopa (also called L-dopa). Nerve cells can use levodopa to make dopamine and replenish the brain's reduced supply. People cannot simply take dopamine pills because dopamine does not easily pass through the blood-brain barrier. (The blood-brain barrier is a protective lining of cells inside blood vessels that regulate the transport of oxygen, glucose, and other substances in the brain.) Usually, people are given levodopa combined with another substance called carbidopa. When added to levodopa, carbidopa prevents the conversion of levodopa into dopamine except for in the brain; this stops or diminishes the side effects due to dopamine in the bloodstream. Levodopa/carbidopa is often very successful at reducing or eliminating the tremors and other motor symptoms of PD during the early stages of the disease. It allows the majority of people with PD to extend the period of time in which they can lead active, productive lives.

Although levodopa/carbidopa helps most people with PD, not all symptoms respond equally to the drug. Levodopa usually helps most with bradykinesia and rigidity. Problems with balance may not respond.

People often see noticeable improvement in their symptoms after starting levodopa/carbidopa therapy. However, they may need to increase the dose gradually for maximum benefit. Levodopa is often so effective that some people may not show symptoms during the early stages of the disease as long as they take the medicine. But levodopa is not a cure. Although it can reduce the symptoms of PD, it does not replace lost nerve cells and it does not stop the progression of the disease.

Levodopa/carbidopa can have a variety of side effects. The most common initial side effects include nausea, low blood pressure, and restlessness. The nausea and vomiting caused by levodopa are greatly reduced by the right combination of levodopa and carbidopa. The drug also can cause drowsiness or sudden sleep onset, which can make driving and other activities dangerous. Long-term use of levodopa sometimes causes hallucinations and psychosis.

Dyskinesias, or involuntary movements such twisting and writhing, commonly develop in people who take levodopa over an extended period. These movements may be either mild or severe. Some doctors start younger individuals with PD on drugs that act directly like dopamine itself and add levodopa later in the course of the disease. The dosage of levodopa is sometimes reduced in order to lessen these drug-induced movements. The drug amantadine may help control dyskinesias but if dyskinesias are severe, surgical treatment such as deep brain stimulation may be considered (see description in "Surgery").

Other difficulties may be encountered later in the disease course. People with PD may begin to notice more pronounced symptoms before their first dose of medication in the morning and between doses as the period of effectiveness after each dose begins to shorten, called the wearing-off effect. People experience sudden, unpredictable "off periods," where the medications do not seem to be working. One approach to alleviating these side effects is to take levodopa more often and in smaller amounts. People with PD should never stop taking levodopa without their physician's input, because rapidly withdrawing the drug can have potentially serious side effects.

In addition to levodopa/carbidopa, there are other available treatments:

- **Dopamine agonists.** These drugs, which include apomorphine, pramipexole, ropinirole, and rotigotine, mimic the role of dopamine in the brain. They can be given alone or with levodopa. They are somewhat less effective than levodopa in treating PD symptoms, but work for longer periods of time. Many of the potential side effects are similar to those associated with the use of levodopa, including drowsiness, sudden sleep onset, hallucinations, confusion, dyskinesias, edema (swelling due to excess fluid in body tissues), nightmares, and vomiting. In rare cases, they can cause an uncontrollable desire to gamble, hypersexuality, or compulsive shopping.

- **MAO-B inhibitors.** These drugs inhibit the enzyme monoamine oxidase B, or MAO-B, which breaks down dopamine in the brain. MAO-B inhibitors cause dopamine to accumulate in surviving nerve cells and reduce the symptoms of PD. Studies supported by the NINDS have shown that selegiline (also called deprenyl) can delay the need for levodopa therapy by up to a year or more. When selegiline is given with levodopa, it appears to enhance and prolong the response to levodopa and thus may reduce wearing-off. Selegiline is usually well-tolerated, although side effects may include nausea, orthostatic hypotension, or insomnia. It should not be taken with the antidepressant fluoxetine or the sedative meperidine, because combining selegiline with these drugs can be harmful. The drug rasagiline is used in treating the motor symptoms of PD with or without levodopa. Whether rasagiline slows progression of PD is still controversial.

- **COMT inhibitors.** COMT stands for catechol-O-methyltransferase, another enzyme that breaks down dopamine. The drug entacapone and tolcapone prolong the effects of levodopa by preventing the breakdown of dopamine. COMT inhibitors can decrease the duration of "off periods" of one's dose of levodopa. The most common side effect is diarrhea. The drugs cause nausea, sleep disturbances, dizziness, urine discoloration, abdominal pain, low blood pressure, or hallucinations. In a few rare cases, tolcapone has caused severe liver disease, and people taking tolcapone need regular monitoring of their liver function.

- **Amantadine.** This antiviral drug can help reduce symptoms of PD and levodopa-induced dyskinesia. It is often used alone in the early stages of the disease. It may also be used with an anticholinergic drug or levodopa. After several months, amantadine effectiveness wears off in up to half of the people taking it. Amantadine side effects may include insomnia, mottled skin, edema, agitation, or hallucinations. Researchers are not certain how amantadine works in PD, but it may increase the effects of dopamine.

- **Anticholinergics.** These drugs, which include trihexyphenidyl, benztropine, and ethopropazine, decrease the activity of the neurotransmitter acetylcholine and can be particularly effective for tremor. Side effects may include dry mouth, constipation, urinary retention, hallucinations, memory loss, blurred vision, and confusion.

When recommending a course of treatment, a doctor will assess how much the symptoms disrupt the person's life and then tailor therapy to the person's particular condition. Since no two people will react the same way to a given drug, it may take time and patience to get the dose just right. Even then, symptoms may not be completely alleviated.

Chapter 19

Vascular Dementia

Chapter Contents

Section 19.1

What Is Vascular Dementia?

This section includes excerpts from "The Dementias: Hope through Research," National Institute on Aging (NIA), September 2013; and text from "Advisory Council on Alzheimer's Research, Care, and Services," U.S. Department of Health and Human Services (HHS), July 27, 2015.

Vascular Dementia and Vascular Cognitive Impairment

Vascular dementia and vascular cognitive impairment (VCI) are caused by injuries to the vessels supplying blood to the brain. These disorders can be caused by brain damage from multiple strokes or any injury to the small vessels carrying blood to the brain. Dementia risk can be significant even when individuals have suffered only small strokes. Vascular dementia and VCI arise as a result of risk factors that similarly increase the risk for cerebrovascular disease (stroke), including atrial fibrillation, hypertension, diabetes, and high cholesterol. Vascular dementia also has been associated with a condition called amyloid angiopathy, in which amyloid plaques accumulate in the blood-vessel walls, causing them to break down and rupture. Symptoms of vascular dementia and VCI can begin suddenly and progress or subside during one's lifetime.

Some types of vascular dementia include:

Cerebral autosomal dominant arteriopathy with subcortical infarcts and leukoencephalopathy (CADASIL)

This inherited form of cardiovascular disease results in a thickening of the walls of small- and medium-sized blood vessels, eventually stemming the flow of blood to the brain. It is associated with mutations of a specific gene called Notch3, which gives instructions to a protein on the surface of the smooth muscle cells that surround blood vessels. CADASIL is associated with multi-infarct dementia, stroke, migraine with aura (migraine preceded by visual symptoms), and mood disorders. The first symptoms can appear in people between ages 20 and 40.

Many people with CADASIL are undiagnosed. People with first-degree relatives who have CADASIL can be tested for genetic mutations to the Notch3 gene to determine their own risk of developing CADASIL.

Multi-infarct dementia

This type of dementia occurs when a person has had many small strokes that damage brain cells. One side of the body may be disproportionately affected, and multi-infarct dementia may impair language or other functions, depending on the region of the brain that is affected. Doctors call these "local" or "focal" symptoms, as opposed to the "global" symptoms seen in Alzheimer disease (AD) that tend to affect several functions and both sides of the body. When the strokes occur on both sides of the brain, however, dementia is more likely than when stroke occurs on one side of the brain. In some cases, a single stroke can damage the brain enough to cause dementia. This so-called single-infarct dementia is more common when stroke affects the left side of the brain—where speech centers are located—and/or when it involves the hippocampus, the part of the brain that is vital for memory.

Subcortical vascular dementia, also called Binswanger disease

This is a rare form of dementia that involves extensive microscopic damage to the small blood vessels and nerve fibers that make up white matter, the "network" part of the brain believed to be critical for relaying messages between regions. The symptoms of Binswanger's are related to the disruption of subcortical neural circuits involving short-term memory, organization, mood, attention, decision making, and appropriate behavior. A characteristic feature of this disease is psychomotor slowness, such as an increase in the time it takes for a person to think of a letter and then write it on a piece of paper.

Other symptoms include urinary incontinence that is unrelated to a urinary tract condition, trouble walking, clumsiness, slowness, lack of facial expression, and speech difficulties. Symptoms tend to begin after age 60, and they progress in a stepwise manner. People with subcortical vascular disease often have high blood pressure, a history of stroke, or evidence of disease of the large blood vessels in the neck or heart valves. Treatment is aimed at preventing additional strokes and may include drugs to control blood pressure.

Vascular and AD Overlap: Autopsy Evidence

- Between 55 and 80% of AD patients have coincident vascular changes in the brain.

- Multiple studies have found less AD neuropathological changes (plaques, tangles) in patients with vascular changes for an equivalent level of cognitive impairment

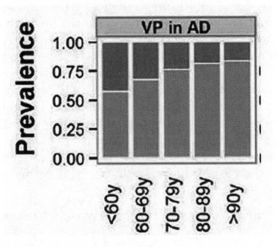

Figure 19.1. *Vascular and AD overlap: Autopsy evidence*

(VP: Vascular Pathology; AD: Alzheimer Disease

Possible Explanations for a Vascular AD Connection

- Vascular disease and Alzheimer disease changes are additive, leading to worse cognition when both are present, OR

- Vascular disease directly leads to AD neuropathological changes

Mechanisms for a Vascular AD Interaction

- Vascular risk factors lead to alterations in cerebral blood vessels and can lead to low cerebral blood flow, especially in the white matter of the brain

- The blood brain barrier can be disrupted in the presence of vascular disease

- Role of the neurovascular unit: Amyloid-ß itself may directly damage blood vessels, further worsening cerebral blood flow

- Vascular disease may make clearance of amyloid-ß harder; the "glymphatic system" is around blood vessels and helps remove brain waste

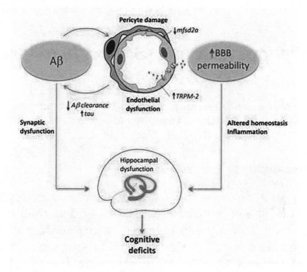

Figure 19.2. *Mechanisms for a Vascular AD Interaction*

Why Is the Vascular Contribution to Dementia and AD Important?

- Vascular disease is preventable
- Vascular disease is very common
- Therefore, this may be a way to prevent AD and other dementia cases

Section 19.2

Binswanger Disease (Subcortical Vascular Dementia)

Text in this section is excerpted from "NINDS Binswanger's Disease Information Page," National Institute of Neurological Disorders and Stroke (NINDS), November 2, 2015.

What Is Binswanger's Disease?

Binswanger's disease (BD), also called *subcortical vascular dementia*, is a type of dementia caused by widespread, microscopic areas of damage to the deep layers of white matter in the brain. The damage is the result of the thickening and narrowing (atherosclerosis) of arteries that feed the subcortical areas of the brain. Atherosclerosis (commonly known as "hardening of the arteries") is a systemic process that affects blood vessels throughout the body. It begins late in the fourth decade of life and increases in severity with age. As the arteries become more and more narrowed, the blood supplied by those arteries decreases and brain tissue dies. A characteristic pattern of BD-damaged brain tissue can be seen with modern brain imaging techniques such as CT scans or magnetic resonance imaging (MRI).

The symptoms associated with BD are related to the disruption of subcortical neural circuits that control what neuroscientists call *executive cognitive functioning*: short-term memory, organization, mood, the regulation of attention, the ability to act or make decisions, and appropriate behavior. The most characteristic feature of BD is psychomotor slowness—an increase in the length of time it takes, for example, for the fingers to turn the thought of a letter into the shape of a letter on a piece of paper. Other symptoms include forgetfulness (but not as severe as the forgetfulness of Alzheimer disease), changes in speech, an unsteady gait, clumsiness or frequent falls, changes in personality or mood (most likely in the form of apathy, irritability, and depression), and urinary symptoms that aren't caused by urological disease. Brain imaging, which reveals the characteristic brain lesions of BD, is essential for a positive diagnosis.

Is There Any Treatment?

There is no specific course of treatment for BD. Treatment is symptomatic. People with depression or anxiety may require antidepressant medications such as the serotonin-specific reuptake inhibitors (SSRI) sertraline or citalopram. Atypical antipsychotic drugs, such as risperidone and olanzapine, can be useful in individuals with agitation and disruptive behavior. Recent drug trials with the drug memantine have shown improved cognition and stabilization of global functioning and behavior. The successful management of hypertension and diabetes can slow the progression of atherosclerosis, and subsequently slow the progress of BD. Because there is no cure, the best treatment is preventive, early in the adult years, by controlling risk factors such as hypertension, diabetes, and smoking.

What Is the Prognosis?

BD is a progressive disease; there is no cure. Changes may be sudden or gradual and then progress in a stepwise manner. BD can often coexist with Alzheimer disease. Behaviors that slow the progression of high blood pressure, diabetes, and atherosclerosis -- such as eating a healthy diet and keeping healthy wake/sleep schedules, exercising, and not smoking or drinking too much alcohol -- can also slow the progression of BD.

Section 19.3

Cerebral Autosomal Dominant Arteriopathy with Subcortical Infarcts and Leukoencephalopathy (CADASIL)

Text in this section is excerpted from "NINDS CADASIL Information Page," National Institute of Neurological Disorders and Stroke (NINDS), December 18, 2013.

What Is CADASIL?

CADASIL (Cerebral Autosomal Dominant Arteriopathy with Subcortical Infarcts and Leukoencephalopathy) is an inherited form of cerebrovascular disease that occurs when the thickening of blood vessel walls blocks the flow of blood to the brain. The disease primarily affects small blood vessels in the white matter of the brain. A mutation in the Notch3 gene alters the muscular walls in these small arteries. CADASIL is characterized by migraine headaches and multiple strokes progressing to dementia. Other symptoms include cognitive deterioration, seizures, vision problems, and psychiatric problems such as severe depression and changes in behavior and personality. Individuals may also be at higher risk of heart attack. Symptoms and disease onset vary widely, with signs typically appearing in the mid-30s. Some individuals may not show signs of the disease until later in life. CADASIL—formerly known by several names, including hereditary multi-infarct dementia— is one cause of vascular cognitive impairment (dementia caused by lack of blood to several areas of the brain). It is an autosomal dominant inheritance disorder, meaning that one parent carries and passes on the defective gene. Most individuals with CADASIL have a family history of the disorder. However, because the genetic test for CADASIL was not available before 2000, many cases were misdiagnosed as multiple sclerosis, Alzheimer disease, or other neurodegenerative diseases.

Is There Any Treatment?

There is no treatment to halt this genetic disorder. Individuals are given supportive care. Migraine headaches may be treated by different

192

drugs and a daily aspirin may reduce stroke and heart attack risk. Drug therapy for depression may be given. Affected individuals who smoke should quit as it can increase the risk of stroke in CADASIL. Other stroke risk factors such as hypertension, hyperlipidemia, diabetes, blood clotting disorders and obstructive sleep apnea also should be aggressively treated.

What Is the Prognosis?

Symptoms usually progress slowly. By age 65, the majority of persons with CADASIL have cognitive problems and dementia. Some will become dependent due to multiple strokes.

Section 19.4

Multi-Infarct Dementia

Text in this section is excerpted from "NINDS Multi-Infarct Dementia Information Page," National Institute of Neurological Disorders and Stroke (NINDS), November 2, 2015.

What Is Multi-Infarct Dementia?

Multi-infarct dementia (MID) is a common cause of memory loss in the elderly. MID is caused by multiple strokes (disruption of blood flow to the brain). Disruption of blood flow leads to damaged brain tissue. Some of these strokes may occur without noticeable clinical symptoms. Doctors refer to these as "silent strokes." An individual having a silent stroke may not even know it is happening, but over time, as more areas of the brain are damaged and more small blood vessels are blocked, the symptoms of MID begin to appear. MID can be diagnosed by an MRI or CT of the brain, along with a neurological examination. Symptoms include confusion or problems with short-term memory; wandering, or getting lost in familiar places; walking with rapid, shuffling steps; losing bladder or bowel control; laughing or crying inappropriately; having difficulty following instructions; and having problems counting money and making monetary transactions. MID, which typically begins between the ages of 60 and 75, affects men more often than women. Because the symptoms of MID are so similar to Alzheimer disease, it can be difficult for a doctor to make a firm diagnosis. Since the diseases often occur together, making a single diagnosis of one or the other is even more problematic.

Is There Any Treatment?

There is no treatment available to reverse brain damage that has been caused by a stroke. Treatment focuses on preventing future strokes by controlling or avoiding the diseases and medical conditions that put people at high risk for stroke: high blood pressure, diabetes, high cholesterol, and cardiovascular disease. The best treatment for MID is prevention early in life eating a healthy diet, exercising, not smoking, moderately using alcohol, and maintaining a healthy weight.

What Is the Prognosis?

The prognosis for individuals with MID is generally poor. The symptoms of the disorder may begin suddenly, often in a stepwise pattern after each small stroke. Some people with MID may even appear to improve for short periods of time, then decline after having more silent strokes. The disorder generally takes a downward course with intermittent periods of rapid deterioration. Death may occur from stroke, heart disease, pneumonia, or other infection.

Chapter 20

Dementia Caused by Infections

Chapter Contents

Section 20.1

Creutzfeldt-Jakob Disease

Text in this section is excerpted from "Creutzfeldt-Jakob Disease
Fact Sheet," National Institute of Neurological Disorders and
Stroke (NINDS), November 2, 2015.

What Is Creutzfeldt-Jakob Disease?

Creutzfeldt-Jakob disease (CJD) is a rare, degenerative, invariably
fatal brain disorder. It affects about one person in every one million
people per year worldwide; in the United States there are about 300
cases per year. CJD usually appears in later life and runs a rapid
course. Typically, onset of symptoms occurs about age 60, and about
90 percent of individuals die within 1 year. In the early stages of
disease, people may have failing memory, behavioral changes, lack of
coordination and visual disturbances. As the illness progresses, mental deterioration becomes pronounced and involuntary movements,
blindness, weakness of extremities, and coma may occur.

There are three major categories of CJD:

- In sporadic CJD, the disease appears even though the person
  has no known risk factors for the disease. This is by far the most
  common type of CJD and accounts for at least 85 percent of
  cases.

- In hereditary CJD, the person has a family history of the disease
  and/or tests positive for a genetic mutation associated with CJD.
  About 5 to 10 percent of cases of CJD in the United States are
  hereditary.

- In acquired CJD, the disease is transmitted by exposure to brain
  or nervous system tissue, usually through certain medical procedures. There is no evidence that CJD is contagious through
  casual contact with a CJD patient. Since CJD was first described
  in 1920, fewer than 1 percent of cases have been acquired CJD.

CJD belongs to a family of human and animal diseases known as
the transmissible spongiform encephalopathies (TSEs). Spongiform

refers to the characteristic appearance of infected brains, which become filled with holes until they resemble sponges under a microscope. CJD is the most common of the known human TSEs. Other human TSEs include kuru, fatal familial insomnia (FFI), and Gerstmann-Strauss-ler-Scheinker disease (GSS). Kuru was identified in people of an isolated tribe in Papua New Guinea and has now almost disappeared. FFI and GSS are extremely rare hereditary diseases, found in just a few families around the world. Other TSEs are found in specific kinds of animals. These include bovine spongiform encephalopathy (BSE), which is found in cows and is often referred to as "mad cow" disease; scrapie, which affects sheep and goats; mink encephalopathy; and feline encephalopathy. Similar diseases have occurred in elk, deer, and exotic zoo animals.

What Are the Symptoms of the Disease?

CJD is characterized by rapidly progressive dementia. Initially, individuals experience problems with muscular coordination; personality changes, including impaired memory, judgment, and thinking; and impaired vision. People with the disease also may experience insomnia, depression, or unusual sensations. CJD does not cause a fever or other flu-like symptoms. As the illness progresses, mental impairment becomes severe. Individuals often develop involuntary muscle jerks called myoclonus, and they may go blind. They eventually lose the ability to move and speak and enter a coma. Pneumonia and other infections often occur in these individuals and can lead to death.

There are several known variants of CJD. These variants differ somewhat in the symptoms and course of the disease. For example, a variant form of the disease-called new variant or variant (nv-CJD, vCJD), described in Great Britain and France-begins primarily with psychiatric symptoms, affects younger individuals than other types of CJD, and has a longer than usual duration from onset of symptoms to death. Another variant, called the pan encephalopathic form, occurs primarily in Japan and has a relatively long course, with symptoms often progressing for several years. Scientists are trying to learn what causes these variations in the symptoms and course of the disease.

Some symptoms of CJD can be similar to symptoms of other progressive neurological disorders, such as Alzheimer or Huntington diseases. However, CJD causes unique changes in brain tissue which can be seen at autopsy. It also tends to cause more rapid deterioration of a person's abilities than Alzheimer disease or most other types of dementia.

How Is CJD Diagnosed?

There is currently no single diagnostic test for CJD. When a doctor suspects CJD, the first concern is to rule out treatable forms of dementia such as encephalitis (inflammation of the brain) or chronic meningitis. A neurological examination will be performed and the doctor may seek consultation with other physicians. Standard diagnostic tests will include a spinal tap to rule out more common causes of dementia and an electroencephalogram (EEG) to record the brain's electrical pattern, which can be particularly valuable because it shows a specific type of abnormality in CJD. Computerized tomography of the brain can help rule out the possibility that the symptoms result from other problems such as stroke or a brain tumor. Magnetic resonance imaging (MRI) brain scans also can reveal characteristic patterns of brain degeneration that can help diagnose CJD.

The only way to confirm a diagnosis of CJD is by brain biopsy or autopsy. In a brain biopsy, a neurosurgeon removes a small piece of tissue from the patient's brain so that it can be examined by a neuropathologist. This procedure may be dangerous for the individual, and the operation does not always obtain tissue from the affected part of the brain. Because a correct diagnosis of CJD does not help the person, a brain biopsy is discouraged unless it is needed to rule out a treatable disorder. In an autopsy, the whole brain is examined after death. Both brain biopsy and autopsy pose a small, but definite, risk that the surgeon or others who handle the brain tissue may become accidentally infected by self-inoculation. Special surgical and disinfection procedures can minimize this risk.

Scientists are working to develop laboratory tests for CJD. One such test, developed at NINDS, is performed on a person's cerebrospinal fluid and detects a protein marker that indicates neuronal degeneration. This can help diagnose CJD in people who already show the clinical symptoms of the disease. This test is much easier and safer than a brain biopsy. The false positive rate is about 5 to 10 percent. Scientists are working to develop this test for use in commercial laboratories. They are also working to develop other tests for this disorder.

How Is the Disease Treated?

There is no treatment that can cure or control CJD. Researchers have tested many drugs, including amantadine, steroids, interferon, acyclovir, antiviral agents, and antibiotics. Studies of a variety of other drugs are now in progress. However, so far none of these treatments has shown any consistent benefit in humans.

Current treatment for CJD is aimed at alleviating symptoms and making the individual as comfortable as possible. Opiate drugs can help relieve pain if it occurs, and the drugs clonazepam and sodium valproate may help relieve myoclonus. During later stages of the disease, changing the person's position frequently can keep him or her comfortable and helps prevent bedsores. A catheter can be used to drain urine if the individual cannot control bladder function, and intravenous fluids and artificial feeding also may be used.

What Causes Creutzfeldt-Jakob Disease?

Some researchers believe an unusual "slow virus" or another organism causes CJD. However, they have never been able to isolate a virus or other organism in people with the disease. Furthermore, the agent that causes CJD has several characteristics that are unusual for known organisms such as viruses and bacteria. It is difficult to kill, it does not appear to contain any genetic information in the form of nucleic acids (DNA or RNA), and it usually has a long incubation period before symptoms appear. In some cases, the incubation period may be as long as 50 years. The leading scientific theory at this time maintains that CJD and the other TSEs are caused by a type of protein called a *prion*.

Prion proteins occur in both a normal form, which is a harmless protein found in the body's cells, and in an infectious form, which causes disease. The harmless and infectious forms of the prion protein have the same sequence of amino acids (the "building blocks" of proteins) but the infectious form of the protein takes a different folded shape than the normal protein. Sporadic CJD may develop because some of a person's normal prions spontaneously change into the infectious form of the protein and then alter the prions in other cells in a chain reaction.

Once they appear, abnormal prion proteins aggregate, or clump together. Investigators think these protein aggregates may lead to the neuron loss and other brain damage seen in CJD. However, they do not know exactly how this damage occurs.

About 5 to 10 percent of all CJD cases are inherited. These cases arise from a mutation, or change, in the gene that controls formation of the normal prion protein. While prions themselves do not contain genetic information and do not require genes to reproduce themselves, infectious prions can arise if a mutation occurs in the gene for the body's normal prion protein. If the prion protein gene is altered in a person's sperm or egg cells, the mutation can be transmitted to the person's offspring. All mutations in the prion protein gene are inherited

199

as dominant traits. Therefore, family history is helpful in considering the diagnosis. Several different mutations in the prion gene have been identified. The particular mutation found in each family affects how frequently the disease appears and what symptoms are most noticeable. However, not all people with mutations in the prion protein gene develop CJD.

How Is CJD Transmitted?

CJD cannot be transmitted through the air or through touching or most other forms of casual contact. Spouses and other household members of sporadic CJD patients have no higher risk of contracting the disease than the general population. However, exposure to brain tissue and spinal cord fluid from infected individuals should be avoided to prevent transmission of the disease through these materials.

In some cases, CJD has spread to other people from grafts of dura mater (a tissue that covers the brain), transplanted corneas, implantation of inadequately sterilized electrodes in the brain, and injections of contaminated pituitary growth hormone derived from human pituitary glands taken from cadavers. Doctors call these cases that are linked to medical procedures iatrogenic cases. Since 1985, all human growth hormone used in the United States has been synthesized by recombinant DNA procedures, which eliminates the risk of transmitting CJD by this route.

The appearance of the new variant of CJD (nv-CJD or vCJD) in several younger than average people in Great Britain and France has led to concern that BSE may be transmitted to humans through consumption of contaminated beef. Although laboratory tests have shown a strong similarity between the prions causing BSE and vCJD, there is no direct proof to support this theory.

Many people are concerned that it may be possible to transmit CJD through blood and related blood products such as plasma. Some animal studies suggest that contaminated blood and related products may transmit the disease, although this has never been shown in humans. If there are infectious agents in these fluids, they are probably in very low concentrations. Scientists do not know how many abnormal prions a person must receive before he or she develops CJD, so they do not know whether these fluids are potentially infectious or not. They do know that, even though millions of people receive blood transfusions each year, there are no reported cases of someone contracting CJD from a transfusion. Even among people with hemophilia, who sometimes receive blood plasma concentrated from thousands of donors, there are no reported cases of CJD.

While there is no evidence that blood from people with sporadic CJD is infectious, studies have found that infectious prions from BSE and vCJD may accumulate in the lymph nodes (which produce white blood cells), the spleen, and the tonsils. These findings suggest that blood transfusions from people with vCJD might transmit the disease. The possibility that blood from people with vCJD may be infectious has led to a policy preventing people in the United States from donating blood if they have resided for more than 3 months in a country or countries where BSE is common.

How Can People Avoid Spreading the Disease?

To reduce the already very low risk of CJD transmission from one person to another, people should never donate blood, tissues, or organs if they have suspected or confirmed CJD, or if they are at increased risk because of a family history of the disease, a dura mater graft, or other factor.

Normal sterilization procedures such as cooking, washing, and boiling do not destroy prions. Caregivers, healthcare workers, and undertakers should take the following precautions when they are working with a person with CJD:

- Cover cuts and abrasions with waterproof dressings.

- Wear surgical gloves when handling a patient's tissues and fluids or dressing the patient's wounds.

- Avoid cutting or sticking themselves with instruments contaminated by the patient's blood or other tissues.

- Use disposable bedclothes and other cloth for contact with the patient. If disposable materials are not available, regular cloth should be soaked in undiluted chlorine bleach for an hour or more, and then washed in a normal fashion after each use.

- Use face protection if there is a risk of splashing contaminated material such as blood or cerebrospinal fluid.

- Soak instruments that have come in contact with the patient in undiluted chlorine bleach for an hour or more, then use an autoclave (pressure cooker) to sterilize them in distilled water for at least one hour at 132-134 degrees Centigrade.

Section 20.2

Acquired Immunodeficiency Syndrome (AIDS) Dementia Complex

Text in this section is excerpted from "Neurological Complications of AIDS Fact Sheet," National Institute of Neurological Disorders and Stroke (NINDS), November 2, 2015.

What is AIDS?

AIDS (acquired immune deficiency syndrome) is a condition that occurs in the most advanced stages of human immunodeficiency virus (HIV) infection. It may take many years for AIDS to develop following the initial HIV infection.

Although AIDS is primarily an immune system disorder, it also affects the nervous system and can lead to a wide range of severe neurological disorders.

How Does AIDS Affect the Nervous System?

The virus does not appear to directly invade nerve cells but it jeopardizes their health and function. The resulting inflammation may damage the brain and spinal cord and cause symptoms such as confusion and forgetfulness, behavioral changes, headaches, progressive weakness, and loss of sensation in the arms and legs. Cognitive motor impairment or damage to the peripheral nerves is also common. Research has shown that the HIV infection can significantly alter the size of certain brain structures involved in learning and information processing.

Other nervous system complications that occur as a result of the disease or the drugs used to treat it include pain, seizures, shingles, spinal cord problems, lack of coordination, difficult or painful swallowing, anxiety disorder, depression, fever, vision loss, gait disorders, destruction of brain tissue, and coma. These symptoms may be mild in the early stages of AIDS but can become progressively severe.

In the United States, neurological complications are seen in more than 50 percent of adults with AIDS. Nervous system complications in children may include developmental delays, loss of previously achieved milestones, brain lesions, nerve pain, smaller than normal skull size, slow growth, eye problems, and recurring bacterial infections.

What Are Some of the Neurological Complications That Are Associated with AIDS?

AIDS-related disorders of the nervous system may be caused directly by the HIV virus, by certain cancers and opportunistic infections (illnesses caused by bacteria, fungi, and other viruses that would not otherwise affect people with healthy immune systems), or by toxic effects of the drugs used to treat symptoms. Other neuro-AIDS disorders of unknown origin may be influenced by but are not caused directly by the virus.

AIDS dementia complex (ADC), or *HIV-associated dementia (HAD)*, occurs primarily in persons with more advanced HIV infection. Symptoms include encephalitis (inflammation of the brain), behavioral changes, and a gradual decline in cognitive function, including trouble with concentration, memory, and attention. Persons with ADC also show progressive slowing of motor function and loss of dexterity and coordination. When left untreated, ADC can be fatal. It is rare when antiretroviral therapy is used. Milder cognitive complaints are common and are termed HIV-associated neurocognitive disorder (HAND). Neuropsychological testing can reveal subtle deficits even in the absence of symptoms.

Central nervous system (CNS) lymphomas are cancerous tumors that either begin in the brain or result from a cancer that has spread from another site in the body. CNS lymphomas are almost always associated with the Epstein-Barr virus (a common human virus in the herpes family). Symptoms include headache, seizures, vision problems, dizziness, speech disturbance, paralysis, and mental deterioration. Individuals may develop one or more CNS lymphomas. Prognosis is poor due to advanced and increasing immunodeficiency, but is better with successful HIV therapy.

Cryptococcal meningitis is seen in about 10 percent of untreated individuals with AIDS and in other persons whose immune systems have been severely suppressed by disease or drugs. It is caused by the fungus Cryptococcus neoformans, which is commonly found in dirt and bird droppings. The fungus first invades the lungs and spreads to the covering of the brain and spinal cord, causing inflammation.

203

Symptoms include fatigue, fever, headache, nausea, memory loss, confusion, drowsiness, and vomiting. If left untreated, patients with cryptococcal meningitis may lapse into a coma and die.

Cytomegalovirus (CMV) infections can occur concurrently with other infections. Symptoms of CMV encephalitis include weakness in the arms and legs, problems with hearing and balance, altered mental states, dementia, peripheral neuropathy, coma, and retinal disease that may lead to blindness. CMV infection of the spinal cord and nerves can result in weakness in the lower limbs and some paralysis, severe lower back pain, and loss of bladder function. It can also cause pneumonia and gastrointestinal disease. This is rarely seen in HIV-treated individuals since advanced immunity is required for CMV to emerge.

Herpes virus infections are often seen in people with AIDS. The herpes zoster virus, which causes chickenpox and shingles, can infect the brain and produce encephalitis and myelitis (inflammation of the spinal cord). It commonly produces shingles, which is an eruption of blisters and intense pain along an area of skin supplied by an infected nerve. In people exposed to herpes zoster, the virus can lay dormant in the nerve tissue for years until it is reactivated as shingles. This reactivation is common in persons with AIDS because of their weakened immune systems. Signs of shingles include painful blisters (like those seen in chickenpox), itching, tingling, and pain in the nerves.

People with AIDS may suffer from several different forms of neuropathy, or nerve pain, each strongly associated with a specific stage of active immunodeficiency disease. Peripheral neuropathy describes damage to the peripheral nerves, the vast communications network that transmits information between the brain and spinal cord to every other part of the body. Peripheral nerves also send sensory information back to the brain and spinal cord. HIV damages the nerve fibers that help conduct signals and can cause several different forms of neuropathy. Distal sensory polyneuropathy causes either a numbing feeling or a mild to painful burning or tingling sensation that normally begins in the legs and feet. These sensations may be particularly strong at night and may spread to the hands. Affected persons have a heightened sensitivity to pain, touch, or other stimuli. Onset usually occurs in the later stages of the HIV infection and may affect the majority of advanced-stage HIV patients.

Neurosyphilis, the result of an insufficiently treated syphilis infection, seems more frequent and more rapidly progressive in people with HIV infection. It may cause slow degeneration of the nerve cells and nerve fibers that carry sensory information to the brain. Symptoms, which may not appear for some decades after the initial infection and vary from person to person, include weakness, diminished reflexes, unsteady gait, progressive degeneration of the joints, loss of coordination, episodes of intense pain and disturbed sensation, personality changes, dementia, deafness, visual impairment, and impaired response to light. The disease is more frequent in men than in women. Onset is common during mid-life.

Progressive multifocal leukoencephalopathy (PML) primarily affects individuals with suppressed immune systems (including nearly 5 percent of people with AIDS). PML is caused by the JC virus, which travels to the brain, infects multiple sites, and destroys the cells that make myelin the fatty protective covering for many of the body's nerve and brain cells. Symptoms include various types of mental deterioration, vision loss, speech disturbances, ataxia (inability to coordinate movements), paralysis, brain lesions, and, ultimately, coma. Some individuals may also have compromised memory and cognition, and seizures may occur. PML is relentlessly progressive and death usually occurs within 6 months of initial symptoms. However, immune reconstitution with highly active antiretroviral therapy allows survival of more than half of HIV-associated PML cases in the current treatment era.

Psychological and neuropsychiatric disorders can occur in different phases of the HIV infection and AIDS and may take various and complex forms. Some illnesses, such as AIDS dementia complex, are caused directly by HIV infection of the brain, while other conditions may be triggered by the drugs used to combat the infection. Individuals may experience anxiety disorder, depressive disorders, increased thoughts of suicide, paranoia, dementia, delirium, cognitive impairment, confusion, hallucinations, behavioral abnormalities, malaise, and acute mania.

Toxoplasma encephalitis, also called cerebral toxoplasmosis, occurs in about 10 percent of untreated AIDS patients. It is caused by the parasite Toxoplasma gondii, which is carried by cats, birds, and other animals and can be found in soil contaminated by cat feces and sometimes in raw or undercooked meat. Once the parasite invades the immune system, it remains there; however, the immune system in a healthy person can fight off the parasite, preventing disease. Symptoms include encephalitis, fever, severe headache that does not respond to treatment, weakness on one side of the body, seizures, lethargy, increased confusion, vision problems, dizziness, problems with speaking and walking, vomiting, and personality changes. Not all patients show signs of the infection. Antibiotic therapy, if used early, will generally control the complication.

Vacuolar myelopathy causes the protective myelin sheath to pull away from nerve cells of the spinal cord, forming small holes called vacuoles in nerve fibers. Symptoms include weak and stiff legs and unsteadiness when walking. Walking becomes more difficult as the disease progresses and many patients eventually require a wheelchair. Some people also develop AIDS dementia. Vacuolar myelopathy may affect up to 30 percent of untreated adults with AIDS and its incidence may be even higher in HIV-infected children.

How Are These Disorders Diagnosed?

Based on the results of the individual's medical history and a general physical exam, the physician will conduct a thorough neurological exam to assess various functions: motor and sensory skills, nerve function, hearing and speech, vision, coordination and balance, mental status, and changes in mood or behavior. The physician may order laboratory tests and one or more of the following procedures to help diagnose neurological complications of AIDS.

Brain imaging can reveal signs of brain inflammation, tumors and CNS lymphomas, nerve damage, internal bleeding or hemorrhage, white matter irregularities, and other brain abnormalities. Several painless imaging procedures are used to help diagnose neurological complications of AIDS.

- *Computed tomography* (also called a CTscan) uses X-rays and a computer to produce two-dimensional images of bone and tissue, including inflammation, certain brain tumors and cysts, brain damage from head injury, and other disorders. It provides more details than an X-ray alone.

- *Magnetic resonance imaging* (MRI) uses a computer, radio waves, and a powerful magnetic field to produce either a detailed three-dimensional picture or a two-dimensional "slice" of body structures, including tissues, organs, bones, and nerves. It does not use ionizing radiation (as does an X-ray) and gives physicians a better look at tissue located near bone.

- *Functional MRI* (fMRI) uses the blood's magnetic properties to pinpoint areas of the brain that are active and to note how long they stay active. It can assess brain damage from head injury or degenerative disorders such as Alzheimer disease and can identify and monitor other neurological disorders, including AIDS dementia complex.

- *Magnetic resonance spectroscopy* (MRS) uses a strong magnetic field to study the biochemical composition and concentration of hydrogen-based molecules, some of which are very specific to nerve cells, in various brain regions. MRS is being used experimentally to identify brain lesions in people with AIDS.

Electromyography, or EMG, is used to diagnose nerve and muscle dysfunction (such as neuropathy and nerve fiber damage caused by the HIV virus) and spinal cord disease. It records spontaneous muscle activity and muscle activity driven by the peripheral nerves.

Biopsy is the removal and examination of tissue from the body. A brain biopsy, which involves the surgical removal of a small piece of the brain or tumor, is used to determine intracranial disorders and tumor type. Unlike most other biopsies, it requires hospitalization. Muscle or nerve biopsies can help diagnose neuromuscular problems, while a brain biopsy can help diagnose a tumor, inflammation, or other irregularity.

Cerebrospinal fluid analysis can detect any bleeding or brain hemorrhage, infections of the brain or spinal cord (such as neurosyphilis), and any harmful buildup of fluid. It can also be used to sample viruses that may be affecting the brain. A sample of the fluid is removed by needle, under local anesthesia, and studied to detect any irregularities.

How Are These Disorders Treated?

No single treatment can cure the neurological complications of AIDS. Some disorders require aggressive therapy while others are treated symptomatically.

Neuropathic pain is often difficult to control. Medicines range from analgesics sold over the counter to antiepileptic drugs, opiates, and some classes of antidepressants. Inflamed tissue can press on nerves, causing pain. Inflammatory and autoimmune conditions leading to neuropathy may be treated with corticosteroids, and procedures such as plasmapheresis (or plasma exchange) can clear the blood of harmful substances that cause inflammation.

Treatment options for AIDS- and HIV-related neuropsychiatric or psychotic disorders include antidepressants and anticonvulsants.

Psychostimulants may also improve depressive symptoms and combat lethargy. Antidementia drugs may relieve confusion and slow mental decline, and benzodiazepines may be prescribed to treat anxiety. Psychotherapy may also help some individuals.

Aggressive antiretroviral therapy is used to treat AIDS dementia complex, vacuolar myopathy, progressive multifocal leukoencephalopathy, and cytomegalovirus encephalitis. HAART, or highly active antiretroviral therapy, combines at least three drugs to reduce the amount of virus circulating in the blood and may also delay the start of some infections.

Other neuro-AIDS treatment options include physical therapy and rehabilitation, radiation therapy and/or chemotherapy to kill or shrink cancerous brain tumors that may be caused by the HIV virus, antifungal or antimalarial drugs to combat certain bacterial infections associated with the disorder, and penicillin to treat neurosyphilis.

Chapter 21

Other Health Conditions That Cause Dementia

Chapter Contents

Section 21.1

Cancer, Delirium, and Dementia

This section includes excerpts from "Collaborative Networks to Advance Delirium Research," National Institute of Health (NIH), September 4, 2015; text from "The Dilemma of Delirium in Older Patients," National Institute on Aging (NIA), April 2, 2015; and text from "Delirium (PDQ®)," National Cancer Institute (NCI), December 12, 2013.

Cancer, Delirium, and Dementia

Delirium, defined as an acute impairment of cognition and attention, is a common complication of severe illness and surgery in older adults. Delirium is associated with multiple adverse outcomes including increased morbidity, mortality, functional and cognitive decline, and institutionalization. While more than 7 million hospitalized Americans suffer from delirium annually, older adults, especially those in ICU and post-operative settings, are more vulnerable than younger patients to developing delirium and its sequelae. Delirium cases are rapidly increasing as more seniors undergo major surgeries and hospitalization for critical illness from underlying multiple chronic conditions. In 2004, hospital-related costs for delirium were estimated at over $8 billion, with post-hospitalization costs topping $150 billion annually. These figures are likely underestimates, as delirium remains markedly underdiagnosed. Moreover, the underlying mechanisms, and thereby potential treatment or prevention targets, are inadequately understood, as is prognosis. Addressing important research gaps may improve approaches for appropriate prevention and management, especially as studies of multicomponent interventions suggest that delirium may be at least 30-40% preventable.

The underlying pathophysiology of delirium remains elusive. As a quintessential geriatric syndrome, delirium represents the convergence of multiple interacting pathways from both diagnosed and sub-clinical conditions culminating in impairment. Further complicating our understanding is the lack of clarity between causal and associated factors for conditions believed to underlie delirium. A variety of hypotheses have been advanced ranging from brain and systemic inflammation to amyloid deposition leading to at-risk brains. In addition, risk for morbidity is increased significantly when delirium and dementia interact, but the mechanistic link is unclear. Delirium occurs in 66-89% of persons with Alzheimer disease (AD) during acute illness and hospitalization and is often dismissed as an inevitable, but transient, condition in AD patients during hospitalization. However, cognitive and functional decline, morbidity, and other adverse outcomes are increased more in the setting of concomitant AD and delirium compared to either condition alone. Moreover, delirium episodes may be misdiagnosed as dementia, resulting in improper care, treatment, and long-term adverse outcomes for patients and caregivers.

There is mounting evidence, however, that delirium may be associated with increased risk for dementia and may contribute to morbidity and death. One recent study found that in a group of 553 people age 85 and older, those with a history of delirium had an eight-fold increase in risk for developing dementia. The researchers also found that among the participants with dementia, delirium was associated with an acceleration of dementia severity, loss of independent functioning, and higher mortality. These findings showed that delirium is a strong risk factor for dementia and cognitive decline in the oldest old.

Cognitive Disorders and Delirium: Causal Factors

There is often more than one cause of delirium in a cancer patient, especially when the cancer is advanced and the patient has many medical conditions. Causes of delirium include the following:

- Organ failure, such as liver or kidney failure.

- Electrolyte imbalances: Electrolytes are important minerals (including salt, potassium, calcium, and phosphorous) in blood and body fluids. These electrolytes are needed to keep the heart, kidneys, nerves, and muscles working the way they should.

- Infections.

- Paraneoplastic syndromes: Symptoms that occur when cancer-fighting antibodies or white blood cells attack normal cells in the nervous system by mistake.

- Side effects of medicines and treatments: Patients with cancer may take medicines with side effects that include delirium and confusion. The effects usually go away after the medicine is stopped.

- Withdrawal from medicines that depress (slow down) the central nervous system (brain and spinal cord).

Patients with cancer are likely to have more than one risk factor for delirium. Identifying risk factors early may help prevent delirium or decrease the time it takes to treat it. Risk factors include the following:

- Serious illness.

- Having more than one disease.

- Older age.

- Dementia.

- Low level of albumin (protein) in the blood, which is often caused by liver problems.

- Infection.

- High level of nitrogen waste products in the blood, which is often caused by kidney problems.

- Taking medicines that affect the mind or behavior.

- Taking high doses of pain medicines, such as opioids.

The risk increases when the patient has more than one risk factor. Older patients with advanced cancer who are hospitalized often have more than one risk factor for delirium.

The Symptoms of Delirium Are a Lot Like Symptoms of Depression and Dementia

Early symptoms of delirium are like symptoms of depression and dementia. Delirium that causes the patient to be inactive may appear to be depression. Delirium and dementia both cause problems with memory, thinking, and judgment. Dementia may be caused by a number of medical conditions, including Alzheimer disease. Differences in the symptoms of delirium and dementia include the following:

- Patients with delirium often show changes in how alert or aware they are. Patients who have dementia usually stay alert and aware until the dementia becomes very advanced.

- Delirium occurs suddenly (within hours or days). Dementia appears gradually (over months to years) and gets worse over time.

Older patients with cancer may have both dementia and delirium. This can make it hard for the doctor to diagnose the problem. If treatment for delirium is given and the symptoms continue, then the diagnosis is more likely dementia. Checking the patient's health and symptoms over time can help diagnose delirium and dementia.

Physical Exams and Other Laboratory Tests Are Used to Diagnose the Causes of Delirium

Doctors will try to find the causes of delirium.

- Physical exam and history: An exam of the body to check general signs of health, including checking for signs of disease, such as lumps or anything else that seems unusual. A history of the patient's health habits, past illnesses including depression, and treatments will also be taken. A physical exam can help rule out a physical condition that may be causing symptoms.

- Laboratory tests: Medical procedures that test samples of tissue, blood, urine, or other substances in the body. These tests help to diagnose disease, plan and check treatment, or monitor the disease over time.

Treatment for Delirium

Treatment Includes Looking at the Causes and Symptoms of Delirium

Both the causes and the symptoms of delirium may be treated. Treatment depends on the following:

- Where the patient is living, such as home, hospital, or nursing home.

- How advanced the cancer is.

- How the delirium symptoms are affecting the patient.

- The wishes of the patient and family.

Treating the causes of delirium usually includes the following:

- Stopping or lowering the dose of medicines that cause delirium.

- Giving fluids to treat dehydration.

- Giving drugs to treat hypercalcemia (too much calcium in the blood).

- Giving antibiotics for infections.

In a terminally ill patient with delirium, the doctor may treat just the symptoms. The doctor will continue to watch the patient closely during treatment.

Treatment without Medicines Can Also Help Relieve Symptoms

Controlling the patient's surroundings may help with mild symptoms of delirium. The following may help:

- Keep the patient's room quiet and well-lit, and put familiar objects in it.
- Put a clock or calendar where the patient can see it.
- Have family members around.
- Keep the same caregivers as much as possible.

Patients who may hurt themselves or others may need to have physical restraints.

Treatment May Include Medicines

Medicines may be used to treat the symptoms of delirium depending on the patient's condition and heart health. These medicines have serious side effects and the patient will be watched closely by a doctor. These medicines include the following:

- Haloperidol
- Olanzapine
- Risperidone
- Lorazepam
- Midazolam

Sedation May Be Used for Delirium at the End of Life or When Delirium Does Not Get Better with Treatment

When the symptoms of delirium are not relieved with standard treatments and the patient is near death, in pain, or has trouble breathing, other treatment may be needed. Sometimes medicines that will sedate (calm) the patient will be used. The family and the health care team will make this decision together.

The decision to use sedation for delirium may be guided by the following:

- The patient will have repeated assessments by experts before the delirium is considered to be refractory (doesn't respond to treatment).

- The decision to sedate the patient is reviewed by a team of health care professionals and not made by one doctor.

- Temporary sedation, for short periods of time such as overnight, is considered before continuous sedation is used.

- The team of health care professionals will work with the family to make sure the team understands the family's views and that the family understands palliative sedation.

Effects of Delirium on the Patient, Family, and Health Care Providers

Delirium may be dangerous to the patient if his or her judgment is affected. Delirium can cause the patient to behave in unusual ways. Even a quiet or calm patient can have a sudden change in mood or become agitated and need more care.

Delirium can be upsetting to the family and caregivers. When the patient becomes agitated, family members often think the patient is in pain, but this may not be the case. Learning about differences between the symptoms of delirium and pain may help the family and caregivers understand how much pain medicine is needed. Health care providers can help the family and caregivers learn about these differences.

Delirium May Affect Physical Health and Communication

Patients with delirium are:

- More likely to fall.

- Sometimes unable to control bladder and/or bowels.

- More likely to become dehydrated (drink too little water to stay healthy).

215

They often need a longer hospital stay than patients without delirium.

The confused mental state of these patients may make them:

- Unable to talk with family members and caregivers about their needs and feelings.

- Unable to make decisions about care.

This makes it harder for health care providers to assess the patient's symptoms. The family may need to make decisions for the patient.

Section 21.2

Dementia: A Symptom of Normal Pressure Hydrocephalus

Text in this section is excerpted from "Hydrocephalus Fact Sheet," National Institute of Neurological Disorders and Stroke (NINDS), July 27, 2015.

What Is Hydrocephalus?

The term hydrocephalus is derived from the Greek words "hydro" meaning water and "cephalus" meaning head. As the name implies, it is a condition in which the primary characteristic is excessive accumulation of fluid in the brain. Although hydrocephalus was once known as "water on the brain," the "water" is actually cerebrospinal fluid (CSF)—a clear fluid that surrounds the brain and spinal cord. The excessive accumulation of CSF results in an abnormal widening of spaces in the brain called ventricles. This widening creates potentially harmful pressure on the tissues of the brain.

The ventricular system is made up of four ventricles connected by narrow passages. Normally, CSF flows through the ventricles, exits into cisterns (closed spaces that serve as reservoirs) at the base of the brain, bathes the surfaces of the brain and spinal cord, and then reabsorbs into the bloodstream.

CSF has three important life-sustaining functions:

1) to keep the brain tissue buoyant, acting as a cushion or "shock absorber";

2) to act as the vehicle for delivering nutrients to the brain and removing waste; and

3) to flow between the cranium and spine and compensate for changes in intracranial blood volume (the amount of blood within the brain).

The balance between production and absorption of CSF is critically important. Because CSF is made continuously, medical conditions that block its normal flow or absorption will result in an over-accumulation of CSF. The resulting pressure of the fluid against brain tissue is what causes hydrocephalus.

What Are the Different Types of Hydrocephalus?

Hydrocephalus may be congenital or acquired. Congenital hydrocephalus is present at birth and may be caused by either events or influences that occur during fetal development, or genetic abnormalities. Acquired hydrocephalus develops at the time of birth or at some point afterward. This type of hydrocephalus can affect individuals of all ages and may be caused by injury or disease.

Hydrocephalus may also be communicating or noncommunicating. Communicating hydrocephalus occurs when the flow of CSF is blocked after it exits the ventricles. This form is called communicating because the CSF can still flow between the ventricles, which remain open. Non-communicating hydrocephalus—also called "obstructive" hydrocephalus—occurs when the flow of CSF is blocked along one or more of the narrow passages connecting the ventricles. One of the most common causes of hydrocephalus is "aqueductal stenosis." In this case, hydrocephalus results from a narrowing of the aqueduct of Sylvius, a small passage between the third and fourth ventricles in the middle of the brain.

There are two other forms of hydrocephalus which do not fit exactly into the categories mentioned above and primarily affect adults: hydrocephalus ex-vacuo and Normal Pressure Hydrocephalus (NPH).

Hydrocephalus ex-vacuo occurs when stroke or traumatic injury cause damage to the brain. In these cases, brain tissue may actually shrink. NPH is an abnormal increase of cerebrospinal fluid in the brain's ventricles that may result from a subarachnoid hemorrhage, head trauma, infection, tumor, or complications of surgery. However, many people develop NPH when none of these factors are present. An estimated 375,000 older Americans have NPH.

Who Gets This Disorder?

The number of people who develop hydrocephalus or who are currently living with it is difficult to establish since the condition occurs in children and adults, and can develop later in life. A 2008 data review found that, in 2003, hydrocephalus accounted for 0.6 percent of all pediatric hospital admissions in the United States. Some estimates report one to two of every 1,000 babies are born with hydrocephalus.

What Causes Hydrocephalus?

The causes of hydrocephalus are still not well understood. Hydrocephalus may result from inherited genetic abnormalities (such as the genetic defect that causes aqueductal stenosis) or developmental disorders (such as those associated with neural tube defects including spina bifida and encephalocele). Other possible causes include complications of premature birth such as intraventricular hemorrhage, diseases such as meningitis, tumors, traumatic head injury, or subarachnoid hemorrhage, which block the exit of CSF from the ventricles to the cisterns or eliminate the passageway for CSF within the cisterns.

What Are the Symptoms?

Symptoms of hydrocephalus vary with age, disease progression, and individual differences in tolerance to the condition. For example, an infant's ability to compensate for increased CSF pressure and enlargement of the ventricles differs from an adult's. The infant skull can expand to accommodate the buildup of CSF because the sutures (the fibrous joints that connect the bones of the skull) have not yet closed.

In infancy, the most obvious indication of hydrocephalus is often a rapid increase in head circumference or an unusually large head size. Other symptoms may include vomiting, sleepiness, irritability, downward deviation of the eyes (also called "sun setting"), and seizures.

Older children and adults may experience different symptoms because their skulls cannot expand to accommodate the buildup of CSF. Symptoms may include headache followed by vomiting, nausea, blurred or double vision, sun setting of the eyes, problems with balance, poor coordination, gait disturbance, urinary incontinence, slowing or loss of developmental progress, lethargy, drowsiness, irritability, or other changes in personality or cognition including memory loss.

Symptoms of normal pressure hydrocephalus include problems with walking, impaired bladder control leading to urinary frequency and/or incontinence, and progressive mental impairment and dementia. An individual with this type of hydrocephalus may have a general slowing of movements or may complain that his or her feet feel "stuck." Because some of these symptoms may also be experienced in other disorders such as Alzheimer disease, Parkinson disease, and Creutzfeldt-Jakob disease, normal pressure hydrocephalus is often incorrectly diagnosed and never properly treated. Doctors may use a variety of tests, including brain scans such as computed tomography (CT) and magnetic resonance imaging (MRI), a spinal tap or lumbar catheter, intracranial pressure monitoring, and neuropsychological tests, to help them accurately diagnose normal pressure hydrocephalus and rule out any other conditions.

The symptoms described in this section account for the most typical ways in which progressive hydrocephalus is noticeable, but it is important to remember that symptoms vary significantly from person to person.

How Is Hydrocephalus Diagnosed?

Hydrocephalus is diagnosed through clinical neurological evaluation and by using cranial imaging techniques such as ultrasonography, CT, MRI, or pressure-monitoring techniques. A physician selects the appropriate diagnostic tool based on an individual's age, clinical presentation, and the presence of known or suspected abnormalities of the brain or spinal cord.

What Is the Current Treatment?

Hydrocephalus is most often treated by surgically inserting a shunt system. This system diverts the flow of CSF from the CNS (central nervous system) to another area of the body where it can be absorbed as part of the normal circulatory process.

A shunt is a flexible but sturdy plastic tube. A shunt system consists of the shunt, a catheter, and a valve. One end of the catheter is placed within a ventricle inside the brain or in the CSF outside the spinal cord. The other end of the catheter is commonly placed within the abdominal cavity, but may also be placed at other sites in the body such as a chamber of the heart or areas around the lung where the CSF can drain and be absorbed. A valve located along the catheter maintains one-way flow and regulates the rate of CSF flow.

A limited number of individuals can be treated with an alternative procedure called third ventriculostomy. In this procedure, a neuro endoscope—a small camera that uses fiber optic technology to visualize small and difficult to reach surgical areas—allows a doctor to view the ventricular surface. Once the scope is guided into position, a small tool makes a tiny hole in the floor of the third ventricle, which allows the CSF to bypass the obstruction and flow toward the site of resorption around the surface of the brain.

What Are the Possible Complications of a Shunt System?

Shunt systems are imperfect devices. Complications may include mechanical failure, infections, obstructions, and the need to lengthen or replace the catheter. Generally, shunt systems require monitoring and regular medical follow up. When complications occur, subsequent surgery to replace the failed part or the entire shunt system may be needed.

Some complications can lead to other problems such as overdraining or underdraining. Overdraining occurs when the shunt allows CSF to drain from the ventricles more quickly than it is produced. Overdraining can cause the ventricles to collapse, tearing blood vessels and causing headache, hemorrhage (subdural hematoma), or slitlike ventricles (slit ventricle syndrome). Underdraining occurs when CSF is not removed quickly enough and the symptoms of hydrocephalus recur. Overdrainage and underdrainage of CSF are addressed by adjusting the drainage pressure of the shunt valve; if the shunt has an adjustable pressure valve these changes can be made by placing a special magnet on the scalp over the valve. In addition to the common symptoms of hydrocephalus, infections from a shunt may also produce symptoms such as a low-grade fever, soreness of the neck or shoulder muscles, and redness or tenderness along the shunt tract. When there is reason to suspect that a shunt system is not functioning properly (for example, if the symptoms of hydrocephalus return), medical attention should be sought immediately.

What Is the Prognosis?

The prognosis for individuals diagnosed with hydrocephalus is difficult to predict, although there is some correlation between the specific cause of the hydrocephalus and the outcome. Prognosis is further clouded by the presence of associated disorders, the timeliness of diagnosis, and the success of treatment. The degree to which relief of CSF pressure following shunt surgery can minimize or reverse damage to the brain is not well understood.

Affected individuals and their families should be aware that hydrocephalus poses risks to both cognitive and physical development. However, many children diagnosed with the disorder benefit from rehabilitation therapies and educational interventions and go on to lead normal lives with few limitations. Treatment by an interdisciplinary team of medical professionals, rehabilitation specialists, and educational experts is critical to a positive outcome. Left untreated, progressive hydrocephalus may be fatal.

The symptoms of normal pressure hydrocephalus usually get worse over time if the condition is not treated, although some people may experience temporary improvements. While the success of treatment with shunts varies from person to person, some people recover almost completely after treatment and have a good quality of life. Early diagnosis and treatment improves the chance of a good recovery.

Part Four

Recognizing, Diagnosing, and Treating Symptoms of Alzheimer Disease and Dementias

Chapter 22

Forgetfulness: Knowing When to Ask for Help

Many people worry about becoming forgetful. They think forgetfulness is the first sign of Alzheimer disease (AD). Over the past few years, scientists have learned a lot about memory and why some kinds of memory problems are serious but others are not.

Age-Related Changes in Memory

Forgetfulness can be a normal part of aging. As people get older, changes occur in all parts of the body, including the brain. As a result, some people may notice that it takes longer to learn new things, they don't remember information as well as they did, or they lose things like their glasses. These usually are signs of mild forgetfulness, not serious memory problems.

Some older adults also find that they don't do as well as younger people on complex memory or learning tests. Scientists have found, though, that given enough time, healthy older people can do as well as younger people do on these tests. In fact, as they age, healthy adults usually improve in areas of mental ability such as vocabulary.

Text in this chapter is excerpted from "Forgetfulness: Knowing When to Ask for Help," National Institute on Aging (NIA), May 2015.

Other Causes of Memory Loss

Some memory problems are related to health issues that may be treatable. For example, medication side effects, vitamin B12 deficiency, chronic alcoholism, tumors or infections in the brain, or blood clots in the brain can cause memory loss or possibly dementia. Some thyroid, kidney, or liver disorders also can lead to memory loss. A doctor should treat serious medical conditions like these as soon as possible.

Emotional problems, such as stress, anxiety, or depression, can make a person more forgetful and can be mistaken for dementia. For instance, someone who has recently retired or who is coping with the death of a spouse, relative, or friend may feel sad, lonely, worried, or bored. Trying to deal with these life changes leaves some people confused or forgetful.

The confusion and forgetfulness caused by emotions usually are temporary and go away when the feelings fade. The emotional problems can be eased by supportive friends and family, but if these feelings last for a long time, it is important to get help from a doctor or counselor. Treatment may include counseling, medication, or both.

More Serious Memory Problems

For some older people, memory problems are a sign of a serious problem, such as mild cognitive impairment or dementia. People who are worried about memory problems should see a doctor. The doctor might conduct or order a thorough physical and mental health evaluation to reach a diagnosis. Often, these evaluations are conducted by a neurologist, a physician who specializes in problems related to the brain and central nervous system.

A complete medical exam for memory loss should review the person's medical history, including the use of prescription and over-the-counter medicines, diet, past medical problems, and general health. A correct diagnosis depends on accurate details, so in addition to talking with the patient, the doctor might ask a family member, caregiver, or close friend for information.

Blood and urine tests can help the doctor find the cause of the memory problems or dementia. The doctor also might do tests for memory loss and test the person's problem-solving and language abilities. A brain scan, such as an MRI, may help rule out some causes of the memory problems.

Amnestic Mild Cognitive Impairment (MCI). Some people with memory problems have a condition called amnestic mild cognitive impairment, or amnestic MCI. People with this condition have more memory problems than normal for people their age, but their symptoms are not as severe as those of **Alzheimer disease**, and they are able to carry out their normal daily activities.

Signs of MCI include losing things often, forgetting to go to important events and appointments, and having trouble coming up with desired words. Family and friends may notice memory lapses, and the person with MCI may worry about losing his or her memory. These worries may prompt the person to see a doctor for diagnosis.

Researchers have found that more people with MCI than those without it go on to develop Alzheimer disease. However, not everyone who has MCI develops Alzheimer disease. Studies are underway to learn why some people with MCI progress to Alzheimer disease and others do not.

There currently is no standard treatment for MCI. Typically, the doctor will regularly monitor and test a person diagnosed with MCI to detect any changes in memory and thinking skills over time. No medications have been approved to treat MCI.

Dementia. Dementia is the loss of thinking, memory, and reasoning skills to such an extent that it seriously affects a person's ability to carry out daily activities. Dementia is not a disease itself but a group of symptoms caused by certain diseases or conditions such as Alzheimer disease. People with dementia lose their mental abilities at different rates.

Keeping Your Memory Sharp

People with some forgetfulness can use a variety of techniques that may help them stay healthy and maintain their memory and mental skills. Here are some tips:

- Plan tasks, make "to do" lists, and use memory aids like notes and calendars. Some people find they remember things better if they mentally connect them to other meaningful things, such as a familiar name, song, book, or TV show.

- Develop interests or hobbies and stay involved in activities that can help both the mind and body.

- Engage in physical activity and exercise. Several studies have associated exercise (such as walking) with better brain function, although more research is needed to say for sure whether exercise can help to maintain brain function or prevent or delay symptoms of Alzheimer disease.

- Limit alcohol use. Although some studies suggest that moderate alcohol use has health benefits, heavy or binge drinking over time can cause memory loss and permanent brain damage.

- Find activities, such as exercise or a hobby, to relieve feelings of stress, anxiety, or depression. If these feelings last for a long time, talk with your doctor.

Symptoms of dementia may include:

- Being unable to remember things

- Asking the same question or repeating the same story over and over

- Becoming lost in familiar places

- Being unable to follow directions

- Getting confused about time, people, and places

- Neglecting personal safety, hygiene, and nutrition

Two of the most common forms of dementia in older people are Alzheimer disease and vascular dementia. These types of dementia cannot be cured at present.

In *Alzheimer disease*, changes in certain parts of the brain result in the death of many nerve cells. Symptoms of Alzheimer disease begin slowly and worsen steadily as damage to nerve cells spreads throughout the brain. As time goes by, forgetfulness gives way to serious problems with thinking, judgment, recognizing family and friends, and the ability to perform daily activities like driving a car or handling money. Eventually, the person needs total care.

In *vascular dementia*, strokes or changes in the brain's blood supply lead to the death of brain tissue. Symptoms of vascular dementia can vary but usually begin suddenly, depending on where in the brain the strokes occurred and how severe they were. The person's memory, language, reasoning, and coordination may be affected. Mood and personality changes are common as well.

It's not possible to reverse damage already caused by a stroke, so it's very important to get medical care right away if someone has signs of a stroke. It's also important to take steps to prevent further strokes, which worsen vascular dementia symptoms. Some people have both Alzheimer disease and vascular dementia.

Treatment for Dementia

A person with dementia should be under a doctor's care. The doctor might be a neurologist, family doctor, internist, geriatrician, or psychiatrist. He or she can treat the patient's physical and behavioral problems (such as aggression, agitation, or wandering) and answer the many questions that the person or family may have.

People with dementia caused by Alzheimer disease may be treated with medications. Four medications are approved by the U.S. Food and Drug Administration (FDA) to treat AD. Donepezil (Aricept®), rivastigmine (Exelon®), and galantamine (Razadyne®) are used to treat mild to moderate Alzheimer disease (donepezil has been approved to treat severe Alzheimer disease as well).

Memantine (Namenda®) is used to treat moderate to severe Alzheimer disease. These drugs may help maintain thinking, memory, and speaking skills, and may lessen certain behavioral problems for a few months to a few years in some people. However, they don't stop Alzheimer disease from progressing. Many studies are investigating medications and other interventions to prevent or delay Alzheimer disease, as well as cognitive decline.

People with vascular dementia should take steps to prevent further strokes. These steps include controlling high blood pressure, monitoring and treating high cholesterol and diabetes, and not smoking. Studies are underway to develop medicines to reduce the severity of memory and thinking problems that come with vascular dementia. Other studies are looking at drugs to relieve certain symptoms of this type of dementia. Family members and friends can help people in the early stages of dementia to continue their daily routines, physical activities, and social contacts. People with dementia should be kept up to date about the details of their lives, such as the time of day, where they live, and what is happening at home or in the world. Memory aids may help. Some families find that a big calendar, a list of daily plans, notes about simple safety measures, and written directions describing how to use common household items are useful aids.

What You Can Do

If you're concerned that you or someone you know has a serious memory problem, talk with your doctor. He or she may be able to diagnose the problem or refer you to a specialist, such as a neurologist or geriatric psychiatrist. Healthcare professionals who specialize in Alzheimer disease and other dementias can recommend ways to manage the problem or suggest treatment or services that might help.

Consider participating in clinical trials or studies. People with Alzheimer disease, MCI, or a family history of Alzheimer disease and healthy people with no memory problems and no family history of Alzheimer disease may be able to take part in clinical trials, which may help themselves or future generations.

Chapter 23

Talking with Your Doctor

Choosing a Doctor You Can Talk to

Finding a main doctor (often called your primary doctor or primary care doctor) who you feel comfortable talking to is the first step in good communication. It is also a way to ensure your good health. This doctor gets to know you and what your health is normally like. He or she can help you make medical decisions that suit your values and daily habits and can keep in touch with the other medical specialists and healthcare providers you may need.

If you don't have a primary doctor or are not at ease with the one you currently see, now may be the time to find a new doctor. Whether you just moved to a new city, changed insurance providers, or had a bad experience with your doctor or medical staff, it is worthwhile to spend time finding a doctor you can trust. People sometimes hesitate to change doctors because they worry about hurting their doctor's feelings. But doctors understand that different people have different needs. They know it is important for everyone to have a doctor with whom they are comfortable.

Primary care doctors frequently are family practitioners, internists, or geriatricians. A geriatrician is a doctor who specializes in older people, but family practitioners and internists may also have a lot of experience with older patients. Here are some suggestions that can help you find a doctor who meets your needs.

Text in this chapter is excerpted from "Talking with Your Doctor," National Institute on Aging (NIA), June 2014.

Decide What You Are Looking for in a Doctor

A good first step is to make a list of qualities that matter to you. Do you care if your doctor is a man or a woman? Is it important that your doctor has evening office hours, is associated with a specific hospital or medical center, or speaks your language? Do you prefer a doctor who has an individual practice or one who is part of a group so you can see one of your doctor's partners if your doctor is not available? After you have made your list, go back over it and decide which qualities are most important and which are nice, but not essential.

Identify Several Possible Doctors

Once you have a general sense of what you are looking for, ask friends and relatives, medical specialists, and other health professionals for the names of doctors with whom they have had good experiences. Rather than just getting a name, ask about the person's experiences. For example, say: "What do you like about Dr. Smith?" and "Does this doctor take time to answer questions?" A doctor whose name comes up often may be a strong possibility.

If you belong to a managed care plan—a health maintenance organization (HMO) or preferred provider organization (PPO)—you may be required to choose a doctor in the plan or else you may have to pay extra to see a doctor outside the network. Most managed care plans will provide information on their doctors' backgrounds and credentials. Some plans have websites with lists of participating doctors from which you can choose.

It may be helpful to develop a list of a few names you can choose from. As you find out more about the doctors on this list, you may rule out some of them. In some cases, a doctor may not be taking new patients and you may have to make another choice.

Learn about Doctors You Are Considering

Once you have narrowed your list to two or three doctors, call their offices. The office staff is a good source of information about the doctor's education and qualifications, office policies, and payment procedures. Pay attention to the office staff—you will have to deal with them often!

You may want to set up an appointment to meet and talk with a doctor you are considering. He or she is likely to charge you for such a visit. After the appointment, ask yourself if this doctor is a person with whom you could work well. If you are not satisfied, schedule a visit with one of your other candidates.

232

When Learning about a Doctor, Consider Asking Questions Like:

- Do you have many older patients?

- How do you feel about involving my family in care decisions?

- Can I call or email you or your staff when I have questions? Do you charge for telephone or email time?

- What are thoughts about complementary or alternative treatments?

When Making a Decision about Which Doctor to Choose, You Might Want to Ask Yourself Questions Like:

- Did a doctor give me chance to ask questions?

- Was the doctor really listening to me?

- Could I understand what the doctor was saying? Was I comfortable asking him or her to say it again?

Make a Choice

Once you've chosen a doctor, make your first actual care appointment. This visit may include a medical history and a physical exam. Be sure to bring your medical records, or have them sent from your former doctor. Bring a list of your current medicines or put the medicines in a bag and take them with you. If you haven't already met the doctor, ask for extra time during this visit to ask any questions you have about the doctor or the practice.

Getting Ready for an Appointment

A basic plan can help you make the most of your appointment whether you are starting with a new doctor or continuing with the doctor you've seen for years. The following tips will make it easier for you and your doctor to cover everything you need to talk about.

List and Prioritize Your Concerns

Make a list of what you want to discuss. For example, do you have a new symptom you want to ask the doctor about? Do you want to get a flu shot? Are you concerned about how a treatment is affecting your daily life? If you have more than a few items to discuss, put them in order and ask about the most important ones first. Don't put off the things that are really on your mind until the end of your appointment—bring them up right away!.

Take Information with You

Some doctors suggest you put all your prescription drugs, over-the-counter medicines, vitamins, and herbal remedies or supplements in a bag and bring them with you. Others recommend you bring a list of everything you take and the dose. You should also take your insurance cards, names and phone numbers of other doctors you see, and your medical records if the doctor doesn't already have them.

Consider Bringing a Family Member or Friend

Sometimes it is helpful to bring a family member or close friend with you. Let your family member or friend know in advance what you want from your visit. Your companion can remind you what you planned to discuss with the doctor if you forget. She or he can take notes for you and can help you remember what the doctor said.

Be Sure You Can See and Hear as Well as Possible

Many older people use glasses or need aids for hearing. Remember to take your eyeglasses to the doctor's visit. If you have a hearing aid, make sure that it is working well and wear it. Let the doctor and staff know if you have a hard time seeing or hearing. For example, you may want to say: *"My hearing makes it hard to understand everything you're saying. It helps a lot when you speak slowly."*

Plan to Update the Doctor

Let your doctor know what has happened in your life since your last visit. If you have been treated in the emergency room or by a specialist, tell the doctor right away. Mention any changes you have noticed in your appetite, weight, sleep, or energy level. Also tell the doctor about any recent changes in any medications you take or the effects they have had on you.

Giving Information

Talking about your health means sharing information about how you feel physically, emotionally, and mentally. Knowing how to describe your symptoms and bring up other concerns will help you become a partner in your health care.

Share Any Symptoms

A symptom is evidence of a disease or disorder in the body. Examples of symptoms include pain, fever, a lump or bump, unexplained weight loss or gain, or having a hard time sleeping.

Be clear and concise when describing your symptoms. Your description helps the doctor identify the problem. A physical exam and medical tests provide valuable information, but your symptoms point the doctor in the right direction.

Your doctor will ask when your symptoms started, what time of day they happen, how long they last (seconds? days?), how often they occur, if they seem to be getting worse or better, and if they keep you from going out or doing your usual activities.

Take the time to make some notes about your symptoms before you call or visit the doctor. Worrying about your symptoms is not a sign of weakness. Being honest about what you are experiencing doesn't mean that you are complaining. The doctor needs to know how you feel.

Questions to Ask Yourself about Your Symptoms:

* What exactly are my symptoms?

* Are the symptoms constant? If not, when do I experience them?

* Does anything I do make the symptoms better? Or worse?

* Do the symptoms affect the daily activities? Which ones? How?

Give Information about Your Medications

It is possible for medicines to interact causing unpleasant and sometimes dangerous side effects. Your doctor needs to know about ALL of the medicines you take, including over-the-counter(nonprescription) drugs and herbal remedies or supplements. Make a list or bring everything with you to your visit—don't forget about eye drops, vitamins, and laxatives. Tell the doctor how often you take each. Describe any drug allergies or reactions you have had. Say which medications work best for you. Be sure your doctor has the phone number of the pharmacy you use.

Tell the Doctor about Your Habits

To provide the best care, your doctor must understand you as a person and know what your life is like. The doctor may ask about where you live, what you eat, how you sleep, what you do each day, what activities you enjoy, what your sex life is like, and if you smoke or drink. Be open and honest with your doctor. It will help him or her to understand your medical conditions fully and recommend the best treatment choices for you.

Voice Other Concerns

Your doctor may ask you how your life is going. This isn't being impolite or nosy. Information about what's happening in your life may be useful medically. Let the doctor know about any major changes or stresses in your life, such as a divorce or the death of a loved one. You don't have to go into detail; you may want to say something like: *"It might be helpful for you to know that my sister passed away since my last visit with you,"* or *"I recently had to sell my home and move in with my daughter."*

Getting Information

Asking questions is key to good communication with your doctor. If you don't ask questions, he or she may assume you already know the answer or that you don't want more information. Don't wait for the doctor to raise a specific question or subject because he or she may not know it's important to you. Be proactive. Ask questions when you don't know the meaning of a word (like aneurysm, hypertension, or infarct) or when instructions aren't clear (for example, does taking medicine with food mean before, during, or after a meal?).

Learn about Medical Tests

Sometimes doctors need to do blood tests, X-rays, or other procedures to find out what is wrong or to learn more about your medical condition. Some tests, such as Pap tests, mammograms, glaucoma tests, and screenings for prostate and colorectal cancer, are done regularly to check for hidden medical problems. Before having a medical test, ask your doctor to explain why it is important, what it will show, and what it will cost. Ask what kind of things you need to do to prepare for the test. For example, you may need to have an empty stomach, or you may have to provide a urine sample. Ask how you will be notified of the test results and how long they will take to come in.

Questions to Ask about Medical Tests:

- Why is the test being done?
- What steps does the test involve?

- Are there any dangers or side-effects?

- How will I find out the results? How long will it take to get the results?

- What will we know after the test?

When the results are ready, make sure the doctor tells you what they are and explains what they mean. You may want to ask your doctor for a written copy of the test results. If the test is done by a specialist, ask to have the results sent to your primary doctor.

Is It Possible to Find Information about Medical Tests Online?

Yes—there is a lot of information online about medical tests. The National Library of Medicine's MedlinePlus website provides links to many trustworthy resources. Visit www.medlineplus.gov and enter "laboratory tests" in the search window at the top of the page. Then, select the link that applies to your situation. You can get information on preparing for lab tests, explanations of different tests, and tips on interpreting lab test results.

Discuss Your Diagnosis and What to Expect

A diagnosis identifies your disease or physical problem. The doctor makes a diagnosis based on the symptoms you are experiencing and the results of the physical exam, laboratory work, and other tests.

If you understand your medical condition, you can help make better decisions about treatment. If you know what to expect, it may be easier for you to deal with the condition. Ask the doctor to tell you the name of the condition and why he or she thinks you have it. Ask how it may affect you and how long it might last. Some medical problems never go away completely. They can't be cured, but they can be treated or managed.

Questions to Ask about Your Diagnosis:

- What may have caused this condition? Will it be permanent?

- How is this condition treated or managed? What will be the long-term effects on my life?

- How can I learn more about my condition?

Find out about Your Medications

Your doctor may prescribe a drug for your condition. Make sure you know the name of the drug and understand why it has been prescribed for you. Ask the doctor to write down how often and for how long you should take it.

Make notes about any other special instructions. There may be foods or drinks you should avoid while you are taking the medicine. Or you may have to take the medicine with food or a whole glass of water. If you are taking other medications, make sure your doctor knows, so he or she can prevent harmful drug interactions.

Sometimes medicines affect older people differently than younger people. Let the doctor know if your medicine doesn't seem to be working or if it is causing problems. It is best not to stop taking the medicine on your own. If you want to stop taking your medicine, check with your doctor first.

If another doctor (for example, a specialist) prescribes a medication for you, call your primary doctor's office and leave a message letting him or her know. Also call to check with your doctor's office before taking any over-the- counter medications. You may find it helpful to keep a chart of all the medicines you take and when you take them.

The pharmacist is also a good source of information about your medicines. In addition to answering questions and helping you select over-the-counter medications, the pharmacist keeps records of all the prescriptions you get filled at that pharmacy. Because your pharmacist keeps these records, it is helpful to use the same store regularly. At your request, the pharmacist can fill your prescriptions in easy-to-open containers and may be able to provide large-print prescription labels.

What Are Side Effects?

"My headache prescription always makes me sleepy."

"Aunt Sarah's cough syrup caused a rash."

Unwanted or unexpected symptoms or feelings that happen when you take a medicine are called side effects.

Some side effects happen just when you start taking a medicine. Some happen only once in a while and you learn how to manage them. But other side effects may make you want to stop taking the medicine. Tell your doctor if this happens. He or she may be able to prescribe a different medicine or help you deal with these side effects in other ways.

Questions to Ask about Medications:

- What are the common side effects? What should I pay attention to?

- When the medicine begin to work?

- What should I do if I miss a dose?

- Should I take it at meals or between meals? Do I need to drink a whole glass of water with it?

- Are the foods, drugs, or activities I should avoid while taking this medicine?

- Will I need a refill? How do I arrange that?

Making Decisions with Your Doctor

Giving and getting information are two important steps in talking with your doctor. The third big step is making decisions about your care.

Find out about Different Treatments

You will benefit most from a treatment when you know what is happening and are involved in making decisions. Make sure you understand what your treatment involves and what it will or will not do. Have the doctor give you directions in writing and feel free to ask questions. For example: *"What are the pros and cons of having surgery at this stage?"* or *"Do I have any other choices?"*

If your doctor suggests a treatment that makes you uncomfortable, ask if there are other treatments that might work. If cost is a concern, ask the doctor if less expensive choices are available. The doctor can work with you to develop a treatment plan that meets your needs.

Here are some things to remember when deciding on a treatment:

- **Discuss Choices.** There are different ways to manage many health conditions, especially chronic conditions like high blood pressure and cholesterol. Ask what your options are.

- **Discuss Risks and Benefits.** Once you know your options, ask about the pros and cons of each one. Find out what side effects might occur, how long the treatment would continue, and how likely it is that the treatment will work for you.

- **Consider Your Own Values and Circumstances.** When thinking about your pros and cons the treatment, don't forget to consider its impact on your overall life. For instance, will one of the side effects interfere with a regular activity that means a lot to you? Is one treatment choice expensive and not covered by your insurance? Doctors need to know about these practical matters and can work with you to develop a treatment plan that meets your needs.

Questions to Ask about Treatment:

- Are there any risk associated with the treatment

- How soon should treatment start? How long will it last?

- Are there other treatments available?

- How much will the treatment cost? Will my insurance cover it?

Learn about Prevention

Doctors and other health professionals may suggest you change your diet, activity level, or other aspects of your life to help you deal with medical conditions. Research has shown that these changes, particularly an increase in exercise, have positive effects on overall health.

Until recently, preventing disease in older people received little attention. But things are changing. We now know that it's never too late to stop smoking, improve your diet, or start exercising. Getting regular checkups and seeing other health professionals such as dentists and eye specialists helps promote good health. Even people who have chronic diseases, like arthritis or diabetes, can prevent further disability and, in some cases, control the progress of the disease.

If a certain disease or health condition runs in your family, ask your doctor if there are steps you can take to help prevent it. If you have a chronic condition, ask how you can manage it and if there are things you can do to prevent it from getting worse. If you want to discuss health and disease prevention with your doctor, say so when you make your next appointment. This lets the doctor plan to spend more time with you.

It is just as important to talk with your doctor about lifestyle changes as it is to talk about treatment. For example: *"I know that you've told me to eat more dairy products, but they really disagree with me. Is there something else I could eat instead?"* or *"Maybe an exercise class would help, but I have no way to get to the senior center. Is there something else you could suggest?"*

As with treatments, consider all the alternatives, look at pros and cons, and remember to take into account your own point of view. Tell your doctor if you feel his or her suggestions won't work for you and explain why. Keep talking with your doctor to come up with a plan that works.

Talking about Exercise

Exercise is often "just what the doctor ordered!" Exercise can:

• Help you have more energy to do the things you want to do.

• Help maintain and improve your physical strength and fitness.

• Help improve mood and relieve depression.

• Help manage and prevent diseases like heart disease, diabetes, some types of cancer, osteoporosis, and disabilities as people grow older.

• Help improve your balance.

Many doctors now recommend that older people try to make physical activity a part of everyday life. When you are making your list of things to talk about with your doctor, add exercise. Ask how exercise would benefit you, if there are any activities you should avoid, and whether your doctor can recommend any specific kinds of exercise.

Questions to Ask about Prevention:

• Is there any way to prevent a condition that runs in my family before it affects me?

• Are there ways to keep my condition from getting worse?

• How will making a change in my habits help me?

• Are there any risks in making this change?

• Are there support groups or community services that might help me?

Involving Your Family and Friends

It can be helpful to take a family member or friend with you when you go to the doctor's office. You may feel more confident if someone else is with you. Also, a relative or friend can help remind you about things you planned to tell or ask the doctor. He or she also can help you remember what the doctor says.

Don't let your companion take too strong a role. The visit is between you and the doctor. You may want some time alone with the doctor to discuss personal matters. If you are alone with the doctor during or right after the physical exam, this might be a good time to raise private concerns. Or, you could ask your family member or friend to stay in the waiting room for part of the appointment. For best results, let your companion know in advance how he or she can be most helpful.

If a relative or friend helps with your care at home, bringing that person along when you visit the doctor may be useful. In addition to the questions you have, your caregiver may have concerns he or she wants to discuss with the doctor. Some things caregivers may find especially helpful to discuss are: what to expect in the future, sources of information and support, community services, and ways they can maintain their own well-being.

Even if a family member or friend can't go with you to your appointment, he or she can still help. For example, the person can serve as your sounding board, helping you practice what you want to say to the doctor before the visit. And after the visit, talking about what the doctor said can remind you of the important points and help you come up with questions to ask next time.

Chapter 24

Diagnosis and Treatment of Dementias

Diagnosis

Doctors first assess whether the individual has an underlying treatable condition such as depression, abnormal thyroid function, drug-induced encephalopathy, normal pressure hydrocephalus, or vitamin B12 deficiency. Early diagnosis is important, as some causes for symptoms can be treated. In many cases, the specific type of dementia that a person has may not be confirmed until after the person has died and the brain is examined.

An assessment generally includes:

- **Patient history.** Typical questions about a person's medical and family history might include asking about whether dementia runs in the family, how and when symptoms began, and if the person is taking certain medications that might cause or exacerbate symptoms.

- **Physical exam.** Measuring blood pressure and other vital signs may help physicians detect conditions that might cause or occur with dementia. Such conditions may be treatable.

Text in this chapter is excerpted from "The Dementias, Hope through Research," National Institute of Neurological Disorders and Stroke (NINDS), November 2, 2015.

- Neurological evaluations. Assessing balance, sensory function, reflexes, vision, eye movements, and other functions helps identify signs of conditions that may affect the diagnosis or are treatable with drugs. Doctors also might use an electroencephalogram, a test that records patterns of electrical activity in the brain, to check for abnormal electrical brain activity.

The following procedures also may be used when diagnosing dementia:

- **Brain scans.** These tests can identify strokes, tumors, and other problems that can cause dementia. Scans also identify changes in the brain's structure and function. The most common scans are computed tomographic (CT) scans and magnetic resonance imaging (MRI). CT scans use X-rays to produce images of the brain and other organs. MRI scans use a computer, magnetic fields, and radio waves to produce detailed images of body structures, including tissues, organs, bones, and nerves.

- **Other types of scans let doctors watch the brain as it functions**. Two of these tests are single photon-emission computed tomography, which can be used to measure blood flow to the brain, and positron emission tomography (PET), which uses radioactive isotopes to provide pictures of brain activity. These scans are used to look for patterns of altered brain activity that are common in dementia. Researchers also use PET imaging with compounds that bind to beta-amyloid to detect levels of the protein, a hallmark of Alzheimer disease (AD), in the living brain.

- **Cognitive and neuropsychological tests**. These tests measure memory, language skills, math skills, and other abilities related to mental functioning. For example, people with AD often show impairment in problem-solving, memory, and the ability to perform once-automatic tasks.

- **Laboratory tests**. Many tests help rule out other conditions. They include measuring levels of sodium and other electrolytes in the blood, a complete blood count, a blood sugar test, urine analysis, a check of vitamin B12 levels, cerebrospinal fluid analysis, drug and alcohol tests, and an analysis of thyroid function. Presymptomatic tests. Some dementias are associated with a known gene defect. In these cases, a genetic test could help people know if they are at risk for dementia. People should talk with family members, their primary health care professional, and a genetic counselor before getting tested.

- **Psychiatric evaluation**. This will help determine if depression or another mental health condition is causing or contributing to a person's symptoms.

Treatment

Some dementias are treatable. However, therapies to stop or slow common neurodegenerative diseases such as AD have largely been unsuccessful, though some drugs are available to manage certain symptoms.

Most drugs for dementia are used to treat symptoms in AD. One class of drugs, called cholinesterase inhibitors, includes donepezil, rivastigmine, and galantamine. These drugs can temporarily improve or stabilize memory and thinking skills in some people by increasing the activity of the cholinergic brain network. The drug memantine is in another class of medications called NMDA receptor agonists, which prevents declines in learning and memory. NMDA receptor agonists work by regulating the activity of the neurotransmitter glutamate. When glutamate activity levels are excessive, neurons may die. Memantine may be combined with a cholinesterase inhibitor for added benefits. These drugs are sometimes used to treat other dementias as well. None of these drugs can stop or reverse the course of the disease.

- **Creutzfeldt-Jakob disease.** There are no treatments to cure or control CJD. Management focuses on reducing symptoms and making people comfortable.

- **Dementia with Lewy bodies.** Drugs available for managing DLB are aimed at relieving symptoms such as stiffness, hallucinations, and delusions. However, many of the agents for treating the physical symptoms, particularly antipsychotics, can make the mental health symptoms worse. Conversely, drugs used to treat mental health symptoms can exacerbate physical symptoms. Studies suggest that AD drugs may benefit people with DLB.

- **Frontotemporal disorder (FTD).** There are no medications approved to treat or prevent FTD and most other types of progressive dementia. Sedatives, antidepressants, and other drugs used to treat Parkinson's and Alzheimer disease symptoms may help manage certain symptoms and behavioral problems associated with the disorders.

- **Parkinson disease dementia.** Some studies suggest that the cholinesterase inhibitors used in people with AD might improve cognitive, behavioral, and psychotic symptoms in people with Parkinson disease dementia. The U.S. Food and Drug Administration (FDA) has approved one Alzheimer disease drug, rivastigmine, to treat cognitive symptoms in PDD.

- **Vascular dementia.** This type of dementia is often managed with drugs to prevent strokes. The aim is to reduce the risk of additional brain damage. Some studies suggest that drugs that improve memory in AD might benefit people with early vascular dementia. Most of the modifiable risk factors that influence development of vascular dementia and VCI are the same risk factors for cerebrovascular disease, such as hypertension, atrial fibrillation, diabetes, and high cholesterol. Interventions that address these risk factors may be incorporated into the management of vascular dementia.

Although scientists have some understanding of these dementias and the mechanisms involved, ongoing research may lead to new ways to diagnose, treat, or perhaps prevent or block disease development. Current areas of research include:

Clinical studies

Clinical studies offer an opportunity to help researchers find better ways to safely detect, treat, or prevent dementias. Various NIH Institutes support clinical studies on AD and related dementias at the NIH research campus in Bethesda, MD, and at medical research centers throughout the United States.

Drugs

A number of agents that might slow the progression of AD and other dementias are in various stages of testing.

The NIA-supported Alzheimer Disease Cooperative Study (ADCS) is a consortium of academic medical centers and clinics set up by NIH in 1991 to collaborate on the development of promising Alzheimer disease treatments and diagnostic tools.

In the latest round of studies, the ADCS will test drug and exercise interventions in people in the early stages of the disease, examine a medication to reduce agitation in people with Alzheimer dementia, and test a cutting-edge approach to speed testing of drugs in clinical trials. Because Alzheimer disease-related brain changes begin years before symptoms appear, the A4 (Anti-amyloid Treatment in Asymptomatic Alzheimer Disease) trial is testing a promising therapy in the early stages of the disorder. This secondary prevention trial will test an amyloid-clearing drug in the symptom-free stage of the disease in 1,000 cognitively healthy older volunteers whose brain scans show abnormal levels of amyloid accumulation. Another of the newly funded ADCS drug trials is the Prazosin for Treating Agitation trial, which will test the use of the generic drug prazosin as a treatment for agitation that may also be well-tolerated in frail and elderly people.

Exercise

Researchers are assessing the effectiveness of a supervised aerobic exercise program to enhance general cognition in adults with age-related cognitive decline. They predict that greater cognitive gains will be made by individuals with more fitness gains. Another study will determine if exercise prevents memory loss from getting worse, and if it improves daily functioning and attitudes of those with probable AD. Researchers also hope to gain a better understanding of the effects of exercise and cognitive training on improving brain function in healthy older adults who may be at risk for developing AD.

Proteins

One feature that several major dementias have in common is an excess in the brain of certain proteins or protein fragments that have taken abnormal forms thought to be toxic to brain cells. NIH-funded research projects are aimed at better understanding the toxic effects of protein buildup and how it is related to the development of AD and related dementias. Some of these protein abnormalities can be detected in cerebrospinal fluid.

For example, an abnormally high accumulation of beta-amyloid protein in the brain is a hallmark of AD. NINDS-funded researchers are determining which neural pathways are affected by beta-amyloid and contribute to the development of Alzheimer disease pathology and symptoms. NINDS funding also led to a genetically engineered rat model of AD that has the full array of brain changes associated with the human disease and may be used to better define causes and effects of AD related to beta-amyloid accumulation. Funding also was provided by NIA, the National Institute of Mental Health (also part of NIH), and other organizations.

In FTD, AD, and other neurodegenerative diseases, the protein tau collects in abnormal tangled masses of filaments that disrupt nerve signaling, cause cell death, and impair cognition. NINDS-funded researchers are determining whether specific forms of tau interfere with nerve cell signaling and decrease memory function. Others are studying how tau pathology spreads from cell to cell. Tau-related investigations are aimed at identifying common mechanisms of FTD, as well as biomarkers (signs that may indicate disease risk and progression, and improve diagnosis) that will speed the development of novel therapeutics for PDD and other forms of dementia.

Similarly, the abnormal accumulation of the protein alpha-synuclein is a hallmark of Parkinson disease and Lewy body dementia. Scientists hope to identify what causes alpha-synuclein to form abnormal aggregates and become toxic to nerve cells, and to understand why the aggregation is an age-related phenomenon in Parkinson disease and other synuclein-related disorders.

Genetics

Several genes—most notably ApoE and the gene for tau (MAPT)—have been implicated in AD and other forms of dementia. Many dementia-related disorders share genetic and other characteristics of AD. Some families share a particular genetic mutation that causes dementia. Researchers are using samples of a person's genetic material, or genome, to identify genes that may be responsible for the development of dementia and AD. For example, NIH-funded researchers recently examined ApoE's role in the development of late-onset AD and found that one of the three forms of the ApoE gene triggers an inflammatory reaction and damages the blood vessels that feed the brain. Other researchers have identified a gene variant of TREM2 that is involved with a form of frontotemporal dementia that runs in families. Additional research may identify novel genes involved with FTD and other neurodegenerative diseases, perhaps leading to therapeutic approaches where delivery of normal genes would improve or restore normal brain function.

Sleep

The sleep and wakefulness cycle plays an integral, but not well understood, role in many dementias, including dementia with Lewy bodies, AD, prion dementias, and PDD. Sleep studies in individuals during periods of excessive daytime sleepiness and nocturnal sleep can help determine if fluctuations in mental status among people with DLB are related to excessive daytime sleepiness. Sleep studies also can assess whether declining cognition is predicted by sleep-related and neurobehavioral markers in parkinsonism.

Conclusion

Currently, there are no cures for the common dementias caused by progressive neurodegeneration, including AD, frontotemporal disorders, and Lewy body dementia. However, some forms of dementia are treatable. A better understanding of dementia disorders, as well as their diagnosis and treatment, will make it possible for affected individuals and their caretakers to live their lives more fully and meet daily challenges. NIH, primarily through research activities funded by NINDS and NIA, continues to make discoveries in the lab, design therapeutic approaches to dementias, and create tools and resources to help speed the development of treatments that can be used in practice. These discoveries may eventually lead to ways to slow disease progression or even cure and prevent the dementias.

Chapter 25

Diagnosing Alzheimer Disease

Chapter Contents

Section 25.1

Alzheimer Disease: Diagnosis

Text in this section is excerpted from "About Alzheimer's Disease: Diagnosis," National Institute on Aging (NIA), December 16, 2011. Reviewed February 2016.

What Should I Do If I'm Worried about Memory Loss or Possible Alzheimer disease (AD)

If you are concerned about changes in memory and thinking or changes in senses, behavior, mood, or movement that do not seem normal in yourself or a family member, talk with a doctor. A doctor can administer a brief memory screening test that can help detect problems, and can also do a complete exam to find out if a physical or mental health issue is causing the problem.

How Is Alzheimer Disease Diagnosed?

Doctors use several methods and tools to help determine whether a person who is having memory problems has "possible Alzheimer disease (AD)" (dementia may be due to another cause), "probable Alzheimer disease" (no other cause for dementia be found), or some other problem.

To diagnose Alzheimer disease, doctors may:

- Ask the person and a family member or friend questions about overall health, past medical problems, ability to carry out daily activities, and changes in behavior and personality

- Conduct tests of memory, problem solving, attention, counting, and language

- Carry out standard medical tests, such as blood and urine tests, to identify other possible causes of the problem

- Perform brain scans, such as computed tomography (CT), magnetic resonance imaging (MRI), or positron emission tomography (PET), to rule out other possible causes for symptoms.

These tests may be repeated to give doctors information about how the person's memory and other cognitive functions are changing over time. Tests can also help diagnose other causes of memory problems, such as mild cognitive impairment and vascular dementia. Alzheimer disease can be definitely diagnosed only after death, by linking clinical measures with an examination of brain tissue in an autopsy.

What Are Options for Further Assessment and Diagnosis

If a primary care doctor suspects mild cognitive impairment or possible Alzheimer disease, he or she may refer you to a specialist who can provide a detailed diagnosis, or you may decide to go to a specialist for further assessment. You can find specialists through memory clinics and centers or through local organizations or referral services. Specialists include:

- Geriatricians, who manage health care in older adults. They know how the body changes as it ages and whether symptoms indicate a serious problem.

- Geriatric psychiatrists, who specialize in the mental and emotional problems of older adults and can assess memory and thinking problems

- Neurologists, who specialize in abnormalities of the brain and central nervous system and can conduct and review brain scans

- Neuropsychologists, who can conduct tests of memory and thinking

Memory clinics and centers, including Alzheimer Disease Research Centers, offer teams of specialists who work together to diagnose the problem. Tests often are done at the clinic or center, which can speed up diagnosis.

You may also want to get a second opinion. Diagnosis of memory and thinking problems can be challenging. Subtle signs and symptoms may be overlooked or unclear. Getting a second opinion helps confirm the diagnosis. Most doctors understand the benefit of a second opinion and will share your records if you permit. A specialist can refer you to another doctor for a second opinion, or you may decide to find one yourself.

What Are the Benefits of Early Diagnosis?

Early, accurate diagnosis is beneficial for several reasons. Beginning treatment early in the disease process may help preserve daily functioning for some time, even though the underlying Alzheimer disease process cannot be stopped or reversed.

Having an early diagnosis helps people with Alzheimer disease and their families:

- plan for the future

- take care of financial and legal matters

- address potential safety issues

- learn about living arrangements

- develop support networks

In addition, an early diagnosis gives people greater opportunities to participate in clinical trials that are testing possible new treatments for Alzheimer disease or other research studies.

What New Methods for Diagnosing Alzheimer Disease Are Being Studied?

Scientists are exploring ways to help physicians diagnose Alzheimer disease earlier and more accurately. The ultimate goal is a reliable, valid, and inexpensive diagnostic test that can be used in any doctor's office.

Some studies focus on changes in personality and mental functioning, measured through memory and recall tests, which might point to early Alzheimer disease or predict whether individuals are at higher risk of developing the disease. Other studies are examining the relationship between early damage to brain tissue and outward clinical signs.

Another very promising area of diagnostic research is the analysis of biomarkers—biological signs of disease found in brain images, cerebrospinal fluid, and blood—to detect early changes in the brains of people with MCI and in cognitively normal people who may be at greater risk for Alzheimer disease. Studies indicate that such early detection may be possible, but more research is needed before these techniques can be relied upon to diagnose Alzheimer disease in everyday medical practice.

Section 25.2

Advances in Detecting Alzheimer Disease

This section includes excerpts from "Advances in
Detecting Alzheimer's Disease," National Institute on
Aging (NIA), October 15, 2013; and text from "Advances
in Detecting Alzheimer's Disease," National Institute on
Aging (NIA), December 21, 2012.

Alzheimer disease (AD)-related changes in the brain can begin
years, even decades, before cognitive impairment becomes evident.
Researchers are developing methods to detect these changes at their
earliest stages. By determining who is at the highest risk for Alzheimer disease, promising interventions can be tested more rapidly and
effectively. Identifying those at high risk will also improve diagnosis in
clinical practice, better serving patients and their families. Scientists
continue to explore three main approaches to early diagnosis: measurements of biomarkers in blood and cerebrospinal fluid, brain imaging,
and standardized clinical tests of memory and thinking abilities to
determine cognitive health. Through the NIA-led Alzheimer Disease
Neuroimaging Initiative and other studies, these efforts are leading
to new ways to detect the onset of the disorder.

Imaging Tau Pathology

Brain imaging experts at the National Institute of Radiological
Sciences in Japan and at the University of Pennsylvania, Philadelphia,
have developed a way to image abnormal forms of the tau protein, a
hallmark of Alzheimer disease, in the living brain.

The researchers tested a number of potential tracer compounds
on an abnormal form of tau in Alzheimer disease mouse models. The
tracer that proved most sensitive, PBB3, was then tested in a clinical
positron emission tomography (PET) study of six volunteers, three of
whom had Alzheimer disease. In the participants with the disorder,
the PBB3 fluorescent tracer was highly visible in the hippocampus
and other brain regions where abnormal tau is known to accumulate.
The compound was equally visible in the brain of a volunteer with

corticobasal degeneration, a disorder marked by abnormal deposits of tau but no amyloid plaques. Tau imaging with PBB3 holds promise for distinguishing Alzheimer disease from other forms of dementia and for testing the effectiveness of drugs targeting abnormal tau.

Visual Changes May Signal Alzheimer Disease Onset

Problems with navigating, or getting lost in a familiar place, are common in both Alzheimer disease and normal aging. However the brain mechanisms behind this problem may be very different in different groups of people. The researchers compared eye and head movements in 15 young and 15 older volunteers with normal cognition, and in 12 older participants with early Alzheimer disease, finding differences in the brain's electrical responses to moving visual patterns. The volunteers were shown a computer display of moving dot patterns designed to simulate what it feels like to move while navigating through an environment. Compared to younger participants, older healthy volunteers had delayed responses to pattern changes, while those with Alzheimer disease had diminished responses. These visual processing differences may be used to develop a test that distinguishes early Alzheimer disease from normal aging.

Cognitive Decline in Middle Age

Cognitive decline may begin earlier in life than researchers had previously believed. A study led by researchers at University College, London, and the Institut National de la Santé et de la Recherche Médicales (INSERM) in Villejuif, France, analyzed 10 years of cognitive test data for more than 10,000 British civil servants participating in the long-running Whitehall II study. Age 45 to 70 years old when the study began, the participants were tested on verbal and mathematical reasoning, verbal memory, verbal fluency, and vocabulary.

Performance in all areas except vocabulary declined over time in all age groups. For example, reasoning test scores declined by 4 percent in the 45- to 49-year-old group and by 10 percent in the 65- to 70-year-old group. Relatively recent improvements in women's educational attainment resulted in higher scores, and although the scores still declined with age, the extent of the decline was less than might have been expected from previous cross-sectional data. This study suggests that efforts to detect and prevent declines in cognitive health may need to start in adults as young as 45 years.

Walking Speed and MCI

Declining gait speed may predict cognitive decline in older adults. However, it can be difficult to recognize and assess gradual changes in walking speed. To obtain continuous daily assessments of gait speed, researchers at the Oregon Health & Sciences University, Portland, OR, used an in-home device that unobtrusively monitors gait speed by collecting measurements from infrared motion sensors.

Over more than 3 years, the researchers collected data from 93 volunteers (average age, 85) who had either normal cognition, amnestic MCI (the form that usually precedes Alzheimer disease), or nonamnestic MCI. They found that participants with amnestic MCI were more likely to experience declines in walking speed. The study suggests that the use of in-home activity monitors offers a new method for detecting changes in motor function that may signal early stages of progression to Alzheimer dementia.

Section 25.3

Diagnostic Guidelines for Alzheimer Disease: Frequently Asked Questions

Text in this section is excerpted from "Diagnostic Guidelines for Alzheimer's Disease: Frequently Asked Questions for the General Public," National Institute on Aging (NIA), June 3, 2011. Reviewed February 2016.

What Are the Main Differences between the 1984 Diagnostic Criteria for Alzheimer Disease and the New Guidelines?

The new guidelines differ from the 1984 diagnostic criteria in a few key ways:

- The new guidelines propose that Alzheimer disease (AD) progresses on a spectrum with three stages—an early, preclinical stage with no symptoms; a middle stage of mild cognitive impairment (MCI); and a final stage of Alzheimer dementia. The 1984 criteria recognized only one stage of disease, Alzheimer dementia.

- The new guidelines expand the criteria for Alzheimer dementia beyond memory loss as the initial or major symptom. They recognize that problems with other aspects of cognition, such as word-finding ability or judgment, may be the first symptom to appear. The 1984 criteria focused on memory loss as the central characteristic of Alzheimer dementia.

- The new guidelines reflect a better understanding of the distinctions between Alzheimer and non-Alzheimer dementias and the possible relationship between Alzheimer disease and cerebrovascular disease (which affects blood vessels that supply the brain). In 1984, these relationships were not well recognized or understood.

- The new guidelines address the use of biomarkers—measures in blood, fluid or imaging that could indicate possible Alzheimer disease. The use of biomarkers for Alzheimer disease is still considered experimental and is appropriate only for use by researchers at this time. The guidelines call for validating and standardizing the use of biomarkers before they can be applied in a clinical setting, like a doctor's office. Biomarkers for Alzheimer disease did not exist when the original criteria were developed in 1984, and have been studied intensively in recent years.

Why Were the Diagnostic Criteria for Alzheimer Disease Revised and Who Led the Effort?

The diagnostic criteria for Alzheimer disease were revised to reflect a better understanding of the disease. During the past 27 years, scientists have learned much about how Alzheimer disease changes the brain, how these changes progress over time, and how they correspond to clinical symptoms. The new guidelines were developed by expert panels convened by the National Institute on Aging and the Alzheimer Association.

How Will Doctors Use the Updated Guidelines to Better Diagnose Alzheimer Disease?

Doctors in clinical practice will use the updated guidelines to better inform their diagnosis of Alzheimer dementia and mild cognitive impairment (MCI). Other aspects of cognition, in addition to memory loss, will now be considered as a possible first symptom of the disorder.

258

At this time, however, the use of neuroimaging and biomarkers is not yet developed enough for clinicians to diagnose the disease in symptom-free people.

My Family Has a History of Alzheimer Disease. Will the New Guidelines Help My Doctor Know If I Will or Will Not One Day Get the Disease?

At this time, doctors cannot predict with any certainty who will or will not develop Alzheimer dementia. Researchers are studying markers in blood and spinal fluid, as well as changes in the brain shown on brain scans, that one day may be able to tell us who is at risk for developing Alzheimer dementia. The guidelines, as used by researchers, will help make this possible.

What Is "Preclinical" Alzheimer Disease?

Preclinical Alzheimer disease is a new concept that indicates that changes in the brain, including deposition of abnormal proteins, can be detected before there are any clinical symptoms. Research will investigate the usefulness of this concept under the new guidelines. The course of Alzheimer disease varies widely from one person to the next, but, generally, scientists have observed that changes in the brain can begin 10 or more years before clinical symptoms like memory loss appear.

What Is Mild Cognitive Impairment? How Is It Different from Alzheimer Dementia?

Mild cognitive impairment (MCI) is a condition characterized by memory issues or other thinking problems that are greater than normal for a person's age and education, but not serious enough to interfere with a person's ability to function independently. Many, but not all, people with MCI progress to Alzheimer dementia. The kinds of problems associated with MCI may also be caused by certain medications, cerebrovascular disease (which affects blood vessels that supply the brain), and other factors. It is important to talk with your doctor because some of the problems brought on by these conditions can be managed or reversed.

How Can Doctors Know When Mild Cognitive Impairment Becomes Early-Stage Alzheimer Dementia?

The Alzheimer disease process progresses slowly, and it can be difficult to identify the transition from MCI to the early stages of dementia. If the symptoms of MCI continue or worsen over time and other cognitive problems become apparent, everyday functions may become compromised, and the patient will have more and more trouble functioning independently. Recently—just as it was a quarter of century ago—the key factor in diagnosing Alzheimer dementia is losing the ability to live independently. It may be, some experts suggest and the new guidelines discuss, that MCI with minor loss of independent function indicates early-stage Alzheimer disease.

Experts can evaluate the extent of cognitive impairment by using neuropsychological tests to measure changes in memory, language, and other cognitive abilities. They also talk to the person and their caregivers and family about any changes in the person's ability to carry out everyday activities, such as paying bills and preparing meals. Not everyone with MCI develops Alzheimer disease. Among people with MCI, impaired ability to learn and retain new information, such as remembering a story or something that happened recently, is associated with an increased likelihood of worsening memory problems leading to Alzheimer dementia.

What Are Biomarkers?

Biomarkers are measures that indicate the presence or absence of disease or factors that can increase or decrease your risk of disease. You are most likely familiar with elevated blood cholesterol as a risk factor for heart disease. In the case of Alzheimer disease, biomarkers being studied include physical changes in the brain, such as shrinkage in specific brain regions, and certain protein levels in blood and cerebrospinal fluid. These changes, which are measured by imaging, blood, and lumbar puncture tests, may detect who is at risk for Alzheimer disease. Biomarkers are also being studied to see how they may be used to measure disease progression or the effect of interventions.

Why Are Some of the New Guidelines to Be Used Only for Research?

At this time, biomarkers are to be used only for research. Investigators are working hard to better understand how biomarkers relate to the underlying disease process and whether biomarker measures can accurately predict who will or will not develop Alzheimer dementia. Biomarker tests also must be standardized to ensure they are measured correctly and consistently before they can be used in all clinical settings.

Can Doctors Use the Guidelines to Diagnose Other Kinds of Dementia besides Alzheimer Disease?

No. The guidelines apply only to Alzheimer disease. In specialized clinical settings and research settings, they may be used to confirm or rule out Alzheimer disease as a cause of cognitive impairment and dementia. Alzheimer disease is the most common form of dementia. Other forms include vascular dementia, which results from strokes or changes in the brain's blood supply; dementia with Lewy bodies; and the frontotemporal disorders. Researchers are still working on the best ways to diagnose these other types of dementia.

Chapter 26

Testing for Alzheimer Disease

Chapter Contents

Section 26.1

Test for Assessing Cognitive Impairment

This section includes excerpts from "Assessing Cognitive Impairment in Older Patients," National Institute on Aging (NIA), October 2014; and text from "Instruments to Detect Cognitive Impairment in Older Adults," National Institute on Aging (NIA), June 2, 2013.

A primary care provider is often the first to address a patient's complaints—or a family's concerns—about memory loss or possible dementia. This section provides information about assessing cognitive impairment in older adults.

With this information, primary care providers can identify emerging cognitive deficits and possible causes, following up with treatment for what may be a reversible health condition. Or, if Alzheimer disease (AD) or another dementia is found, they can help patients and their caregivers prepare for the future.

Why Is It Important to Assess Cognitive Impairment in Older Adults?

Cognitive impairment in older adults has a variety of possible causes, including medication side effects, metabolic and/or endocrine derangements, delirium due to intercurrent illness, depression, and dementia, with Alzheimer dementia being most common. Some causes, like medication side effects and depression, can be reversed with treatment. Others, such as Alzheimer disease, cannot be reversed, but symptoms can be treated for a period of time and families can be prepared for predictable changes.

Most patients with memory, other cognitive, or behavior complaints want a diagnosis to understand the nature of their problem and what to expect. Some patients (or families) are reluctant to mention such complaints because they fear a diagnosis of dementia and the future it portends. In these cases, a primary care provider can explain the benefits of finding out what may be causing the patient's health concerns.

Pharmacological treatment options for Alzheimer disease-related memory loss and other cognitive symptoms are limited, and none can stop or reverse the course of the disease. However, assessing cognitive impairment and identifying its cause, particularly at an early stage, offers several benefits.

Many people who are developing or have dementia do not receive a diagnosis. One study showed that physicians were unaware of cognitive impairment in more than 40 percent of their cognitively impaired patients. Another study found that more than half of patients with dementia had not received a clinical cognitive evaluation by a physician. The failure to evaluate memory or cognitive complaints is likely to hinder treatment of underlying disease and comorbid conditions, and may present safety issues for the patient and others. In many cases, the cognitive problem will worsen over time.

Benefits of Early Screening

- **If screening is negative:** Concerns may be alleviated, at least at that point in time.

- **If screening is positive and further evaluation is warranted:** The patient and physician can take the next step of identifying the cause of impairment (for example, medication side effects, metabolic and/or endocrine imbalance, delirium, depression, Alzheimer disease). This may result in:

- Treating the underlying disease or health condition

- Managing comorbid conditions more effectively

- Averting or addressing potential safety issues

- Allowing the patient to create or update advance directives and plan long-term care

- Ensuring the patient has a caregiver or someone to help with medical, legal, and financial concerns

- Ensuring the caregiver receives appropriate information and referrals

- Encouraging participation in clinical research

When Is Screening Indicated?

The U.S. Preventive Services Task Force (USPSTF), in its recent review and recommendation regarding routine screening for cognitive impairment, noted that "although the overall evidence on routine screening is insufficient, clinicians should remain alert to early signs or symptoms of cognitive impairment (for example, problems with memory or language) and evaluate as appropriate." The Dementia Screening Indicator can help guide clinician decisions about when it may be appropriate to screen for cognitive impairment in the primary care setting.

Trained staff using readily available screening tools need only 10 minutes or less to initially assess a patient for cognitive impairment. While screening results alone are insufficient to diagnose dementia, they are an important first step. The AD8 and Mini-Cog are among many possible tools.

Assessment for cognitive impairment can be performed at any visit but is now a required component of the Medicare Annual Wellness. Coverage for wellness and, importantly, for follow-up visits is available to any patient who has had Medicare Part B coverage for at least 12 months.

How Is Cognitive Impairment Evaluated?

Positive screening results warrant further evaluation. A combination of cognitive testing and information from a person who has frequent contact with the patient, such as a spouse or other care provider, is the best way to more fully assess cognitive impairment.

A primary care provider may conduct an evaluation or refer to a specialist such as a geriatrician, neurologist, geriatric psychiatrist, or neuropsychologist. If available, a local memory disorders clinic or Alzheimer Disease Center may also accept referrals.

Genetic testing, neuroimaging, and biomarker testing are not generally recommended for clinical use at this time. These tests are primarily conducted in research settings.

Interviews to assess memory, behavior, mood, and functional status (especially complex actions such as driving and managing money) are best conducted with the patient alone, so that family members or companions cannot prompt the patient. Information can also be gleaned from the patient's behavior on arrival in the doctor's office and interactions with staff.

Note that patients who are only mildly impaired may be adept at covering up their cognitive deficits and reluctant to address the problem.

Family members or close companions can also be good sources of information. Inviting them to speak privately may allow for a more candid discussion. Per HIPAA (Health Insurance Portability and Accountability Act) regulations, the patient should give permission in advance. An alternative would be to invite the family member or close companion to be in the examining room during the patient's interview and contribute additional information after the patient has spoken. Brief, easy-to-administer informant screening tools, such as the short IQCODE (Informant Questionnaire on Cognitive Decline in the Elderly) or the AD8, are available.

Points to Remember

- Patients should be screened for cognitive impairment if:

  - the person, family members, or others express concerns about changes in his or her memory or thinking, or

  - you observe problems/changes in the patient's memory or thinking, or

  - the patient is age 80 or older.

  Other risk factors that could indicate the need for cognitive-impairment screening include: low education, history of type 2 diabetes, stroke, depression, and trouble managing money or medications.

- Instruments for brief screening are available and can be used in an office visit.

- Patients, particularly those who express a concern, likely want to know what the underlying problem is.

- Refer to a specialist if needed.

Instruments to Detect Cognitive Impairment in Older Adults

Table 26.1. Instruments to Detect Cognitive Impairment in Older Adults

Abbrev	Name	Domains Assessed
3MS	Modified Mini-Mental State Examination	Memory Language Function Attention Visual Context/ Visual-Spatial Additional Domains
7MS	7-Minute Screen	Memory Language Function Attention Cultural Experience Visual Context/ Visual-Spatial Additional Domains

Table 26.1. Continued

Abbrev	Name	Domains Assessed
AD8	Ascertain Dementia 8	Memory Executive Function Language Function Cultural Experience Visual Context/ Visual-Spatial Additional Domains
BIDD	Brief Instrument for Dementia Detection	No information identified
CAMCOG	Cambridge Cognitive Examination	Memory Language Function Attention Visual Context/ Visual-Spatial Additional Domains
CDT	Clock Drawing Test	Memory Executive Function Language Function Attention Visual Context/ Visual-Spatial Additional Domains
GPCOG	General Practitioner Assessment of Cognition	Memory Executive Function Language Function Visual Context/ Visual-Spatial Additional Domains
IQCODE	Informant Questionnaire on Cognitive Decline in the Elderly	Executive Function Cultural Experience Additional Domains
MMSE	Mini-Mental State Examination	Memory Executive Function Language Function Attention Speed of Processing Cultural Experience Visual Context/ Visual-Spatial Additional Domains

Section 26.2

Positron Emission Tomography (PET) and Single Photon Emission Computed Tomography

Text in this section is excerpted from "Nuclear Medicine," National Institute of Biomedical Imaging and Bioengineering (NIBIB), July 2013.

What Is Nuclear Medicine?

Nuclear medicine is a medical specialty that uses radioactive tracers (radiopharmaceuticals) to assess bodily functions and to diagnose and treat disease. Specially designed cameras allow doctors to track the path of these radioactive tracers. Single Photon Emission Computed Tomography or SPECT and Positron Emission Tomography or PET scans are the two most common imaging modalities in nuclear medicine.

What Are Radioactive Tracers?

Radioactive tracers are made up of carrier molecules that are bonded tightly to a radioactive atom. These carrier molecules vary greatly depending on the purpose of the scan. Some tracers employ molecules that interact with a specific protein or sugar in the body and can even employ the patient's own cells. For example, in cases where doctors need to know the exact source of intestinal bleeding they may radiolabel (add radioactive atoms) to a sample of red blood cells taken from the patient and then use a SPECT scan to follow the path of the blood after it has been reinjected into the patient. Any accumulation of radioactivity in the intestines informs doctors of where the problem lies.

For most diagnostic studies in nuclear medicine, the radioactive tracer is administered to a patient by intravenous injection, but a radioactive tracer may also be administered by inhalation, by oral ingestion, or by direct injection into an organ. The mode of tracer administration will depend on the disease process that is to be studied.

269

Approved tracers are called radiopharmaceuticals since they must meet FDA's exacting standards for safety and appropriate performance for the approved clinical use. The Nuclear Medicine Physician will select the tracer that will provide the most specific and reliable information for a patient's particular problem. The tracer that is used determines whether the patient receives a SPECT or PET scan.

What Is Single Photon Emission Computed Tomography (SPECT)?

SPECT imaging instruments provide 3 dimensional (tomographic) images of the distribution of radioactive tracer molecules that have been introduced into the patient's body. The 3D image data sets are computer generated from a large number of projection images of the body recorded at different angles. SPECT imagers have gamma camera detectors that can detect the gamma emissions from the isotopes that have been injected into the patient. Gamma rays are a form of light that move at a different wavelength than visible light. The cameras are mounted on a rotating gantry that allows the detectors to be moved in a tight circle around a patient who is lying motionless on a palette.

What Is Positron Emission Tomography (PET)?

PET scans also use radiopharmaceuticals to create 3 dimensional images. The main difference between SPECT and PET scans is the type of radiotracers used. While SPECT scans measure gamma rays, the decay of the radiotracers used with PET scans produce small particles called positrons. A positron is a particle with roughly the same mass as electron but oppositely charged. These react with electrons in the body and when these two particles combine they annihilate each other. This annihilation produces a small amount of energy in the form of two photons that shoot off in opposite directions. The detectors in the PET scanner measure these photons and use this information to create images of internal organs.

What Are Nuclear Medicine Scans Used For?

SPECT scans are primarily used to diagnose and track the progression of heart disease, such as blocked coronary arteries. There are also radiotracers to detect disorders in bone, gall bladder disease and intestinal bleeding. Recently SPECT agents have become available for aiding in the correct diagnosis of Parkinson disease in the brain, and distinguishing this malady from other anatomically-related movement disorders and dementias.

Recently, a PET probe was approved by the FDA to aid in the accurate diagnosis of Alzheimer disease, which until recently could only be diagnosed with accuracy only after a patient's death. In the absence of this PET imaging test, Alzheimer disease can be difficult to distinguish from vascular dementia or other forms of dementia that affect older people.

The major purpose of PET scans is to detect cancer and monitor its progression, response to treatment, and to detect metastases. Glucose utilization is dependent on the intensity of cellular and tissue activity so it is much higher in rapidly dividing cancer cells. In fact, the degree of aggressiveness for most cancers is roughly paralleled by their rate of glucose utilization. In the last 15 years, slightly modified radiolabeled glucose molecules (F-18 labeled deoxy-glucose or FDG) have been shown to be the best available tracer for detecting cancer and its metastatic spread in the body.

A combination instrument that produces both CT and PET scans of the same body regions in one examination (PET/ CT Scanner) has become the primary imaging tool for the staging of most cancers worldwide.

Section 26.3

Magnetic Resonance Imaging (MRI)

Text in this section is excerpted from "Magnetic Resonance Imaging (MRI)," National Institute of Biomedical Imaging and Bioengineering (NIBIB), May 4, 2013.

What is Magnetic Resonance Imaging?

Magnetic Resonance Imaging (MRI) is a non-invasive imaging technology that produces three dimensional detailed anatomical images without the use of damaging radiation. It is often used for disease detection, diagnosis, and treatment monitoring. It is based on sophisticated technology that excites and detects the change in the direction of the rotational axis of protons found in the water that makes up living tissues.

How Does MRI Work?

MRIs employ powerful magnets which produce a strong magnetic field that forces protons in the body to align with that field. When a radiofrequency current is then pulsed through the patient, the protons are stimulated, and spin out of equilibrium, straining against the pull of the magnetic field. When the radiofrequency field is turned off, the MRI sensors are able to detect the energy released as the protons realign with the magnetic field. The time it takes for the protons to realign with the magnetic field, as well as the amount of energy released, changes depending on the environment and the chemical nature of the molecules. Physicians are able to tell the difference between various types of tissues based on these magnetic properties.

To obtain an MRI image, a patient is placed inside a large magnet and must remain very still during the imaging process in order not to blur the image. Contrast agents (often containing the element Gadolinium) may be given to a patient intravenously before or during the MRI to increase the speed at which protons realign with the magnetic field. The faster the protons realign, the brighter the image.

What Is MRI Used For?

MRI scanners are particularly well suited to image the non-bony parts or soft tissues of the body. They differ from computed tomography (CT), in that they do not use the damaging ionizing radiation of X-rays. The brain, spinal cord and nerves, as well as muscles, ligaments, and tendons are seen much more clearly with MRI than with regular X-rays and CT; for this reason MRI is often used to image knee and shoulder injuries.

In the brain, MRI can differentiate between white matter and grey matter and can also be used to diagnose aneurysms and tumors. Because MRI does not use X-rays or other radiation, it is the imaging modality of choice when frequent imaging is required for diagnosis or therapy, especially in the brain. However, MRI is more expensive than X-ray imaging or CT scanning.

One kind of specialized MRI is functional Magnetic Resonance Imaging (fMRI.) This is used to observe brain structures and determine which areas of the brain "activate" (consume more oxygen) during various cognitive tasks. It is used to advance the understanding of brain organization and offers a potential new standard for assessing neurological status and neurosurgical risk.

Are There Risks?

Although MRI does not emit the damaging ionizing radiation that is found in X-ray and CT imaging, it does employ a strong magnetic field. The magnetic field extends beyond the machine and exerts very powerful forces on objects of iron, some steels, and other magnetizable objects; it is strong enough to fling a wheelchair across the room. Patients should notify their physicians of any form of medical or implant prior to an MR scan.

When having an MRI scan, the following should be taken into consideration:

- **People with implants, particularly those containing iron,**—pacemakers, vagus nerve stimulators, implantable cardioverter- defibrillators, loop recorders, insulin pumps, cochlear implants, deep brain stimulators, and capsules from capsule endoscopy should not enter an MRI machine.

- **Noise**—loud noise commonly referred to as clicking and beeping, as well as sound intensity up to 120 decibels in certain MR scanners, may require special ear protection.

- **Nerve Stimulation**—a twitching sensation sometimes results from the rapidly switched fields in the MRI.

- **Contrast agents**—patients with severe renal failure who require dialysis may risk a rare but serious illness called nephrogenic systemic fibrosis that may be linked to the use of certain gadolinium-containing agents, such as gadodiamide and others. Although a causal link has not been established, current guidelines in the United States recommend that dialysis patients should only receive gadolinium agents when essential, and that dialysis should be performed as soon as possible after the scan to remove the agent from the body promptly.

- **Pregnancy**—while no effects have been demonstrated on the fetus, it is recommended that MRI scans be avoided as a precaution especially in the first trimester of pregnancy when the fetus' organs are being formed and contrast agents, if used, could enter the fetal bloodstream.

- **Claustrophobia**—people with even mild claustrophobia may find it difficult to tolerate long scan times inside the machine. Familiarization with the machine and process, as well as visualization techniques, sedation, and anesthesia provide patients with mechanisms to overcome their discomfort. Additional coping mechanisms include listening to music or watching a video or movie, closing or covering the eyes, and holding a panic button. The open MRI is a machine that is open on the sides rather than a tube closed at one end, so it does not fully surround the patient. It was developed to accommodate the needs of patients who are uncomfortable with the narrow tunnel and noises of the traditional MRI and for patients whose size or weight make the traditional MRI impractical. Newer open MRI technology provides high quality images for many but not all types of examinations.

Section 26.4

Biomarker Testing for Alzheimer Disease

This section includes excerpts from "Biomarkers Can Predict Risk for Alzheimer's Several Years before Symptoms Appear," National Institute on Aging (NIA), June 15, 2013; and text from "Alzheimer's Disease Progress Report," National Institute on Aging (NIA), December 2015.

Biomarkers Can Predict Risk for Alzheimer Disease Several Years before Symptoms Appear

Brain imaging and spinal-fluid testing can help predict which cognitively normal older people will develop Alzheimer disease (AD) as many as 7.5 years before symptoms appear, according to a new study supported in part by the NIA. The findings confirm the power of biomarkers as predictors of disease risk in the earliest, symptom-free stages of Alzheimer disease. These biomarkers may prove to be valuable tools in testing promising treatments in future studies.

While not typically used in clinical practice, investigators worldwide are studying, refining, and standardizing biomarkers aimed at identifying who is at risk for developing Alzheimer disease, the most common form of dementia in older adults. The biomarkers in this study include positron emission tomography (PET) scans of the brain to detect deposits of the telltale protein beta-amyloid, as well as levels of beta-amyloid and another protein, tau, found in cerebrospinal fluid.

The research team, at Washington University School of Medicine in St. Louis, tracked the cognition of 201 dementia-free volunteers, ages 45 to 88, at the school's Alzheimer Disease Research Center. The researchers found that abnormal levels of biomarkers identified in PET scans and lumbar punctures could predict who would develop cognitive impairment among the volunteers who were followed for an average of 3.7 years, but in some cases as long as 7.5 years.

Some 28 volunteers (14 percent) of the group developed memory loss and other signs of cognitive impairment. Abnormal levels of all biomarkers predicted the development of Alzheimer dementia equally well, the study found. Older participants, men, and African Americans who developed dementia did so faster than those who were younger, female, and white, the researchers report. In a few cases, participants with abnormal biomarker levels remained cognitively normal, perhaps because of "cognitive reserve," the ability of some brains to cope with or stave off decline.

Blood Biomarkers May Predict Future Dementia Risk

A panel of 10 blood lipids might be used to predict future cognitive impairment in asymptomatic older adults, according to researchers who observed 525 otherwise healthy participants, age 70 and older, for 5 years. Forty-six of the participants met the clinical criteria for mild cognitive impairment or Alzheimer disease at the start of the study, and 28 others (called "converters") developed clinical symptoms over the course of the study.

The researchers analyzed blood samples donated by the volunteers. Among the thousands of metabolites (products of cellular metabolism) the researchers measured, they identified 10 lipids that distinguished the converters from those who remained cognitively healthy. To validate the finding, they studied another 40 participants and confirmed that the 10-lipid panel predicted with 90 percent accuracy who among the cognitively healthy group would later develop mild cognitive impairment or Alzheimer disease.

If the results of this study are confirmed in larger and more ethnically diverse groups of subjects, blood lipid tests may offer an easy and inexpensive way to predict risk for Alzheimer disease.

The Way Forward in Biomarker Research

Advances in imaging and fluid biomarkers over the past decade have led to remarkable results. Researchers can now "see" Alzheimer disease-related pathology and structural and functional changes in the living brain, tract disease onset and progression, and use these approaches for testing the effectiveness of promising drugs. To build on these successes, researchers hope to concentrate studies in this area by:

- Developing and validating a full range of translatable biomarkers for use in preclinical and clinical drug development

- Advancing the use of novel positron emission tomography ligands, as well as cerebrospinal fluid (CSF) and blood biomarkers, to identify and access Alzheimer disease pathologies, including tau, inflammation, and synaptic dysfunction

- Developing minimally invasive biomarkers (for example, EEG, blood) for detection and monitoring of Alzheimer disease-related pathology in the brain

- Developing and refining sensitive clinical and neuropsychological assessment measures to detect and track early-stage disease.

Chapter 27

Overview of Alzheimer Disease Interventions

About Alzheimer Disease: Treatment

How Is Alzheimer Disease Treated?

Alzheimer disease (AD) is complex, and it is unlikely that any one drug or other intervention can successfully treat it. Current approaches focus on helping people maintain mental function, manage behavioral symptoms, and slow or delay the symptoms of disease.

What Drugs Are Currently Available to Treat Alzheimer Disease (AD)?

Several medications are approved by the U.S. Food and Drug Administration to treat symptoms of Alzheimer disease. Donepezil (Aricept®), rivastigmine (Exelon®), and galantamine (Razadyne®) are used to treat mild to moderate AD (donepezil can be used for severe AD as well). Memantine (Namenda®), is used to treat moderate to severe AD.

These drugs work by regulating neurotransmitters, the brain chemicals that transmit messages between neurons. They may help maintain thinking, memory, and communication skills and help with

This chapter includes excerpts from "About Alzheimer's Disease: Treatment," National Institute on Aging (NIA), May 15, 2015; and text from "Alzheimer's Disease Progress Report," National Institute on Aging (NIA), December 2015.

certain behavioral problems. However, these drugs don't change the underlying disease process. They are effective for some but not all people and may help only for a limited time.

No published study directly compares the four approved drugs. Because they work in a similar way, it is not expected that switching from one of these drugs to another will produce significantly different results. However, a patient may respond better to one drug than another.

Are There Treatments Available for Managing Behavioral Symptoms?

Common behavioral symptoms of Alzheimer disease include sleeplessness, wandering, agitation, anxiety, and depression. Scientists are learning why these symptoms occur and are studying new treatments—drug and nondrug—to manage them. Research has shown that treating behavioral symptoms can make people with Alzheimer disease more comfortable and makes things easier for caregivers.

What Potential New Treatments Are Being Researched?

Alzheimer disease research has developed to a point where scientists can look beyond treating symptoms to think about addressing underlying disease processes. In ongoing clinical trials, scientists are developing and testing several possible interventions, including immunization therapy, drug therapies, cognitive training, physical activity, and treatments used for cardiovascular disease and diabetes.

Recent progress in drug discovery and development includes a number of studies indicating how new approaches may modify underlying mechanisms of disease. Pursuit of innovative research in this area will lead more quickly to design of new therapies and their testing.

Recent studies have shown:

Cancer Drug Offers Hope for Alzheimer

NIH's National Center for Advancing Translational Sciences (NCATS) is supporting the testing of an experimental drug, originally developed to fight cancer, that may prove effective against Alzheimer disease. The drug, saracatinib, proved safe in human trials but was shelved by the biopharmaceutical company AstraZeneca when it proved unsuccessful at targeting a family of enzymes (called src kinases) involved in the spread of cancer.

In 2012, researchers discovered that a related kinase called Fyn may play a key role in Alzheimer disease. They found that mis-folded beta-amyloid protein—a hallmark of Alzheimer—interacts with another protein to activate Fyn excessively and spur the loss of synapses.

The scientists wanted to test whether a precisely targeted com-pound, such as saracatinib, could block Fyn. They reached out to NCATS's Discovering New Therapeutic Uses for Existing Molecules program, a pioneering partnership between NIH and industry in which pharmaceutical companies offer compounds that have failed to the sci-entific community to repurpose for the development of new therapies. AstraZeneca provided saracatinib at no cost. The researchers gave the compound to mice with Alzheimer disease-like symptoms for 4 weeks and found they could turn off Fyn, get brain synapses firing again, and reverse memory loss. Because saracatinib had already passed human safety tests, the researchers are now conducting a Phase II clinical trial to test its effectiveness in about 150 people with mild Alzheimer disease.

New Compounds Stabilize Neurons

Neurons are supported internally by networks of microtubules, microscopic rods of protein that help maintain a neuron's complex structure and shuttle nutrients around inside it. The protein tau nor-mally stabilizes microtubules, but the abnormal forms of tau that accumulate in AD cause microtubules to fall apart.

Drugs that stabilize microtubules have shown therapeutic benefit in AD model mice. However, when given orally, they became inactive and/ or had the potentially lethal side effect of blocking the P-glycoprotein transporter, a protein that helps clear drugs and toxins from the body.

Researchers recently identified two new classes of compounds that substantially enhanced the stability of brain microtubules in normal mice within 4 to 6 days. These two new classes of microtubule-sta-bilizing agents can be taken orally, cross into the brain, and do not block the P-glycoprotein transporter. These results offer insights on the development and testing of compounds that may prevent damage to neurons.

Drug Seems to Suppress Brain Inflammation

In Alzheimer disease, the brain shows signs of chronic inflamma-tion, a tissue response to toxic proteins or cellular injury. The inflam-matory response is mounted by glial cells (the support cells of the brain) through the release of proteins called cytokines. In the short term, inflammation promotes tissue repair. But if the inflammatory response persists for months or years, as it does in Alzheimer and other neurodegenerative diseases, it can ultimately contribute to neuronal damage.

Researchers recently developed a drug called MW 181 to try to control destructive inflammation in neurons. It targets the enzyme p38 MAPK, which helps trigger the production of proinflammatory and potentially damaging cytokines by glia and other cell types.

The researchers showed that the drug delivered orally in mice inhibited the targeted enzyme. They then administered the drug to mice shortly before injecting them with a bacterial membrane molecule that provokes a strong brain inflammatory response. The drug significantly suppressed the production of several pro-inflammatory cytokines in the brain. These results, while preliminary, offer promise for taking the compound into an early-stage human trial.

Protein May Help Neurons Repair Damaged DNA

In people with Alzheimer disease, the ability to repair damaged neurons is severely impaired. Scientists in the National Institute on Aging (NIA) Intramural Research Program, Baltimore, studied whether and how brain-derived neurotrophic factor (BDNF), a protein that protects neurons, could affect the ability of brain cells to repair DNA damaged by oxidative stress.

Previous animal studies have shown that exercise can increase the low levels of BDNF found in Alzheimer disease mouse models. The NIA team found that mice exercising on running wheels increased BDNF by activating the CREB protein, which then stimulated the production of APE1, an enzyme that helps repair DNA.

These findings provide a possible explanation for the protective effect of exercise on cognition that has been observed in some studies and offer further rationale for ongoing and new studies of exercise to prevent cognitive decline. In addition, these findings suggest that exercise may enhance the ability of neurons to repair oxidative damage to DNA and that APE1 may be a promising new therapeutic target.

New Insights on Causes of Early—Onset Alzheimer Disease

Mutations in the presenilin-1 gene are the most common cause of inherited, early-onset forms of Alzheimer disease. Numerous studies have suggested that the mutations increase activity of gamma secretase, an enzyme involved in the development of abnormal levels of amyloid plaques in the brain. However, clinical trials testing drugs that block gamma-secretase have so far failed to halt the disease.

NIH-supported researchers developed a new animal model to better understand how these genetic changes may lead to the development of Alzheimer disease. They replaced the normal mouse presenilin-1 gene with Alzheimer disease-causing forms of the human gene and discovered that the mutation may cause the disease by decreasing—rather than increasing—gamma-secretase activity. These new insights into a mechanism involved in Alzheimer disease suggest that developing therapies that promote gamma secretase activity may be a promising avenue of research.

What Are Clinical Trials?

People who want to help scientists test possible treatments may be able to take part in clinical trials, which are research studies that test the safety, side effects, and effectiveness of a medication or other intervention in humans. Study volunteers help scientists learn about the brain in healthy aging and in Alzheimer disease. Results of clinical trials are used to improve prevention and treatment approaches.

Chapter 28

Alzheimer Disease Medications

Medicines to Treat AD Symptoms and Behaviors

People with Alzheimer Disease (AD) May Take Medications to Treat:

- The disease itself

- Mood or other behavior changes

- Other medical conditions they may have

Caregivers need to know about **each** medicine that a person with AD takes.

Ask the Doctor or Pharmacist the Questions below and Write down the Answers:

- Why is this medicine being used?

- What positive effects should I look for, and when?

- How long will the person need to take it?

- How much should he or she take each day?

This chapter includes excerpts from "Caring for a Person with Alzheimer's Disease: Your Easy-to-Use Guide," National Institute on Aging (NIA), July 2012; and text from "Alzheimer's Disease Medications: Fact Sheet," National Institute on Aging (NIA), June 2015.

- When does the person need to take the medicine?
- What are the side effects?
- What can I do about these side effects?
- Can the medicine be crushed and mixed into foods such as applesauce?
- Can I get the medicine in a liquid form?
- Can this medicine cause problems if taken with other medicines?

Reminders to Take Medicine

People with AD often need help taking their medicine. If the person still lives alone, you may need to call and remind him or her. It's also helpful to buy a pillbox and put pills for each day in the box. That way all the pills for the day are in one place. You can get pillboxes at the drugstore. **As the disease gets worse, you will need to keep track of his or her medicines. You also will need to make sure they take the medicine or you will need to give them the medicine.** Ask the doctor or pharmacist about when to give the medications.

Alzheimer Disease Medications

Several prescription drugs are currently approved by the U.S. Food and Drug Administration (FDA) to treat people who have been diagnosed with Alzheimer disease. Treating the symptoms of Alzheimer disease can provide patients with comfort, dignity, and independence for a longer period of time and can encourage and assist their caregivers as well.

It is important to understand that none of these medications stops the disease itself.

Treatment for Mild to Moderate Alzheimer Disease

Medications called cholinesterase inhibitors are prescribed for mild to moderate Alzheimer disease. These drugs may help delay or prevent symptoms from becoming worse for a limited time and may help control some behavioral symptoms. The medications include Razadyne® (galantamine), Exelon® (rivastigmine), and Aricept® (donepezil). Scientists do not yet fully understand how cholinesterase inhibitors work to treat Alzheimer disease, but research indicates that they prevent the breakdown of acetylcholine, a brain chemical believed to be important for memory and thinking. As Alzheimer disease progresses, the brain produces less and less acetylcholine; therefore, cholinesterase inhibitors may eventually lose their effect.

No published study directly compares these drugs. Because they work in a similar way, switching from one of these drugs to another probably will not produce significantly different results. However, an Alzheimer disease patient may respond better to one drug than another.

Treatment for Moderate to Severe Alzheimer Disease

A medication known as Namenda® (memantine), an N-methyl D-aspartate (NMDA) antagonist, is prescribed to treat moderate to severe Alzheimer disease. This drug's main effect is to delay progression of some of the symptoms of moderate to severe Alzheimer disease. It may allow patients to maintain certain daily functions a little longer than they would without the medication. For example, Namenda® may help a patient in the later stages of the disease maintain his or her ability to use the bathroom independently for several more months, a benefit for both patients and caregivers.

The FDA has also approved Aricept® and Namzaric®, a combination of Namenda® and donepezil, for the treatment of moderate to severe Alzheimer disease.

Namenda® is believed to work by regulating glutamate, an important brain chemical. When produced in excessive amounts, glutamate may lead to brain cell death. Because NMDA antagonists work very differently from cholinesterase inhibitors, the two types of drugs can be prescribed in combination.

Dosage and Side Effects

Doctors usually start patients at low drug doses and gradually increase the dosage based on how well a patient tolerates the drug. There is some evidence that certain patients may benefit from higher doses of the cholinesterase inhibitors. However, the higher the dose, the more likely are side effects. The recommended effective dosages of drugs prescribed to treat the symptoms of Alzheimer and the drugs' possible side effects are summarized in the table.

Patients should be monitored when a drug is started. Report any unusual symptoms to the prescribing doctor right away. It is important to follow the doctor's instructions when taking any medication,

Table 28.1. Medications to Treat Alzheimer Disease

Medications to Treat Alzheimer Disease

This brief summary does not include all information important for patient use and should not be used as a substitute for professional medical advice. Consult the prescribing doctor and read the package insert before using these or any other medications or supplements.

Drug Name	Drug Type and Use	How It Works	Common Side Effects	Manufacturer's Recommended Dosage
Aricept® (donepezil)	Cholinesterase inhibitor prescribed to treat symptoms of mild, moderate, and severe Alzheimer	Prevents the breakdown of acetylcholine in the brain	Nausea, vomiting, diarrhea, muscle cramps, fatigue, weight loss	• Tablet*: Initial dose of 5 mg once a day • May increase dose to 10 mg/day after 4-6 weeks if well tolerated, then to • 23 mg/day after at least 3 months • Orally disintegrating tablet*: Same dosage as above • 23-mg dose available as brand-name tablet only
Exelon® (rivastigmine)	Cholinesterase inhibitor prescribed to treat symptoms of mild to moderate Alzheimer (patch is also for severe Alzheimer)	Prevents the breakdown of acetylcholine and butyrylcholine (a brain chemical similar to acetylcholine) in the brain	Nausea, vomiting, diarrhea, weight loss, decreased appetite, muscle weakness	• Capsule*: Initial dose of 3 mg/day (1.5 mg twice a day) • May increase dose to 6 mg/day (3 mg twice a day), 9 mg (4.5 mg twice a day), and 12 mg/day (6 mg twice a day) at minimum 2-week intervals if well tolerated

Table 28.1. Continued

Medications to Treat Alzheimer Disease

This brief summary does not include all information important for patient use and should not be used as a substitute for professional medical advice. Consult the prescribing doctorand read the package insert before using these or any other medications or supplements.

Drug Name	Drug Type and Use	How It Works	Common Side Effects	Manufacturer's Recommended Dosage
				• Patch: Initial dose of 4.6 mg once a day; may increase dose to 9.5 mg once a day and 13.3 mg once a day at minimum 4-week intervals if well tolerated • Oral solution: Same dosage as capsule
Namenda® (memantine)	N-methyl D-aspartate (NMDA) antagonist prescribed to treat symptoms of moderate to severe Alzheimer.	Blocks the toxic effects associated with excess glutamate and regulates glutamate activation	Dizziness, headache, diarrhea, constipation, confusion	• Tablet: Initial dose of 5 mg once a day • May increase dose to 10 mg/day (5 mg twice a day), 15 mg/day (5 mg and 10 mg as separate doses), and 20 mg/day (10 mg twice a day) at minimum 1-week intervals if well tolerated • Oral solution: Same dosage as above • Extended-release capsule: Initial dose of 7 mg once a day; may increase dose to 14 mg/day, 21mg/day, and 28 mg/day at minimum 1-week intervals if well tolerated

Table 28.1. Continued

Medications to Treat Alzheimer Disease

This brief summary does not include all information important for patient use and should not be used as a substitute for professional medical advice. Consult the prescribing doctorand read the package insert before using these or any other medications or supplements.

Drug Name	Drug Type and Use	How It Works	Common Side Effects	Manufacturer's Recommended Dosage
Namzaric® (memantine extended release and donepezil)	NMDA antagonist and cholinesterase inhibitor prescribed to treat symptoms of moderate to severe Alzheimer	Blocks the toxic effects associated with excess glutamate and prevents the breakdown of acetylcholine in the brain	Headache, nausea, vomiting, diarrhea, dizziness, decreased appetite	• Capsule: 28 mg memantine extended-release + 10 mg donepezil once a day • 14 mg memantine extended-release + 10 mg donepezil once a day (for patients with severe renal impairment)
Razadyne® (galantamine)	Cholinesterase inhibitor prescribed to treat symptoms of mild to moderate Alzheimer	Prevents the breakdown of acetylcholine and stimulates nicotinic receptors to release more acetylcholine in the brain	Nausea, vomiting, diarrhea, weight loss, decreased appetite, muscle weakness	• Tablet*: Initial dose of 8 mg/day (4 mg twice a day) • May increase dos e to 16 mg/day (8 mg twice a day) and 24 mg/day (12 mg twice a day) at minimum 4-week intervals if well tolerated • Oral solution*: Same dosage as above • Extended-release capsule*: Same dosage as above but taken once a day

*Available as a generic drug.

Testing New Alzheimer Drugs

Clinical trials are the best way to find out if promising new treatments are safe and effective in humans. Volunteers are needed for many Alzheimer trials conducted around the United States. To learn more, talk with your doctor or visit the ADEAR Center's listing of clinical trials at www.nia.nih.gov/alzheimers/clinical-trials. More information is available at www.nia.nih.gov/alzheimers/volunteer.

---

including vitamins and herbal supplements. Also, let the doctor know before adding or changing any medications.

Medicines to Treat Behavior Problems Related to AD

Examples of behavior problems that can occur in AD are restlessness, anxiety, depression, trouble sleeping, and aggression. Experts agree that medicines to treat these behavior problems should be used only after other strategies that don't use medicine have been tried. Some of these tips are listed in Challenge: changes in personality and behavior. If they don't work and the person with AD continues to be upset, restless, depressed, or aggressive, he or she may need medicine. Talk with the doctor about which medicines are safest and most effective to help with these problems.

Remember the following Tips about Medicines:

• Use the lowest dose possible.

• Watch for side effects. Be prepared to stop the medicine if they occur.

• Allow the medicine a few weeks to take effect.

Below is a list of medicines used to help with depression, aggression, restlessness, and anxiety.

Antidepressants are drugs used to treat depression and worry (also called anxiety).

289

Examples of these medicines include:

- Celexa®, brand name; citalopram, generic name
- Remeron®, brand name; mirtazepine, generic name
- Zoloft®, brand name; sertraline, generic name

Anticonvulsants are drugs sometimes used to treat severe aggression.

Examples of these medicines include:

- Depakote®, brand name; sodium valproate, generic name
- Tegretol®, brand name; carbamazepine, generic name
- Trileptal®, brand name; oxcarbazepine, generic name

Medicines to Be Used with Caution

There are some medicines, such as sleep aids, anti-anxiety drugs, and antipsychotics, that the person with AD should take only:

- After the doctor has explained all the risks and side effects of the medicine
- After other, safer medicines have not helped treat the problem

You will need to watch closely for side effects from these medications.

Sleep aids are used to help people get to sleep and stay asleep. People with AD should NOT use these drugs on a regular basis because they make the person more confused and more likely to fall.
Examples of these medicines include:

- Ambien®, brand name; zolpidem, generic name
- Lunesta®, brand name; eszopiclone, generic name
- Sonata®, brand name; zaleplon, generic name

Anti-anxiety drugs are used to treat agitation. These drugs can cause sleepiness, dizziness, falls, and confusion. Therefore, doctors recommend using them only for short periods of time.

Examples of these medicines include:

- Ativan®, brand name; lorazepam, generic name
- Klonopin®, brand name; clonazepam, generic name

Antipsychotics are drugs used to treat paranoia, hallucinations, agitation, and aggression. Side effects of using these drugs can be serious, including increased risk of death in some older people with dementia. They should **ONLY** be given to people with AD when the doctor agrees that the symptoms are severe.

Examples of these medicines include:

* Risperdal®, brand name; risperidone, generic name

* Seroquel®, brand name; quetiapine, generic name

* Zyprexa®, brand name; olanzapine, generic name

Medicines That People with AD Should Not Take

Anticholinergic drugs are used to treat many medical problems such as sleeping problems, stomach cramps, incontinence, asthma, motion sickness, and muscle spasms. Side effects, such as confusion, can be serious for a person with AD. These drugs should **NOT** be given to a person with AD. You might talk with the person's doctor about other, safer drugs.

Examples of these drugs include:

* Atrovent®, brand name; ipratropium, generic name

* Combivent®, brand name; ipratropium and albuterol, generic names

* DuoNeb®, brand name; ipratropium and albuterol, generic names

* Spiriva®, brand name; tiotropium, generic name

Medicines to Treat Other Medical Conditions

Many people with AD also have other medical problems such as diabetes, high blood pressure, or heart disease. They may take different medicines for these problems. It's important to track all the medicines they take. Make a list of their medicines and take the list with you when you visit their doctors.

Chapter 29

Non-Pharmacological Therapies for Alzheimer Disease

Reminiscence Therapy

Summary: With the exception of one small trial (N=17) that showed a benefit on mood, this limited body of evidence of small trials does not support the use of reminiscence therapy for the treatment of behavioral symptoms of dementia.

Details: Reminiscence therapy involves the discussion of past activities, events and experiences with another person or group of people. Reminiscence therapy uses materials such as old newspapers, photographs, household and other familiar items from the past to stimulate memories and enable people to share and value their experiences. General reminiscence in a group context aims to enhance interaction, whereas life review usually involves individual sessions in which the person is guided chronologically through life experiences and encouraged to evaluate them. Studies have suggested that reminiscence work assists in reducing depression in older people, and both of these approaches might plausibly have an impact on mood and well-being.

Text in this chapter is excerpted from "A Systematic Evidence Review of Non-Pharmacological Interventions for Behavioral Symptoms of Dementia," Department of Veterans Affairs (VA), March 2011. Reviewed February 2016.

We found one systematic review that focused on reminiscence therapy as a treatment for dementia. Four RCTs that included a combined total of 144 subjects were included in the findings of this review. Three of the RCTs assessed behavioral symptoms and found no effect of reminiscence therapy on these symptoms. One RCT (N=17) compared the effects of 12 individual weekly sessions of reminiscence therapy with no treatment, and found statistically significant improvements in depression at six weeks in the treatment group, but found no differences in other behavioral symptoms between groups.

A systematic review examining a variety of interventions included three small RCTs (combined N=38) of reminiscence therapy, and found no clear benefit. Other reviews that examined reminiscence therapy in addition to other interventions similarly found no effects of reminiscence therapy on behavioral symptoms.

Simulated Presence Therapy (SPT)

Summary: The findings of the included studies are mixed, and well-conducted studies are lacking. This body of research did not find consistent evidence that SPT reduces behavioral symptoms of dementia. In addition, there is some indication that SPT may worsen behavioral symptoms of dementia in some individuals.

Details: Simulated presence therapy (SPT) involves the use of audiotapes made by family members containing scripted "telephone conversations" about cherished memories from earlier life, in an effort to tap remote memory, improve behavioral symptoms, and enhance quality of life among persons with dementia.

Our search identified one systematic review that focused on SPT for the treatment of behavioral symptoms of dementia. A meta-analysis found a statistically significant effect of SPT on disruptive, agitated, or depressed behaviors from pre- to post-intervention, but this analysis was based on three small quasi-experimental studies (ranging from six to nine subjects in each) and one small RCT (N=30). Furthermore, there was significant statistical heterogeneity between studies and substantial variation in the research designs used, the measures used to assess challenging behavior, and the administration of SPT.

The review identified three additional studies that could not be combined in the meta-analysis; of these, two studies found that SPT was effective in reducing challenging behaviors, and the third found no overall benefit and that the response to SPT may differ among individuals. Furthermore, three studies identified in the review reported that SPT actually increased agitation or disruptive behaviors in some participants. The authors of the review noted the importance of assessing participants' suitability for emotion-oriented approaches and monitoring their responses closely.

A review of multiple interventions included one non-randomized controlled study of SPT vs. recorded readings from a newspaper and found no statistically significant differences in monitored behaviors.

Validation Therapy

Summary: The findings are mixed, and the evidence is insufficient to draw conclusions about the efficacy of the treatment of validation therapy for dementia.

Details: Validation therapy is based on the general principle of validation, the acceptance of the reality and personal truth of another's experience, and incorporates a range of specific techniques. Validation therapy is intended to give the individual an opportunity to resolve unfinished conflicts by encouraging and validating expression of feelings.

One systematic review focused on validation therapy for the treatment of dementia. The review included three RCTs with a combined total of 146 subjects. Comparison groups in the studies included usual care, social contact (activities such as music, art, literature, dance, and games), and reality orientation. One study compared the effects of validation therapy, reality orientation, and usual care on behavioral symptoms among 31 nursing home residents. Participants in the treatment group received 30-minute validation sessions, five days a week, for six weeks. At the end of the treatment period, the study found a significant difference in Behavior Assessment Tool (BAT) scores in favor of validation therapy compared to usual care, but there were no significant differences between validation therapy and reality orientation therapy.

The second study compared usual care to validation therapy (30-minute sessions, four days per week for 52 weeks) given to 27 residents of a large VA Medical Center (VAMC). The study found no significant differences in behavior after nine months of therapy. In a study of 88 patients from four nursing homes, a beneficial effect on depression was observed at 12 months in favor of validation therapy compared with social contact, but there was no difference compared to usual care.

Three additional systematic reviews that examined validation therapy in addition to other forms of therapy found no statistically significant findings in favor of validation therapy for reducing behavioral symptoms of dementia.

Acupuncture

Summary: There are currently no good quality trials evaluating acupuncture for the treatment of behavioral symptoms associated with dementia.

Details: Acupuncture is an ancient Chinese method which has been used for both the prevention and treatment of diseases for over 3,000 years. One systematic review evaluated acupuncture in patients with vascular dementia. The review found 17 RCTs, but found them all to be ineligible for the following reasons:

1. the control group received some form of Western medicine in six studies;

2. there was inadequate randomization in four studies;

3. acupuncture was used in conjunction with another therapy and the effects of acupuncture could not be evaluated separately in six studies; and

4. insufficient information was available for one study. Because none of the identified RCTs met inclusion criteria for this review, the effectiveness and safety of acupuncture could not be analyzed.

The authors of the review emphasized the need for randomized placebo-controlled trials of acupuncture.

Aromatherapy

Summary: There is limited evidence that aromatherapy may be an effective treatment for the behavioral symptom of agitation.

Details: Aromatherapy consists of the use of fragrant oils from plants. Aromatherapy has been used in attempts to reduce behavioral symptoms, to promote sleep, and to stimulate motivational behavior in people with dementia. Much of the literature on aromatherapy comes from qualitative research and small scale non-randomized trials.

One systematic review focused solely on aromatherapy, but only one RCT met its inclusion criteria. This clustered RCT included

72 participants with severe dementia in eight nursing homes. The four-week study examined the effects of topical Melissa oil, and sunflower oil was used at control nursing homes. Though the study found a significant decrease in measures of agitation and neuropsychiatric symptoms, there was no significant decrease in aggression, and important differences among participants such as medication use were not accounted for.

A study cited in another systematic review similarly found that aromatherapy was associated with decreased agitation among dementia patients. In this study of 15 individuals, two percent lavender oil or water vapor was sprayed in a communal area of a dementia ward for two hours a day, on alternating days for 10 sessions. Agitation was assessed during the last hour of each session using the Pittsburgh Agitation Scale, by an observer who wore a nose clip in an effort to be blinded to the intervention. Median behavior scores were 20 percent lower while exposed to lavender compared to water vapor, and the difference was statistically significant (p= 0.016).

Light Therapy

Summary: There is insufficient evidence to draw any conclusions about the effectiveness of bright light therapy in managing sleep, behavior, or mood disturbances associated with dementia.

Details: Rest-activity and sleep-wake cycles are controlled by the endogenous circadian rhythm generated by the suprachiasmatic nuclei (SCN) of the hypothalamus. Degenerative changes in the SCN appear to be a biological basis of circadian disturbances in people with dementia. In addition to the internal regulatory loss, elderly people (especially those with dementia) experience a reduction in sensory input because they are visually less sensitive to light and have less exposure to bright environmental light. Evidence suggests that circadian disturbances may be reversed by stimulation of the SCN by light.

One Cochrane review examined RCTs of the effects of light therapy on sleep, behavior, and mood disturbances among patients with dementia in long-term care facilities. Only two studies met methodological and design criteria for inclusion in the review. One small RCT compared dawn-dusk simulation (maximum 400 lux) to dim red light (<5 lux) for three weeks among 13 nursing home residents. There were no significant differences in any outcome: nocturnal sleep duration, night-time activity, sleep latency (defined as the amount of time between reclining in bed and the onset of sleep), agitation (Neuropsychiatric Inventory; NPI), and depression (Geriatric Depression

Scale; GDS) measured at the end of light therapy and three weeks post-treatment.

Another RCT randomly assigned 92 nursing home residents with severe Alzheimer disease (AD) to receive morning bright light, evening bright light, or morning dim red light for 10 days. The study found no differences between groups in sleep duration or agitation at the end of therapy and at five days post-treatment.

An older systematic review included four studies of bright light therapy, three of which reported beneficial effects on agitation and nocturnal restlessness during bright light treatment (1500–2500 lux). The studies were limited by small sample size (N < 24), and three of the studies had samples of 10 subjects or fewer.

Massage and Touch Therapy

Summary: Though the true effect of massage and touch on behavioral symptoms is uncertain, this very small body of evidence preliminarily suggests that hand massage and touch may be a viable treatment option, especially given the ease of implementation and minimal training involved.

Details: Massage and touch are among the interventions used in dementia care with the aim of reducing depression, anxiety, aggression and other related psychological and behavioral manifestations. Expressive touch such as patting or holding a client's hand involves emotional intent, for example, to calm a patient or to show concern, as opposed to instrumental/task-associated touch within nursing care.

A 2005 review focused on RCTs of massage and touch therapies for dementia. Eligibility criteria required that studies used a RCT design, employed blinding of outcome assessors, and measured changes in agitated behavior. Of 34 references identified by the search, only two small RCTs met these criteria. One RCT of 42 institutionalized patients with organic brain syndrome compared verbal encouragement with touch to verbal encouragement alone during meals, and found that touch therapy was associated with a significant increase in mean calorie and protein intake. The second RCT assessed the effect of hand massage vs. calming music, and simultaneous hand massage and calming music vs. no intervention. Sixty-eight participants were randomly assigned to one of four groups. Interventions consisted of a single 10-minute treatment. Researchers found a greater decrease in agitated behavior (CMAI score) compared with baseline during treatment, immediately after treatment, and one hour after treatment among the groups receiving hand massage compared to the group receiving no treatment. Findings were similar for hand massage, calming music, or both.

Another systematic review that examined touch interventions among other treatments for dementia identified a small RCT that found that an expressive touch intervention that involved 5.5 minutes a day of touching, including 2.5 minutes a day of gentle massage and 3 minutes a day of intermittent touching with someone talking, over a 10-day period decreased disturbed behavior from baseline immediately and for 5 days after the intervention.

Music Therapy

Summary: Music interventions have potential for reducing agitation in persons with dementia in the short-term. Well-conducted studies are lacking, and trials with adequate sample size and rigorous methodology are needed. Some interventions such as listening to recorded music during mealtimes are simple and low-cost, and they may be feasible in VA settings. The feasibility and cost-effectiveness of more resource-intensive interventions, such as individual patient interactions with a professional music therapist, need to be evaluated.

Details: People with dementia may retain the ability to sing old songs, and musical abilities appear to be preserved in individuals with dementia who were musicians despite aphasia and memory loss. Information presented in a song context appears to enhance retention and recall of information, and structured music activities can promote interaction and communication. Music therapy can, therefore, potentially enhance cognitive skills as well as social/emotional skills, and may also serve as an alternative to medication for managing behavioral symptoms of AD.

There is a wide range of music interventions for older people with dementia, including listening to different types of music, instrument playing, or group exercise while listening to music. The range of music interventions includes activities administered by a professional music therapist, as well as the presentation of recorded music by a variety of caregivers, to patients privately or in a group setting.

The literature search for music and music therapy interventions for behavioral symptoms identified 18 reviews that included a total of 104 primary studies. Among these reviews, we selected four systematic reviews, based on quality, recency, and relevance. The most rigorous systematic review was a Cochrane review that conducted a literature search through September 2005, and included three RCTs.

Three other systematic reviews included a wider range of study designs not limited to RCTs.

The Cochrane review determined that trials were poor in quality, citing inadequate reporting of methods of randomization and blinding, as well as inappropriate methods of data analysis in two of the studies. Reviewers concluded that no study presented any quantitative results in sufficient detail to justify the original investigators' conclusions that music listening was more effective than control on behavioral symptoms. In one study, when bathing was accompanied by listening to preferred music (as compared with no music), residents demonstrated significantly less aggressive behaviors. Gerdner (2000) reports that agitation was significantly less frequent during and after music therapy when each patient listened to his or her preferred music compared with standard classical music. Groene (1993) reported that the amount of time a wandering subject remained seated or in close proximity to the session area was longer for music sessions than for reading sessions.

Systematic reviews that included a wider range of study designs consistently concluded that music therapy decreases agitation in the short-term, although there was no evidence of long-term effects. One systematic review examined studies published through 2000, and another included music interventions (including of the same studies) published through 2003. A systematic review of eight studies that specifically examined the use of preferred or individualized music found reductions in agitated behaviors that were statistically significant in all but one study.

Methodological limitations in the music intervention studies include lack of randomization, observational methods and sampling techniques, problems with internal validity, and confounding due to the possible effects of the music intervention on staff. Some studies employed momentary time sampling techniques, where the observer records whether or not the behavior is occurring at the end of a pre-specified time period. This sampling method may tend to overestimate continuous behaviors and underestimate discrete episodes of behavior. Internal validity was questionable in two studies in which some participants were transferred to "geri-chairs" that prevent the patient from leaving the chair due to a fixed tray across the chair arms. A reduction in agitation behaviors in these studies was attributed to the effects of music, despite the fact that the use of these chairs would directly affect pacing behaviors.

In another study, the effects of the music intervention on staff behavior was an unexpected confounder. This study compared the use of taped music to no music during meal times, and it measured the amount of food eaten by participants. The participants' consumption of food increased during the music conditions, but the staff served more food during the music conditions as well. The effect of music on increasing food intake could not be clearly separated from the fact that the patients had received more food on their plates.

Snoezelen Multisensory Stimulation Therapy

Summary: There is no consistent evidence demonstrating a durable effect of multisensory stimulation (MSS) therapy on behavioral symptoms of dementia. Preliminary findings of short-term benefits and the reported pleasantness of the treatment of MSS, however, suggest that future research may be warranted.

Details: MSS, otherwise known as Snoezelen therapy, is based on the premise that neuropsychiatric symptoms may result from periods of sensory deprivation. MSS uses multiple stimuli during a treatment session aimed at stimulating the primary senses of sight, hearing, touch, taste and smell. MSS combines the use of such treatments as lights, tactile surfaces, music, and aroma. Interventions generally occur in specially designed rooms with a variety of sensory based materials. A typical MSS room provides taped music, aroma, bubble tubes, fiber optic sprays and moving shapes projected across walls. MSS has become a popular intervention for behavioral symptoms in persons with dementia, but the application of MSS varies in form, procedures, and in frequency of treatment.

One systematic review included two RCTs in which MSS was used for a total of 246 individuals with dementia aged 60 and older. The first study compared eight 30-minute MSS sessions to activity sessions that were based on individual subjects' preferences and abilities, but with no obvious sensory inputs. No significant effects on mood were found either immediately after intervention or at one-month post-follow-up. The second study compared a 24-hour exposure to MSS with usual care. Although patients appeared to find MSS enjoyable, the study found no long-term significant effects on behavior or mood.

Other systematic reviews identified four additional RCTs and reported mixed results. One study administered MSS in specially designed rooms in 30- to 60-minute sessions and found that during the four-week treatment period, disruptive behavior outside the treatment setting briefly improved but did not last once the treatment had stopped. Two studies conducted MSS sessions for 30 to 60 minutes for three consecutive days and found that subjects were less apathetic when remaining in a multisensory stimulation room compared with remaining in the living room or receiving activity therapy. Lastly, one small (N=20) repeated-measures study set in a day-care center and mental health nursing home exposed patients to three 40-minute sessions of either MSS or reminiscence therapy and found no significant differences in behavior symptoms during or after treatment.

Chapter 30

Recent Alzheimer Disease Research

Chapter Contents

Section 30.1

Progress in Understanding Alzheimer Genetics

Text in this section is excerpted from "Alzheimer's Disease Progress Report," National Institute on Aging (NIA), December 2015.

Recent discoveries have not only identified more genes involved in Alzheimer Disease (AD), but also have helped us figure out what they may do. Discovering the mechanisms involved in Alzheimer onset and progression, as well as disease-related brain changes, directs us to pathways that might be targeted to help stop disease or protect against it.

Figure 30.1. *Genetic Regions of Interest in Alzheimer Disease By year of discovery*

Recent examples illustrate how such discoveries are moving this area of research forward:

Longevity Gene May Boost Cognition

Scientists had previously shown that people who have a variant of the longevity gene KLOTHO have improved brain skills such as thinking, learning, and memory. The gene activates production of a protein found in both the kidney and the brain. Researchers looked at the impact of a variant of the KLOTHO gene, called KL-VS, on cognitive performance in more than 700 cognitively normal volunteers age 52 to 85. Compared with participants who carried no copies of the KL-VS form, those with one copy had higher blood levels of the klotho protein and performed better on tests of multiple brain functions, including attention, problem solving, visuospatial ability, learning, and memory. To better understand why, the scientists studied mice genetically engineered to overproduce the klotho protein. Not only did these mice live up to 30 percent longer, they outperformed control mice on tests of learning and memory. The modified mice showed higher-than-normal brain levels of a receptor for the neurotransmitter glutamate, which enhances cognitive function. When this action was blocked in the mice, cognitive function returned to control levels. This study suggests that drugs targeting the klotho protein could improve cognition in people at risk for Alzheimer disease.

Genetically Reprogrammed Cells Offer New Insights into Alzheimer Disease

While animal models have provided important information about the basic biology of Alzheimer disease, scientists are working hard to develop better human models of the disease. The recent development of induced pluripotent stem cells (iPSCs) is a major step forward in biomedical research. iPSCs are adult human skin cells that have been genetically reprogrammed to resemble embryonic stem cells, and they can be manipulated in tissue culture to produce any type of cell desired.

In Alzheimer disease research, iPSCs have advanced our under-standing of how gene mutations influence early-onset Alzheimer disease, a rare form that occurs in people in their 30s, 40s, and 50s. These insights inform our basic knowledge of both early-and late-onset disease. Two recent studies are cases in point.

In one study, scientists studied iPSCs donated by people carrying the so-called London mutation in the gene for amyloid precursor protein (APP). Named for the home city of the family in which it was discovered, the London mutation is the most common APP mutation associated with early-onset Alzheimer disease.

The scientists stimulated mutant and control iPSCs to develop into brain cells and then compared their APP-processing pathways. The mutant cells increased production of beta-amyloid 42, a toxic form of the protein involved in forming amyloid plaques, and higher levels of tau. The findings suggest a direct link between the biochemical pathways responsible for generating beta-amyloid and tau and revealed the effects of the most common form of the APP mutation.

A second research team used iPSCs to study how mutations in a different gene—presenilin-1 (PSEN1), the most common cause of early-onset Alzheimer—might wreak havoc. They generated neurons from skin cells donated by volunteers from two families carrying PSEN1 mutations. The cells in tissue culture resembled those in the brains of humans with the PSEN1 mutation in that they produced a higher-than-normal ratio of beta-amyloid 42. The researchers also discovered 14 genes that were activated at significantly higher or lower levels in mutant iPSCs brain cells and identified three genes, NLRP2, ASB9, and NDP, involved in inflammation, energy production, and the generation of new neurons. These and other intriguing studies show the promise of iPSC technology for unraveling the molecular mechanisms of both early-and late-onset Alzheimer disease. Ultimately, these findings could point to new and more precise therapeutic targets.

Alzheimer disease in a Dish

It is extraordinarily difficult to mimic the brain's complexity in standard laboratory models. Now, NIH-funded researchers have developed a new model that for the first time contains the two proteins that are hallmarks of Alzheimer disease. Using genetic engineering to spur the growth of neural stem cells in a gel, the cells formed into three-dimensional networks with the amyloid plaques and tau tangles found in the human brain. This process took just 6 weeks, compared with the year it takes for plaque alone to form in a mouse model. The researchers then used this new model, called "Alzheimer in a dish, " to show that blocking the formation of amyloid plaques with certain drugs prevents tau tangles from forming inside neurons. This finding lends support to the hypothesis that amyloid triggers the cascade of events that leads to Alzheimer dementia. It also provides new encouragement that a category of drugs called beta-secretase and gamma-secretase inhibitors might ultimately benefit patients if given early enough in the course of the disease. This new model will inform efforts to test existing and novel drugs as potential therapies, and it may be used to develop models of other neurodegenerative diseases.

Epigenetics

The epigenome—chemical modifications, or marks, on DNA that turn gene activity on and off—may influence Alzheimer disease. The epigenome can be modified by lifestyle and environmental influences, and studies such as the one described here are fueling scientists' speculation that epigenetic changes might contribute to Alzheimer disease.

Epigenome changes linked to Alzheimer disease

Scientists looked at samples from 708 donated brains from the NIA-supported Religious Orders Study and Rush Memory and Aging Project. About 60 percent of the brains displayed Alzheimer disease pathology. They analyzed DNA sequences from the brains for a specific chemical change—methylation, a process that can control how a gene is turned on or off—and correlated that change with amyloid plaque burden, a hallmark of Alzheimer disease.

The researchers found greater methylation levels correlated with Alzheimer disease pathology in 71 of the 400,000-plus chemical modifications analyzed. These 71 markers were found in gene variants already associated with Alzheimer and others suspected to be. These include genes thought to be involved in regulating processing of beta-amyloid and several others that have been linked to cell function.

They estimated that those methylation-related epigenetic changes accounted for about 29 percent of the plaque burden in the participants. This compares to the effect of all known Alzheimer genes, which accounted for just 14 percent of the plaque burden in this group. This intriguing new avenue of research exploring how the epigenome influences a person's risk for developing Alzheimer—and ways to target related toxic changes—is a focus of the NIH research agenda.

Section 30.2

Genetic Advances in Alzheimer Disease Research

Text in this section is excerpted from "The Genetics of Alzheimer's Disease," National Institute on Aging (NIA), October 15, 2013.

Age and genetics are the best-known risk factors for Alzheimer disease. Most people with Alzheimer do not start showing symptoms until age 60 or older. However, in rare cases, people develop Alzheimer disease much earlier, between the ages of 30 and 60. This "early-onset" form of Alzheimer always runs in families. It is caused by a mutation in one of three genes inherited from a parent that causes abnormal proteins to be formed.

In early-onset Alzheimer disease, mutations on chromosome 21 cause the formation of abnormal amyloid precursor protein (APP), a mutation on chromosome 14 causes abnormal presenilin 1 to be made, and a mutation on chromosome 1 leads to abnormal presenilin 2. Scientists know that each of these mutations plays a role in the cleavage of APP, a protein whose precise function is not yet known. This breakdown is part of a process that generates harmful forms of beta-amyloid that lead to amyloid plaques, a hallmark of the disease.

The more common "late-onset" form of the disease typically occurs after age 65. While no single gene mutation is known to cause this form of Alzheimer, evidence of a hereditary component is mounting. Environmental and lifestyle factors may also contribute to the risk of developing late-onset Alzheimer.

The apolipoprotein E (APOE) gene is the strongest common genetic risk factor identified to date for late-onset Alzheimer. The APOE gene, found on chromosome 19, comes in three different forms, or alleles: ε2, ε3, and ε4. The APOE ε2 allele is the least common form, found in 5 percent to 10 percent of people, and appears to reduce risk. The APOE ε3 allele, the most common form, is found in 70 percent to 80 percent of the population and appears to play a neutral role in the disease. The APOE ε4 allele, found in 10 percent to 15 percent of the population, increases risk for Alzheimer disease by three- to eight-fold, depending on whether a person has one or two copies of the allele. The APOE ε4 allele is also associated with an earlier age of disease onset.

APOE ε4 is called a risk-factor gene because it increases a person's risk of developing the disease but is not the direct cause. Inheriting an APOE ε4 allele does not mean that a person will definitely develop Alzheimer. Some people with an APOE ε4 allele never get the disease, and many who develop Alzheimer do not have any APOE ε4 alleles.

Technology, Collaboration Key to Genetic Advances

Researchers are working collaboratively on genome-wide association studies (GWAS) to identify other genes that may influence Alzheimer disease. Technological advances have enabled them to detect subtle gene variants involved in this complex disorder by scanning thousands of DNA samples from people with Alzheimer disease as well as unaffected individuals. By identifying genetic factors that may confer risk or protection, we gain insights into the molecular mechanisms and disease pathways that influence disease onset and progression.

Until 2009, APOE ε4 was the only known genetic risk factor for Alzheimer, but now GWAS researchers have detected and confirmed a growing list of others: PICALM, CLU, CR1, BIN1, MS4A, CD2AP, EPHA1, ABCA7, SORL1, and TREM2. In 2013, this list expanded to include another 11 genes, described below.

Scientists are using other techniques as well. Whole genome sequencing, which identified the TREM2 gene, captures genetic variations in an entire complement of a person's DNA. Researchers are also looking for genes that protect against developing the disease. This year, they identified one such protective gene, a variant of the APP gene, described below. These discoveries are helping to uncover the cellular pathways involved in Alzheimer and could lead to new avenues for therapeutic approaches.

International GWAS Identifies 11 New Gene Risk Factors

In October 2013, the International Genomic Alzheimer Project (IGAP) announced the results of a GWAS that offer important new insights into the disease pathways involved in late-onset Alzheimer disease. IGAP, comprised of four research consortia in the United States and Europe and supported in part by the National Institutes of Health (NIH), scanned the DNA of more than 74,000 volunteers—the largest genetic GWAS yet conducted in Alzheimer research. The researchers shared DNA samples and data sets in a collaborative effort that resulted in the identification of 11 new genes. The study also brought to light another 13 variants that merit further analysis.

The IGAP findings strengthened evidence about the involvement of certain pathways in the disease, such as the role of SORL1 in amyloid deposition, a hallmark of the disease. The results also shed light on new gene risk factors that may influence several cell functions, such as the ability of microglial cells to respond to inflammation.

The researchers identified the new genes by analyzing previously studied and newly collected DNA data from 74,076 older volunteers from 15 countries. The newly discovered risk genes (HLA-DRB5/HLA0DRB1, PTK2B, SLC24A4-0RING3, DSG2, INPP5D, MEF2C, NME8, ZCWPW1, CELF1, FERMT2, and CASS4) and previously identified variants are now being examined for the roles they play in Alzheimer disease. For example, investigators are exploring how SORL1 and CASS4 influence amyloid, how CASS4 and FERMT2 affect tau, and how some of these genes impact lipid transport, synaptic function, and other cell functions.

The National Institute on Aging (NIA)-funded Alzheimer Disease Genetics Consortium (ADGC), at the University of Pennsylvania School of Medicine, Philadelphia, is one of the four IGAP founding partners. Its goal is to identify genetic variants associated with risk for Alzheimer. Other NIA research infrastructure resources have supported the ADGC by making available DNA samples, data sets containing biomedical and demographic information about participants, and genetic analysis data.

The other three founding partners of IGAP are the Cohorts for Heart and Aging Research in Genomic Epidemiology, supported in part by several NIH institutes and NIH-supported databases from the AGES-Reykjavik Study and the Atherosclerosis Risk in Communities Study; the European Alzheimer Disease Initiative in France; and Genetic and Environmental Research in Alzheimer Disease in Wales.

Microglial Gene Triples Alzheimer Disease Risk

Alzheimer disease geneticists discovered rare mutations in a gene called TREM2 (triggering receptor expressed on myeloid cells) that increase Alzheimer disease risk as much as threefold. Scientists had previously found that both copies of the TREM2 gene are mutated in some cases of frontotemporal dementia. To learn if mutations in just one copy of the gene might be associated with Alzheimer disease, the scientists, from University College London and NIA, analyzed thousands of DNA sequences from people with and without Alzheimer disease; the data came from the investigator's' own collections and several other large collections from around the world.

The analysis identified a set of TREM2 mutations that occurred at much higher frequencies in people with Alzheimer than in controls. Unlike APOE ε4, the TREM2 mutations are very rare in the general population. Nonetheless, the discovery of these mutations sheds new light on the biology of Alzheimer.

The protein encoded by the TREM2 gene is found on the cell membranes of microglia, the major class of immune cells in the brain. Microglia help maintain brain health by attacking and removing infectious agents. They also digest cellular debris, including beta-amyloid, and participate in the ongoing remodeling of communication between cells that is vital for learning and memory. This finding points to microglial cell dysfunction as a major route by which the disease can develop and will no doubt prompt researchers to probe further the biology of microglia.

Protective Gene Mutation and Beta-Amyloid in Alzheimer Disease

The discovery of a rare gene mutation that protects people against Alzheimer provides some of the strongest evidence yet that overproduction of beta-amyloid plays a role in the disease. The A673T mutation, which lies in the gene for APP, was discovered when researchers at deCode Genetics in Iceland scanned the DNA sequence of the APP gene in 1,795 Icelanders. The mutation, which is extremely uncommon, slows the rate at which the APP protein is processed to generate the more toxic forms of beta-amyloid.

To look at how the gene mutation affects cognition, the researchers studied 3,700 nondemented nursing home residents between 80 and 100 years of age. The 41 volunteers in the group who carried the APP gene mutation had better cognitive scores than those of peers of similar age who did not have the protective gene mutation. This discovery lends fresh hope to the idea that beta-amyloid-lowering drugs could prove useful in treating Alzheimer.

Natural Selection and Alzheimer Disease Risk Genes

The apolipoprotein E (APOE) ε4 allele is the strongest known genetic risk factor for late-onset Alzheimer. Nonetheless, natural selection has favored inheritance of the APOE gene during recent human evolution.

Researchers at Harvard Medical School, Boston, and Rush University, Chicago, analyzed data from two large-scale GWAS and discovered that the inheritance patterns of four Alzheimer susceptibility genes (PICALM, BIN1, CD2AP, EPHA1) also show evidence of positive selection during recent evolution. The researchers suggest that these genes signal the body to produce specific proteins that, interacting with other proteins, serve a common function—perhaps an immune function—that benefits humans during evolution. Since these Alzheimer disease susceptibility genes did not affect reproductive status, they were carried through numerous generations to recent days' population, which is living longer and thus developing the disease.

Brain Imaging and New Insights into Alzheimer Genetics

Efforts to understand the genetic basis of Alzheimer disease are challenging because of the complexity of diagnosing the disorder.

No two people with Alzheimer show exactly the same cognitive or behavioral symptoms, and symptoms may fluctuate from day to day. However, imaging studies of people with dementia are identifying common patterns of Alzheimer-related brain changes. Images of these brain changes, which tend to be more stable and can be measured more accurately than clinical symptoms, are offering new insights into the genetic basis of Alzheimer.

The brains of people with Alzheimer show a breakdown of functional connections within the default mode network, a group of brain areas used when the mind "wanders," as in daydreaming. In a functional magnetic resonance imaging (fMRI) study of nearly 350 cognitively normal participants age 45 to 91, researchers at Washington University, St. Louis, found early signs of breakdown in the default mode network in people with a family history of late-onset Alzheimer disease. None of the study participants carried the APOE ε4 allele, the strongest genetic risk factor for Alzheimer disease. This study suggests that other genes, in addition to APOE ε4, contribute to the risk of Alzheimer in people with a family history of the disease. Also, testing for declines in the default mode network may help identify those at increased risk.

Alzheimer disease is also marked by reduced blood flow to certain brain regions. University of Wisconsin, Madison, researchers used MRI to study blood flow in the brains of more than 250 middle-aged people. Those with a maternal history of late-onset Alzheimer disease showed Alzheimer-like changes in brain blood flow patterns, including reduced blood flow to the hippocampus and certain regions of the cortex. Further investigation is needed to examine any possible influence of a maternal history of Alzheimer disease.

Gene Variants Influence Hippocampal Volume

Hippocampal atrophy, a recognized biological marker of Alzheimer disease, is influenced by various vascular and metabolic factors. Hippocampal volume is a heritable, measurable trait that shows detectable changes throughout life. Researchers at Boston University and other institutions explored genetic influences on hippocampal volume by conducting a GWAS analysis in the Cohorts for Heart and Aging Research in Genomic Epidemiology Consortium in dementia-free people from community-based studies.

The investigators detected genetic loci associated with hippocampal volume, implicating genes related to the health and normal functioning of neurons (list genes), cell death (HRK), development

(WIF1), oxidative stress (MSR3B), protein clearance (FBXW8), and neurogenesis (ASTN2), as well as enzymes targeted by new diabetes medications (DPP4). This finding suggests genetic influences on hippocampal size and possibly the risk of cognitive decline and dementia.

Researchers from Boston University and other institutions looked for genes associated with patterns of brain degeneration commonly seen in people with Alzheimer disease, including degeneration of the hippocampus, a brain region important for learning and memory. They analyzed MRI scans from more than 1,600 older individuals with Alzheimer, mild cognitive impairment, or normal cognition who are participating in the Alzheimer Disease Neuroimaging Initiative.

The research team identified four genes associated with degeneration of the hippocampus, including three new genes not previously suspected to be involved in Alzheimer: F5, SELP, and SYNPR. The F5 and SELP genes direct the production of the proteins Factor V and P-selectin, which are involved in blood clotting and blood vessel function, respectively. SYNPR is involved in production of a protein that is vital to normal functioning of synapses.

Section 30.3

Vascular System

Text in this section is excerpted from "Alzheimer Disease Progress Report," National Institute on Aging (NIA), December 2015.

Scientists for some time have been interested in how the body's vast network of small and large blood vessels the vascular system may be involved in the development of dementia and the clinical symptoms of Alzheimer disease (AD). Some scientists are focusing on what happens to the brain's blood vessels in aging and Alzheimer disease. Others are zeroing in on the relationship between Alzheimer disease and vascular problems in other parts of the body, such as cardiovascular disease, stroke, and diabetes.

Recent NIA funded studies including the following:

Beta-Amyloid Impairs the Function of the Blood-Brain Barrier

Researchers used transgenic mice to study how beta-amyloid protein interacts with pericytes, cells that are important for controlling the movement of molecules into and out of blood vessels in the brain. They found that beta-amyloid deposits impaired the normal pericyte function of removing the protein from the brain, which then led to further accumulation of the protein. Pericyte deficiency also led to the development of tau pathology and an early loss of neurons that is not normally seen in these transgenic mice. These findings suggest that pericytes may be a viable target for therapeutic intervention.

Lymphatic Drainage System Is Discovered in the Brain

Scientists have long believed that although the brain maintains a functional immune system, it lacks the type of lymphatic vessels that drain cellular debris from other tissues in the body. NIH-supported investigators recently made a significant discovery that overturns this scientific dogma.

In mice, the investigators developed a new method to mount the membranes covering the brain on a single slide so they could be examined as a unit. While examining the membranes, the investigators noticed what appeared to be lymphatic vessels, and further testing confirmed this fact. The well-hidden vessels follow a major blood vessel into the sinus cavity, an area that is notoriously difficult to image.

The discovery of this remarkable "brain drain " raises a number of research possibilities. For one thing, the vessels appear different in older mice than in younger ones, so researchers are intrigued by the roles they may play in the aging process. In the case of Alzheimer disease, the investigators theorize that the vessels may not efficiently remove abnormal proteins.

More research is needed to determine whether the vessels are unable to remove large chunks of amyloid-beta and tau, or if they lose this ability over time. Further, this discovery may have major implications for an array of other brain diseases, including autoimmune diseases and autism.

Section 30.4

Amylin Deposits in the Brain and Alzheimer Disease Risk

Text in this section is excerpted from "Amylin Deposits in the Brain May Link Dementia and Diabetes," National Institute on Aging (NIA), July 30, 2013.

Deposits of a hormone called amylin in the brain may indicate risk for developing dementia and type 2 diabetes, according to a study published online in the Annals of Neurology. The analysis by researchers at the NIA-funded Alzheimer's Disease Center at the University of California, Davis, is the first to identify amylin deposits in post-mortem brain tissue from older people who had been diagnosed with Alzheimer disease (AD) or vascular dementia and diabetes. The findings also indicated that amylin may play a similar role in the Alzheimer disease process as amyloid protein, a hallmark of the disorder.

Amylin (also known as islet amyloid polypeptide) is a hormone expressed and secreted with insulin. It influences blood sugar levels; when too much is secreted, risk for developing diabetes increases. These new findings show that amylin deposits can also build up and form plaques in the brain, similar to amyloid plaques found in Alzheimer disease.

The researchers examined post-mortem brain tissue from three groups of volunteers older than 70 years: those who had diabetes and dementia (vascular dementia or Alzheimer), those who had Alzheimer but no diabetes, and those free of these disorders. Investigators found significant amylin deposits in the brain tissue of people with both dementia and diabetes. Surprisingly, they also found amylin in people with Alzheimer but without diabetes—perhaps because these individuals had undiagnosed insulin resistance. The healthy controls had few amylin deposits.

The study, led by Dr. Florin Despa, may explain why people with diabetes are at risk for dementia. Like amyloid, amylin circulates in the blood and, during the disease process, is overproduced and not cleared normally, building up in the brain. Over time, both proteins lead to the loss of brain cells and brain damage. Amylin buildup in the brain's blood vessels may also play a role in amyloid buildup and contribute to risk for Alzheimer, the study found.

Chapter 31

Participating in Alzheimer Disease Clinical Trials and Studies

Introduction

This is an exciting time for Alzheimer disease (AD) clinical research. Thanks to advances in our understanding of this brain disorder and powerful new tools for "seeing" and diagnosing it in people, scientists are making great strides in identifying potential new ways to help diagnose, treat, and even prevent Alzheimer disease. These advances are possible because thousands of people have participated in Alzheimer disease clinical trials and other studies to learn more about the disease and test treatments. We know what we know because of them.

You may have heard of clinical trials and research studies but are not sure what they are or if you want to join one. This booklet provides information to help you decide if participating in a clinical trial or study is right for you, a friend, or family member.

Whatever the motivation, when you choose to participate in research, you become a partner in scientific discovery. Your contribution can help future generations lead healthier lives. Major medical

Text in this chapter is excerpted from "Participating in Alzheimer's Research," National Institute on Aging (NIA), August 2014.

breakthroughs could not happen without the generosity of clinical trial participants—young and old.

You can make a difference by participating in research.

Today, at least 70,000 volunteers are urgently needed to participate in more than 150 active clinical trials and studies in the United States that are testing ways to understand, treat, prevent, or cure Alzheimer disease. All kinds of people, including healthy volunteers, are needed.

Types of Clinical Research

Clinical research is medical research involving people. There are two types, clinical studies and clinical trials.

Clinical Studies

Clinical (sometimes called observational) studies observe people in normal settings. Researchers gather information, group volunteers according to broad characteristics, and compare changes over time. Alzheimer disease studies may help identify new possibilities for clinical trials.

For example, the Alzheimer Disease Neuroimaging Initiative studies brain images and biomarkers (biological signs of disease) in people with normal cognitive aging, mild cognitive impairment—a disorder that may precede Alzheimer disease—and early-stage Alzheimer disease to better understand the disease and its progression. The researchers discovered that certain changes in blood or cerebrospinal fluid may signal early Alzheimer disease in people with normal cognition. Now, that knowledge is being used to test treatments for Alzheimer disease before symptoms, like changes in memory, begin.

Clinical Trials

Clinical trials test interventions, such as drugs or devices, as well as diet or lifestyle changes. Drug testing is the focus of many clinical trials. Currently, more than 70 drugs are in clinical trials for Alzheimer disease, and more are awaiting U.S. Food and Drug Administration (FDA) approval to begin testing in people.

Clinical trials are the primary way that researchers find out if a promising treatment is safe and effective in people. Clinical trials also can evaluate which treatments are more effective than others.

Before FDA-approved clinical trials begin, scientists perform laboratory tests and studies in animals to test a potential therapy's safety and efficacy. If these studies show favorable results, the FDA gives approval for the intervention to be tested in humans.

Clinical trials advance through four phases to test a treatment, find the appropriate dosage, and look for side effects. If, after the first three phases, researchers find a drug or other intervention to be safe and effective, the FDA approves it for clinical use and continues to monitor its effects.

Common Questions about Participating in Research

How Can I Find out about Alzheimer Disease Trials and Studies?

- Ask your doctor, who may know about local research studies that may be right for you.

- Sign up for a registry or a matching service to be invited to participate in studies or trials when they are available in your area.

- Contact Alzheimer disease centers or memory or neurology clinics in your community. They may be conducting trials.

- Visit the Alzheimer Disease Education and Referral (ADEAR) Center clinical trials finder, www.nia.nih.gov/alzheimers/clinical-trials.

- Look for announcements in newspapers and other media.

- Search www.clinicaltrials.gov.

Why Would I Participate in a Clinical Trial?

There are many reasons why you might choose to join an Alzheimer disease clinical trial. You may want to:

- Help others, including future family members, who may be at risk for Alzheimer disease

- Receive regular monitoring by medical professionals

- Learn about Alzheimer disease and your health

- Test new treatments that might work better than those currently available

- Get information about support groups and resources

What Else Should I Consider?

While there are benefits to participating in a clinical trial or study, there are some risks and other issues to consider as well.

Risk. Researchers make every effort to ensure participants' safety. But, all clinical trials have some risk. Before joining a clinical trial, the research team will explain what you can expect, including possible side effects or other risks. That way, you can make an informed decision about joining the trial.

Expectations and motivations. Single clinical trials and studies generally do not have miraculous results, and participants may not benefit directly. With a complex disease like Alzheimer, it is unlikely that one drug will cure or prevent the disease.

Uncertainty. Some people are concerned that they are not permitted to know whether they are getting the experimental treatment or a placebo (inactive treatment), or may not know the results right away. Open communication with study staff can help you understand why the study is set up this way and what you can expect.

Time commitment and location. Clinical trials and studies last days to years. They usually require multiple visits to study sites, such as private research facilities, teaching hospitals, Alzheimer disease research centers, or doctors' offices. Some studies pay participants a fee and/or reimburse travel expenses.

Study partner requirement. Many Alzheimer disease trials require a caregiver or family member who has regular contact with the person to accompany the participant to study appointments. This study partner can give insight into changes in the person over time.

Steps in Clinical Trial Participation

Here's what happens in a trial.

1. Study staff explain the trial in detail and gather more information about you.

2. Once you have had all your questions answered and agree to participate, you sign an informed consent form.

3. You are screened to make sure you qualify for the trial.

4. If accepted into the trial, you schedule a first visit (called the "baseline" visit). The researchers conduct cognitive and/or physical tests during this visit.

5. You are randomly assigned to a treatment or control group.

6. You and your family members follow the trial procedures and report any issues or concerns to researchers.

7. You may visit the research site at regularly scheduled times for new cognitive, physical, or other evaluations and discussions with staff. At these visits, the research team collects information about effects of the intervention and your safety and well-being.

8. You continue to see your regular physician for usual health care throughout the study.

How Will My Safety Be Protected?

Congress has passed laws to protect study participants. Today, researchers are required to follow strict rules to make sure that every participant is safe and information remains confidential. These rules are enforced by the Federal Government. Here are some of the safeguards in place:

Institutional Review Board (IRB). Every study site must have IRB oversight to ensure participants are not exposed to unnecessary risk. The IRB must include at least one public member.

Data and Safety Monitoring (DSM) committee. In addition to the IRB, clinical trials with potential safety concerns are monitored by a DSM committee. If the committee finds that the experimental treatment is not working or is harming participants, it will stop the trial right away.

Informed consent. Before a volunteer agrees to participate, researchers must explain the details of the study: purpose, duration, required procedures, risks, and potential benefits.

Right to withdraw. Even if volunteers sign up to participate in a research study, they can decide to withdraw at any time during the study.

Privacy. Researchers must keep health and personal information private.

Questions to Ask about Clinical Trials and Studies

Here are some questions to ask the research team when you are thinking about a trial or study.

• What is the purpose

• What tests and treatments will be given

- What are the risks What side effects might occur
- How long will the study last How much time will it take at each visit
- Where and when will the testing occur
- Can I continue treatments for Alzheimer disease and other conditions as prescribed by my regular doctor
- How will you keep my doctor informed about my participation in the trial
- Does the study compare standard and experimental treatments
- How will the trial affect my everyday activities
- If I withdraw, will this affect my normal care
- Will I learn the results of my tests of the study overall
- What are the chances that I will receive a placebo
- What steps ensure my privacy
- Will my expenses be reimbursed
- Will I be paid

Part Five

Living with Alzheimer Disease and Dementias

Chapter 32

Talking about Your Diagnosis

Chapter Contents

Section 32.1

Telling Others about an Alzheimer Disease Diagnosis

Text in this section is excerpted from "Helping Family
and Friends Understand Alzheimer's Disease," National Institute
on Aging (NIA), July 2012.

Talking about Your Diagnosis

When you learn that someone has Alzheimer disease (AD), you may wonder when and how to tell your family and friends. You may be worried about how others will react to or treat the person. Realize that family and friends often sense that something is wrong before they are told. Alzheimer disease is hard to keep secret.

There's no single right way to tell others about Alzheimer disease. When the time seems right, be honest with family, friends, and others. Use this as a chance to educate them about Alzheimer disease. You can:

- Tell friends and family about Alzheimer disease and its effects.

- Share articles, websites, and other information about the disease.

- Tell them what they can do to help. Let them know you need breaks.

When a family member has Alzheimer disease, it affects everyone in the family, including children and grandchildren. It's important to talk to them about what is happening.

Tips for Communicating

You can help family and friends understand how to interact with the person with Alzheimer disease. Here are some tips:

- Help family and friends realize what the person can still do and how much he or she still can understand.

- Give visitors suggestions about how to start talking with the person. For example, make eye contact and say, "Hello George, I'm John. We used to work together."

- Help them avoid correcting the person with Alzheimer disease if he or she makes a mistake or forgets something. Instead, ask visitors to respond to the feelings expressed or talk about something different.

- Help family and friends plan fun activities with the person, such as going to family reunions or visiting old friends. A photo album or other activity can help if the person is bored or confused and needs to be distracted.

Remind visitors to:

- Visit at times of day when the person with Alzheimer disease is at his or her best.

- Be calm and quiet. Don't use a loud voice or talk to the person as if he or she were a child.

- Respect the person's personal space, and don't get too close.

- Not take it personally if the person does not recognize you, is unkind, or gets angry. He or she is acting out of confusion.

When You're Out in Public

Some caregivers carry a card that explains why the person with Alzheimer disease might say or do odd things. For example, the card could read, "My family member has Alzheimer disease. He or she might say or do things that are unexpected. Thank you for your understanding."

The card allows you to let others know about the person's Alzheimer disease without the person hearing you. It also means you don't have to keep explaining things.

Section 32.2

Talking to Children about Alzheimer Disease

Text in this section is excerpted from "Helping Kids Understand
Alzheimer's Disease," National Institute on Aging (NIA), July 2012.

Talking to Children about Alzheimer Disease

When a family member has Alzheimer disease (AD), it affects everyone in the family, including children and grandchildren. It's important
to talk to them about what is happening. How much and what kind of
information you share depends on the child's age and relationship to
the person with Alzheimer disease.

Helping Kids Cope

Here are some tips to help kids understand what is happening:

- Answer their questions simply and honestly. For example, you
  might tell a young child, "Grandma has an illness that makes it
  hard for her to remember things."

- Help them know that their feelings of sadness and anger are
  normal.

- Comfort them. Tell them no one caused the disease.

Talk with kids about their concerns and feelings. Some may not
talk about their negative feelings, but you may see changes in how
they act. Problems at school, with friends, or at home can be a sign
that they are upset. A school counselor or social worker can help your
child understand what is happening and learn how to cope.

A teenager might find it hard to accept how the person with Alzheimer disease has changed. He or she may find the changes upsetting
or embarrassing and not want to be around the person. Don't force
them to spend time with the person who has Alzheimer disease. This
could make things worse.

Spending Time Together and Alone

It's important to show kids that they can still talk with the person with Alzheimer disease and help him or her enjoy activities. Doing fun things together can help both the child and the person with Alzheimer disease. Here are some things they might do:

- Do simple arts and crafts
- Play music or sing
- Look through photo albums
- Read stories out loud

If kids live in the same house as someone with Alzheimer disease:

- Don't expect a young child to help take care of or "babysit" the person.
- Make sure they have time for their own interests and needs, such as playing with friends, going to school activities, or doing homework.
- Make sure you spend time with them, so they don't feel that all your attention is on the person with Alzheimer disease.
- Be honest about your feelings when you talk with kids, but don't overwhelm them.

If the stress of living with someone who has Alzheimer disease becomes too great, think about placing the person with Alzheimer disease into a respite care facility. Then, both you and your kids can get a much-needed break.

Chapter 33

Getting Support for Alzheimer Disease

Finding Alzheimer Disease Capable Care

As Alzheimer disease (AD) progresses, you may need to consider in-home assistance or residential care facilities. There are several easy-to-use tools to help you figure out your needs and find care assistance.

Deciding Where to Live

Staying at Home: Most people prefer to stay at home for as long as possible. Staying at home often requires two elements: 1) finding care providers who will come to the home; and 2) adapting the home to reduce obstacles that hinder care giving and make the home unsafe for a person with Alzheimer disease. In many cases, small changes to the home can make it possible to live at home longer.

- Eldercare.gov has answers on how to modify your home for caregiving.

- The Alzheimer Association CareFinder is an interactive tool that recommends care options and provides a list of questions to ask when screening a care provider.

This chapter includes excerpts from "Finding Alzheimer's Capable Care," U.S. Department of Health and Human Services (HHS), May 15, 2012; and text from "Caregiver Resources," U.S. Department of Health and Human Services (HHS), May 15, 2012. Reviewed February 2016.

- The Eldercare Locator allows you to find help in your community by searching by zip code, or city and state.

Home-and Community-Based Services

- The Alzheimer Association has a list of services that may be included in home- and community-based services waivers.

Respite Care

- The Alzheimer Association explains available types of care centers and resources to find care facilities.

Types of Licensed Residences in Your Area

Residential Care: If staying at home is no longer an option, there are different kinds of facilities that take care of people with Alzheimer disease.

- Medicare's Nursing Home Compare can help you find and compare nursing homes.

- The Eldercare Locator provides answers to common questions and information about assisted living facility.

- The Alzheimer Association's Senior Housing Finder has various filters to search for a care facility, including city and state, county, zip code or options.

- The Alzheimer Foundation of America provides names and links to dementia care settings that meet its national standards.

Caregiver Resources

Most people want to stay in their communities and live in their homes as long as possible. Communities and states offer different services. This page offers ideas to get you started finding support in your area.

Finding Local Resources

Federal and States Programs (Other than Medicaid): Many communities have programs to assist people with Alzheimer disease in a number of different ways. One of the best ways to determine what government assistance is available is to contact your local Area Agency on Aging.

The local Area Agency on Aging may be able to connect you with services such as Meals on Wheels, transportation services to help get to doctors' appointments, or support groups for people with Alzheimer disease and their caregivers, and other home care programs. These resources are particularly important if you choose to remain in your home.

- The Eldercare Locator helps find help on a variety of subjects and can be filtered by topic area or geographic location.

- The Alzheimer Association's 24/7 Helpline provides information and support to people with memory loss, caregivers, healthcare professionals, and the public at 1-800-272-3900.

- The U.S. Department of Veterans Affairs can help you find help near your home via their zip code locator or their Caregiver Support Line when caring for a veteran.

- NIH's Alzheimer Disease Education and Referral Center can be contacted five days a week via phone at 1-800-438-4380 or via email at adear@nia.nih.gov.

Counseling and Support

Getting information and counseling from reliable sources, such as community organizations and support groups, can help both people with Alzheimer disease and family members adjust to the challenges of the disease and reduce stress.

Counseling can help you understand how a person with Alzheimer disease is changing, and help you figure out how to deal with those changes. By learning some tips from people who have experience with this disease, caregivers can be better prepared and less stressed as new challenges come up.

Support groups can connect you with people who are facing similar circumstances. Participating in groups or talking with someone on the phone can help reduce feelings of isolation.

Finding the right counseling for you and the person you are taking care of is an important piece of the care and treatment puzzle.

- The Alzheimer Foundation's toll-free hotline provides information and counseling by licensed social workers and can refer you to community resources across the nation.

- The Alzheimer Association's 24/7 Helpline is available to caregivers, families and individuals with Alzheimer disease.

- WebMD's Alzheimer Disease Health Center has an overview of types of support services and counseling options for people affected by the disease.

- The National Institutes of Health (NIH) has a guide that offers practical advice for caregiving at all stages, including how to cope with changes in personality and communication, making your home safe, where to get help, medical decisions, and coping with the last stages of the disease.

- The U.S. Department of Veterans Affairs' Caregiver Support Line can provide assistance when caring for a veteran and connect you with a local Caregiver Support Coordinator.

Chapter 34

Preventing Cognitive Decline If You Have Alzheimer Disease or Dementia

Chapter Contents

Section 34.1

Nutrition, Exercise, and Therapeutic Recommendations

Text in this section is excerpted from "Preventing Alzheimer's Disease," National Institute on Aging (NIA), September 2012.

Do Exercise and Physical Activity Protect the Brain?

Exercise and other types of physical activity have many benefits. Studies show that they are good for our hearts, waistlines, and ability to carry out everyday activities. Epidemiological studies and some intervention studies suggest that physical exercise may also play a role in reducing risk for Alzheimer disease (AD) and age-related cognitive decline.

Animal studies point to why this might be so. Exercise increases both the number of small blood vessels that supply blood to the brain and the number of connections between nerve cells in older rats and mice. In addition, researchers have found that exercise raises the level of a nerve growth factor (a protein key to brain health) in an area of the brain that is important to memory and learning.

Researchers have also shown that exercise can stimulate the human brain's ability to maintain old network connections and make new ones that are vital to healthy cognition. In a year-long study, 65 older people exercised daily, doing either an aerobic exercise program of walking for 40 minutes or a non aerobic program of stretching and toning exercises. At the end of the trial, the walking group showed improved connectivity in the part of the brain engaged in daydreaming, envisioning the future, and recalling the past. The walking group also improved on executive function, the ability to plan and organize tasks such as cooking a meal.

Several other clinical trials are exploring further the effect of physical activity on the risk of Alzheimer disease and cognitive decline. Other NIA-supported research is examining whether exercise can delay the development of Alzheimer disease in people with MCI. Findings from these and other clinical trials will show more definitively whether exercise helps protect our brains from cognitive impairment.

Does Diet Matter?

A number of studies suggest that eating certain foods may help keep the brain healthy—and that others can be detrimental to cognitive health. A diet that includes lots of fruits, vegetables, and whole grains and is low in fat and added sugar can reduce the risk of many chronic diseases, including heart disease and type 2 diabetes. Researchers are looking at whether a healthy diet also can help preserve cognitive function or reduce the risk of Alzheimer disease.

Studies have found, for example, that a diet rich in vegetables, especially green leafy vegetables and cruciferous vegetables like broccoli, is associated with a reduced rate of cognitive decline. One epidemiological study reported that people who ate a "Mediterranean diet" had a 28 percent lower risk of developing MCI and a 48 percent lower risk of progressing from MCI to Alzheimer disease. A Mediterranean diet includes vegetables, legumes, fruits, cereals, fish, olive oil, mild to moderate amounts of alcohol, and low amounts of saturated fats, dairy products, meat, and poultry.

While some foods may stave off cognitive decline, other foods, such as saturated fats and refined carbohydrates (white sugar, for example), may pose a problem. In one study, scientists fed rats a "Western" diet high in fats and simple carbohydrates for 90 days. The results: rats fed this high-energy diet performed significantly worse on certain memory tests than rats fed a diet containing one-third the fat. Notably, the rats scored poorly on tests that involve the hippocampus, a part of the brain that plays a major role in learning and memory. Some scientists have focused on DHA (docosahexaenoic acid), an omega-3 fatty acid found in salmon and certain other fish. Studies in mice specially bred to have features of Alzheimer disease found that DHA reduces beta-amyloid plaques, abnormal protein deposits in the brain that are a hallmark of Alzheimer disease. Although a clinical trial of DHA showed no impact on people with mild to moderate Alzheimer disease, it is possible that DHA supplements could be effective if started before cognitive symptoms appear.

These findings are of great interest and suggest possible areas for future study. The NIA supports clinical trials to examine the relationship between several dietary components and Alzheimer disease and cognitive decline.

What Is the Effect of Other Chronic Diseases?

Age-related diseases and conditions—such as vascular disease, high blood pressure, heart disease, and type 2 diabetes—may increase the risk of Alzheimer disease and cognitive decline. Many studies are looking at whether this risk can be reduced by preventing or controlling these diseases and conditions through medication or changes in diet and exercise.

Much of the evidence about possible ties between vascular diseases and Alzheimer disease risk comes from observational studies. For example, high cholesterol levels and obesity during midlife—known risk factors for heart disease—have also been linked to increased risk of Alzheimer disease. High blood pressure may be another risk factor.

One NIH clinical trial is looking at how lowering blood pressure to or below current recommended levels may affect cognitive decline and the development of MCI and Alzheimer disease. Participants are older adults with high systolic blood pressure who have a history of heart disease or stroke, or are at risk for those conditions.

Diabetes is another disease that has been linked to Alzheimer disease. Previous research suggests that abnormal insulin production (insulin is the hormone involved in diabetes) contributes to Alzheimer disease-related brain changes. Can restoring normal insulin function in the brain provide cognitive benefits?

The results so far are mixed. One large NIH-funded clinical trial compared intensive glucose-lowering treatment with standard treatment in nearly 3,000 older adults with diabetes. After 40 months, the two groups showed no significant difference in cognitive function. But pilot testing of an insulin nasal spray has shown promising results. A clinical trial is testing this potential treatment in older adults with MCI or mild to moderate Alzheimer disease to see if it can improve memory and daily functioning.

Additional studies and clinical trials are looking at cardiovascular and diabetes medications to see if they might prevent Alzheimer disease. These therapies include aspirin, medications used to treat high blood pressure and other heart conditions, and the diabetes drugs metformin and pioglitazone.

What about Vitamins and Dietary Supplements?

Can any vitamins or dietary supplements protect the brain from Alzheimer disease and cognitive decline? One area of research focuses on antioxidants, natural substances that appear to fight damage caused by molecules called free radicals. Other studies are looking at a compound called resveratrol.

As a person ages, free radicals can build up in nerve cells, causing damage that might contribute to Alzheimer disease. Some epidemiological and laboratory studies suggest that antioxidants from food or dietary supplements help prevent this oxidative damage—and lower the risk of Alzheimer disease—but other studies have shown no effect. Vitamin E, vitamin C, B vitamins, ginkgo biloba, and coenzyme Q have all been tested in clinical trials, but none has proven effective in preventing or slowing down Alzheimer disease.

Resveratrol, a compound found in red grapes as well as supplements, appears to have properties that may help protect the brain. Observational studies have shown that moderate consumption of red wine is associated with a lower incidence of Alzheimer disease, and animal studies have shown that resveratrol can reduce beta-amyloid deposits in the brain. Resveratrol also appears to affect the biological processes of aging-related diseases, including Alzheimer disease. An NIA-supported clinical trial will test the effects of resveratrol in people with Alzheimer disease.

Is Keeping Your Brain Active Important?

Staying cognitively active throughout life—via social engagement or intellectual stimulation—is associated with a lower risk of Alzheimer disease. Several observational studies link continued cognitive health with social engagement through work, volunteering, or living with someone. Mentally stimulating activities such as reading books and magazines, going to lectures, and playing games are also linked to keeping the mind sharp.

In a large study of healthy older people, researchers found a relationship between more frequent social activity and better cognitive function. It is not clear whether improved cognition resulted from the social interaction itself or from related factors, such as increased intellectual stimulation, that generally accompany social interaction. Other studies are exploring these relationships.

Intellectually stimulating activities may also reduce the risk of Alzheimer disease, studies show. One large observational study looked at the impact of ordinary activities like listening to the radio, reading newspapers, playing puzzle games, and visiting museums. Investigators asked more than 700 older nuns, priests, and religious brothers to describe the amount of time they spent doing these activities. After 4 years, the risk of developing Alzheimer disease was 47 percent lower, on average, for those who did the activities most often than for those who did them least frequently.

A more recent study showed that people with less education who engaged in activities like reading, doing crossword puzzles, and writing letters performed as well on memory tests as their better-educated peers. Having fewer years of education has been associated with a higher risk of dementia. More research is needed to see if everyday cognitive activities can reduce the risk of cognitive decline in people with less education.

Formal cognitive training also seems to have cognitive benefits. In the Advanced Cognitive Training for Independent and Vital Elderly (ACTIVE) trial, for example, healthy adults 65 and older participated in 10 sessions of memory training, reasoning training, or processing-speed training. The sessions improved participants' mental skills in the area in which they were trained. These improvements persisted 10 years after the training was complete.

Another approach is testing the impact of formal cognitive training, with and without aerobic exercise. For example, an NIA-funded clinical trial is investigating the effectiveness of cognitive training, alone and combined with aerobic exercise, in people with MCI to see if it can prevent or delay Alzheimer disease. Other trials are underway in healthy older adults to see if exercise and/or cognitive training (for example, a demanding video game) can delay or prevent age-related cognitive decline.

Other types of formal cognitive training are being studied in healthy older adults to explore their impact on age-related cognitive decline. Types of training being tested in NIA-funded trials include learning digital photography or quilting and volunteering at local schools.

How Might an Active Brain Prevent Alzheimer Disease?

The reasons for the apparent link between social engagement or intellectual stimulation and Alzheimer disease risk aren't entirely clear, but scientists offer these possibilities:

- Such activities may protect the brain by establishing "cognitive reserve," the brain's ability to operate effectively even when it is damaged or some brain function is disrupted.

- These activities may help the brain become more adaptable in some mental functions, so it can compensate for declines in other functions.

- People who engage in these activities may have other lifestyle factors that protect them against Alzheimer disease.

- Less engagement with other people or in intellectually stimulating activities could be the result of very early effects of Alzheimer disease rather than its cause.

Other Clues to Alzheimer Disease Prevention

The quest for ways to prevent Alzheimer disease is part of a broad research program that is exploring a number of possibilities. For example, scientists are looking at caregiver stress and physical frailty as possible risk factors for Alzheimer disease and MCI. Other areas of interest include hormones and immunization.

Hormones

Scientists are studying hormones—especially those taken by older women as menopausal hormone therapy—for their potential ability to prevent or delay Alzheimer disease and age-related cognitive decline. Several clinical trials are testing forms of estrogen as well as testosterone and other hormones in both healthy older adults and those with MCI.

Hormones such as estrogen and progesterone have important effects on the brain, many of which could relate to cognitive aging and Alzheimer disease. Over the years, research has led to conflicting reports as to whether menopausal hormone therapy can prevent cognitive decline in postmenopausal women.

Some animal and observational studies comparing women who did and did not take estrogen have shown that the hormone may benefit cognition. However, clinical trials of estrogen and progestin in older women have generally failed to show similar beneficial effects. In fact, one large study showed that prolonged treatment with these hormones actually increased the risk of dementia in women 65 and older.

Researchers now wonder if it may be better for women to start taking hormones closer to menopause. NIA funded clinical trials are studying the timing of menopausal hormone therapy on cognition and other health factors.

Other hormones being studied in clinical trials for their effects on Alzheimer disease and cognitive decline include testosterone, which is being tested in older men with MCI and low levels of the hormone; growth hormone releasing hormone (GHRH), in healthy older adults and those with early MCI; and DHEA, in healthy postmenopausal women.

Immunization

The idea of a vaccine to prevent Alzheimer disease is under scrutiny as well. Early vaccine studies in mice were so successful in reducing deposits of Alzheimer disease-related proteins in the brain and improving performance on memory tests that investigators conducted preliminary clinical trials in humans with Alzheimer disease. These studies had to be stopped, however, because life-threatening brain inflammation occurred in some participants.

Scientists continue to refine this approach, hoping to maintain the vaccine's possible benefits while reducing side effects. Several pharmaceutical companies are testing potential vaccines for safety and effectiveness in clinical trials.

The NIA is also supporting a clinical trial testing whether intravenous immunoglobulin (IVIg), a blood product containing naturally occurring antibodies that is used to treat immune-system disorders, may improve cognition by clearing Alzheimer disease plaques from the brain.

Section 34.2

Effect of Physical Activities on Cognitive Functions

This section includes excerpts from "Exercise and Physical Activity,"
National Institute on Aging (NIA), July 2012; and text from "Physical
Activity and Alzheimer Disease-Related Hippocampal Atrophy,"
National Institute on Aging (NIA), August 4, 2014.

Being active and getting exercise helps people with Alzheimer disease (AD) feel better. Exercise helps keep their muscles, joints, and heart in good shape. It also helps people stay at a healthy weight and have regular toilet and sleep habits. You can exercise together to make it more fun. You want someone with Alzheimer disease to do as much as possible for himself or herself. At the same time, you need to make sure that the person is safe when active.

Getting Started

Here are some tips for helping the person with Alzheimer disease stay active:

- Be realistic about how much activity can be done at one time. Several 10-minute "mini-workouts" may be best.

- Take a walk together each day. Exercise is good for caregivers, too!

- Make sure the person with Alzheimer disease has an ID bracelet with your phone number if he or she walks alone.

- Check your local TV guide to see if there is a program to help older adults exercise, or watch exercise videos/DVDs made for older people.

- Add music to the exercises if it helps the person with Alzheimer disease. Dance to the music if possible.

- Break exercises into simple, easy-to-follow steps.

- Make sure the person wears comfortable clothes and shoes that fit well and are made for exercise.

- Make sure he or she drinks water or juice after exercise.

Gentle Exercise

Some people with Alzheimer disease may not be able to get around well. This is another problem that becomes more challenging to deal with as the disease gets worse. Some possible reasons for this include:

- Trouble with endurance

- Poor coordination

- Sore feet or muscles

- Illness

- Depression or general lack of interest

Even if people have trouble walking, they may be able to:

- Do simple tasks around the home, such as sweeping and dusting.

- Use a stationary bike.

- Use soft rubber exercise balls or balloons for stretching or throwing back and forth.

- Use stretching bands, which you can buy in sporting goods stores. Be sure to follow the instructions.

- Lift weights or household items such as soup cans.

Physical Activity and Alzheimer Disease-Related Hippocampal Atrophy

Physical activity may help prevent atrophy of the hippocampus, a brain region important for learning and memory that often shrinks in the brains of people with Alzheimer disease. A recent study that looked at the rate of atrophy over 18 months in cognitively normal older adults suggests that physical activity may help prevent or delay this Alzheimer disease-related change.

The NIA-funded study by researchers at the Cleveland Clinic's Schey Center for Cognitive Neuroimaging is the first to show the protective effects physical activity may have on the hippocampus in older adults at genetic risk for Alzheimer disease. It also adds to past findings that physical activity, from gardening to walking to structured exercise programs, may benefit cognitive function in older adults.

Researchers studied 97 cognitively normal adults, age 65 to 89, some of whom had a family history of dementia. They were divided into four groups based on their self-reported levels of physical activity (low or high) and the presence or absence of the apolipoprotein E (APOE) ε4 gene form, the strongest known genetic risk factor for Alzheimer disease. Individuals with low physical activity said they walked or did other low-intensity activities on 2 or fewer days per week; those with high activity said they engaged in moderate or vigorous activity, such as brisk walking or swimming, on 3 or more days per week.

All participants underwent magnetic resonance imaging (MRI) of the brain to measure the size of the hippocampus—a part of the brain that shrinks as Alzheimer disease progresses—and other brain structures, as well as neurobehavioral testing to measure cognition and daily functioning. MRI scans were done at the beginning of the study and after 18 months. At the study end, researchers found the size of the hippocampus decreased by 3 percent in the group with high genetic risk and low physical activity. Hippocampal size remained stable in the group with low genetic risk and in participants with high genetic risk/high physical activity. Physical activity did not appear to affect several other brain areas, including the amygdala, thalamus, and cortical white matter.

While promising, more research is needed to confirm these findings. Researchers want to learn how physical activity influences hippocampal atrophy in people at high genetic risk of Alzheimer disease. Animal studies suggest several possibilities, including the impact of physical activity on cholinergic function, brain inflammation, and cerebral blood flow.

Section 34.3

Alternative Medicine Therapies for Cognitive Functions

This section includes excerpts from "Alzheimer's Disease at a Glance," National Center for Complementary and Integrative Health (NCCIH), November 2014; and text from "5 Things To Know About Complementary Health Practices for Cognitive Function, Dementia, and Alzheimer's Disease," National Center for Complementary and Integrative Health (NCCIH), November 2014.

What the Science Says

Following are some of the complementary health approaches that have been studied in recent years.

- Fish Oil/Omega-3s. Among the nutritional and dietary factors studied to prevent cognitive decline in older adults, the most consistent positive research findings are for omega-3 fatty acids, often measured as how much fish people ate. However, taking omega-3 supplements did not have any beneficial effects on the cognitive functioning of older people without dementia.

- Ginkgo. An NCCIH-funded study of the well-characterized ginkgo supplement EGb-761 found that it didn't lower the incidence of dementia, including Alzheimer disease (AD), in older adults. Further analysis of the same data showed that ginkgo did not slow cognitive decline, lower blood pressure, or reduce the incidence of hypertension. In this clinical trial, known as the Ginkgo Evaluation of Memory study, researchers recruited more than 3,000 volunteers age 75 and older who took 240 mg of ginkgo daily. Participants were followed for an average of approximately 6 years.

- B-vitamins. Results of short-term studies suggest that B-vitamin supplements do not help cognitive functioning in adults age 50 or older with or without dementia. The vitamins studied were B12, B6, and folic acid, taken alone or in combination.

- Curcumin, which comes from turmeric, has anti-inflammatory and antioxidant properties that might affect chemical processes in the brain associated with Alzheimer disease, laboratory studies have suggested. However, the few clinical trials (studies done in people) that have looked at the effects of curcumin on Alzheimer disease have not found a benefit.

- Melatonin. People with dementia can become agitated and have trouble sleeping. Supplements of melatonin, which is a naturally occurring hormone that helps regulate sleep, are being studied to see if they improve sleep in some people with dementia. However, in one study researchers noted that melatonin supplements may worsen mood in people with dementia.

- For caregivers, taking a mindfulness meditation class or a caregiver education class reduced stress more than just getting time off from providing care, a small, 2010 NCCIH-funded study showed.

Side Effects and Risks

- Don't use complementary approaches as a reason to postpone seeing a healthcare provider about memory loss. Treatable conditions, such as depression, bad reactions to medications, or thyroid, liver, or kidney problems, can cause memory impairment.

- Keep in mind that although many dietary supplements (and some prescription drugs) come from natural sources, "natural" does not always mean "safe."

- Some dietary supplements have been found to interact with medications, whether prescription or over-the-counter. For example, the herbal supplement St. John's wort interacts with many medications, making them less effective. Your healthcare provider can advise you.

5 Things to Know about Complementary Health Practices for Cognitive Function, Dementia, and Alzheimer Disease

Many people, particularly older individuals, worry about forgetfulness and whether it is the first sign of dementia or Alzheimer disease. In fact, forgetfulness has many causes. It can also be a normal part of aging, or related to various treatable health issues or to emotional problems, such as stress, anxiety, or depression. The National Institute on Aging has a lot of information on the aging brain as well as cognitive function, dementia, and Alzheimer disease. Although no treatment is proven to stop dementia or Alzheimer disease, some conventional drugs may limit worsening of symptoms for a period of time in the early stages of the disease.

Many dietary supplements are marketed with claims that they enhance memory or improve brain function and health. To date, research has yielded no convincing evidence that any dietary supplement can reverse or slow the progression of dementia or Alzheimer disease. Additional research on dietary supplements, as well as several mind and body practices such as music therapy and mental imagery, which have shown promise in basic research or preliminary clinical studies, is underway.

Here are few things to know about current research on complementary health approaches for cognitive function, dementia, and Alzheimer disease.

- To date there is no convincing evidence from a large body of research that any dietary supplement can prevent worsening of cognitive impairment associated with dementia or Alzheimer disease. This includes studies of ginkgo, omega-3 fatty acids/fish oil, vitamins B and E, Asian ginseng, grape seed extract, and curcumin. Additional research on some of these supplements is underway.

- Preliminary studies of some mind and body practices such as music therapy suggest they may be helpful for some of the symptoms related to dementia, such as agitation and depression. Several studies on music therapy in people with Alzheimer disease have shown improvement in agitation, depression, and quality of life.

- Mindfulness-based stress reduction programs may be helpful in reducing stress among caregivers of patients with dementia. To reduce caregiver stress, studies suggest that a mindfulness-based stress reduction program is more helpful for improving mental health than attending an education and support program or just taking time off from providing care.

- Don't use complementary health approaches as a reason to postpone seeing a healthcare provider about memory loss. Treatable conditions, such as depression, bad reactions to medications, or thyroid, liver, or kidney problems, can impair memory.

- Some complementary health approaches interact with medications and can have serious side effects. If you are considering replacing conventional medications with other approaches, talk to your health care provider.

Chapter 35

Common Medical Problems in People with Alzheimer Disease

A person with Alzheimer disease (AD) may have other medical problems over time, as we all do. These problems can cause more confusion and behavior changes. The person may not be able to tell you what is wrong. You need to watch for signs of illness and tell the doctor about what you see.

The Most Common Medical Problems

Fever

Having a fever means that the person's temperature is 2 degrees above his or her normal temperature.

A fever may be a sign of:

- Infection, caused by germs
- Dehydration, caused by a lack of fluids
- Heat stroke
- Constipation (discussed later in this section)

Don't use a glass thermometer because the person might bite down on the glass. Use a digital thermometer, which you can buy at a grocery store or drugstore.

Text in this chapter is excerpted from "Caring for a Person with Alzheimer's Disease," National Institute on Aging (NIA), May 2015.

Flu and Pneumonia

These diseases spread quickly from one person to another, and people with AD are more likely to get them. **Make sure that the person gets a flu shot each year and a pneumonia shot once after age 65. Some older people need to get more than one pneumonia vaccine.** The shots lower the chances that the person will get flu or pneumonia.

Flu and pneumonia may cause:

- Fever (Not everyone with pneumonia has a fever.)
- Chills
- Aches and pains
- Vomiting
- Coughing
- Breathing trouble

Falls

As AD gets worse, the person may have trouble walking and keeping his or her balance. He or she also may have changes in depth perception, which is the ability to understand distances. For example, someone with AD may try to step down when walking from a carpeted to a tile floor. This puts him or her at risk for falls.

To reduce the chance of a fall:

- Clean up clutter.
- Remove throw rugs.
- Use chairs with arms.
- Put grab bars in the bathroom.
- Use good lighting.
- Make sure the person wears sturdy shoes with good traction.

Dehydration

Our bodies must have a certain amount of water to work well. If a person is sick or doesn't drink enough fluid, he or she may become dehydrated.

Signs of dehydration to look for include:

- Dry mouth

- Dizziness

- Hallucinations (Don't forget that hallucinations may be caused by the AD itself.)

- Rapid heart rate

Be aware of how much fluid the person is drinking. This is even more important during hot weather or in homes without air conditioning. Also, look for signs of dehydration during the winter months when heat in your home can create a lot of dry air.

Constipation

People can have constipation—trouble having a bowel movement—when they:

- Change what they eat

- Take certain medicines, including Namenda®

- Get less exercise than usual

- Drink less fluid than usual

Try to get the person to drink at least 6 glasses of liquid a day.

Besides water, other good sources of liquid include:

- Juice, especially prune juice

- Gelatin, such as Jell-O®

- Soup

- Melted ice cream

- Decaffeinated coffee and tea

- Liquid cereal, such as Cream of Wheat®

Have the person eat foods high in fiber. Foods like dried apricots, raisins, or prunes; some dry cereals; or soybeans might help ease constipation.

If possible, make sure that the person gets some exercise each day, such as walking. Call the doctor if you notice a change in the person's bowel habits.

Diarrhea

Some medicines, such as Aricept®, Razadyne®, and Exelon®, may cause diarrhea—loose bowel movements. Certain medical problems also may cause diarrhea. Make sure the person takes in lots of fluids when he or she has diarrhea. Also, be sure to let the doctor know about this problem.

Incontinence

Incontinence means a person can't control his or her bladder and/or bowels. This may happen at any stage of AD, but it is more often a problem in the later stages. Signs of this problem are leaking urine, problems emptying the bladder, and soiled underwear and bed sheets. Be sure to let the doctor know if this happens. He or she may be able to treat the cause of the problem.

Here are some examples of things that can be treated:

- Urinary tract infection
- Enlarged prostate gland
- Too little fluid in the body (dehydration)
- Diabetes that isn't being treated
- Taking too many water pills
- Drinking too much caffeine
- Taking medicines that make it hard to hold urine

When you talk to the doctor, be ready to answer the following questions:

- What medicines is the person taking?
- Does the person leak urine when he or she laughs, coughs, or lifts something?
- Does the person urinate often?
- Can the person get to the bathroom in time?
- Is the person urinating in places other than the bathroom?
- Is the person soiling his or her clothes or bed sheets each night?
- Do these problems happen each day or once in awhile?

Here are some ways you can deal with incontinence:

- Remind the person to go to the bathroom every 2 to 3 hours.

- Show him or her the way to the bathroom, or take him or her.

- Make sure that the person wears loose, comfortable clothing that is easy to remove.

- Limit fluids after 6 p.m. if problems happen at night. Do not give the person fluids with caffeine, such as coffee or tea.

- Give the person fresh fruit before bedtime instead of fluids if he or she is thirsty.

- Mark the bathroom door with a big sign that reads "Toilet" or "Bathroom."

- Use a stable toilet seat that is at a good height. Using a colorful toilet seat may help the person identify the toilet. You can buy raised toilet seats at medical supply stores.

- Help the person when he or she needs to use a public bathroom. This may mean going into the stall with the person or using a family or private bathroom.

Things you may want to buy:

- Use adult disposable briefs or underwear, bed protectors, and waterproof mattress covers. You can buy these items at drug-stores and medical supply stores.

- Use a drainable pouch for the person who can't control his or her bowel movements. Talk to the nurse about how to use this product.

Some people find it helpful to keep a record of how much food and fluid the person takes in and how often he or she goes to the bathroom. You can use this information to make a schedule of when he or she needs to go to the bathroom.

Dental Problems

As AD gets worse, people need help taking care of their teeth or dentures.

Check the person's mouth for any problems such as:

- Sores

- Decayed teeth
- Food "pocketed" in the cheek or on the roof of the mouth
- Lumps

Be sure to take the person for dental checkups. Some people need medicine to calm them before they can see the dentist.

Other Medical Problems

People with AD can have the same medical problems as many older adults. Research suggests that some of these medical problems may be related to AD.

For example, some heart and blood circulation problems, stroke, and diabetes are more common in people who have AD than in the general population. Diseases caused by infections also are common.

Be sure to take the person to the doctor for regular checkups.

Chapter 36

Pain and Dementia

Acute Pain and Chronic Pain

Dementia is known primarily for its effects on memory. However, 80 percent of people with dementia also have behavioral disturbances. These behaviors are often not addressed, leading to increased use of nursing homes, higher incidence of injury (to both individuals and caregivers), and the use of tranquilizing medications. Pain is present in about half of people with dementia and is associated with significant negative outcomes, including aggression, increased health care use, inactivity, and isolation.

There are two kinds of pain. Acute pain begins suddenly, lasts for a short time, and goes away as your body heals. You might feel acute pain after surgery or if you have a broken bone, infected tooth, or kidney stone.

Pain that lasts for several months or years is called chronic (or persistent) pain. This pain often affects older people. Examples include rheumatoid arthritis (RA) and sciatica. In some cases, chronic pain follows after acute pain from an injury or other health issue has gone away, like postherpetic neuralgia after shingles.

Living with any type of pain can be very hard. It can cause many other problems. For instance, pain can:

• Get in the way of your daily activities

This chapter includes excerpts from "Pain: You Can Get Help," National Institute on Aging (NIA), June 25, 2015; and text from "Preventing Aggression in Veterans with Dementia," National Institute on Aging (NIA), June 28, 2013.

- Disturb your sleep and eating habits
- Make it difficult to continue working
- Cause depression or anxiety

Describing Pain

Many people have a hard time describing pain. Think about these questions when you explain how the pain feels:

- Where does it hurt?
- When did it start? Does the pain come and go?
- What does it feel like? Is the pain sharp, dull, or burning? Would you use some other word to describe it?
- Do you have other symptoms?
- When do you feel the pain? In the morning? In the evening? After eating?
- Is there anything you do that makes the pain feel better or worse? For example, does using a heating pad or ice pack help? Does changing your position from lying down to sitting up make it better? Have you tried any over-the-counter medications for it?

Your doctor or nurse may ask you to rate your pain on a scale of 0 to 10, with 0 being no pain and 10 being the worst pain you can imagine. Or, your doctor may ask if the pain is mild, moderate, or severe. Some doctors or nurses have pictures of faces that show different expressions of pain. You point to the face that shows how you feel.

Attitudes about Pain

Everyone reacts to pain differently. Many older people have been told not to talk about their aches and pains. Some people feel they should be brave and not complain when they hurt. Other people are quick to report pain and ask for help.

Worrying about pain is a common problem. This worry can make you afraid to stay active, and it can separate you from your friends and family. Working with your doctor, you can find ways to continue to take part in physical and social activities despite being in pain.

Some people put off going to the doctor because they think pain is just part of aging and nothing can help. This is not true! It is important to see a doctor if you have a new pain. Finding a way to manage your pain is often easier if it is addressed early.

Treating Pain

Treating, or managing, chronic pain is important. The good news is that there are ways to care for pain. Some treatments involve medications, and some do not. Your doctor may make a treatment plan that is specific for your needs.

Most treatment plans do not just focus on reducing pain. They also include ways to support daily function while living with pain.

Pain doesn't always go away overnight. Talk with your doctor about how long it may take before you feel better. Often, you have to stick with a treatment plan before you get relief. It's important to stay on a schedule. Sometimes this is called "staying ahead" or "keeping on top" of your pain. As your pain lessens, you can likely become more active and will see your mood lift and sleep improve.

Medicines to Treat Pain

Your doctor may prescribe one or more of the following pain medications:

- **Acetaminophen** may help all types of pain, especially mild to moderate pain. Acetaminophen is found in over-the-counter and prescription medicines. People who drink a lot of alcohol or who have liver disease should not take acetaminophen. Be sure to talk with your doctor about whether it is safe for you to take and what would be the right dose.

- **Nonsteroidal anti-inflammatory drugs (NSAIDs)** include medications like aspirin, naproxen, and ibuprofen. Some types of NSAIDs can cause side effects, like internal bleeding, which make them unsafe for many older adults. For instance, you may not be able to take ibuprofen if you have high blood pressure or had a stroke. Talk to your doctor before taking NSAIDs to see if they are safe for you.

- **Narcotics** (also called opioids) are used for severe pain and require a doctor's prescription. They may be habit-forming. Examples of narcotics are codeine, morphine, and oxycodone.

- **Other medications** are sometimes used to treat pain. These include antidepressants, anticonvulsive medicines, local painkillers like nerve blocks or patches, and ointments and creams.

As people age, they are at risk for developing more serious side effects from medication. It's important to take exactly the amount of pain medicine your doctor prescribes.

Mixing any pain medication with alcohol or other drugs, such as tranquilizers, can be dangerous. Make sure your doctor knows all the medicines you take, including over-the-counter drugs and herbal supplements, as well as the amount of alcohol you drink.

Remember: If you think the medicine is not working, don't change it on your own. Talk to your doctor or nurse. You might say, "I've been taking the medication as you directed, but it still hurts too much to play with my grandchildren. Is there anything else I can try?"

What Other Treatments Help with Pain?

In addition to drugs, there are a variety of complementary and alternative approaches that may provide relief. Talk to your doctor about these treatments. It may take both medicine and other treatments to feel better.

- **Acupuncture** uses hair-thin needles to stimulate specific points on the body to relieve pain.

- **Biofeedback** helps you learn to control your heart rate, blood pressure, and muscle tension. This may help reduce your pain and stress level.

- **Cognitive behavioral therapy** is a form of short-term counseling that may help reduce your reaction to pain.

- **Distraction** can help you cope with pain by learning new skills that may take your mind off your discomfort.

- **Electrical nerve stimulation** uses electrical impulses in order to relieve pain.

- **Guided imagery** uses directed thoughts to create mental pictures that may help you relax, manage anxiety, sleep better, and have less pain.

- **Hypnosis** uses focused attention to help manage pain.

- **Massage therapy** can release tension in tight muscles.

- **Physical therapy** uses a variety of techniques to help manage everyday activities with less pain and teaches you ways to improve flexibility and strength.

Helping Yourself

There are things you can do yourself that might help you feel better. Try to:

- Keep a healthy weight. Putting on extra pounds can slow healing and make some pain worse. Keeping a healthy weight might help with knee pain, or pain in the back, hips, or feet.

- Be active. Try to keep moving. Pain might make you inactive, which can lead to a cycle of more pain and loss of function. Mild activity can help.

- Get enough sleep. It will improve healing and your mood.

- Avoid tobacco, caffeine, and alcohol. They can get in the way of your treatment and increase your pain.

- Join a pain support group. Sometimes, it can help to talk to other people about how they deal with pain. You can share your ideas and thoughts while learning from others.

- Participate in activities you enjoy. Taking part in activities that you find relaxing, like listening to music or doing art, might help take your mind off of some of the pain.

Alzheimer Disease and Pain

People who have Alzheimer disease (AD) may not be able to tell you when they're in pain. When you're caring for someone with Alzheimer disease, watch for clues. A person's face may show signs of being in pain or feeling ill. You may also notice sudden changes in behavior such as increased yelling, striking out, or spending more time in bed. It's important to find out if there is something wrong. If you're not sure what to do, call the doctor for help.

Pain at the End of Life

Not everyone who is dying is in pain. But if a person has pain at the end of life, there are ways to help. Experts often believe it's best to focus on making the person comfortable, without worrying about possible addiction or drug dependence.

Speak to a palliative care or pain management specialist if you are concerned about pain for yourself or a loved one. These specialists are trained to manage pain and other symptoms for people with serious illnesses.

Caring for Someone in Pain

It's hard to see a loved one hurting. Caring for a person in pain can leave you feeling tired and discouraged. To keep from feeling overwhelmed, you might consider asking other family members and friends for help. Or, some community service organizations might offer short-term, or respite, care.

Some Facts about Pain

- **Most people don't have to live with pain.** There are pain treatments. While not all pain can be cured, most pain can be managed. If your doctor has not been able to help you, ask to see a pain specialist.

- **Most people who properly take doctor-prescribed narcotic drugs for pain relief do not become addicted.** If you take your medicine exactly the way your doctor tells you, then you are not likely to develop an addiction problem. Let your doctor know if you have a personal or family history of substance abuse.

- **The side effects from pain medicine usually are not worse than the pain.** Side effects from pain medicine like constipation, dry mouth, and drowsiness may be a problem when you first begin taking the medicine. These problems can often be treated and may go away as your body gets used to the medicine.

- **Your doctor will not think you're a whiner or a sissy if you talk about your pain.** If you are in pain, tell your doctor so you can get the help you need.

- **If you use pain medicine now, it will still work when you need it later.** Using medicine at the first sign of pain may help control your pain later.

- **Pain is not "all in your head."** No one but you knows how your pain feels. If you're in pain, talk with your doctor.

Chapter 37

Sleep Problems and Alzheimer Disease

Sleep Patterns May Signal Alzheimer Disease Risk

People with Alzheimer disease (AD) often have insomnia, nighttime wandering, daytime napping, or other problems with sleeping and/or staying awake. Researchers at Washington University School of Medicine in St. Louis found that preclinical signs of Alzheimer are also associated with poor sleep quality. The researchers monitored sleep-wake patterns in 142 cognitively normal participants (average age, 66) by using actigraphy (devices worn on the wrist that record movement) and measuring beta-amyloid levels in their cerebrospinal fluid (CSF). Thirty-two of the participants had significantly reduced CSF beta-amyloid levels, a sign of brain beta-amyloid deposition seen in the preclinical stages of Alzheimer disease. That group also had worse sleep quality (they spent more time awake when in bed) and more frequent daytime napping than individuals with normal CSF beta-amyloid levels.

NIA researchers, in collaboration with the Johns Hopkins Bloomberg School of Public Health, Baltimore, found reduced sleep quantity and poorer sleep quality in people with elevated brain beta-amyloid

This chapter includes excerpts from "Identifying Risk Factors for Cognitive Decline and Alzheimer's," National Institute on Aging (NIA), February 15, 2014; and text from "A Good Night's Sleep," National Institute on Aging (NIA), December 22, 2015.

deposition. The researchers studied 70 adults (average age, 76) enrolled in the Baltimore Longitudinal Study of Aging. The participants' sleep patterns were assessed using questionnaires, and their levels of brain beta-amyloid were measured by positron emission tomography scans. Those with more brain beta-amyloid deposition reported fewer average hours of sleep per night and more restless sleep.

Conversely, better sleep may reduce one's risk of Alzheimer disease, according to a study by researchers at the University of Toronto, Ontario, Canada, and the Rush Alzheimer Disease Center, Chicago. The researchers studied 698 volunteers (average age, 82) who were not demented at the start of the study. The participants' sleep was monitored by actigraphy for 10 days at the start of the study, and their cognition was tested annually for 3 to 6 years. During that period, 98 of the participants developed Alzheimer disease. As has been found in many other studies, the APOE ε4 carriers were much more likely than noncarriers to develop Alzheimer disease (two- to four-fold more likely, in this study). However, APOE ε4 carriers who showed restful sleep at the start of the study were only half as likely to develop Alzheimer disease as those who slept more poorly.

The researchers also analyzed post mortem brain tissue from 201 participants who died during the course of the study. They found that APOE ε4 carriers showed much more severe tau pathology than did noncarriers, but APOE ε4 carriers who slept better had less tau pathology than those who slept worse.

It is not yet clear whether sleep disturbances contribute directly to the Alzheimer disease process, are a secondary result of it, or both. However, these studies raise the possibility that interventions to improve sleep in older people could reduce their risk of developing Alzheimer disease.

Getting a Good Night's Sleep

Being older doesn't mean you have to feel tired all the time. There are many things you can do to help you get a good night's sleep. Here are some ideas:

- Follow a regular sleep schedule. Go to sleep and get up at the same time each day, even on weekends. Try to avoid napping in the late afternoon or evening, as it may keep you awake at night.

- Develop a bedtime routine. Take time to relax before bedtime each night. Some people watch television, read a book, listen to soothing music, or soak in a warm bath.

- Keep your bedroom dark, not too hot or too cold, and as quiet as possible.

- Have a comfortable mattress, a pillow you like, and enough blankets for the season.

- Exercise at regular times each day but not within 3 hours of your bedtime.

- Make an effort to get outside in the sunlight each day.

- Be careful about when and how much you eat. Large meals close to bedtime may keep you awake, but a light snack in the evening can help you get a good night's sleep.

- Stay away from caffeine late in the day. Caffeine (found in coffee, tea, soda, and hot chocolate) can keep you awake.

- Drink fewer beverages in the evening. Waking up to go to the bathroom and turning on a bright light break up your sleep.

- Remember that alcohol won't help you sleep. Even small amounts make it harder to stay asleep.

- Use your bedroom only for sleeping. After turning off the light, give yourself about 20 minutes to fall asleep. If you're still awake and not drowsy, get out of bed. When you feel sleepy, go back to bed.

Safe Sleeping

Try to set up a safe and restful place to sleep. Make sure you have smoke alarms on each floor of your house or apartment. Lock the outside doors before going to bed. Other ideas for a safe night's sleep are:

- Keep a telephone with emergency phone numbers by your bed.

- Have a good lamp within reach that turns on easily.

- Put a glass of water next to the bed in case you wake up thirsty.

- Use nightlights in the bathroom and hall.

- Don't smoke, especially in bed.

- Remove area rugs so you won't trip if you get out of bed in the middle of the night.

- Don't fall asleep with a heating pad on; it may burn.

Sweet Dreams

There are some tricks to help you fall asleep. You don't really have to count sheep—but you could try counting slowly to 100. Some people find that playing mental games makes them sleepy. For example, tell yourself it's 5 minutes before you have to get up, and you're just trying to get a few extra winks.

Other people find that relaxing their body puts them to sleep. You might start by telling yourself that your toes feel light as feathers and then work your way up the rest of the body saying the same words. You may drift off to sleep before getting to the top of your head.

If you feel tired and unable to do your activities for more than 2 or 3 weeks, you may have a sleep problem. Talk to your doctor about changes you can make to get a better night's sleep.

Instructions for Caregivers

Alzheimer disease often changes a person's sleeping habits. For example, some people with Alzheimer disease sleep too much; others don't sleep enough. Some people wake up many times during the night; others wander or yell at night. The person with Alzheimer disease isn't the only one who loses sleep. Caregivers may have sleepless nights, leaving them tired for the challenges they face.

If you're caring for someone with Alzheimer disease, there are steps you can take for his or her safety and that might help you sleep better at night. Try the following:

- Make sure the floor is clear of objects.

- Lock up any medicines.

- Attach grab bars in the bathroom.

- Place a gate across the stairs.

Chapter 38

Sexuality and Alzheimer Disease

Changes in Intimacy and Sexuality Intimacy is the special bond we share with a person we love and respect. It includes the way we talk and act toward one another. This bond can exist between spouses or partners, family members, and friends. Alzheimer disease (AD) often changes the intimacy between people.

Sexuality is one type of intimacy. It is an important way that spouses or partners express their feelings physically for one another.

AD can cause changes in intimacy and sexuality in both the person with AD and the caregiver. The person with AD may be stressed by the changes in his or her memory and behaviors. Fear, worry, depression, anger, and low self-esteem (how much the person likes himself or herself) are common. The person may become dependent and cling to you. He or she may not remember your life together and feelings toward one another. Sometimes the person may even fall in love with someone else.

You, the caregiver, may pull away from the person in both an emotional and physical sense. You may be upset by the demands of caregiving.

Text in this chapter is excerpted from "Caring for a Person with Alzheimer's Disease," National Institute on Aging (NIA), May 2015.

You also may feel frustrated by the person's constant forgetfulness, repeated questions, and other bothersome behaviors.

Most caregivers learn how to cope with these challenges, but it takes time. Some learn to live with the illness and find new meaning in their relationships with people who have AD.

How to Cope with Changes in Intimacy?

Remember that most people with AD need to feel that someone loves and cares about them. They also need to spend time with other people as well as you. Your efforts to take care of these needs can help the person with AD to feel happy and safe.

It's important to reassure the person that:

- You love him or her.

- You will keep him or her safe.

- Others also care about him or her.

When intimacy changes, the following tips may help you cope with your own needs:

- Talk with a doctor, social worker, or clergy member about these changes. It may feel awkward to talk about such personal issues, but it can help.

- Talk about your concerns in a support group.

- Think more about the positive parts of the relationship.

How to Cope with Changes in Sexuality?

The well spouse/partner or the person with AD may lose interest in having sex. This change can make you feel lonely or frustrated. Here are some possible reasons for changes in sexual interest.

The well spouse/partner may feel that:

- It's not okay to have sex with someone who has AD

- The person with AD seems like a stranger

- The person with AD seems to forget that the spouse/partner is there or how to make love

A person with AD may have:

- Side effects from medications that affect his or her sexual interest

- Memory loss, changes in the brain, or depression that affects his or her interest in sex

Here are some suggestions for coping with changes in sexuality:

- Explore new ways of spending time together.

- Focus on other ways to show affection. Some caregivers find that snuggling or holding hands reduces their need for a sexual relationship.

- Focus on other ways to show affection.

- Try other nonsexual forms of touching, such as giving a massage, hugging, and dancing.

- Consider other ways to meet your sexual needs. Some caregivers report that they masturbate to meet their needs.

Chapter 39

Living Alone with Alzheimer Disease or Dementia

Unmet Care Needs for People with Dementia Who Live Alone

People with Alzheimer disease (AD) and other dementias who live alone have care needs that differ and that are dependent on factors including the extent of their cognitive and functional abilities, availability of a caregiver, access to adequate care and services, and coordination of care. People with dementia generally report fewer unmet care needs than their caregivers. The number of reported unmet care needs is related to the severity of their dementia and their living situation. Some reasons for unmet needs in community-dwelling people with dementia, including those living alone, are lack of knowledge of existing services and that some of the services are insufficient and not customized to the person's needs or preferences.

Many people with dementia who live alone are at risk for self-neglect. Self-neglect is when a vulnerable adult is unable to practice basic self-care, including but not limited to provision of food, clothing, or shelter, and management of health care needs; physical and mental health maintenance, emotional well-being, and general safety; or

---

Text in this chapter is excerpted from "Identifying and Meeting the Needs of Individuals with Dementia Who Live Alone," Administration for Community Living (ACL), September 2015.

manage financial affairs. Signs of self-neglect include dehydration, malnutrition, untreated medical conditions, poor personal hygiene, unsafe or unsanitary living conditions, inappropriate or inadequate clothing, and inadequate housing or homelessness.

In a survey conducted by the National Association of Professional Geriatric Care Managers, 92 percent of care managers said that elder self-neglect was a significant problem in their community and 94 percent of care managers indicated that elder self-neglect is a largely hidden problem with cases frequently going unreported. According to a national survey on vulnerable adult abuse conducted by the National Center on Elder Abuse, self-neglect is the highest category of abuse investigated and substantiated by APS.

Self-neglect in older adults includes both medical and social care needs and has implications for public health. Cases of self-neglect can be among the most difficult to address and manage. At times, a person will resist interventions, deny or under estimate the severity and importance of his or her cognitive deficits, and have little or no awareness regarding his or her circumstances thus placing them at greater risk for adverse outcomes. Service providers working with these individuals are presented with the ethical dilemma of balancing efforts to support individual autonomy with efforts to ensure safety, with the understanding that there is "no perfect environment" for someone with dementia living alone and that "a certain amount of risk is inevitable".

People with dementia who live alone may underuse needed long-term services and supports. In a study of African American older adults with dementia living in the community, social workers rated 61 percent of the persons with dementia living alone as receiving inadequate support and supervision, compared with 25 percent of persons with dementia living with others. A recent study from Sweden indicated that a large number of people with Alzheimer disease or other dementia living alone had severe cognitive and functional impairment, but use of home help services did not match the severity of cognitive impairment.

Ability to Manage Personal Care Needs and Daily Activities

Among individuals with dementia, the ability to live alone is dependent on their physical ability and cognitive capacity to perform daily activities independently. reported that individuals with dementia who lived alone had significantly more unmet needs than those living with others, particularly in the areas of looking after home, food, self-care, and accidental self-harm. One study indicated that activity of daily living impairment was more common among subjects who lived with others but nearly half of the individuals with dementia living alone were found to have two or more impairments in instrumental activities of daily living.

People living alone with dementia are also at greater risk for malnutrition than those living with others. A study of individuals with dementia and their caregivers (about half of whom lived separate from each other) showed that the nutritional status of older people with dementia is strongly and positively associated with the nutritional status of caregivers. Accordingly, it is recommended that nutritional interventions in the context of dementia should address the caregiving dyad and not strictly the person with dementia.

Medication nonadherence is a complex problem with various risk factors, particularly in older adults living alone. Accidental injuries from errors in medication self-administration are more likely for people with dementia than injury from fires/burns and wandering. According to one study, the majority of self-medication errors occurred in administering the medication, modifying the medication regimen, or not following clinical advice about medication use. These errors were attributed to cognitive deficits, sensory or physical problems with dispensers, or the complexity of the regimen.

In a study of 339 elderly participants with cognitive impairment who lived alone and took at least one medication, 17.4 percent had at least one report of medication nonadherence. The most frequently occurring medical consequences were essential hypertension (13.0%), exacerbation of diabetes mellitus (13.0%), complications of heart disease (8.7%), constipation (8.7%), and edema (8.7%). Eleven (47.8%) of the 23 who had a medical consequence also required an emergency medical service.

Indications that a person with dementia living alone is not able to adequately manage his or her personal care needs and daily activities include frequent emergency medical visits, little or no food in the home, unkempt appearance, dirty clothes, and inappropriate clothing for the weather. Intervention strategies include referral for pharmacist or nurse medication reconciliation, home-delivered meals, arranging for home care services, and notifying the police and fire departments of the person's condition and providing contact information.

Home Safety Issues

Alzheimer disease and other dementias result in deficiencies that can reduce an individual's ability to remain safe at home, such as impairments in balance and mobility, judgment, sense of time and place, orientation and recognition of environmental cues, and changes in vision or hearing. As a result of impaired judgment, visual and spatial perception deficits, and disorientation, cognitive impairment increases the risk of falls by almost two-fold. Falls are the most common source of in-home accidents leading to morbidity and mortality. Falls are also the leading source of in-home injury in dementia. Signs that a person is at risk for falling include confusion, poor balance and unsteady gait, and four or more prescription medications.

Compulsive hoarding or extreme clutter and debris in the home can contribute to an individual's inability to manage his or her own daily activities and self-care. Food preparation becomes difficult if the person cannot access cooking appliances or even cupboards where food is stored. A significantly cluttered environment can lead to unsanitary living conditions and poses safety risks such as fire or falls/trips hazards. The living conditions affect not only the individual and family members but also neighbors and can become a public health concern.

Safety considerations and adaptations to the home to reduce safety risks include removal of throw rugs that may be a trip hazard, placement of latches on kitchen cabinets and drawers to keep knives and cleaning products out of reach, monitoring the environment for rearranging or removing furniture, removal of clutter and organization of areas of the home, installation of a ramp and grab bars in the bathroom, and widening doorways. Various types of assistive technology can also be used to prevent injuries in the home such as gas detectors, room air temperature monitors, and devices that monitor water levels to prevent accidents and damage from flooding. Technology is available to alert a caregiver or emergency response system when the person with dementia has fallen. These systems may monitor for activity in the home or may detect falls through a floor impact sensor.

Wandering

Wandering is a serious safety risk for people with dementia living alone because the likelihood of a person returning home safely largely depends on others recognizing that the person is missing or that something is unusual and reporting it to the appropriate authorities. Rowe and Glover (2001) define "unattended wandering" as forays into the community without the supervision of a caregiver. The professionals interviewed indicated that those at greatest risk are individuals with dementia living alone or living with a caregiver who leaves them alone while attending to other family or job responsibilities.

The Alzheimer Association (2015b) suggests that families make a plan if someone with dementia goes missing. Strategies include keeping a list of people to call on for help, a recent close-up photo, a list of places where the person may wander, and enrolling the person in an identification program. A missing person's report should be filed immediately so that police can begin to search for the individual.

Global positioning systems (GPS) and other assistive technologies are being used to monitor and locate people with dementia at risk of wandering. A person can wear a location device as a watch or pendant, carry it like a mobile phone, or even mount it to the car. As the technology advances, people with dementia are being engaged in the process of design with the hope of leading to devices that are more acceptable, user-friendly, and relevant to their needs. There are some limitations to using these devices. GPS and other assistive technologies are dependent on transmission and reception capability to be effective and buildings or other objects can impede signal transmission. In addition, a person with dementia may not like wearing or carrying a device and may remove it.

Although a location device may increase personal freedom and provide peace of mind to the person with dementia and those close to him or her, the decision to use one raises ethical issues regarding personal autonomy and privacy. Some have also suggested that having a location device may lead family members or friends to check in with the person less often. Experts have also suggested that the person with dementia be involved in decision-making and that this decision should be made in a formal structured meeting facilitated by a professional team.

Ability to Respond to Emergencies

The ability of persons with dementia to respond to crisis situations in the home is another important safety concern. One study found that older people who die as a result of a fire are more likely to be living alone than other older people. Another study of 38 people with dementia who are living at home demonstrated that those living alone were perceived to be more at risk than those living with someone, and the most commonly reported risks included fire, nutrition, and medication management.

Dementia increases the risk for fire-related death. found that the majority of persons with burn injuries among persons with dementia were unsupervised at the time of injury and were burned while performing routine activities of daily living, such as cooking or bathing.

The causes of burn injuries were predominantly bathroom or kitchen scalding and flame burns, suggesting that routine cooking and bathroom activities are of concern when an individual with dementia is alone.

Living alone with dementia increases the risk of mortality associated with accidental injuries because of impaired insight and problem-solving ability, the absence of a caregiver and delayed medical help. Difficulties in using the telephone are common among individuals with dementia living alone, so when emergencies do arise calling for help may not be possible.

Home and community-based services providers need to understand how to respond in an emergency, to the unique needs of someone with dementia who lives alone. Emergency personnel at the time of the crisis situation should have access to concise, accurate information 13 about the person's medical conditions, medications and dosage, and other important information. Home and community-based services providers should be trained on working with first responders such as fire personnel or police to assist with finding individuals in emergency situations, effective communication strategies for people with dementia, and effective approaches when offers of assistance meet resistance.

Social Isolation and Loneliness

Relationships with others and having the support of family and friends are important to sustain people with dementia who live alone. In a qualitative study of 15 people with dementia who live alone, the participants indicated that having a strong social support network was the most important factor for helping them cope with living alone (Harris, 2006). The study participants were concerned about maintaining their independence, continuing to drive, and being involved in decision-making for as long as possible. Most were comfortable living alone but they did experience feelings of loneliness. The author suggests that services for people with dementia living alone need to be sensitive to the person's needs and wishes, and not just about responding to safety concerns.

A more recent study found that people with dementia who live alone with an unmet care need did not manage everyday life when they felt lonely. Feelings of loneliness may negatively impact a person's ability to act and engage in everyday activities. The presence of a home care worker, for the purpose of performing a task, did not relieve feelings of loneliness. One of the participants in the study described the home care worker as being rushed and expressed a wish for a longer visit to allow for companionship and conversation. The authors also found that without the presence of others, the person with dementia seemed to lack initiative and experienced difficulties in managing everyday life. The authors highlight the importance of the presence of caregivers for those who live alone with dementia that address needs for socialization and not solely focus on specific tasks or physical needs.

If there is no one in the home to observe changes in the person's cognitive and functional abilities, the progressive decline associated with Alzheimer disease or a related dementia may go unnoticed until it is a problem. Changes in the ability to plan, organize, and follow through with daily activities and personal care needs are likely to lead to self-neglect because of the individual's lack of insight and poor judgment.

Even when someone who lives alone gets support from family and friends, it may not be enough to manage all of his or her daily needs. One study found that persons with dementia living alone had significantly more unmet needs than those living with others in the areas of looking after home, nutrition, self-care, daytime activities, companionship, psychological distress, eyesight/hearing, and accidental self-harm. Another study that assessed African Americans with dementia living alone found that neighbors and friends were more often the primary care providers. Neighbors and friends, when compared to caregivers living with the person, were less likely to help with tasks that were time-consuming or required more intimate care.

Soniat and Pollack (1993) describe non traditional support systems for individuals with dementia who live alone with no close family as "makeshift networks of neighbors and agencies." Those involved in helping a person stay in the community may have narrowly defined roles and the various members of the network may not even know each other or coordinate the care they provide. When there is no relationship history, as with a family member or close friend, the support person may not have any emotional ties or commitment to the individual with dementia that keeps them involved in caregiving. The caregiving relationship may end when the support person gets frustrated and decides to move on.

Chapter 40

Medicare and Alzheimer Disease

Chapter Contents

Section 40.1

Understanding Medicare

Text in this section is excerpted from "What's Medicare?"
Centers for Medicare and Medicaid Services (CMS), June 2015;
and text from "Medicine & You," Centers for Medicare and
Medicaid Services (CMS), October 1, 2015.

What is Medicare?

Medicare is health insurance for:

- People 65 or older

- People under 65 with certain disabilities

- People of any age with End-Stage Renal Disease (ESRD) (permanent kidney failure requiring dialysis or a kidney transplant)

What Are the Different Parts of Medicare?

Part A (Hospital Insurance) helps cover:

- Inpatient care in hospitals

- Skilled nursing facility (SNF) care

- Hospice care

- Home health care

Usually, you don't pay a monthly premium for Part A coverage if you or your spouse paid Medicare taxes while working. This is sometimes called premium-free Part A. If you aren't eligible for premium-free Part A, you may be able to buy Part A, and pay a premium.

Part B (Medical Insurance) helps cover:

- Services from doctors and other health care providers

- Outpatient care

- Home health care

- Durable medical equipment (DME)

- Some preventive services

Most people pay the standard monthly Part B premium.

Part C (Medicare Advantage):

- Includes all benefits and services covered under Parts A and B

- Usually includes Medicare prescription drug coverage (Part D) as part of the plan

- Run by Medicare-approved private insurance companies

- May include extra benefits and services for an extra cost

Part D (Medicare Prescription Drug Coverage):

- Helps cover the cost of prescription drugs

- Run by Medicare-approved private insurance companies

- May help lower your prescription drug costs and help protect against higher costs in the future

What is Medicaid?

Medicaid is a joint federal and state program that helps with medical costs for some people with limited income and resources. Medicaid may also cover services not normally covered by Medicare (like long term supports and services and personal care services). Each state has different rules about eligibility and applying for Medicaid. If you qualify for Medicaid in your state, you automatically qualify for Extra Help paying your Medicare prescription drug coverage (Part D).

You may be eligible for Medicaid if you have limited income and are any of these:

- 65 or older

- A child under 19

- Pregnant

- Living with a disability

- A parent or adult caring for a child

- An adult without dependent children (in certain states)

- An eligible immigrant

In many states, more parents and other adults can get coverage now. If you were turned down in the past, you can try again and may qualify now.

When you enroll, you can get the health care benefits you need, like:

- Doctor visits

- Hospital stays

- Long-term services and supports

- Preventive care, including immunizations, mammograms, colonoscopies, and other needed care

- Prenatal and maternity care

- Mental health care

- Necessary medications

- Vision and dental care (for children)

What Are the Different Parts of Medicare?

Medicare Part A (Hospital Insurance) helps cover:

- Inpatient care in hospitals

- Skilled nursing facility care

- Hospice care

- Home health care

Medicare Part B (Medical Insurance) helps cover:

- Services from doctors and other health care providers

- Outpatient care

- Home health care

- Durable medical equipment

- Some preventive services

Medicare Part C (Medicare Advantage):

- Includes all benefits and services covered under Part A and Part B

- Usually includes Medicare prescription drug coverage (Part D) as part of the plan

- Run by Medicare-approved private insurance companies

- May include extra benefits and services for an extra cost

Medicare Part D (Medicare Prescription Drug Coverage):

- Helps cover the cost of prescription drugs

- Run by Medicare-approved private insurance companies

- May help lower your prescription drug costs and help protect against higher costs in the future

How Can I Get My Medicare Coverage?

When you first enroll in Medicare, you have Original Medicare. However, you can choose different ways to get your Medicare coverage:

1. You can stay in Original Medicare. If you want prescription drug coverage, you must join a Medicare Prescription Drug Plan (Part D). If you don't join a Medicare drug plan when you're first eligible, and you don't have other creditable prescription drug coverage (for example, from an employer or union), you may pay a late enrollment penalty if you choose to join later.

2. You can choose to join a Medicare Advantage Plan (like an HMO or PPO) if one's available in your area. The Medicare Advantage Plan may include Medicare prescription drug coverage. In most cases, you must take the drug coverage that comes with the Medicare health plan if it's offered. In some types of plans that don't offer drug coverage, you may be able to join a Medicare Prescription Drug Plan.

What Are My Medicare Coverage Choices?

There are 2 main choices for how you get your Medicare coverage. Use these steps to help you decide.

Step 1: Decide If You Want Original Medicare or a Medicare Advantage Plan.

Original Medicare Includes Part a (Hospital Insurance) and/or Part B (Medical Insurance)

- Medicare provides this coverage directly.

- You have your choice of doctors, hospitals, and other providers that accept Medicare.

- Generally, you or your supplemental coverage pay deductibles and coinsurance.

- You usually pay a monthly premium for Part B.

Medicare Advantage (Part C) Includes BOTH Part a (Hospital Insurance) and Part B (Medical Insurance)

- Private insurance companies approved by Medicare provide this coverage.

- In most plans, you need to use plan doctors, hospitals, and other providers or you may pay more or all of the costs.

- You may pay a monthly premium (in addition to your Part B premium), deductible, copayments, or coinsurance for covered services.

- Costs, extra coverage, and rules vary by plan.

Step 2: Decide If You Want Prescription Drug Coverage (Part D).

- If you want drug coverage, you must join a Medicare Prescription Drug Plan. You usually pay a monthly premium.

- These plans are run by private companies approved by Medicare.

- If you want drug coverage, and it's offered by your Medicare Advantage Plan, in most cases, you must get it through your plan.

- In some types of plans that don't offer drug coverage, you can join a Medicare Prescription Drug Plan.

Step 3: Decide If You Want Supplemental Coverage.

- You may want to get coverage that fills gaps in Original Medicare coverage. You can choose to buy a Medicare Supplement Insurance (Medigap) policy from a private company.

- Costs vary by policy and company.

- Employers/unions may offer similar coverage.

What Should I Consider When Choosing or Changing My Coverage?

Convenience

Where are the doctors' offices? What are their hours? Do the doctors use electronic health records or prescribe electronically? Which pharmacies can you use? Is the pharmacy you use in the plan's network? If it's in the network and your plan offers preferred cost sharing, does your pharmacy offer preferred cost sharing? You may pay less for some drugs at pharmacies that offer preferred cost sharing.

Cost

How much are your premiums, deductibles, and other costs? How much do you pay for services like hospital stays or doctor visits? Is there a yearly limit on what you pay out-of-pocket? Your costs may vary and may be different if you don't follow the coverage rules.

Coverage

How well does the plan cover the services you need?

Doctor and Hospital Choice

Do your doctors and other health care providers accept the type of coverage you have? Are the doctors you want to see accepting new patients? Do you need to get referrals? Do you have to choose your hospital and health care providers from a network? If so, is your doctor in the network? Can you go outside of the network?

Prescription Drugs

Do you need to join a Medicare drug plan? Are your drugs covered under the plan's formulary? Are there any coverage rules that apply to your prescriptions? (like prior authorization, step therapy, quantity limits, etc.)

Quality of Care

Are you satisfied with your medical care? The quality of care and services offered by plans and other health care providers can vary. Medicare has information to help you compare how well plans and providers work to give you the best care possible.

Travel

Will you have coverage in another state or outside the United States?

Your Other Coverage

Do you have, or are you eligible for, other types of health or prescription drug coverage? (like from a former or current employer or union) If so, read the materials from your insurer or plan, or call them to find out how the coverage works with, or is affected by, Medicare. If you have coverage through a former or current employer or union or other source, talk to your benefits administrator, insurer, or plan before making any changes to your coverage. If you drop your coverage, you may not be able to get it back.

What If I Need Help Deciding How to Get My Medicare?

1. Visit the Medicare Plan Finder at Medicare.gov/find-a-plan. With the Medicare Plan Finder, you can compare plans by plan type and find out the coverage, benefits, and estimated costs for each plan. You can also find out how Medicare has rated the plans' quality and performance. You can use the Medicare Plan Finder to enroll in a Medicare Prescription Drug Plan, Medicare Advantage Plan, or Medicare Supplement Insurance (Medigap) policy. Here's what you may see

Figure 40.1. *Medicare Plan Finder at Medicare.gov*

Get personalized counseling about choosing coverage.

1. Call 1-800-MEDICARE (1-800-633-4227) and say "Agent." TTY users should call 1-877-486-2048. If you need help in a language other than English or Spanish, let the customer service representative know.

Where Can I Get My Questions Answered?

1-800-MEDICARE (1-800-633-4227)

Get general or claims-specific Medicare information, request documents in alternate formats, and make changes to your Medicare coverage. If you need help in a language other than English or Spanish, say "Agent" to talk to a customer service representative.

TTY: 1-877-486-2048
Medicare.gov

Benefits Coordination & Recovery Center (BCRC)

Contact the BCRC to report changes in your insurance information or to let Medicare know if you have other insurance. You can also find out if Medicare or your other insurance pays first.

1-855-798-2627
TTY: 1-855-797-2627

Beneficiary and Family Centered Care Quality

Improvement Organization (BFCC-QIO) Contact a BFCC-QIO to ask questions or report complaints about the quality of care for a Medicare-covered service you got, or if you think Medicare coverage for your service is ending too soon (for example, if your hospital says that you must be discharged and you disagree). Visit Medicare.gov/contacts, or call 1-800-MEDICARE (1-800-633-4227) to get the phone number of your BFCC-QIO. TTY users should call 1-877-486-2048.

Department of Defense

Get information about TRICARE for Life (TFL) and the TRICARE Pharmacy Program.

TFL
1-866-773-0404
TTY: 1-866-773-0405
tricare.mil/tfl
tricare4u.com

Tricare Pharmacy Program
1-877-363-1303
TTY: 1-877-540-6261
tricare.mil/pharmacy
express-scripts.com/tricare

Department of Health and Human Services
Office for Civil Rights

Contact if you think you were discriminated against or if your health information privacy rights were violated.

1-800-368-1019

TTY: 1-800-537-7697
hhs.gov/ocr

Department of Veterans Affairs

Contact if you're a veteran or have served in the U.S. military and you have questions about VA benefits.

1-800-827-1000
TTY: 1-800-829-4833
va.gov

Office of Personnel Management

Get information about the Federal Employee Health Benefits (FEHB) Program for current and retired federal employees.

Retirees: 1-888-767-6738
TTY: 1-800-878-5707
opm.gov/healthcare-insurance
Active federal employees: Contact your Benefits Officer.
Visit apps.opm.gov/abo for a list of Benefits Officers.

Railroad Retirement Board (RRB)

If you have benefits from the RRB, call them to change your address or name, check eligibility, enroll in Medicare, replace your Medicare card, or report a death.

1-877-772-5772
TTY: 1-312-751-4701
rrb.gov

Social Security

Find out if you're eligible for Part A and/or Part B and how to enroll, get a replacement Medicare or Social Security card, report a change to your address or name, apply for Extra Help with Medicare prescription drug costs, ask questions about Part A and Part B premiums, and report a death.

1-800-772-1213
TTY: 1-800-325-0778
socialsecurity.gov

Section 40.2

Choosing a Medicare Drug Plan for People with Alzheimer Disease

This section includes excerpts from "Things to Think about
When You Compare Medicare Drug Coverage," Centers for
Medicare and Medicaid Services (CMS), September 2015; and text
from "Paying for Medical Care and Daily Living Services," U.S.
Department of Health and Human Services (HHS), May 15, 2012.
Reviewed February 2016.

Paying for Medical Care and Daily Living Services

Alzheimer disease (AD) care can be extremely expensive. It's important to know what to expect and what resources are available to you. Care for a person with Alzheimer disease is broken down into two categories, each with different sources of payment. Medical expenses are usually paid separately from the non-medical services that are needed to make it possible for someone with Alzheimer disease to live at home as long as possible.

Medical Expenses

People with Alzheimer disease require regular medical care as well as some special care that might include medications or other inter-ventions. Medical services are often covered under medical insurance (either Medicare or private health insurance). It may be important to examine the health coverage to determine the extent of coverage limitations or co-pays and deductibles.

Medicare

- Medicare's website provides details about Medicare coverage in general.

- The National Clearinghouse for Long Term Care Information provides details about Medicare-related to long-term care needs.

- Medicare has information on Medicare Drug plans.

- The zip code finder helps locate a Medigap Policy in your area.

Private Health Insurance

If the person with Alzheimer disease has private health insurance it is important to contact the insurer and learn what lifetime maximums or other limitations you may encounter. Knowing what you are covered for in advance will help avoid surprises when coverage is denied.

Long-Term Care

Long-term care refers to a set of services and supports for activities of daily living such as dressing, bathing, eating and moving around. Medicare does not generally pay for long-term care and Medicaid is only available under specific circumstances.

Almost half of the formal long-term care provided in the U.S. is paid for out-of-pocket. While not every person with Alzheimer disease needs long-term care, it is important to develop a plan because it can be very expensive. A list of long-term care services and their definitions is available.

Medicaid

Medicaid is a state/federal program that pays for long-term care services. The program is administered by each state so eligibility criteria and services may differ from one state to another.

It is important to learn what the rules are in your state. Each state also provides a somewhat different set of services. Nursing homes are always covered but coverage for in-home services varies.

- The National Clearinghouse for Long Term Care Information provides an overview of the Medicaid program and a link to state-based Medicaid resources.

Programs for Veterans with Alzheimer Disease

- The U.S. Department of Veterans Affairs' Geriatrics and Extended Care resources include an overview of eligibility, and details on home- and community-based services, nursing homes and other residential care.

- The U.S. Department of Veterans Affairs offers support and resources to caregivers.

- The Family Caregiver Alliance's FAQ External Web Site Policy provides answers to individuals who provide caregiving services to veterans.

Private Long-Term Care Insurance

The National Clearinghouse for Long-Term Care Information has an overview of long-term care options, details on cost, how to buy insurance, and provides information on state partnership programs.

Things to Think about When You Compare Medicare Drug Coverage

There are 2 ways to get Medicare prescription drug coverage. You can join a Medicare Prescription Drug Plan and keep your health coverage under Original Medicare. Some Medicare Advantage Plans (like HMOs or PPOs) offer Medicare drug coverage. If you join a Medicare Advantage Plan that includes prescription drug coverage, you get your Medicare benefits through a private insurance company. Whichever you choose, prescription drug coverage can vary by cost, coverage, convenience, and quality. Some of these things might be more important to you than others, depending on your situation and prescription drug needs. No matter which type of Medicare drug plan you join, your plan will send you information about plan changes each fall. You should review your prescription drug needs and compare Medicare drug plans during Medicare Open Enrollment. You can make changes to your coverage between October 15 and December 7.

Cost

When you get Medicare prescription drug coverage, you pay part of the costs, and Medicare pays part of the costs. Your costs will vary depending on which Medicare drug plan you choose and whether or not you get Extra Help. You should look at your current prescription drug costs to find a Medicare drug plan that works with your financial situation.

Monthly premium

Most drug plans charge a monthly fee that varies by plan. You pay this fee in addition to the Medicare Part B (Medical Insurance) premium. If you have the type of Medicare Advantage Plan or Medicare Cost Plan that includes Medicare prescription drug coverage, the monthly premium you pay to your plan may include an amount for prescription drug coverage.

Consider automatic premium deduction

When you join a drug plan, think about having your premiums automatically deducted from your Social Security payment. Automatic premium deduction has many benefits:

• It takes the worry out of remembering to pay your premiums.

• Your premiums will get paid on time.

• You'll be helping the environment by not getting a paper bill from your plan.

Yearly deductible

This is the amount you must pay before your drug plan begins to pay its share of your covered drugs. Some drug plans don't have a deductible.

Copayment/Coinsurance

This is the amount you pay for each of your prescriptions after you've paid the deductible (if the plan has one). Some Medicare drug plans have different levels or "tiers" of coinsurance or copayments, with different costs for different types of drugs. Coinsurance means you pay a percentage (25%, for example) of the cost of the drug. With a copayment, you pay a set amount ($10, for example) for all drugs on a tier. For example, you might have to pay a lower copayment for generic drugs than brand-name drugs, or lower coinsurance for some brand-name drugs than for others.

Coverage gap

Most Medicare drug plans have a coverage gap (also called the "donut hole"). This means that there's a temporary limit on what the drug plan will cover for drugs. The coverage gap begins after you and your drug plan have spent a certain amount for covered drugs. In 2016, once you enter the coverage gap, you pay 45% of the plan's cost for covered brand-name drugs and 58% of the plan's cost for covered generic drugs until you reach the end of the coverage gap. Not everyone will enter the coverage gap.

These amounts all count toward you getting out of the coverage gap:

• Your yearly deductible, coinsurance, and copayments

- The discount you get on brand-name drugs in the coverage gap

- What you pay in the coverage gap

These amounts don't count toward you getting out of the coverage gap:

- Your drug plan premium

- What you pay for non-covered drugs

- What's paid by other insurance

Some plans offer additional coverage during the gap, like for generic drugs, but they may charge a higher monthly premium. Check with the plan first to see if your drugs would be covered during the gap.

In addition to the discount on covered brand-name prescription drugs, there will be increasing coverage for drugs in the coverage gap each year until the gap closes in 2020.

Catastrophic coverage

Once you get out of the coverage gap, you automatically get "catastrophic coverage." Catastrophic coverage means that you only pay a small coinsurance amount or copayment for covered drugs for the rest of the year.

Late enrollment penalty

If you don't join a Medicare drug plan when you're first eligible, and you don't have other creditable prescription drug coverage or get Extra Help, you'll likely pay a Part D late enrollment penalty. Creditable prescription drug coverage is coverage (for example, from an employer or union) that's expected to pay, on average, at least as much as Medicare's standard prescription drug coverage. If you're subject to the penalty, you may have to pay it each month for as long as you have Medicare drug coverage.

Coverage

Review your prescription drug needs, and look for a plan that meets these needs. Plans may vary in what drugs they cover, and some may have special rules that you must follow before a drug is covered.

Formulary

A formulary is a list of the drugs that a Medicare drug plan covers. It includes how much you pay for each drug. If the plan uses tiers, the formulary lists which drugs are in each tier. Formularies include both generic and brand-name drugs. In general, each Medicare drug plan's formulary must include most types of drugs that people with Medicare use. However, each drug plan has its own formulary, so you should check to make sure your drugs are covered.

Coverage rules

Medicare drug plans may require "prior authorization." This means that before the Medicare drug plan will cover certain prescriptions, your doctor must contact the plan for approval. Your doctor may need to provide additional information about why the drug is medically necessary for you before you can fill the prescription. Plans may also require "step therapy" on certain drugs. This means you must try one or more similar, lower cost drugs before the plan will cover the prescribed drug. Plans may also set "quantity limits"—limits on how much medication you can get.

Convenience

Check with each Medicare drug plan you're considering to make sure your current pharmacy is in the plan's network or there are pharmacies convenient to you. Some Medicare drug plans charge lower copayments or coinsurance amounts at some pharmacies in their network than at others. Also, some Medicare drug plans may offer a mail-order program that will allow you to have drugs sent directly to your home. You should consider the most cost effective and convenient way to have your prescriptions filled.

Important: Even if you're not changing plans, make sure your pharmacy is still in your plan's network next year. Plans may change their network pharmacies each year.

Quality

In addition to a plan's costs, coverage, and convenience, you should also review the quality ratings for plans before you decide which one best meets your needs. Medicare uses information from member satisfaction surveys, plans, and health care providers to give overall performance star ratings to plans. A plan can get a rating between 1–5 stars. A 5-star rating is considered excellent. These ratings are listed on the Medicare Plan Finder at Medicare. gov/find-a-plan.

5-Star Special Enrollment Period

You can switch to a Medicare Advantage Plan or a Medicare Prescription Drug Plan that has 5 stars for its overall plan rating once from December 8–November 30. The overall plan ratings are available at Medicare.gov/find-a-plan. Medicare updates these ratings each fall for the following year. These ratings can change each year.

- You can only switch to a 5-star Medicare Prescription Drug Plan if one is available in your area.

- You can only use this Special Enrollment Period once during the above timeframe.

Table 40.1. Here Are Some Common Situations to Consider

common situations to consider	
If you...	**You might want to...**
...currently take specific prescription drugs.	...look at drug plans that have included your drugs on their formularies. Then, compare costs.
...want extra protection from high prescription drug costs.	...look for plans that offer coverage in the coverage gap, and then check with those plans to be sure your drugs would be covered during the gap. (The plans may charge a higher monthly premium.)
...want your drug expenses to be balanced throughout the year.	...look at plans with low or no deductibles or with additional coverage in the coverage gap.
...take a lot of generic prescriptions.	...look at plans with tiers that charge you nothing or low copayments for generic prescriptions.
...don't have many drug costs now, but want coverage for peace of mind and to avoid future penalties.	...look for plans with low monthly premiums for drug coverage. If you need prescriptions in the future, all plans still must cover most drugs used by people with Medicare.
...like the extra benefits and lower costs that are available by getting your health care and prescription drug coverage from one plan and are willing to accept the plan's restrictions on what doctors, hospitals, and other health care providers you can use.	...look for Medicare Advantage Plans with prescription drug coverage.

What Should I Do before Making a Decision?

Each year, you have the opportunity to join or switch Medicare drug plans during Medicare Open Enrollment. You can make changes between October 1 and December 7. If you switch plans during this time, your coverage with the new plan will start on January 1. As you make a decision about your health and prescription drug coverage, remember to review your current health and prescription drug plans. Health and drug plan benefits and costs can change each year. Look at other plans in your area to see if one may better meet your needs. If you want to keep our current plan, and it's still being offered next year, you don't need to do anything for your enrollment to continue.

Where Can I Get Help?

To help you compare Medicare drug plans, think about what you need in terms of cost, coverage, convenience, and quality. Then, visit Medicare.gov/find-a-plan to see which plans are available in your area.

To get personalized information, you need:

- Your Medicare card that has your Medicare number and Medicare effective date (Medicare Part A (Hospital Insurance) or Medicare Part B (Medical Insurance))

- Date of birth

- Last name

- ZIP code

To get general Medicare drug plan information or to find out what plans are available in your area, just answer a few simple questions. You can also enter your current prescription drug information to get more detailed cost information.

Note: This tool provides useful information to help you review Medicare drug plans based on your current drug needs. The drug costs displayed are estimates and may vary based on the specific quantity, strength and/or dosage of medication, whether you buy your prescriptions at the pharmacy or through mail order, and the pharmacy you use.

- Call 1-800-MEDICARE (1-800-633-4227). TTY users should call 1-877-486-2048.

- Call your State Health Insurance Assistance Program (SHIP) for personalized counseling at no cost to you. Visit shiptacenter. org, or call 1-800-MEDICARE to find the phone number for your state.

Important: If you have employer or union coverage, call your benefits administrator before you make any changes to your coverage.

Chapter 41

Getting Your Affairs in Order

Chapter Contents

Section 41.1

Planning for the Future

This section includes excerpts from "Getting Your Affairs In Order,"
National Institute on Aging (NIA), December 23, 2015; and text
from "Making a Plan to Manage the Disease," U.S.
Department of Health and Human Services (HHS),
May 16, 2012. Reviewed February 2016.

Ben has been married for 47 years. He always managed the family's money. But since his stroke, Ben can't walk or talk. His wife, Shirley, feels overwhelmed. Of course, she's worried about Ben's health. But on top of that, she has no idea what bills should be paid or when they are due.

Across town, 80-year-old Louise lives alone. One night, she fell in the kitchen and broke her hip. She spent a week in the hospital and 2 months in a rehabilitation nursing home. Even though her son lives across the country, he was able to pay her bills and handle her Medicare questions right away. That's because, several years ago, Louise and her son made a plan about what he should do in case Louise had a medical emergency.

Plan for the Future

No one ever plans to be sick or disabled. Yet, it's just this kind of planning that can make all the difference in an emergency. Long before she fell, Louise had put all her important papers in one place and told her son where to find them. She gave him the name of her lawyer as well as a list of people he could contact at her bank, doctor's office, insurance company, and investment firm. She made sure he had copies of her Medicare and other health insurance cards. She added her son's name to her checking account, allowing him to write checks from that account. His name is on her safe deposit box at the bank as well. Louise made sure Medicare and her doctor had written permission to talk with her son about her health and insurance claims.

On the other hand, Ben always took care of family money matters, and he never talked about the details with Shirley. No one but Ben knew that his life insurance policy was in a box in the closet or that the car title and deed to the house were filed in his desk drawer. Ben never expected that his wife would have to take over. His lack of planning has made a tough job even tougher for Shirley.

Legal Documents

There are many different types of legal documents that can help you plan how your affairs will be handled in the future. Many of these documents have names that sound alike, so make sure you are getting the documents you want. Also, State laws do vary, so find out about the rules, requirements, and forms used in your State.

- **Wills** and **trusts** let you name the person you want your money and property to go to after you die.
- **Advance directives** let you make arrangements for your care if you become sick. There are two ways to do this:
- A **living will** gives you a say in your health care if you are too sick to make your wishes known. In a living will, you can state what kind of care you do or don't want. This can make it easier for family members to make tough healthcare decisions for you.
- A **durable power of attorney for health care** lets you name the person you want to make medical decisions for you if you can't make them yourself. Make sure the person you name is willing to make those decisions for you.

For legal matters, there are two ways to give someone you trust the power to act in your place:

- A **general power of attorney** lets you give someone else the authority to act on your behalf, but this power will end if you are unable to make your own decisions.
- A **"durable" power of attorney** allows you to name someone to act on your behalf for any legal task, but it stays in place if you become unable to make your own decisions.

Steps for Getting Your Affairs in Order

- **Put your important papers and copies of legal documents in one place.** You could set up a file, put everything in a desk or dresser drawer, or just list the information and location of papers in a notebook. If your papers are in a bank safe deposit box, keep copies in a file at home. Check each year to see if there's anything new to add.

- **Tell a trusted family member or friend where you put all your important papers.** You don't need to tell this friend or family member about your personal affairs, but someone should know where you keep your papers in case of an emergency. If you don't have a relative or friend you trust, ask a lawyer to help.

- **Give consent in advance for your doctor or lawyer to talk with your caregiver as needed.** There may be questions about your care, a bill, or a health insurance claim. Without your consent, your caregiver may not be able to get needed information. You can give your okay in advance to Medicare, a credit card company, your bank, or your doctor. You may need to sign and return a form.

What Exactly Is an "Important Paper"?

The answer to this question may be different for every family. The following lists can help you decide what is important for you. Remember, this is a starting place. You may have other information to add. For example, if you have a pet, you will want to include the name and address of your vet.

Please remember to include complete information about the following:

Personal Records

- Full legal name
- Social Security number
- Legal residence
- Date and place of birth
- Names and addresses of spouse and children
- Location of birth and death certificates and certificates of marriage, divorce, citizenship, and adoption
- Employers and dates of employment
- Education and military records

400

- Names and phone numbers of religious contacts
- Memberships in groups and awards received
- Names and phone numbers of close friends, relatives, and lawyer or financial advisor
- Names and phone numbers of doctors
- Medications taken regularly
- Location of living will and other legal documents

Financial records

- Sources of income and assets (pension from your employer, IRAs, 401(k)s, interest, etc.)
- Social Security and Medicare information
- Insurance information (life, health, long-term care, home, car) with policy numbers and agents' names and phone numbers
- Names of your banks and account numbers (checking, savings, credit union)
- Investment income (stocks, bonds, property) and stockbrokers' names and phone numbers
- Copy of most recent income tax return
- Location of most up-to-date will with an original signature
- Liabilities, including property tax—what is owed, to whom, when payments are due
- Mortgages and debts—how and when paid
- Location of original deed of trust for home and car title and registration
- Credit and debit card names and numbers
- Location of safe deposit box and key

Resources

You may want to talk with a lawyer about setting up a general power of attorney, durable power of attorney, joint account, trust, or advance directive. Be sure to ask about the fees before you make an appointment.

You should be able to find a directory of local lawyers at your library, or you can contact your local bar association for names of lawyers in your area. An informed family member may be able to help you manage some of these issues.

Making a Plan to Manage the Disease

Once a diagnosis has been made, it is important to work closely with your doctor and any other caregivers to map out a plan to manage the disease.

Developing a Plan

A comprehensive financial and legal plan is important. It is helpful to plan as early as possible. Some families use the services of an elder law attorney.

A plan should consider:

- Legal and Estate Planning: There may come a time when a person with Alzheimer disease can no longer make decisions for themselves. This can create a hardship for a caregiver trying to conduct financial transactions and make medical decisions. This is one place where advance planning can be very helpful. There are several types of legal documents that can be written before they are needed to try to prevent legal pitfalls from making a difficult time for families even worse. The legal documents and the legal issues you will need to consider often differ based on state laws and the current situation of the person with Alzheimer disease. For a guide to understanding options in this area, please visit the following links:

- The Alzheimer Foundation of America provides details on guardianship proceedings and how they are reached.

- The Alzheimer Association gives an overview of important legal documents and tips on locating an attorney.

- Identification of Local Assistance Programs: It is important to know what resources you can count on as the disease progresses and the amount and type of care that is needed changes. Please view the local resources in caregiver resources and finding Alzheimer disease capable care to identify resources in your community.

- Optimal Living Arrangements: Many families choose to stay at home for as long as possible. In many cases subtle changes to the home can make staying a more viable option. These changes can remove obstacles that hinder care giving duties. Often the changes are designed to make the home safer for people with dementia. Information on how to modify your home to facilitate caregiving can be found in Caregiver Resources.

- Social Security Disability Insurance: People who are younger than 65 with Alzheimer disease can apply for Social Security Disability. The Social Security Administration recently added Early-Onset Alzheimer Disease as one of the conditions that qualifies for the Compassionate Allowance Program. This program helps speed the processing of applications of people with certain conditions. Information on how to apply for Social Security and the Compassionate Allowance Program is available.

- Paying For Care: Paying for medical care and long-term care services can be a major issue for family caregivers. Understanding what is covered by Medicare and what you may have to pay out-of-pocket will help you prepare for the often significant cost that can accompany caregiving.

Section 41.2

Legal, Health Care, and Financial Planning for People with Alzheimer Disease

Text in this section is excerpted from "Legal and Financial Planning for People with Alzheimer's Disease: Fact Sheet," National Institute on Aging (NIA), August 2013.

Many people are unprepared to deal with the legal and financial consequences of a serious illness such as Alzheimer disease. Legal and medical experts encourage people recently diagnosed with a serious illness particularly one that is expected to cause declining mental and physical health to examine and update their financial and health care arrangements as soon as possible. Basic legal and financial instruments, such as a will, a living trust, and advance directives, are available to ensure that the person's late-stage or end-of-life healthcare and financial decisions are carried out.

A complication of diseases such as Alzheimer disease is that the person may lack or gradually lose the ability to think clearly. This change affects his or her ability to participate meaningfully in decision making and makes early legal and financial planning even more important. Although difficult questions often arise, advance planning can help people with Alzheimer disease and their families clarify their wishes and make well-informed decisions about healthcare and financial arrangements.

When possible, advance planning should take place soon after a diagnosis of early-stage Alzheimer disease while the person can participate in discussions. People with early-stage disease are often capable of understanding many aspects and consequences of legal decision making. However, legal and medical experts say that many forms of planning can help the person and his or her family even if the person is diagnosed with later-stage Alzheimer disease.

There are good reasons to retain the services of a lawyer when preparing advance planning documents. For example, a lawyer can help interpret different State laws and suggest ways to ensure that the person's and family's wishes are carried out. It's important to understand that laws vary by State, and changes in situation—for instance, a divorce, relocation, or death in the family—can influence how documents are prepared and maintained.

Legal, Financial, and Health Care Planning Documents

When families begin the legal planning process, there are a number of strategies and legal documents they need to discuss.

Depending on the family situation and the applicable State laws, some or all of the following terms and documents may be introduced by the lawyer hired to assist in this process. Broadly speaking, these documents can be divided into two groups:

- documents that communicate the health care wishes of someone who may no longer be able to make healthcare decisions
- documents that communicate the financial management and estate plan wishes of someone who may no longer be able to make financial decisions

Advance Directives for Health Care

Advance directives for health care are documents that communicate the health care wishes of a person with Alzheimer disease. These decisions are then carried out after the person no longer can make decisions. In most cases, these documents must be prepared while the person is legally able to execute them.

A **Living Will** records a person's wishes for medical treatment near the end of life. It may do the following:

- specify the extent of life-sustaining treatment and major health care the person wants

- help a terminal patient die with dignity

- protect the physician or hospital from liability for carrying out the patient's instructions

- specify how much discretion the person gives to his or her proxy (discussed below) about end-of-life decisions

A **Durable Power of Attorney for Health Care** designates a person, sometimes called an agent or proxy, to make health care decisions when the person with Alzheimer disease no longer can do so. Depending on State laws and the person's preferences, the proxy might be authorized to:

- refuse or agree to treatments

- change health care providers

- remove the person from an institution

- decide about making organ donations

- decide about starting or continuing life support (if not specified in a living will)

- decide whether the person with Alzheimer disease will end life at home or in a facility

- have access to medical records

A **Do Not Resuscitate (DNR)** Order instructs health care professionals not to perform cardiopulmonary resuscitation if a person's heart stops or if he or she stops breathing. A DNR order is signed by a doctor and put in a person's medical chart.

Advance Directives for Financial and Estate Management

Advance directives for financial and estate management must be created while the person with Alzheimer disease still can make these decisions (sometimes referred to as "having legal capacity" to make decisions).

These directives may include some or all of the following:

A **Will** indicates how a person's assets and estate will be distributed upon death. It also can specify:

- arrangements for care of minors
- gifts
- trusts to manage the estate
- funeral and/or burial arrangements

Medical and legal experts say that the newly diagnosed person with Alzheimer disease and his or her family should move quickly to make or update a will and secure the estate.

A **Durable Power of Attorney for Finances** names someone to make financial decisions when the person with Alzheimer disease can no longer do so. It can help people with the disease and their families avoid court actions that may take away control of financial affairs.

A **Living Trust** provides instructions about the person's estate and appoints someone, called the trustee, to hold title to property and funds for the beneficiaries. The trustee follows these instructions after the person no longer can manage his or her affairs.

The person with Alzheimer disease also can name the trustee as the health care proxy through the durable power of attorney for health care.

A living trust can:

- include a wide range of property
- provide a detailed plan for property disposition
- avoid the expense and delay of probate (in which the courts establish the validity of a will)
- state how property should be distributed when the last beneficiary dies and whether the trust should continue to benefit others

Who Can Help?

Health Care Providers—Health care providers cannot act as legal or financial advisors, but they can encourage planning discussions between patients and their families. Qualified clinicians can also guide patients, families, the care team, attorneys, and judges regarding the patient's ability to make decisions.

Elder Law Attorneys (ELAs)—An ELA helps older people and families:

- interpret State laws
- plan how their wishes will be carried out
- understand their financial options
- learn how to preserve financial assets while caring for a loved one

The National Academy of Elder Law Attorneys and the American Bar Association can help families find qualified ELAs.

Geriatric Care Managers (GCMs) GCMs are trained social workers or nurses who can help people with Alzheimer disease and their families:

- discuss difficult topics and complex issues
- address emotional concerns
- make short- and long-term plans
- evaluate in-home care needs
- select care personnel
- coordinate medical services
- evaluate other living arrangements
- provide caregiver stress relief

Other Advance Planning Advice

Start discussions early. The rate of decline differs for each person with Alzheimer disease, and his or her ability to be involved in planning will decline over time. People in the early stages of the disease may be able to understand the issues, but they may also be defensive or emotionally unable to deal with difficult questions.

Remember that not all people are diagnosed at an early stage. Decision making already may be difficult when Alzheimer disease is diagnosed.

Review plans over time. Changes in personal situations—such as a divorce, relocation, or death in the family—and in State laws can affect how legal documents are prepared and maintained. Review plans regularly, and update documents as needed.

Reduce anxiety about funeral and burial arrangements. Advance planning for the funeral and burial can provide a sense of peace and reduce anxiety for both the person with Alzheimer disease and the family.

Resources for Low-Income Families

Families who cannot afford a lawyer still can do advance planning. Samples of basic health planning documents can be downloaded from State government websites. Area Agency on Aging officials may provide legal advice or help. Other possible sources of legal assistance and referral include State legal aid offices, the State bar association, local non-profit agencies, foundations, and social service agencies.

Summary

Facing Alzheimer disease can be emotionally wrenching for all concerned. A legal expert and members of the health care team can help the person and family address end-of-life issues. Advance health care and financial planning can help people diagnosed with Alzheimer disease and their families confront tough questions about future treatment, caregiving, and legal arrangements.

Table 41.1. Overview of Medical, Legal, and Financial Planning Documents

Medical Document	How It Is Used
Living Will	Describes and instructs how the person wants end-of-life health care managed
Durable Power of Attorney for Health Care	Gives a designated person the authority to make health care decisions on behalf of the person with Alzheimer disease
Do Not Resuscitate Form	Instructs health care professionals not to perform CPR in case of stopped heart or stopped breathing

Table 41.1. Continued

Legal/Financial Document	How It Is Used
Will	Indicates how a person's assets and estate will be distributed among beneficiaries after his/her death
Durable Power of Attorney for Finances	Gives a designated person the authority to make legal/financial decisions on behalf of the person with Alzheimer disease
Living Trust	Gives a designated person (trustee) the authority to hold and distribute property and funds for the person with Alzheimer disease

Section 41.3

Making End-of-Life Choices

Text in this section is excerpted from "End of Life:
Helping with Comfort and Care," National Institute on
Aging (NIA), January 22, 2015.

End of Life: Helping with Comfort and Care

Planning for End-of-Life Care Decisions

Because of advances in medicine, each of us, as well as our families and friends, may face many decisions about the dying process. As hard as it might be to face the idea of your own death, you might take time to consider how your individual values relate to your idea of a good death. By deciding what end-of-life care best suits your needs when you are healthy, you can help those close to you make the right choices when the time comes. This not only respects your values, but also allows those closest to you the comfort of feeling as though they can be helpful.

There are several ways to make sure others know the kind of care you want when dying.

Talking about End-of-Life Wishes

The simplest, but not always the easiest, way is to talk about end-of-life care before an illness. Discussing your thoughts, values, and desires will help people who are close to you to know what end-of-life care you want. For example, you could discuss how you feel about using life-prolonging measures or where you would like to be cared for. For some people, it makes sense to bring this up at a small family gathering. Others may find that telling their family they have made a will (or updated an existing one) provides an opportunity to bring up this subject with other family members. Doctors should be told about these wishes as well. As hard as it might be to talk about your end-of-life wishes, knowing your preferences ahead of time can make decision making easier for your family. You may also have some comfort knowing that your family can choose what you want.

On the other hand, if your parents are aging and you are concerned about what they want, you might introduce the subject. You can try to explain that having this conversation will help you care for them and do what they want. You might start by talking about what you think their values are, instead of talking about specific treatments. Try saying something like, "when Uncle Walt had a stroke and died, I thought you seemed upset that his kids wanted to put him on a respirator." Or, "I've always wondered why Grandpa didn't die at home. Do you know?" Encourage your parents to share the type of care they would choose to have at the end of life, rather than what they don't want. There is no right or wrong plan, only what they would like. If they are reluctant to have this conversation, don't force it, but try to bring it up again at a later time.

Advance Directives and Other Documents

Written instructions letting others know the type of care you want if you are seriously ill or dying are called advance directives. These include a living will and health care power of attorney. A living will records your end-of-life care wishes in case you are no longer able to speak for yourself. You might want to talk with your doctor or other health care provider before preparing a living will. That way you will have a better understanding of what types of decisions might need to be made. Make sure your doctor and family have seen your living will and understand your instructions.

Because a living will cannot give guidance for every possible situation, you probably want to name someone to make care decisions for you if you are unable to do so for yourself. You might choose a family member, friend, lawyer, or someone in your religious community. You can do this either in the advance directives or through a durable power of attorney for health care that names a health care proxy, who is also called a representative, surrogate, agent, or attorney-in-fact. "Durable" means it remains in effect even if you are unable to make decisions. A durable power of attorney for health care is useful if you don't want to be specific—if you would rather let the health care proxy evaluate each situation or treatment option independently. A durable power of attorney for health care is also important if your health care proxy, the person you want to make choices for you, is not a legal member of your family. Of course, you should make sure the person and alternate(s) you have named understand your views about end-of-life care. If you don't name someone, the state you live in probably has an order of priority based on family relationships to determine who decides for you. A few states let people name a health care proxy by telling their doctor, without paperwork.

Don't confuse a durable power of attorney for health care with a durable power of attorney. The first is limited to decisions related to health care, while the latter covers decisions regarding property or financial matters.

A lawyer can prepare these papers, or you can do them yourself. Forms are available from your local or State government, from private groups, or on the Internet. Often these forms need to be witnessed. That means that people who are not related to you watch as you sign and date the paperwork and then sign and date it themselves as proof that the signature is indeed yours. Make sure you give copies to your primary doctor and your health care proxy. Have copies in your files as well. Hospitals might ask for a copy when you are admitted, even if you are not seriously ill.

Sometimes people change their mind as they get older or after they become ill. Review the decisions in your advance directives from time to time and make changes if your views or your health needs have changed. Be sure to discuss these changes with your health care proxy and your doctor. Replace all copies of the older version with the updated ones, witnessed and signed if appropriate.

You should also give permission to your doctors and insurance companies to share your personal information with your health care proxy. This lets that person discuss your case with your doctor and handle insurance issues that may come up.

Do you live in one state, but spend a lot of time in another? Maybe you live in the north and spend winter months in a southern state. Or possibly your children and grandchildren live in a different state and you visit them often. Because states' rules and regulations may differ, make sure your forms are legal in both your home state and the state you travel to often. If not, make an advance directive with copies for that state also. And make sure your family there has a copy.

Part Six

Caregiver Concerns

Chapter 42

Techniques for Communicating with Someone with Alzheimer Disease or Dementia

How to Cope with Changes in Communication Skills?

The first step is to understand that the disease causes changes in these skills. The second step is to try some tips that may make communication easier. For example, keep the following suggestions in mind as you go about day-to-day care.

To Connect with a Person Who Has Alzheimer Disease (AD):

• Make eye contact to get his or her attention, and call the person by name.

• Be aware of your tone and how loud your voice is, how you look at the person, and your "body language." Body language is the message you send just by the way you hold your body. For example, if you stand with your arms folded very tightly, you may send a message that you are tense or angry.

Text in this chapter is excerpted from "Caring for a Person with Alzheimer's Disease," National Institute on Aging (NIA), May 2015.

- Encourage a two-way conversation for as long as possible. This helps the person with AD feel better about himself or herself.

- Use other methods besides speaking to help the person, such as gentle touching to guide him or her.

- Try distracting someone with AD if communication creates problems. For example, offer a fun activity such as a snack or a walk around the neighborhood.

To Encourage the Person with AD to Communicate with You:

- Show a warm, loving, matter-of-fact manner.

- Hold the person's hand while you talk.

- Be open to the person's concerns, even if he or she is hard to understand.

- Let him or her make some decisions and stay involved.

- Be patient with angry outbursts. Remember, it's the illness "talking."

- If you become frustrated, take a "timeout" for yourself.

To Speak Effectively with a Person Who Has AD:

- Offer simple, step-by-step instructions.

- Repeat instructions and allow more time for a response. Try not to interrupt.

- Don't talk about the person as if he or she isn't there.

- Don't talk to the person using "baby talk" or a "baby voice."

Here Are Some Examples of What You Can Say:

- "Let's try this way," instead of pointing out mistakes

- "Please do this," instead of "Don't do this"

- "Thanks for helping," even if the results aren't perfect

You Also Can:

- Ask questions that require a yes or no answer. For example, you could say, "Are you tired?" instead of "How do you feel?"

- Limit the number of choices. For example, you could say, "Would you like a hamburger or chicken for dinner?" instead of "What would you like for dinner?"

- Use different words if he or she doesn't understand what you say the first time. For example, if you ask the person whether he or she is hungry and you don't get a response, you could say, "Dinner is ready now. Let's eat."

- Try not to say, "Don't you remember?" or "I told you."

Chapter 43

Long-Distance Caregiving

Talk about Caregiving Responsibilities

First, try to define the caregiving responsibilities. You could start by setting up a family meeting and, if it makes sense, include the care recipient in the discussion. This is best done when there is not an emergency. A calm conversation about what kind of care is wanted and needed now, and what might be needed in the future, can help avoid a lot of confusion.

Decide who will be responsible for which tasks. Many families find the best first step is to name a primary caregiver, even if one is not needed immediately. That way the primary caregiver can step in if there is a crisis.

Agree in advance how each of your efforts can complement one another so that you can be an effective team. Ideally, each of you will be able to take on tasks best suited to your skills or interests.

Who Is a Long-Distance Caregiver?

Anyone, anywhere, can be a long-distance caregiver, no matter your gender, income, age, social status, or employment. If you are living an

This chapter includes excerpts from "Long-Distance Caregiving—Getting Started," National Institute on Aging (NIA), January 22, 2015; text from "Long-Distance Caregiving—a Family Affair," National Institute on Aging (NIA), January 22, 2015; and text from "Managing Personality and Behavior Changes," National Institute on Aging (NIA), July 2012.

hour or more away from a person who needs your help, you're probably a long-distance caregiver.

What Can I Really Do from Far Away?

Long-distance caregivers take on different roles.
You may:

- Help with finances, money management, or bill paying

- Arrange for in-home care—hire professional caregivers or home health or nursing aides and help get needed durable medical equipment

- Locate care in an assisted living facility or nursing home (also known as a skilled nursing facility)

- Provide emotional support and occasional respite care for a primary caregiver, the person who takes on most of the everyday caregiving responsibilities

- Serve as an information coordinator—research health problems or medicines, help navigate through a maze of new needs, and clarify insurance benefits and claims

- Keep family and friends updated and informed

- Create a plan and get paperwork in order in case of an emergency Over time, as your family member's needs change, so will your role as long-distance caregiver.

I'm New to Long-Distance Caregiving—What Should I Do First?

To get started:

- Ask the primary caregiver, if there is one, and the care recipient how you can be most helpful

- Talk to friends who are caregivers to see if they have suggestions about ways to help

- Find out more about local resources that might be useful

- Develop a good understanding of the person's health issues and other needs

- Visit as often as you can; not only might you notice something that needs to be done and can be taken care of from a distance, but you can also relieve a primary caregiver for a short time

Many of us don't automatically have a lot of caregiver skills. Information about training opportunities is available. Some local chapters of the American Red Cross might offer courses, as do some nonprofit organizations focused on caregiving. Medicare and Medicaid will sometimes pay for this training. See Where can I find local resources for my family member? to find local services for older adults and their families.

As a Caregiver, What Do I Need to Know about My Family Member's Health?

Learn as much as you can about your family member's condition and any treatment. This can help you understand what is going on, anticipate the course of an illness, prevent crises, and assist in healthcare management. It can also make talking with the doctor easier.

Get written permission, as needed under the HIPAA Privacy Rule, to receive medical and financial information. To the extent possible, the family member with permission should be the one to talk with all healthcare providers. Try putting together a notebook, on paper or online, that includes all the vital information about medical care, social services, contact numbers, financial issues, and so on. Make copies for other caregivers, and keep it up-to-date.

Splitting Caregiving Responsibilities—Consider Your Strengths

When thinking about who should be responsible for what, start with your strengths. Consider what you are particularly good at and how those skills might help in the current situation:

- Are you good at finding information, keeping people up-to-date on changing conditions, and offering cheer, whether on the phone or with a computer?

- Are you good at supervising and leading others?

- Are you comfortable speaking with medical staff and interpreting what they say to others?

- Is your strongest suit doing the numbers—paying bills, keeping track of bank statements, and reviewing insurance policies and reimbursement reports?

- Are you the one in the family who can fix anything, while no one else knows the difference between pliers and a wrench?

How Can I Be Most Helpful during My Visit?

Talk to the care recipient ahead of time and find out what he or she would like to do during your visit. Also check with the primary caregiver, if appropriate, to learn what he or she needs, such as handling some caregiving responsibilities while you are in town. This may help you set clear-cut and realistic goals for the visit. Decide on the priorities and leave other tasks to another visit.

Remember to actually spend time visiting with your family member. Try to make time to do things unrelated to being a caregiver, like watching a movie, playing a game, or taking a drive. Finding time to do something simple and relaxing can help everyone—it can be fun and build family memories. And, try to let outside distractions wait until you are home again.

How Can I Stay Connected from Far Away?

Try to find people who live near your loved one and can provide a realistic view of what is going on. This may be your other parent. A social worker may be able to provide updates and help with making decisions. Many families schedule conference calls with doctors, the assisted living facility team, or nursing home staff so several relatives can be in one conversation and get the same up-to-date information about health and progress.

Don't underestimate the value of a phone and email contact list. It is a simple way to keep everyone updated on your parent's' needs.

You may also want to give the person you care for a cell phone (and make sure he or she knows how to use it). Or, if your family member lives in a nursing home, consider having a private phone line installed in his or her room. Program telephone numbers of doctors, friends, family members, and yourself into the phone, and perhaps provide a list of the speed-dial numbers to keep with the phone. Such simple strategies can be a lifeline. But try to be prepared should you find yourself inundated with calls from your parent.

Supporting a Local Caregiver from Far Away

A spouse or the sibling who lives closest to an aging parent often becomes the primary caregiver. Long-distance caregivers can help by providing emotional support and occasional respite to the primary caregiver. Ask the primary caregiver what you can do to help. Staying in contact with your parents by phone or email might also take some pressure off your parent or sibling. Just listening may not sound like much help, but often it is. Long-distance caregivers can also play a part in arranging for professional caregivers, hiring home health and nursing aides, or locating care in an assisted living facility or nursing home (also known as a skilled nursing facility).

Long-distance caregivers may find they can be helpful by handling things online—for example, researching health problems or medicines, paying bills, or keeping family and friends updated. Some long-distance caregivers help a parent pay for care; others step in to manage finances.

Helping a Parent Who Is the Primary Caregiver

A primary caregiver—especially a spouse—may be hesitant to ask for help or a break. Be sure to acknowledge how important the caregiver has been for the care recipient. Also, discuss the physical and emotional effects caregiving can have on people. Although caregiving can be satisfying, it also can be very hard work.

Offer to arrange for respite care. Respite care will give your parent a break from caregiving responsibilities. It can be arranged for just an afternoon or for several days. Care can be provided in the family home, through an adult day services program, or at a skilled nursing facility.

The ARCH National Respite Locator Service can help you find services in your parents' community. You might suggest contacting the Well Spouse Association. It offers support to the wives, husbands, and partners of chronically ill or disabled people and has a nationwide listing of local support groups.

Where Can I Find Local Resources for My Family Member?

Searching online is a good way to start collecting resources. Here are a few potentially helpful places to look:

- Eldercare Locator, 1-800-677-1116 (toll-free)
- National Institute on Aging website
- Family Care Navigator
- Your state government's website

You might also check with local senior centers.

Where Can I Learn More?

Would you like to learn more about long-distance caregiving? The National Institute on Aging's (NIA) booklets *So Far Away:*

Twenty Questions and Answers About Long-Distance Caregiving and Caring for a Person with Alzheimer Disease can help. See Related Publications below. NIA also has a special section of its website featuring health and aging information for caregivers.

Managing Personality and Behavior Changes

Alzheimer disease causes brain cells to die, so the brain works less well over time. This changes how a person acts. This tip sheet has suggestions that may help you understand and cope with changes in personality and behavior in a person with Alzheimer disease.

Common Changes in Personality and Behavior

Common personality and behavior changes you may see include:

- Getting upset, worried, and angry more easily
- Acting depressed or not interested in things
- Hiding things or believing other people are hiding things
- Imagining things that aren't there
- Wandering away from home
- Pacing a lot
- Showing unusual sexual behavior
- Hitting you or other people
- Misunderstanding what he or she sees or hears

You also may notice that the person stops caring about how he or she looks, stops bathing, and wants to wear the same clothes every day.

In addition to changes in the brain, other things may affect how people with Alzheimer disease behave:

- Feelings such as sadness, fear, stress, confusion, or anxiety
- Health-related problems, including illness, pain, new medications, or lack of sleep
- Other physical issues like infections, constipation, hunger or thirst, or problems seeing or hearing
- Problems in their surroundings, like too much noise or being in an unfamiliar place

If you don't know what is causing the problem, call the doctor. It could be caused by a physical or medical issue.

Keep Things Simple...and Other Tips

Caregivers cannot stop Alzheimer disease-related changes in personality and behavior, but they can learn to cope with them. Here are some tips:

- Keep things simple. Ask or say one thing at a time.

- Have a daily routine, so the person knows when certain things will happen.

- Reassure the person that he or she is safe and you are there to help.

- Focus on his or her feelings rather than words. For example, say, "You seem worried."

- Don't argue or try to reason with the person.

- Try not to show your frustration or anger. If you get upset, take deep breaths and count to 10. If it's safe, leave the room for a few minutes.

- Use humor when you can.

- Give people who pace a lot a safe place to walk.

- Try using music, singing, or dancing to distract the person.

- Ask for help. For instance, say, "Let's set the table" or "I need help folding the clothes."

Talk with the person's doctor about problems like hitting, biting, depression, or hallucinations. Medications are available to treat some behavioral symptoms.

Chapter 44

Planning the Day for Someone with Dementia

Providing Everyday Care for People with Alzheimer Disease (AD)

Activity and Exercise

Being active and getting exercise helps people with Alzheimer disease (AD) feel better. Exercise helps keep their muscles, joints, and heart in good shape. It also helps people stay at a healthy weight and have regular toilet and sleep habits. You can exercise together to make it more fun.

You want someone with AD to do as much as possible for himself or herself. At the same time, you also need to make sure that the person is safe when active.

Here are some tips for helping the person with AD stay active:

- Take a walk together each day. Exercise is good for caregivers, too!

- Make sure the person with AD has an ID bracelet with your phone number if he or she walks alone.

- Check your local TV guide to see if there is a program to help older adults exercise.

- Add music to the exercises if it helps the person with AD. Dance to the music if possible.

Text in this chapter is excerpted from "Caring for a Person with Alzheimer's Disease," National Institute on Aging (NIA), May 2015.

- Watch exercise videos/DVDs made for older people. Try exercising together.

- Make sure he or she wears comfortable clothes and shoes that fit well and are made for exercise.

- Make sure the person drinks water or juice after exercise.

Some people with AD may not be able to get around well. This is another problem that becomes more challenging to deal with as the disease gets worse.

Some possible reasons for this include:

- Trouble with endurance

- Poor coordination

- Sore feet or muscles

- Illness

- Depression or general lack of interest

Even if people have trouble walking, they may be able to:

- Do simple tasks around the home, such as sweeping and dusting.

- Use a stationary bike.

- Use soft rubber exercise balls or balloons for stretching or throwing back and forth.

- Use stretching bands, which you can buy in sporting goods stores. Be sure to follow the instructions.

Healthy Eating

Eating healthy foods helps us stay well. It's even more important for people with AD. Here are some tips for healthy eating.

When the person with AD lives with you:

- Buy healthy foods such as vegetables, fruits, and whole-grain products. Be sure to buy foods that the person likes and can eat.

- Buy food that is easy to prepare, such as pre-made salads and single food portions.

- Have someone else make meals if possible.

- Use a service such as Meals on Wheels, which will bring meals right to your home.

When a person with early-stage AD lives alone:

- Follow the steps above.

- Buy foods that the person doesn't need to cook.

- Call to remind him or her to eat. In the early stage of AD, the person's eating habits usually don't change. When changes do occur, living alone may not be safe anymore.

Look for these signs to see if living alone is no longer safe for the person with AD:

- The person forgets to eat.

- Food has burned because it was left on the stove.

- The oven isn't turned off.

Everyday Care

At some point, people with AD will need help bathing, combing their hair, brushing their teeth, and getting dressed. Because these are private activities, people may not want help. They may feel embarrassed about being naked in front of caregivers. They also may feel angry about not being able to care for themselves. Below are suggestions that may help with everyday care.

Bathing

Helping someone with AD take a bath or shower can be one of the hardest things you do. Planning can help make the person's bath time better for both of you.

The person with AD may be afraid. If so, follow the person's lifelong bathing habits, such as doing the bath or shower in the morning or before going to bed. Here are other tips for bathing.

Safety tips:

- Never leave a confused or frail person alone in the tub or shower.

- Always check the water temperature before he or she gets in the tub or shower.

- Use plastic containers for shampoo or soap to prevent them from breaking.

- Use a hand-held showerhead.

- Use a rubber bath mat and put safety bars in the tub.

- Use a sturdy shower chair in the tub or shower. This will support a person who is unsteady, and it could prevent falls. You can get shower chairs at drug stores and medical supply stores.

Before a bath or shower:

- Get the soap, washcloth, towels, and shampoo ready.

- Make sure the bathroom is warm and well lighted. Play soft music if it helps to relax the person.

- Be matter-of-fact about bathing. Say, "It's time for a bath now." Don't argue about the need for a bath or shower.

- Be gentle and respectful. Tell the person what you are going to do, step-by-step.

- Make sure the water temperature in the bath or shower is comfortable.

- Don't use bath oil. It can make the tub slippery and may cause urinary tract infections

During a bath or shower:

- Allow the person with AD to do as much as possible. This protects his or her dignity and helps the person feel more in control.

- Put a towel over the person's shoulders or lap. This helps him or her feel less exposed. Then use a sponge or washcloth to clean under the towel.

- Distract the person by talking about something else if he or she becomes upset.

- Give him or her a washcloth to hold. This makes it less likely that the person will try to hit you.

After a bath or shower:

- Prevent rashes or infections by patting the person's skin with a towel. Make sure the person is completely dry. Be sure to dry between folds of skin.

- If the person has trouble with incontinence, use a protective ointment, such as Vaseline®, around the rectum, vagina, or penis.

- If the person with AD has trouble getting in and out of the bathtub, do a sponge bath instead.

Other bathing tips:

- Give the person a full bath two or three times a week. For most people, a sponge bath to clean the face, hands, feet, underarms, and genital or "private" area is all you need to do every day.

- Washing the person's hair in the sink may be easier than doing it in the shower or bathtub. You can buy a hose attachment for the sink.

- Get professional help with bathing if it becomes too hard for you to do on your own.

Grooming

For the most part, when people feel good about how they look, they feel better. Helping people with AD brush their teeth, shave, or put on makeup often means they can feel more like themselves. Here are some grooming tips.

Mouth care:

Good mouth care helps prevent dental problems such as cavities and gum disease.

- Show the person how to brush his or her teeth. Go step-by-step. For example, pick up the toothpaste, take the top off, put the toothpaste on the toothbrush, and then brush. Remember to let the person do as much as possible.

- Brush your teeth at the same time.

- Help the person clean his or her dentures. Make sure he or she uses the denture cleaning material the right way.

- Ask the person to rinse his or her mouth with water after each meal and use mouthwash once a day.

- Try a long-handled, angled, or electric toothbrush if you need to brush the person's teeth.

- Take the person to see a dentist. Some dentists specialize in treating people with AD. Be sure to follow the dentist's advice about how often to make an appointment.

Other grooming tips:

- Encourage a woman to wear makeup if she has always used it. If needed, help her put on powder and lipstick. Don't use eye makeup.

431

- Encourage a man to shave, and help him as needed. Use an electric razor for safety.

- Take the person to the barber or beauty shop. Some barbers or hair stylists may come to your home.
- Keep the person's nails clean and trimmed.

Dressing

People with AD often need more time to dress. It can be hard for them to choose their clothes. They might wear the wrong clothing for the season. They also might wear colors that don't go together or forget to put on a piece of clothing. Allow the person to dress on his or her own for as long as possible.

Other tips include the following:

- Lay out clothes in the order the person should put them on, such as underwear first, then pants, then a shirt, and then a sweater.

- Hand the person one thing at a time or give step-by-step dressing instructions.

- Put away some clothes in another room to reduce the number of choices. Keep only one or two outfits in the closet or dresser.

- Keep the closet locked if needed. This prevents some of the problems people may have while getting dressed.

- Buy three or four sets of the same clothes, if the person wants to wear the same clothing every day.

- Buy loose-fitting, comfortable clothing. Avoid girdles, control-top pantyhose, knee-high nylons, garters, high heels, tight socks, and bras for women. Sports bras are comfortable and provide good support. Short cotton socks and loose cotton underwear are best. Sweat pants and shorts with elastic waistbands are helpful.

- Use Velcro® tape or large zipper pulls for clothing, instead of shoelaces, buttons, or buckles. Try slip-on shoes that won't slide off or shoes with Velcro® straps.

Adapting Activities for People with AD

Doing things we enjoy gives us pleasure and adds meaning to our lives. People with AD need to be active and do things they enjoy.

However, don't expect too much. It's not easy for them to plan their days and do different tasks.

Here are two reasons:

- They may have trouble deciding what to do each day. This could make them fearful and worried or quiet and withdrawn.

- They may have trouble starting tasks. Remember, the person is not being lazy. He or she might need help organizing the day or doing an activity.

Daily Activities

Doing things we enjoy gives us pleasure and adds meaning to our lives. People with AD need to be active and do things they enjoy. However, don't expect too much. It's not easy for them to plan their days and do different tasks.

Here are two reasons:

- They may have trouble deciding what to do each day. This could make them fearful and worried or quiet and withdrawn.

- They may have trouble starting tasks. Remember, the person is not being lazy. He or she might need help organizing the day or doing an activity.

Going Out

Early in the disease, people with AD may still enjoy the same kinds of outings they enjoyed in the past. Keep going on these outings as long as you are comfortable doing them.

Plan outings for the time of day when the person is at his or her best. Keep outings from becoming too long. You want to note how tired the person with AD gets after a certain amount of time (1/2 hour, 1 hour, 2 hours, etc.).

The person might enjoy outings to a:

- Favorite restaurant

- Zoo, park, or shopping mall

- Swimming pool (during a slow time of day at the pool)

- Museum, theater, or art exhibits for short trips

Remember that you can use a business-size card, as shown below, to tell others about the person's disease. Sharing the information with

433

store clerks or restaurant staff can make outings more comfortable for everyone.

Eating Out

Going out to eat can be a welcome change. But, it also can have some challenges. Planning can help. You need to think about the layout of the restaurant, the menu, the noise level, waiting times, and the helpfulness of staff. Below are some tips for eating out with the person who has AD.

Before choosing a restaurant, ask yourself:

- Does the person with AD know the restaurant well?

- Is it quiet or noisy most of time?

- Are tables easy to get to? Do you need to wait before you can be seated?

- Is the service quick enough to keep the person from getting restless?

- Does the restroom meet the person's needs?

- Are foods the person with AD likes on the menu?

- Is the staff understanding and helpful?

Before going to the restaurant, decide:

- If it is a good day to go.

- When is the best time to go. Going out earlier in the day may be best, so the person is not too tired. Service may be quicker, and there may be fewer people. If you decide to go later, try to get the person to take a nap first.

- What you will take with you. You may need to take utensils, a towel, wipes, or toilet items that the person already uses. If so, make sure this is OK with the restaurant.

At the restaurant:

- Tell the waiter or waitress about any special needs, such as extra spoons, bowls, or napkins.

- Ask for a table near the washroom and in a quiet area.

- Seat the person with his or her back to the busy areas.

- Help the person choose his or her meal, if needed. Suggest food you know the person likes. Read parts of the menu or show the person a picture of the food. Limit the number of choices.

- Ask the waiter or waitress to fill glasses half full or leave the drinks for you to serve.

- Order some finger food or snacks to hold the attention of the person with AD.

- Go with the person to the restroom. Go into the stall if the person needs help.

Traveling

Taking the person with AD on a trip is a challenge. Traveling can make the person more worried and confused. Planning can make travel easier for everyone. Below are some tips that you may find helpful.

Before you leave on the trip:

- Talk with your doctor about medicines to calm someone who gets upset while traveling.

- Find someone to help you at the airport or train station.

- Keep important documents with you in a safe place. These include: insurance cards, passports, doctor's name and phone number, list of medicines, and a copy of medical records.

- Pack items the person enjoys looking at or holding for comfort.

- Travel with another family member or friend.

- Take an extra set of clothing in a carry-on bag.

After you arrive:

- Allow lots of time for each thing you want to do. Do not plan too many activities.

- Plan rest periods.

- Follow a routine like the one you use at home. For example, try to have the person eat, rest, and go to bed at the same time he or she does at home.

- Keep a well-lighted path to the toilet, and leave the bathroom light on all night.

- Be prepared to cut your visit short. People with memory problems may wander around a place they don't know well.

In case someone with AD gets lost:

- Make sure they wear or have something with them that tells who they are, such as an ID bracelet.
- Carry a recent photo of the person with you on the trip.

Spiritual Activities

Like you, the person with AD may have spiritual needs. If so, you can help the person stay part of his or her faith community. This can help the person feel connected to others and remember pleasant times.

Here are some tips for helping a person with AD who has spiritual needs:

- Involve the person in spiritual activities that he or she has known well. These might include worship, religious or other readings, sacred music, prayer, and holiday rituals.
- Tell people in your faith community that the person has AD. Encourage them to talk with the person and show him or her that they still care.
- Play religious or other music that is important to the person. It may bring back old memories. Even if the person with AD has a problem finding the right words to speak, he or she still may be able to sing songs or hymns from the past.

Holidays

Many caregivers have mixed feelings about holidays. They may have happy memories of the past. But, they also may worry about the extra demands that holidays make on their time and energy.

Here are some suggestions to help you find a balance between doing many holiday-related things and resting:

- Celebrate holidays that are important to you. Include the person with AD as much as possible.
- Understand that things will be different. Be realistic about what you can do.
- Ask friends and family to visit. Limit the number of visitors at any one time. Plan visits when the person usually is at his or her best.

- Avoid crowds, changes in routine, and strange places that may make the person with AD feel confused or nervous.

- Do your best to enjoy yourself. Find time for the holiday activities you like to do. Ask a friend or family member to spend time with the person while you're out.

- Make sure there is a space where the person can rest when he or she goes to larger gatherings such as weddings or family reunions.

Visitors

Visitors are important to people with AD. They may not always remember who visitors are, but they often enjoy the company.

Here are ideas to share with a person planning to visit someone with AD:

- Plan the visit when the person with AD is at his or her best.

- Consider bringing along some kind of activity, such as a well-known book or photo album to look at. This can help if the person is bored or confused and needs to be distracted. But, be prepared to skip the activity if it is not needed.

- Be calm and quiet. Don't use a loud voice or talk to the person as if he or she were a child.

- Respect the person's personal space, and don't get too close.

- Make eye contact and call the person by name to get his or her attention.

- Remind the person who you are if he or she doesn't seem to know you.

- Don't argue if the person is confused. Respond to the feelings that they express. Try to distract the person by talking about something different.

- Remember not to take it personally if the person doesn't recognize you, is unkind, or gets angry. He or she is acting out of confusion.

Chapter 45

Safety Issues for People with Alzheimer Disease

Chapter Contents

Section 45.1

Safety at Home

This section includes excerpts from "About Alzheimer's Disease:
Caregiving," National Institute on Aging (NIA), January
2013; and text from "Home Safety for People with Alzheimer's
Disease," National Institute on Aging (NIA), August 2010.
Reviewed February 2016.

Home Safety

Over time, people with Alzheimer disease (AD) become less able to
manage around the house. As a caregiver, you can do many things to
make the person's home a safer place. Think prevention—help avoid
accidents by controlling possible problems.

While some Alzheimer disease behaviors can be managed medically,
many, such as wandering and agitation, cannot. It is more effective to
change the person's surroundings—for example, to remove dangerous
items—than to try to change behaviors. Changing the home environment can give the person more freedom to move around independently
and safely.

Basic Safety for Every Room

Add the following items to the person's home if they are not already
in place:

- Smoke and carbon monoxide detectors in or near the kitchen
  and in all bedrooms

- Emergency phone numbers and the person's address near all
  phones

- Safety knobs and an automatic shut-off switch on the stove

- Childproof plugs for unused electrical outlets and childproof
  latches on cabinet doors

You can buy home safety products at stores carrying hardware,
electronics, medical supplies, and children's items.

Lock up or remove these potentially dangerous items from the home:

- Medicines

- Alcohol

- Cleaning and household products, such as paint thinner and matches

- Poisonous plants—contact the National Poison Control Center at 1-800-222-1222 or www.poison.org to find out which houseplants are poisonous.

- Guns and other weapons, scissors, knives, power tools, and machinery

- Gasoline cans and other dangerous items in the garage

Moving around the House

Try these tips to prevent falls and injuries:

- Simplify the home. Too much furniture can make it hard to move around freely.

- Get rid of clutter, such as piles of newspapers and magazines.

- Have a sturdy handrail on stairways.

- Put carpet on stairs, or mark the edges of steps with brightly colored tape so the person can see them more easily. Alzheimer Disease Education and Referral Center

- Put a gate across the stairs if the person has balance problems.

- Remove small throw rugs. Use rugs with nonskid backing instead.

- Make sure cords to electrical outlets are out of the way or tacked to baseboards.

- Clean up spills right away.

Make sure the person with Alzheimer disease has good floor traction for walking. To make floors less slippery, leave floors unpolished or install non skid strips. Shoes and slippers with good traction also help the person move around safely.

Outside Approaches to the House

- Keep steps sturdy and textured to prevent falls in wet or icy weather.

- Mark the edges of steps with bright or reflective tape.

- Consider installing a ramp with handrails as an alternative to steps.

- Eliminate uneven surfaces or walkways, hoses, and other objects that may cause a person to trip.

- Restrict access to a swimming pool by fencing it with a locked gate, covering it, and closely supervising it when in use.

- In the patio area, remove the fuel source and fire starters from any grills when not in use, and supervise use when the person with Alzheimer disease is present.

- Place a small bench or table by the entry door to hold parcels while unlocking the door.

- Make sure outside lighting is adequate. Light sensors that turn on lights automatically as you approach the house may be useful. They also may be used in other parts of the home.

- Prune bushes and foliage well away from walkways and doorways.

- Consider a NO SOLICITING sign for the front gate or door.

Entryway

- Remove scatter rugs and throw rugs.

- Use textured strips or nonskid wax on hardwood and tile floors to prevent slipping.

Kitchen

- Install childproof door latches on storage cabinets and drawers designated for breakable or dangerous items. Lock away all household cleaning products, matches, knives, scissors, blades, small appliances, and anything valuable.

- If prescription or nonprescription drugs are kept in the kitchen, store them in a locked cabinet.

- Remove scatter rugs and foam pads from the floor.

- Install safety knobs and an automatic shut-off switch on the stove.

- Do not use or store flammable liquids in the kitchen. Lock them in the garage or in an outside storage unit.

- Keep a night-light in the kitchen.

- Remove or secure the family "junk drawer." A person with Alzheimer disease may eat small items such as matches, hardware, erasers, and plastics.

- Remove artificial fruits and vegetables or food-shaped kitchen magnets, which might appear to be edible.

- Insert a drain trap in the kitchen sink to catch anything that may otherwise become lost or clog the plumbing.

- Consider disconnecting the garbage disposal. People with Alzheimer disease may place objects or their own hands in the disposal.

Bedroom

- Anticipate the reasons a person with Alzheimer disease might get out of bed, such as hunger, thirst, going to the bathroom, restlessness, and pain. Try to meet these needs by offering food and fluids and scheduling ample toileting.

- Use a night-light.

- Use a monitoring device (like those used for infants) to alert you to any sounds indicating a fall or other need for help. This also is an effective device for bathrooms.

- Remove scatter rugs and throw rugs.

- Remove portable space heaters. If you use portable fans, be sure that objects cannot be placed in the blades.

- Be cautious when using electric mattress pads, electric blankets, electric sheets, and heating pads, all of which can cause burns and fires. Keep controls out of reach.

- If the person with Alzheimer disease is at risk of falling out of bed, place mats next to the bed, as long as they do not create a greater risk of accident.

- Use transfer or mobility aids.

- If you are considering using a hospital-type bed with rails and/ or wheels, read the Food and Drug Administration's up-to-date safety information at www.fda.gov/cdrh/beds.

Bathroom

- Do not leave a severely impaired person with Alzheimer disease alone in the bathroom.

- Remove the lock from the bathroom door to prevent the person with Alzheimer disease from getting locked inside.

- Place nonskid adhesive strips, decals, or mats in the tub and shower. If the bathroom is uncarpeted, consider placing these strips next to the tub, toilet, and sink.

- Use washable wall-to-wall bathroom carpeting to prevent slipping on wet tile floors.

- Use a raised toilet seat with handrails, or install grab bars beside the toilet.

- Install grab bars in the tub/shower. A grab bar in contrasting color to the wall is easier to see.

- Use a foam rubber faucet cover (often used for small children) in the tub to prevent serious injury should the person with Alzheimer disease fall.

- Use a plastic shower stool and a handheld shower head to make bathing easier.

- In the shower, tub, and sink, use a single faucet that mixes hot and cold water to avoid burns.

- Set the water heater at 120 degrees Fahrenheit to avoid scalding tap water.

- Insert drain traps in sinks to catch small items that may be lost or flushed down the drain.

- Store medications (prescription and nonprescription) in a locked cabinet. Check medication dates and throw away outdated medications.

- Remove cleaning products from under the sink, or lock them away.

- Use a night-light.

- Remove small electrical appliances from the bathroom. Cover electrical outlets.

- If a man with Alzheimer disease uses an use electric razor, have him use a mirror outside the bathroom to avoid water contact.

Living Room

- Clear electrical cords from all areas where people walk.

- Remove scatter rugs and throw rugs. Repair or replace torn carpet.

- Place decals at eye level on sliding glass doors, picture windows, and furniture with large glass panels to identify the glass pane.

- Do not leave the person with Alzheimer disease alone with an open fire in the fireplace. Consider alternative heating sources.

- Keep matches and cigarette lighters out of reach.

- Keep the remote controls for the television, DVD player, and stereo system out of sight.

Laundry Room

- Keep the door to the laundry room locked if possible.

- Lock all laundry products in a cabinet.

- Remove large knobs from the washer and dryer if the person with Alzheimer disease tampers with machinery.

- Close and latch the doors and lids to the washer and dryer to prevent objects from being placed in the machines.

Garage / Shed / Basement

- Lock access to all garages, sheds, and basements if possible.

- Inside a garage or shed, keep all potentially dangerous items, such as tools, tackle, machines, and sporting equipment, either locked away in cabinets or in appropriate boxes or cases.

- Secure and lock all motor vehicles and keep them out of sight if possible. Consider covering vehicles, including bicycles, that are not frequently used. This may reduce the possibility that the person with Alzheimer disease will think about leaving.

- Keep all toxic materials, such as paint, fertilizers, gasoline, or cleaning supplies, out of view. Either put them in a high, dry place, or lock them in a cabinet.

- If the person with Alzheimer disease is permitted in a garage, shed, or basement, preferably with supervision, make sure the area is well lit and that stairs have a handrail and are safe to walk up and down. Keep walkways clear of debris and clutter, and place overhanging items out of reach.

Minimize Danger

People with Alzheimer disease may not see, smell, touch, hear, and/or taste things as they used to. You can do things around the house to make life safer and easier for the person. For example:

- Check all rooms for adequate lighting. Use nightlights in bathrooms, bedrooms, and hallways.

- Be careful about small pets. The person may not see the pet and trip over it.

- Reset the water heater to 120 degrees Fahrenheit to prevent burns.

- Label hot-water faucets red and cold-water faucets blue, or write the words "hot" and "cold" near them.

- Install grab bars in the tub/shower and beside the toilet.

- Put signs near the oven, toaster, and other things that get hot. The sign could say, "Stop!" or "Don't Touch—Very Hot!"

You can also try these tips:

- Check foods in the refrigerator often. Throw out any that have gone bad.

- Put away or lock up things like toothpaste, lotions, shampoos, rubbing alcohol, soap, or perfume. They may look and smell like food to a person with Alzheimer disease.

- If the person wears a hearing aid, check the batteries and settings often. You may want to re-evaluate the safety of the person's home as behavior and abilities change.

Section 45.2

Wandering

Text in this section is excerpted from "Caring for a Person with Alzheimer's Disease," National Institute on Aging (NIA), May 2015.

How to Cope with Wandering?

Many people with Alzheimer disease (AD) wander away from their home or caregiver. As the caregiver, you need to know how to limit wandering and prevent the person from becoming lost. This will help keep the person safe and give you greater peace of mind.

How to Cope with Rummaging and Hiding Things?

Someone with AD may start rummaging or searching through cabinets, drawers, closets, the refrigerator, and other places where things are stored. He or she also may hide items around the house. This behavior can be annoying or even dangerous for the caregiver or family members. If you get angry, try to remember that this behavior is part of the disease.

In some cases, there might be a logical reason for this behavior. For instance, the person may be looking for something specific, although he or she may not be able to tell you what it is. He or she may be hungry or bored. Try to understand what is causing the behavior so you can fit your response to the cause.

Here Are Some Other Steps to Take

- Lock up dangerous or toxic products, or place them out of the person's sight and reach.

- Remove spoiled food from the refrigerator and cabinets. Someone with AD may look for snacks, but lack the judgment or sense of taste to stay away from spoiled foods.

- Remove valuable items that could be misplaced or hidden by the person, like important papers, checkbooks, charge cards, jewelry, and keys.

- People with AD often hide, lose, or throw away mail. If this is a serious problem, consider getting a post office box. If you have a yard with a fence and a locked gate, place your mailbox outside the gate.

- Keep the person with AD from going into unused rooms. This limits his or her rummaging through and hiding things.

- Search the house to learn where the person often hides things. Once you find these places, check them often, out of sight of the person.

- Keep all trash cans covered or out of sight. People with AD may not remember the purpose of the container or may rummage through it.

- Check trash containers before you empty them, in case something has been hidden there or thrown away by accident.

You also can create a special place where the person with AD can rummage freely or sort things. This could be a chest of drawers, a bag of objects, or a basket of clothing to fold or unfold. Give him or her a personal box, chest, or cupboard to store special objects. You may have to remind the person where to find his or her personal storage place.

Section 45.3

Driving Safety

Text in this section is excerpted from "Caring for a Person with Alzheimer's Disease," National Institute on Aging (NIA), May 2015.

Good drivers are alert, think clearly, and make good decisions. When the person with Alzheimer disease (AD) is not able to do these things, he or she should stop driving. But, he or she may not want to stop or even think there is a problem. As the caregiver, you will need to talk with the person about why he or she needs to stop driving. Do this in a caring way. Understand how unhappy the person with AD may be that he or she has reached this new stage.

Be ready to find other ways that the person can travel on his or her own, for as long as possible. Your local Area Agency on Aging has information about transportation services in your area. These services may include free or low-cost buses, taxi service, or carpools for older people. Some churches and community groups have volunteers who take seniors wherever they want to go.

Here Are Some Things You Need to Know about Driving and Memory Loss

- A person with some memory loss may be able to drive safely sometimes. But, he or she may not be able to react quickly when faced with a surprise on the road. This can be dangerous. If the person's reaction time slows, then you need to stop the person from driving.

- The person may be able to drive short distances on local streets during the day, but may not be able to drive safely at night or on a freeway. If this is the case, then limit the times and places that the person can drive.

- Some people with memory problems decide on their own not to drive. Others don't want to stop driving and may deny that they have a problem.

Here Are Some Signs That the Person Should Stop Driving

- New dents and scratches on the car.

- Taking a long time to do a simple errand and not being able to explain why. That may indicate that the person got lost.

Also, consider asking a friend or family member to follow the person. What he or she sees can give you a better sense of how well the person with AD is driving.

Here Are Some Ways to Stop People with AD from Driving

- Try talking about your concerns with the person.

- Ask your doctor to tell him or her to stop driving. The doctor can write, "Do not drive" on a prescription pad and you can show this to the person. Some State Departments of Motor Vehicles require doctors to tell them if the person with AD should no longer drive.

- Ask family or friends to drive the person.

- Take him or her to get a driving test.

- Hide the car keys, move the car, take out the distributor cap, or disconnect the battery if the person won't stop driving.

- Find out about services that help people with disabilities get around their community. Look in the blue pages of your local telephone book, contact your local Area Agency on Aging office, or call the Community Transportation Association at 1-800-891-0590.

- If the person won't stop driving, contact your State Department of Motor Vehicles. Ask about a medical review for a person who may not be able to drive safely. He or she may be asked to retake a driving test. In some cases, the person's license could be taken away.

Section 45.4

Going to the Hospital

Text in this section is excerpted from "Alzheimer's Caregiving Tips,"
National Institute on Aging (NIA), January 2013.

A trip to the hospital can be stressful for people with Alzheimer disease (AD) and their caregivers. Being prepared for emergency and planned hospital visits can relieve some of that stress. This tip sheet suggests ways to make hospital visits easier.

A trip to the emergency room (ER) can tire and frighten a person with Alzheimer disease. Here are some ways to cope:

- Ask a friend or family member to go with you or meet you in the ER. He or she can stay with the person while you answer questions.

- Be ready to explain the symptoms and events leading up to the ER visit—possibly more than once to different staff members.

- Tell ER staff that the person has AD. Explain how best to talk with the person.

- Be patient. It could be a long wait if the reason for your visit is not life-threatening.
- Comfort the person. Stay calm and positive.
- If the person must stay overnight in the hospital, try to have a friend or family member stay with him or her.

Do not leave the emergency room without a plan. If you are sent home, make sure you understand all instructions for follow-up care.

What to Pack

An emergency bag with the following items, packed ahead of time, can make a visit to the ER go more smoothly:

- Health insurance cards
- Lists of current medical conditions, medicines being taken, and allergies
- Health care providers' names and phone numbers
- Copies of health care advance directives
- "Personal information sheet" stating the person's preferred name and language; contact information for key family members and friends; need for glasses, dentures, or hearing aids; behaviors of concern; how the person communicates needs and expresses emotions; and living situation
- Snacks and bottles of water
- Incontinence briefs if usually worn, moist wipes, and plastic bags
- Comforting objects or music player with earphones

Before a Planned Hospital Stay

Keep in mind that hospitals are not typically well designed for patients with dementia. Preparation can make all the difference. Here are some tips.

- Build a care team of family, friends, and/or professional caregivers to support the person during the hospital stay. Do not try to do it all alone.
- Ask the doctor if the procedure can be done during an outpatient visit. If not, ask if tests can be done before admission to the hospital to shorten the hospital stay.

451

- General anesthesia can have side effects, so see if local anesthesia is an option.

- Ask if regular medications can be continued during the hospital stay.

- Ask for a private room, with a reclining chair or bed, if insurance will cover it. It will be calmer than a shared room.

- Shortly before leaving home, tell the person with Alzheimer disease that the two of you are going to spend a short time in the hospital.

During the Hospital

Stay While the person with AD is in the hospital:

- Ask doctors to limit questions to the person, who may not be able to answer accurately. Instead, talk with the doctor in private, outside the person's room.

- Help hospital staff understand the person's normal functioning and behavior. Ask them to avoid using physical restraints or medications to control behaviors.

- Tell the doctor immediately if the person seems suddenly worse or different. Medical problems such as fever, infection, medication side effects, and dehydration can cause delirium, a state of extreme confusion and disorientation.

- Ask friends and family to make calls, or use e-mail or online tools to keep others informed about the person's progress.

Section 45.5

Caring for Someone with Dementia in a Disaster

Text in this section is excerpted from "Alzheimer's Caregiving Tips,"
National Institute on Aging (NIA), October 2012.

Disaster Preparedness

People with Alzheimer disease (AD) can be especially vulnerable during disasters such as severe weather, fires, floods, earthquakes, and other emergency situations. It is important for caregivers to have a disaster plan that includes the special needs of the person with Alzheimer disease.

In general, you should prepare to meet the needs of your family for 3 to 7 days, including having supplies and backup options if you lose basic services such as water or electricity. Organizations such as the Federal Emergency Management Agency (FEMA, www.fema.gov) and the American Red Cross (www.redcross.org) provide information about making a general disaster plan.

Gather Supplies

As you assemble supplies for your family's disaster kit, consider the needs of the person with AD. Be sure to store all supplies in a watertight container. The kit might contain:

- Incontinence undergarments, wipes, and lotions

- Pillow, toy, or something the person can hold onto

- Favorite snacks and high-nutrient drinks

- Physician's name, address, and phone number

- Copies of legal, medical, insurance, and Social Security information

- Ziplock bags to hold medications and documents

- Recent photos of the person

453

Other supplies you may need are:

- Warm clothing and sturdy shoes
- Spare eyeglasses and hearing-aid batteries
- Medications
- Flashlights and extra batteries

If You Must Leave Home

In some situations, you may decide to "ride out" a natural disaster at home. In others, you may need to move to a safer place, like a community shelter or someone's home.

Relocation may make the person with Alzheimer disease very anxious. Be sensitive to his or her emotions. Stay close, offer your hand, or give the person reassuring hugs.

To plan for an evacuation:

- Know how to get to the nearest emergency shelters.
- If you don't drive or driving is dangerous, arrange for someone to transport your group.
- Make sure the person with Alzheimer disease wears an ID bracelet.
- Take both general supplies and your Alzheimer disease emergency kit.
- Pack familiar, comforting items. If possible, plan to take along the household pet.
- Save emergency numbers in your cell phone, and keep it charged.
- Plan to keep neighbors, friends, and family informed about your location.
- If conditions are noisy or chaotic, try to find a quieter place.

If You Are Separated

It's very important to stay with a person with Alzheimer disease in a disaster. Do not count on the person to stay in one place while you go to get help. However, the unexpected can happen, so it is a good idea to plan for possible separation:

- Enroll the person in the MedicAlert® + Alzheimer Association Safe Return® Program—an identification and support service for people who may become lost.

- Prepare for wandering. Place labels in garments to aid in identification. Keep an article of the person's clothing in a plastic bag to help dogs find him or her.

- Identify specific neighbors or nearby family and friends who would be willing to help in a crisis. Make a plan of action with them should the person with Alzheimer disease be unattended during a crisis.

- Give someone you trust a house key and list of emergency phone numbers.

- Provide local police and emergency services with photos of the person with Alzheimer disease and copies of his or her medical documents, so they are aware of the person's needs.

Section 45.6

Understanding Elder Abuse

Text in this section is excerpted from "AgePage,"
National Institute on Aging (NIA), February 2015.

Elder Abuse

Abuse can happen to anyone—no matter the person's age, sex, race, religion, or ethnic or cultural background. Many older people are victims of elder abuse, sometimes called elder mistreatment.

Abuse can happen in many places, including the older person's home, a family member's house, an assisted living facility, or a nursing home.

Types of Abuse

There are many types of abuse:

- Physical abuse happens when someone causes bodily harm by hitting, pushing, or slapping.

- Emotional abuse, sometimes called psychological abuse, can include a caregiver saying hurtful words, yelling, threatening, or repeatedly ignoring the older person. Keeping that person from seeing close friends and relatives is another form of emotional abuse.

- Neglect occurs when the caregiver does not try to respond to the older person's needs.

- Abandonment is leaving a senior alone without planning for his or her care.

- Sexual abuse involves a caregiver forcing an older adult to watch or be part of sexual acts.

Money Matters: Financial Abuse and Healthcare Fraud

Financial abuse happens when money or belongings are stolen. It can include forging checks, taking someone else's retirement and Social Security benefits, or using another person's credit cards and bank accounts. It also includes changing names on a will, bank account, life insurance policy, or title to a house without permission from the older person. Financial abuse is becoming a widespread and hard-to-detect issue. Even someone you've never met can steal your financial information using the Internet or email. Be careful about sharing any financial information online—you don't know who sees it.

Healthcare fraud can be committed by doctors, hospital staff, and other healthcare workers. It includes overcharging, billing twice for the same service, falsifying Medicaid or Medicare claims, or charging for care that wasn't provided. Older adults and caregivers should keep an eye out for this type of fraud.

Who Is Being Abused?

Most victims of abuse are women, but some are men. Likely targets are older people who have no family or friends nearby and people with disabilities, memory problems, or dementia.

Abuse can happen to any older person, but often affects those who depend on others for help with activities of everyday life—including bathing, dressing, and taking medicine. People who are frail may appear to be easy victims.

What Are Signs of Abuse?

You may see signs of abuse or neglect when you visit an older person at home or in an eldercare facility. You may notice the person:

- Has trouble sleeping

- Seems depressed or confused
- Loses weight for no reason
- Displays signs of trauma, like rocking back and forth
- Acts agitated or violent F Becomes withdrawn F Stops taking part in activities he or she enjoys
- Has unexplained bruises, burns, or scars
- Looks messy, with unwashed hair or dirty clothes
- Develops bed sores or other preventable conditions

If you see signs of abuse, try talking with the older person to find out what's going on. For instance, the abuse may be from another resident and not from someone who works at the nursing home or assisted living facility. Most importantly, get help.

Who Can Help?

Elder abuse will not stop on its own. Someone else needs to step in and help. Many older people are too ashamed to report mistreatment. Or, they're afraid if they make a report it will get back to the abuser and make the situation worse.

If you think someone you know is being abused—physically, emotionally, or financially—talk with him or her when the two of you are alone. You could say you think something is wrong and you're worried. Offer to take him or her to get help, for instance, at a local adult protective services agency.

Many local, state, and national social service agencies can help with emotional, legal, and financial problems.

The Administration for Community Living has a National Center on Elder Abuse where you can learn about how to report abuse, where to get help, and state laws that deal with abuse and neglect. Go to www.ncea.aoa.gov for more information. Or, call the Eldercare Locator weekdays at 1-800-677-1116.

Most states require that doctors and lawyers report elder mistreatment. Family and friends can also report it. Do not wait. Help is available.

What Is the Long-Term Effect of Abuse?

Most physical wounds heal in time. But any type of mistreatment can leave the abused person feeling fearful and depressed. Sometimes, the victim thinks the abuse is his or her fault.

Protective services agencies can suggest support groups and counseling that can help the abused person heal the emotional wounds.

Chapter 46

Caregiving and Taking Care of Yourself

Caring for Yourself

Taking care of yourself is one of the most important things you can do as a caregiver. This could mean asking family members and friends to help out, doing things you enjoy, using adult day care services, or getting help from a local home health care agency. Taking these actions can bring you some relief. It also may help keep you from getting ill or depressed.

How to Take Care of Yourself

Here are some ways you can take care of yourself:

- Ask for help when you need it.

- Join a caregiver's support group.

- Take breaks each day.

- Spend time with friends.

- Keep up with your hobbies and interests.

- Eat healthy foods.

Text in this chapter is excerpted from "Caring for a Person with Alzheimer's Disease," National Institute on Aging (NIA), May 2015.

- Get exercise as often as you can.

- See your doctor on a regular basis.

- Keep your health, legal, and financial information up-to-date.

Getting Help

Everyone needs help at times. It's okay to ask for help and to take time for yourself. However, many caregivers find it hard to ask for help. You may feel:

- You should be able to do everything yourself

- That it's not all right to leave the person with someone else

- No one will help even if you ask

- You don't have the money to pay someone to watch the person for an hour or two

If you have trouble asking for help, try using some of the tips below.

- It's okay to ask for help from family, friends, and others. I don't have to do everything myself.

- Ask people to help out in specific ways like making a meal, visiting the person, or taking the person out for a short time.

- Join a support group to share advice and understanding with other caregivers.

- Call for help from home health care or adult day care services when you need it.

- Use national and local resources to find out how to pay for some of this help.

You may want to join a support group of Alzheimer disease (AD) caregivers in your area or on the Internet. These groups meet in person or online to share experiences and tips and to give each other support. Ask your doctor, check online, or look in the phone book for a local chapter of the Alzheimer Association.

Your Emotional Health

You may be busy caring for the person with AD and don't take time to think about your emotional health. But, you need to. Caring for a person with AD takes a lot of time and effort. Your job as caregiver can become even harder when the person you're caring for gets angry with you, hurts your feelings, or forgets who you are. Sometimes, you may feel really discouraged, sad, lonely, frustrated, confused, or angry. **These feelings are normal.**

Here are some things you can say to yourself that might help you feel better:

- I'm doing the best I can.

- What I'm doing would be hard for anyone.

- I'm not perfect, and that's okay.

- I can't control some things that happen.

- Sometimes, I just need to do what works for right now.

Even when I do everything I can think of, the person with AD will still have problem behaviors because of the illness, not because of what I do.

- I will enjoy the moments when we can be together in peace.

- I will try to get help from a counselor if caregiving becomes too much for me.

Meeting Your Spiritual Needs

Many of us have spiritual needs. Going to a church, temple, or mosque helps some people meet their spiritual needs. They like to be part of a faith community. For others, simply having a sense that larger forces are at work in the world helps meet their spiritual needs. As the caregiver of a person with AD, you may need more spiritual resources than others do.

Meeting your spiritual needs can help you:

- Cope better as a caregiver

- Know yourself and your needs

- Feel recognized, valued, and loved

- Become involved with others

- Find a sense of balance and peace

461

Other caregivers made these suggestions to help you cope with your feelings and spiritual needs:

- Understand that you may feel powerless and hopeless about what's happening to the person you care for.

- Understand that you may feel a sense of loss and sadness.

- Understand why you've chosen to take care of the person with AD. Ask yourself if you made this choice out of love, loyalty, a sense of duty, a religious obligation, financial concerns, fear, a habit, or self-punishment.

- Let yourself feel day-to-day "uplifts." These might include good feelings about the person you care for, support from other caring people, or time to spend on your own interests and hobbies.

- Keep a connection to something "higher than yourself." This may be a belief in a higher power, religious beliefs, or a belief that something good comes from every life experience.

Chapter 47

Respite Care: Giving Caregivers a Break

Getting Help with Caregiving

Some caregivers need help when the person is in the early stages of Alzheimer Disease (AD). Other caregivers look for help when the person is in the later stages of AD. It's okay to seek help whenever you need it.

As the person moves through the stages of AD, he or she will need more care. One reason is that medicines used to treat AD can only control symptoms; they cannot cure the disease. Symptoms, such as memory loss and confusion, will get worse over time.

Because of this, you will need more help. You may feel that asking for help shows weakness or a lack of caring, but the opposite is true. Asking for help shows your strength. It means you know your limits and when to seek support.

Build a Support System

According to many caregivers, building a local support system is a key way to get help. Your support system might include your caregiver support group, the local chapter of the Alzheimer Association, family, friends, and faith groups.

Text in this chapter is excerpted from "Caring for a Person with Alzheimer's Disease," National Institute on Aging (NIA), May 2015.

Direct Services—Groups That Help with Everyday Care in the Home

Here is a list of services that can help you care for the person with AD at home. Find out if these services are offered in your area. Also, contact Medicare to see if they cover the cost of any of these services.

Home Health Care Services

What they do:

Send a home health aide to your home to help you care for a person with AD. These aides provide care and/or company for the person. They may come for a few hours or stay for 24 hours. Some home health aides are better trained and supervised than others.

What to know about costs:

- Home health services charge by the hour.

- Medicare covers some home health service costs.

- Most insurance plans do not cover these costs.

- You must pay all costs not covered by Medicare, Medicaid, or insurance.

How to find them:

- Ask your doctor or other health care professional about good home health care services in your area.

- Look in your phone book under "home health care."

Here are some questions you might ask before signing a home health care agreement:

- Is your service licensed and accredited?

- What is the cost of your services?

- What is included and not included in your services?

- How many days a week and hours a day will an aide come to my home?

- How do you check the background and experience of your home health aides?

- How do you train your home health aides?

- Can I get special help in an emergency?

- What types of emergency care can you provide?

- Whom do I contact if there is a problem?

Meal Services

What they do:

- Bring hot meals to the person's home or your home. The delivery staff do not feed the person.

What to know about costs:

- The person with AD must qualify for the service based on local guidelines.

- Some groups do not charge for their services. Others may charge a small fee.

How to find them:

- The Eldercare Locator can help at 1-800-677-1116 or www.eldercare.gov. Or, call the Meals on Wheels organization at 1-888-998-6325 or visit their website at www.mowaa.org.

Adult Day Care Services

What they do:

- Provide a safe environment, activities, and staff who pay attention to the needs of the person with AD in an adult day care facility

- Provide a much-needed break for you

- Provide transportation—the facility may pick up the person, take him or her to day care, and then return the person home

What to know about costs:

- Adult day care services charge by the hour.

- Most insurance plans don't cover these costs. You must pay all costs not covered by insurance.

How to find them:

- Call the National Adult Day Services Association at 1-877-745-1440, or visit their website at www.nadsa.org. You also can call the Eldercare Locator at 1-800-677-1116, or visit their website at www.eldercare.gov.

Respite Services

What they do:

- Provide short stays, from a few days to a few weeks, in a nursing home or other place for the person with AD

- Allow you to get a break to rest or go on a vacation

What to know about costs:

- Respite services charge by the number of days or weeks that services are provided.

- Medicare or Medicaid may cover the cost of up to 5 days in a row of respite care in an inpatient facility.

- Most insurance plans do not cover these costs.

- You must pay all costs not covered by Medicare, Medicaid, or insurance.

How to find them:

- Visit the National Respite Locator Service at http://archrespite. org/respitelocator.

Geriatric Care Managers

What they do:

- Make a home visit and suggest needed services

- Help you get needed services

What to know about costs:

- Geriatric care managers charge by the hour.

- Most insurance plans don't cover these costs.

- Medicare does not pay for this service.

- You will probably have to pay for this service.

How to find them:

- Call the National Association of Professional Geriatric Care Managers at 1-520-881-8008, or visit its website at www.caremanager.org.

Counseling from a Mental Health or Social Work Professional

What they do:

- Help you deal with any stress you may be feeling

- Help you understand your feelings, such as anger, sadness, or feeling out of control and overwhelmed

- Help develop plans for unexpected or sudden events

What to know about costs:

- Professional mental health counselors charge by the hour. There may be big differences in the rates you would be charged from one counselor to another.

- Some insurance companies will cover some of these costs.

- Medicare or Medicaid may cover some of these costs.

- You must pay all costs not covered by Medicare, Medicaid, or insurance.

How to find them:

- It's a good idea to ask your health insurance staff which counselors and services, if any, your insurance plan covers. Then check with your doctor, local family service agencies, and community mental health agencies for referrals to counselors.

Hospice Services

What they do:

- Provide care for a person who is near the end of life

- Keep the person who is dying as comfortable and pain-free as possible

- Provide care in the home or in a hospice facility

- Support the family in providing in-home or end-of-life care

What to know about costs:

- Hospice services charge by the number of days or weeks that services are provided.

- Medicare or Medicaid may cover hospice costs.

- Most insurance plans do not cover these costs.

- You must pay all costs not covered by Medicare, Medicaid, or insurance.

How to find them:

- National Association for Home Care and Hospice at 1-202-547-7424 or www.nahcagencylocator.com

- Hospice Foundation of America at 1-800-854-3402 or www.hospicefoundation.org

- National Hospice and Palliative Care Organization at 1-800-658-8898 or www.nhpco.org/find-hospice

Chapter 48

Hiring In-Home Care Providers

Home Health Care

Home health care helps older adults live independently for as long as possible, even with an illness or injury. It covers a wide range of services and can often delay the need for long-term nursing home care.

Home health care may include occupational and physical therapy, speech therapy, and skilled nursing. It may involve helping older adults with activities of daily living, such as bathing, dressing, and eating. It can also include assistance with cooking, cleaning, other housekeeping, and monitoring one's medication regimen.

It is important to understand the difference between home health care and home care services. Although home health care may include some home care services, it is medical in nature. Home care services include chores and house cleaning, whereas home health care usually involves helping someone to recover from an illness or injury. Home health care professionals are often licensed practical nurses, therapists, or home health aides. Most of them work for home health agencies, hospitals, or public health departments licensed by the state.

This chapter includes excerpts from "Home Health Care," Administration on Aging (AOA), October 15, 2012; and text from "Alzheimer's Caregiving," National Institute on Aging (NIA),, October 2015.

Most people with Alzheimer disease (AD) are cared for at home by family members. Within families, caregiving is provided most often by wives and husbands, followed by daughters.

As Alzheimer disease (AD) gets worse, the person will need more and more care. Because of this, you will need more help. It's okay to seek help whenever you need it.

Building a local support system is a key way to get help. This system might include a caregiver support group, the local chapter of the Alzheimer Association, family, friends, and faith groups. To learn where to get help in your community, contact

- the Alzheimer Disease Education and Referral (ADEAR) Center, 1-800-438-4380 or visit **www.nia.nih.gov/alzheimers**

- the Alzheimer Association at 1-800-272-3900.

Various professional services can help with everyday care in the home of someone with AD. Medicare, Medicaid, and other health insurance plans may help pay for these services. Contact Eldercare Locator to find the services you need in your area by calling 1-800-677-1116 or visiting www.eldercare.gov.

Home Health Care Services

Home health care agencies send a home health aide or nurse to your home to help you care for a person with AD. They may come for a few hours or stay for 24 hours and are paid by the hour. Some home health aides are better trained and supervised than others. Ask your doctor or other health care professional about good home health care services in your area. Get as much information as possible about a service before you sign an agreement. Also, ask for and check references.

Ensuring Quality Care

As with any important purchase, it is wise to talk with friends, neighbors, and your local Area Agency on Aging (AAA) to learn more about the home health care agencies in your community. Consider using the following questions to guide your search.

- How long has the agency served this community?

- Does the agency have a brochure describing services and costs? If so, take or download it.

- Is the agency an approved Medicare provider?

- Does a national accrediting body, such as the Joint Commission for the Accreditation of Healthcare Organizations, certify the quality of care?

- Does the agency have a current license to practice (if required by the state)?

- Does the agency offer a "Bill of Rights" that describes the rights and responsibilities of both the agency and the person receiving care?

- Does the agency prepare a care plan for the patient (with input from the patient, his or her doctor, and family members)? Will the agency update the plan as necessary?

- How closely do supervisors oversee care to ensure quality?

- Are agency staff members available around the clock, seven days a week, if necessary?

- Does the agency have a nursing supervisor available for on-call assistance at all times?

- Whom does the agency call if the home health care worker cannot come when scheduled?

- How does the agency ensure patient confidentiality?

- How are agency caregivers hired and trained?

- How does the agency screen prospective employees?

- Will the agency provide a list of references for its caregivers?

- What is the procedure for resolving problems, if they occur? Whom can I call with questions or complaints?

- Is there a sliding fee schedule based on ability to pay, and is financial assistance available to pay for services?

When purchasing home health care directly from an individual provider (instead of an agency), it is even more important to conduct thorough screening. This should include an interview with the home health caregiver. You should also request references. Prepare for the interview by making a list of the older adult's special needs. For example, the patient may require help getting into or out of a wheelchair. If so, the caregiver must be able to provide appropriate assistance.

Whether you arrange for home health care through an agency or hire an independent aide, it helps to spend time preparing the person who will provide care. Ideally, you will spend a day with the caregiver, before the job formally begins, to discuss what is involved in the daily routine. At a minimum, inform the caregiver (verbally and in writing) of the following things that he or she should know.

- Health conditions, including illnesses and injuries
- Signs of an emergency medical situation
- General likes and dislikes
- Medication, including how and when each must be taken
- Need for dentures, eyeglasses, canes, walkers, hearing aids, etc.
- Possible behavior problems and how best to handle them
- Mobility issues (trouble walking, getting into or out of a wheel-chair, etc.)
- Allergies, special diets, or other nutritional needs
- Therapeutic exercises with detailed instructions

Meal Services

Woman delivery meal to man at home. The delivery staff does not feed the person. The person with Alzheimer disease must qualify for the service based on local guidelines. Some groups do not charge for their services. Others may charge a small fee. For information, call Eldercare Locator at 1-800-677-1116 or go to **www.eldercare.gov**. You may also contact Meals on Wheels at 1-888-998-6325.

Adult Day Care Services

Adult day care services provide a safe environment, activities, and staff who take care of the person with AD at their own facility. This provides a much-needed break for you. Many programs provide transportation between the person's home and the facility.

Adult day care services generally charge by the hour. Most insurance plans do not cover these costs. To find adult day care services in your area, contact the National Adult Day Services Association at 1-877-745-1440.

Respite Services

Respite services provide short stays, from a few days to a few weeks, in a nursing home or other place for the person with AD. This care allows you to get a break or go on a vacation.

Respite services charge by the number of days or weeks that services are provided. Medicare or Medicaid may cover the cost of up to 5 days in a row of respite care in an inpatient facility. Most private insurance plans do not cover these costs. To find respite services in your community, call the National Respite Locator Service at 1-800-773-5433 (toll-free).

Geriatric Care Managers

Geriatric care managers visit your home to assess your needs and suggest and arrange home-care services. They charge by the hour. Most insurance plans don't cover these costs. To find a geriatric care manager, contact the National Association of Professional Geriatric Care Managers at 1-520-881-8008.

Mental Health Professionals and Social Workers

Mental health professionals and social workers help you deal with any stress you may be feeling. They help you understand feelings, such as anger, sadness, or feeling out of control. They can also help you make plans for unexpected or sudden events.

Mental health professionals charge by the hour. Medicare, Medicaid, and some private health insurance plans may cover some of these costs. Ask your health insurance plan which mental health counselors and services it covers. Then check with your doctor, local family service agencies, and community mental health agencies for referrals to counselors.

A Word of Caution

Although most states require home health care agencies to perform criminal background checks on their workers and carefully screen applicants, actual regulations will vary depending on where you live. Therefore, before contacting a home health care agency, you may want to call your local area agency on aging or department of public health to learn what laws apply in your state.

Paying for Care

The cost of home health care varies across and within states. In addition, costs will fluctuate based on the type of health care professional required. Home care services can be paid directly by patients and their families or through a variety of public and private sources. Sources for home health care funding include Medicare, Medicaid, the Older Americans Act, the Veterans Administration, and private insurance.

Chapter 49

Choosing a Nursing Home

Finding the Right Place for the Person with Alzheimer Disease (AD)

Sometimes you can no longer care for the person with Alzheimer disease (AD) at home. The person may need around-the-clock care. Or, he or she may be incontinent, aggressive, or wander a lot. It may not be possible for you to meet all of his or her needs at home anymore. When that happens, you may want to look for another place for the person with AD to live. You may feel guilty or upset about this decision, but remember that many caregivers reach this point as the disease worsens. Moving the person to a care facility may give you greater peace of mind. You will know that the person with AD is safe and getting good care.

Choosing the right place is a big decision. It's hard to know where to start.

Below we list steps you can take to find the right place:

1. Gather information

- Talk with your support group members, social worker, doctor, family members, and friends about facilities in your area.

- Make a list of questions to ask about the facility.

- Call to set up a time to visit.

This chapter includes excerpts from "Caring for a Person with Alzheimer's Disease," National Institute on Aging (NIA), May 2015; and text from "Your Guide to Choosing a Nursing Home or Other Long-Term Care," Centers for Medicare and Medicaid Services (CMS), August 15, 2015.

2. Visit assisted living facilities and nursing homes
Make several visits at different times of the day and evening.
Ask yourself:

- How does the staff care for the residents?

- Is the staff friendly?

- Does the place feel comfortable?

- How do the people who live there look?

- Do they look clean and well cared for?

- Are mealtimes comfortable?

- Is the facility clean and well maintained?

- Does it smell bad?

- How do staff members speak to residents—with respect?

Ask the staff:

- What activities are planned for residents?

- How many staff members are at the facility? How many of them are trained to provide medical care if needed?

- How many people in the facility have AD?

- Does the facility have a special unit for people with AD? If so, what kinds of services does it provide?

- Is there a doctor who checks on residents on a regular basis? How often?

- You also may want to ask staff:

- What is a typical day like for the person with AD?

- Is there a safe place for the person to go outside?

- What is included in the fee?

- How does my loved one get to medical appointments?

Talk with other caregivers who have a loved one at the facility. Find out what they think about the place.

Find out about total costs of care. Each facility is different. You want to find out if long-term care insurance, Medicaid, or Medicare will pay for any of the costs. Remember that Medicare only covers nursing home costs for a short time after the person with AD has been in the hospital for a certain amount of time.

If you're asked to sign a contract, make sure you understand what you are agreeing to.

Assisted Living Facilities

Assisted living facilities have rooms or apartments. They're for people who can mostly take care of themselves, but may need some help. Some assisted living facilities have special AD units. These units have staff who check on and care for people with AD. You will need to pay for the cost of the room or apartment, and you may need to pay extra for any special care. Some assisted living facilities are part of a larger organization that also offers other levels of care. For example, continuing care retirement communities also offer independent living and skilled nursing care.

Group Homes

A group home is a home for people who can no longer take care of themselves. Several people who can't care for themselves live in the home. At least one caregiver is on site at all times.

The staff takes care of the people living there: making meals, helping with grooming and medication, and providing other care. You will need to pay the costs of the person with AD living in this kind of home. Remember that these homes may not be inspected or regulated, but may still provide good care. Check out the home and the staff. Visit at different times of the day and evening to see how the staff takes care of the residents. Also check to see how clean and comfortable the home is. You'll want to look at how the residents get along with one another and with the staff.

Nursing Homes

Nursing homes are for people who can't care for themselves anymore. Some nursing homes have special AD care units. These units are often in separate sections of the building where staff members have special training to care for people with AD. Some units try to make the person feel more like he or she is at home. They provide special activities, meals, and medical care. In many cases, you will have to pay for nursing home care. Most nursing homes accept Medicaid as payment. Also, long-term care insurance may cover some of the nursing home costs. Nursing homes are inspected and regulated by State governments.

Compare the Quality of the Nursing Homes You're Considering.

Medicare's Nursing Home Compare

Compare the care that nursing homes provide to help find the nursing home that meets your needs. Visit Medicare.gov/nursinghome-compare to compare the nursing home quality of every Medicare-and Medicaid-certified nursing home in the country.

Consider the information on Nursing Home Compare carefully. Use it along with other information you gather about nursing homes.

Note: Information on Nursing Home Compare isn't an endorsement or advertisement for any particular nursing home.

Other Ways to Find out about Nursing Home Quality

You may want to use a variety of resources when choosing a nursing home:

- Visit the nursing homes you're considering, if possible, or have someone visit for you.

- Call your Long-Term Care Ombudsman.

- Call your state health department or state licensing agency (look in the blue pages in the phone book or on the internet). Ask if they have written information on the quality of care given in local nursing homes. You can also ask for a copy of the full survey or the last complaint investigation report.

- Look at survey findings (CMS Form 2567) for the facility. They can be found on Nursing Home Compare at Medicare.gov/nursinghomecompare. Nursing homes may post survey findings in the lobby area.

Visit the Nursing Homes You're Interested in or Have Someone Visit for You.

Before you visit any nursing homes, consider what's important to you and think about the questions below. Some of these questions ask about rights and protections that are guaranteed to you as a nursing home resident, like being treated in a respectful way. Other questions ask about preferences that may not be guaranteed, like bringing a pet into a nursing home. Be sure to think about what's important to you before you pick a nursing home.

Quality of Life

- Will I be treated in a respectful way?

- How will the nursing home help me participate in social, recreational, religious, or cultural activities that are important to me? Can I decide when I want to participate?

- Do I get to choose what time to get up, go to sleep, or bathe?

- Can I have visitors at any time? Will the nursing home let me see visitors who may come to visit at early or late hours?

- Is transportation provided to community activities?

- Can I bring my pet, or can my pet visit?

- Can I decorate my living space any way I want?

- How will the nursing home make sure I have privacy when I have visitors or personal care services?

- Would I be able to leave the facility for a few hours or days if I choose to do so? Are there procedures for leaving?

- Are there a variety of activities/programming being offered in the facility?

Quality of Care

- What's a plan of care, and what does it look like?

- Who makes the plan of care, and how do they know what I want, need, or what should be in the plan?

- Will I be included in planning my care? —Will my interests and preferences be included in the care plan? —Will I be able to change the plan if I feel there's a need? —Will I be able to choose which of my family members or friends will be involved in the planning process? —Will I get a copy of my care plan?

- Who are the doctors who will care for me? Can I still see my personal doctors? Who will help me arrange transportation if I choose to continue to see my personal doctors and they don't visit the nursing home?

- Who will give me the care I need?

- If a resident has a problem with confusion and wanders, how does the staff handle this type of behavior to protect the residents?

- Does the nursing home's inspection report show quality of care problems (deficiencies)?
- What does the quality information on Nursing Home Compare at Medicare.gov/nursinghomecompare show about how well this nursing home cares for its residents?

Location

- Is the nursing home close to my family and friends so they can visit often?

Availability

- Is a bed available now, or can I add my name to a waiting list?

Note: Nursing homes don't have to accept all applications, but they must comply with local, state, and federal civil rights laws that prohibit discrimination.

Staffing

- Is there enough staff to give me the care I need?
- Will I have the same staff people take care of me day to day or do they change?
- Does the nursing home post information about the number of nursing staff, including Certified Nursing Assistants (CNAs)? Are they willing to show me if I ask to see it? (Note: Nursing homes are required to post this information.)
- How many residents is a CNA assigned to work with during each shift (day and night) and during meals?
- What type of therapy is available at this facility? Are therapy staff available?
- Is there a social worker available? Can I meet him or her? Note: Nursing homes must provide medically related social services, but if the nursing home has less than 120 beds, it doesn't have to have a full-time social worker on staff.

Religious and Cultural Preference

- Does the nursing home offer the religious or cultural support I need? If not, what type of arrangements will they provide to meet my needs?

- Do they provide special diet options that my faith practice may require?

Food and Dining

- Does the nursing home have food service that I would be happy with?

- Does the nursing home provide a pleasant dining experience?

- Does the staff help residents eat and drink at mealtimes if help is needed?

- What types of meals does the nursing home serve? (Note: Ask the nursing home if you can see a menu.)

- Can I get food and drinks I like at any time? What if I don't like the food that's served?

- Do residents have a choice of food items at each meal? Are there options and substitutes available if I don't like a particular meal?

- Can the nursing home provide for my dietary needs?

Language

- Is my primary language spoken by staff that will work directly with me and fellow residents?

- If not, is an interpreter available or another system in place to help me communicate my needs?

Policies

- Are there resident policies I must follow?

- Will I get a written copy of these policies?

Note: Resident policies are rules that all residents must follow. For example, smoking may not be allowed in or on the premises of some nursing homes.

Security

- Does the nursing home provide a safe environment?

- Will my personal belongings be secure in my room?

- Is the nursing home locked at night?

Preventive Care

- Does the nursing home make sure residents get preventive care to help keep them healthy? Are specialists like eye doctors, ear doctors, dentists, and podiatrists (foot doctors) available to see residents on a regular basis? Does the facility help make arrangements to see these specialists? (Note: Nursing homes must either provide treatment, or help you make appointments and provide transportation for you to see specialists.)

- Does the nursing home have a screening program for vaccinations, like flu (influenza) and pneumonia? (Note: Nursing homes are required to provide flu shots each year, but you have the right to refuse if you don't want the shot, have already been immunized during the immunization period, or if the shots are medically contraindicated.)

- How will I get access to oral care in the nursing home?

- How will I get access to mental health care in the nursing home?

Hospitals

- Does the nursing home have an arrangement with a nearby hospital for emergencies?

- Can my doctor care for me at that hospital?

Licensing

- Are the nursing home and current administrator licensed in my state?

Note: This means nursing homes have met certain standards set by a state or local government agency.

Certification (Certified)

- Is the nursing home Medicare- and/or Medicaid-certified

Note: "Certified" means the nursing home meets Medicare and/or Medicaid regulations and the nursing home has passed and continues to pass an inspection survey done by the State Survey Agency. If they're certified, make sure they haven't recently lost their certification or are about to lose their certification. Also, some nursing homes may only have a certain "distinct part" of their building certified for Medicare or Medicaid residents.

Services

What services does the nursing home provide? Does the nursing home have the services I need?

Charges and Fees

- Will the nursing home tell me in writing about their services, charges, and fees before I move into the home?

Note: Medicare- and/or Medicaid-certified nursing homes must tell you this information in writing. Get a copy of the fee schedule to find out which services are available, which are included in your monthly fee, and which services cost extra. Then, compare nursing home costs.

- Is there a basic fee for room, meals, and personal care?

- Are there extra charges for other services, like beauty shop services?

Health and Fire Safety Inspection Reports

- Does the nursing home have the most recent health and fire inspection reports for me to look at?

Note: Ask the staff to provide these reports. They tell you how well the nursing home meets federal health and safety regulations. The nursing home must have the report of the most recent state or federal survey of the facility available for you to look at. Reports can also be found on most state agency websites, as well as on Nursing Home Compare at Medicare.gov/nursinghomecompare.

Resident, Family, and Satisfaction

- Can I talk to staff, residents, and family members of residents? Will I be able to ask them if they're satisfied with the nursing home and its services?

Note: Any resident or family member of a resident has the right to refuse to talk to you. However, staff should be able to visit with you if they're not involved in care or service duties at the time. Also, many facilities have staff, resident, and family satisfaction surveys. You may want to ask to see the most recent survey results.

How to Make Moving Day Easier?

Moving is very stressful. Moving the person with AD to an assisted living facility, group home, or nursing home is a big change for both the person and the caregiver. You may feel many emotions, from a sense of loss to guilt and sadness. You also may feel relieved. It is okay to have all these feelings. A social worker may be able to help you plan for and adjust to moving day. It's important to have support during this difficult step.

Here are some things that may help:

- Know that the day can be very stressful.

- Talk to a social worker about your feelings about moving the person into a new place. Find out how to help the person with AD adjust.

- Get to know the staff before the person moves into a facility.

- Talk with the staff about ways to make the change to the assisted living facility or nursing home go better.

- Don't argue with the person with AD about why he or she needs to be there.

Be an Advocate

Once the person has moved to his or her new home, check and see how the person is doing. As the caregiver, you probably know the person best. Look for signs that the person may need more attention, is taking too much medication, or may not be getting the care they need. Build a relationship with staff so that you work together as partners.

Chapter 50

Hospitalization and Alzheimer Disease

A trip to the hospital with a person who has memory loss or demen- tia can be stressful for both of you.

Below, you will find: steps you can take now to make hospital vis- its less traumatic; tips on making your relative or care partner more comfortable once you arrive at the hospital; and suggestions on how to work with hospital staff and doctors.

Hospital Emergencies: What You Can Do Now

Planning ahead is key to making an unexpected or planned trip to the hospital easier for you and your care partner. Here is what you should do now:

- Think about and discuss hospitalization before it happens and as the disease and associated memory loss progress.

- Hospitalization is a choice. Talk about when hospice may be a better and more appropriate alternative.

- Register your relative for a MedicAlert® + Alzheimer Associa- tion Safe Return® bracelet through your local Alzheimer Associ- ation chapter. People who are lost may be taken to an emergency

Text in this chapter is excerpted from "Hospitalization Happens: A Guide to Hospital Visits for Individuals with Memory Loss," National Institute on Aging (NIA), March 31, 2015.

room. This bracelet will speed up the process of reconnecting you with your care partner.

- Know who you can depend on. You need a family member or trusted friend to stay with your care partner when he or she is admitted to the emergency room or hospital. Arrange to have at least two dependable family members, neighbors, or friends you can call on to go with you or meet you at the hospital at a moment's notice so that one person can take care of the paperwork and the other can stay with your care partner.

Pack an Emergency Bag Containing the Following:

Personal Information Sheet

Create a document that includes the following information about your care partner:

- Preferred name and language (some people may revert to native languages in late-stage Alzheimer disease)
- Contact information for doctors, key family members, clergy and helpful friends (also program into cell phone, if applicable)
- Illness or medical conditions
- All current medicines and dosage instructions; update whenever there is a change
- Any medicines that have ever caused a bad reaction
- Any allergies to medicines or foods; special diets
- Need for glasses, dentures or hearing aids
- Degree of impairment and amount of assistance needed for activities
- Family information, living situation, major life events
- Work, leisure and spiritual history
- Daily schedule and patterns, self-care preferences
- Favorite foods, music, and things your care partner likes to touch and see
- Behaviors of concern; how your relative communicates needs and expresses emotions

Paperwork

Include copies of important documents such as:

- Insurance cards (include policy numbers and pre-authorization phone numbers)
- Medicaid and/or Medicare cards
- Durable Power of Attorney, Health Care Power of Attorney, Living Will and/or an original DNR (do not resuscitate) order

Supplies for the Care Partner

- A change of clothing, toiletries and personal medications
- Extra adult briefs (e.g., Depends), if usually worn. These may not be available in the emergency room if needed
- Moist hand wipes such as Wet Ones; plastic bags for soiled clothing and/or adult briefs
- Reassuring or comforting objects
- An iPod, MP3 or CD player; earphones or speakers

Supplies for the Caregiver

- A change of clothing, toiletries and personal medications
- Pain medicine such as Advil, Tylenol or aspirin. A trip to the emergency room may take longer than you think. Stress can lead to a headache or other symptoms.
- A pad of paper and pen to write down information and directions given to you by hospital staff. Keep a log of your care partner's symptoms and problems. You may be asked the same questions by many people. Show them what you have written instead of repeating your answers.
- A sealed snack such as a pack of crackers and a bottle of water or juice for you and your care partner. You may have to wait for quite a while.
- A small amount of cash.
- A note on the outside of the emergency bag to remind you to take your cell phone and charger with you.

By taking these steps in advance, you can reduce the stress and confusion that often accompany a hospital visit, particularly if the visit is an unplanned trip to the emergency room.

At the Emergency Room

A trip to the emergency room may fatigue or even frighten your care partner. There are some important things to remember:

- Be patient. It could be a long wait if the reason for your visit is not life-threatening.

- Recognize that results from lab tests take time.

- Offer physical and emotional comfort and verbal reassurance to your relative. Stay calm and positive. How you are feeling will get absorbed by others.

- Realize that just because you do not see staff at work does not mean they are not working.

- Be aware that emergency room staff often have limited training in Alzheimer disease and related dementias, so try to help them better understand your care partner.

- Encourage hospital staff to see your relative as an individual and not just another patient with dementia who is confused and disoriented from the disease.

- Do not assume your care partner will be admitted to the hospital.

Do not leave the emergency room to go home without a follow-up plan. If you are sent home, make sure you have all instructions for follow-up care.

Before a Hospital Stay

If your relative is going to the hospital for a planned stay, you have time to prepare and get more information from your doctor. Ask your doctor if the procedure can be done as an outpatient visit. If not, ask if tests can be done before going to the hospital to shorten the hospital stay. Ask if your doctor plans to talk with other doctors. If so, find out if your care partner can see these specialists before going into the hospital.

You should also ask questions about anesthesia, catheters and IV's. General anesthesia can have side effects. Ask if local anesthesia is an option and ask to be allowed in the recovery room. Insist that regular AD medications be continued throughout the hospital stay unless contraindicated. Discourage stopping cholinesterase inhibitors (Aricept, Exelon, Razadyne).

With Alzheimer disease and related dementias, it is wise to accept that hospitalization is a "when" and not an "if" event. Due to the nature of the disease, it is very probable that, at some point, the person you are caring for will be hospitalized. Medical facilities are not typically well designed for those with dementia, and advance planning and preparation can make all the difference.

Build a team for care and support during a hospital stay. Develop roles for each person (spokesperson, hands-on caregivers, comfort people, home and personal affairs manager, communication center person). Do not try to do it alone. Now may be the time to have one-on-one caregivers on site if money or resources permit. They can help make sure medications and/or physical restraints are not used to control behaviors that can be managed with redirection or distraction.

Before your hospital visit, prepare a list of questions and concerns for your doctor.

Before Going to the Hospital

- If your insurance allows, ask if a private room is available. It will be more quiet and calm. Request a reclining chair or bed for you or a companion/respite provider.

- Shortly before going to the hospital, decide the best way to tell your care partner that the two of you are going to spend a short time in the hospital.

- Involve your care partner in the planning process as much as possible.

- Do not talk about the hospital stay in front of your care partner as if he or she is not there. This can be upsetting and embarrassing.

- Plan ahead. Make a schedule with family, friends and/or a professional respite care provider to take turns staying with your care partner while in the hospital. This is particularly important if your relative needs continuous supervision.

During the Hospital Stay

- Ask the hospital staff to avoid using physical restraints.

- Have a family member, trusted friend or hired caregiver with your care partner at all times if possible—even during medical tests. This may be hard to do, but it will help keep your care partner calm and less frightened, making the hospital stay easier.

- Use a "telephone tree," email or online tools to keep others posted of progress. This can greatly reduce stress and make sure that you do not receive calls just as you get your care partner settled down. You may need to turn the ringer on the phone down or off during rest times.

- Ask doctors to limit the questions directed to your relative, who may not be able to answer accurately. Instead, arrange to answer questions from the doctor in private, outside your care partner's room.

- Modify the hospital room for best performance.

- Help your relative fill out menu requests. Open food containers and remove trays. Assist with eating as needed.

- Remind your care partner to drink fluids. Offer fluids regularly and have him or her make frequent trips to the bathroom.

- Assume your care partner will experience difficulty finding the bathroom and/or using a call button, bed adjustment buttons or the phone.

- Communicate with your care partner in the way he or she will best understand or respond.

- Recognize that an unfamiliar place, medicines, invasive tests and surgery will make a person with dementia more confused. Your relative will likely need more assistance with personal care activities.

- Take deep breaths and schedule breaks for yourself.

- Be aware of acute or sudden confusion or delirium, which can be caused by serious medical problems such as fever, infection, medications and/or dehydration. Inform the doctor as soon as possible if your care partner seems suddenly worse or different. Make sure you advocate for the person you are caring for, others may not recognize the difference in your relative's condition.

If Anxiety or Agitation Occurs

Try some of the following:

- Remove personal clothes from sight.
- Post reminders or cues if this comforts your care partner.
- Turn off the television, telephone ringer and intercom. Minimize background noise to prevent overstimulation.
- Talk in a calm voice and offer reassurance. Repeat answers to questions when needed.
- Provide a comforting touch or distract your care partner with offers of snacks and beverages.
- Consider "unexpressed pain" (i.e., furrowed brow, clenched teeth or fists, kicking). Assume your relative has pain if the condition or procedure is normally associated with pain. Ask for pain evaluation and treatment every four hours without your care partner having to ask for it—especially if he or she has labored breathing, loud moaning, crying or grimacing, or if you are unable to console or distract your care partner.
- Listen to soothing music or try comforting rituals such as reading, praying, singing or reminiscing.
- Slow down; try not to rush your care partner.
- Avoid talking about subjects or events that may upset your care partner.

Working with Hospital Staff

Remember that not everyone in the hospital knows the same basic facts about memory loss and Alzheimer disease or related dementias. You may need to help teach hospital staff what approach works best with your care partner, what distresses or upsets him or her, and ways to reduce this distress.

You can help the staff by providing them with a personal information sheet that includes your care partner's normal routine, how he or she prefers to be addressed (e.g., Miss Minnie, Dr. James, Jane, Mr. Miller, etc.), personal habits, likes and dislikes, possible behaviors (what might trigger them and how best to respond), and nonverbal signs of pain or discomfort.

Help staff understand what your care partner's "baseline" is (prior level of functioning) to help differentiate between dementia and acute confusion or delirium.

491

You should:

- Make the personal information sheet easy to read with headings and short, simple statements. Place a copy with the chart in the hospital room and at the nurse's station.

- With the hospital staff, decide who will do what for your care partner. For example, you may want to be the one who provides assistance with bathing, eating or using the bathroom.

- Inform the staff about any hearing difficulties and/or other communication problems your relative may experience and offer ideas for what works best in those instances.

- Make sure your care partner is safe. Tell the staff about any previous issues with wandering, getting lost, falls, suspiciousness and/or delusional behavior.

- Not assume the staff knows your care partner's needs. Inform them in a polite, calm manner.

- Ask questions when you do not understand certain hospital procedures and tests or when you have any concerns. Do not be afraid to be an advocate for your relative.

- Plan early for discharge. Ask the hospital discharge planner about eligibility for home health services, equipment or other long-term care options. Prepare for an increased level of caregiving.

Realize that hospital staff are providing care for many people. Practice the art of patience.

Chapter 51

Understanding Health Care Decisions

Dementia at the End of Life

As they reach the end of life, people suffering from conditions like Alzheimer disease (AD) or Parkinson disease can present special problems for caregivers. People live with these diseases for years, becoming increasingly disabled. Because they do not die soon after they are diagnosed, it can be hard to think of these as terminal diseases. But they do contribute to death.

Illnesses like AD make it difficult for those who want to provide supportive care at the end of life to know what is needed. Because people with advanced dementia can no longer communicate, they cannot share their concerns. Is Uncle Bert refusing food because he is not hungry or because he's confused? Why does Grandma Ruth seem agitated? Is she in pain and needs medication to relieve it, but can't tell you?

As these conditions progress, they also obstruct efforts to provide emotional or spiritual comfort. How can you let Grandpa know how much his life has meant to you? How do you make peace with your mother if she no longer knows who you are? Someone who has severe memory loss might not take spiritual comfort from sharing family memories or understand when others express what an important part

Text in this chapter is excerpted from "End of Life, Helping with Comfort and Care," National Institute on Aging (NIA), September 2012.

of their life this person has been. Palliative care or hospice can be helpful in many ways to families of people with dementia.

Sensory connections—targeting someone's senses, like hearing, touch, or sight—can bring comfort to people with AD. Being touched or massaged and listening to music, "white" noise, or sounds from nature seem to soothe some people and lessen their agitation.

When an illness like Alzheimer disease is first diagnosed, if everyone understands that there is no cure, then plans for the end of life can be made before thinking and speaking abilities fail and people can no longer legally complete documents like advance directives. That didn't happen in Ethel's family. She had been forgetful for years, but even after her family knew that AD was the cause of her forgetfulness, they never talked about what the future would bring. As time passed and the disease eroded Ethel's memory and her ability to think and speak, she became less and less able to share her concerns and desires with those close to her. This made it hard for her daughter Barbara to know what Ethel needed or wanted. Barbara's decisions, therefore, had to be based on what she knew about her mom's values and priorities, rather than on what Ethel actually said she would like.

Quality of life is an important issue when making health care decisions for people with Alzheimer disease. For example, there are medicines available that might slow the progression of this devastating disease for a short time in some patients, generally early in the illness. However, in more advanced AD, some caregivers might not want these drugs prescribed. They may believe that the quality of life is already so diminished and that the medicine is unlikely to make a difference. If the drug has serious side effects, they are even more likely to decide against it.

End-of-life care decisions are more complicated for caregivers if the dying person has not expressed the kind of end-of-life care he or she would prefer. Someone newly diagnosed with Alzheimer disease might not be able to imagine the later stages of the disease. Ethel was like that. She and Barbara never talked about things like feeding tubes, machines that help with breathing, antibiotics for pneumonia, or transfers to the hospital. So when doctors raised some of these questions, Barbara didn't know how to best reflect her mother's wishes. When making care decisions for someone else near the end of life, it is important to consider how a treatment will benefit the person and what the side effects and risks might be. Sometimes you might decide to try the health care team's suggestion for a short time. Other times you might decide that the best choice is to do nothing.

Alzheimer disease and similar conditions often progress slowly and unpredictably. Experts suggest that signs of the final stage of Alzheimer disease include some of the following:

- Being unable to move around on one's own

- Being unable to speak or make oneself understood

- Needing help with most, if not all, daily activities

- Eating problems such as difficulty swallowing or no appetite

Because of their unique experience with what happens at the end of life, hospice and palliative care experts might also be of help identifying when someone in the final stage of Alzheimer disease is beginning to die.

Caring for people with Alzheimer disease at home can be demanding and stressful for the family caregiver. Depression is a problem for some family caregivers, as is fatigue, because many feel they are always "on call."

More than half of one group of family caregivers reported cutting back on work hours or giving up their jobs because of the demands of caregiving. Most of those family members taking care of dying Alzheimer disease patients at home expressed relief when death happened—for themselves and for the person who died. It is important to realize such feelings are normal. Hospice—whether used at home or in a facility—gives family caregivers needed support near the end of life, as well as help with their grief, both before and after their family member dies.

Questions to Ask

You will want to understand how the available medical options presented by the health care team fit into your family's particular needs. You might want to ask questions such as:

1. How will the approach the doctor is suggesting affect your relative's quality of life? Will it make a difference?

2. If considering hospice for your relative with Alzheimer disease, does the facility have special experience with people with dementia?

Understanding Health Care Decisions

It can be overwhelming to be asked to make health care decisions for someone who is dying and no longer able to make his or her own decisions. It is even more difficult if you do not have written or even verbal guidance. How do you decide what type of care is right for someone? Even when you have written documents, some decisions still might not be clear.

Two approaches might be useful. One is to put yourself in the place of the person who is dying and try to choose as he or she would. That is called *substituted judgment*. Sheila's ninety-year-old mother, Esther, was in a coma after having a major stroke. The doctor said damage to Esther's brain was widespread and she needed to be put on a breathing machine (ventilator) or she would probably die. The doctor asked Sheila if she wanted that to be done. Sheila remembered how her mother disapproved when an elderly neighbor was put on a similar machine after a stroke. She decided to say no, and her mother died peacefully a few hours later. Some experts believe that decisions should be based on substituted judgement whenever possible, but decision-makers sometimes combine that with another method.

The other approach, known as *best interests*, is to decide what would be best for the dying person. Jim's father, Sam, is eighty and has lung cancer, as well as advanced Parkinson disease. He is in a nursing facility and doesn't seem to recognize Jim when he visits. Sam's doctor suggested that surgery to remove part of a lung might slow down the course of the cancer and give Sam more time. But, Jim thought, "What kind of time? What would that time do for Dad?" Jim decided that putting his dad through surgery and recovery was not in Sam's best interests.

If you are making decisions for someone at the end of life and trying to use one of these approaches, it may be helpful to think about the following:

- Has the dying person ever talked about what he or she would want at the end of life?

- Has he or she expressed an opinion about how someone else was being treated?

- What were his or her values in life? What gave meaning to life? Maybe it was being close to family—watching them grow and making memories together. Perhaps just being alive was the most important thing.

As a decision-maker without specific guidance from the dying person, you need as much information as possible on which to base your actions. You might ask the doctor:

- What can we expect to happen in the next few hours, days, or weeks?

- Why is this new test being suggested?

- Will it change the current treatment plan?

- Will a new treatment help my relative get better?

- How would the new treatment change his or her quality of life?

- Will it give more quality time with family and friends?

- How long will this treatment take to make a difference?

- If we choose to try this treatment, can we stop it at any time? For any reason?

- What are the side effects of the approach you are suggesting?

- If we try this new treatment and it doesn't work, what then?

- If we don't try this treatment, what will happen?

- Is the improvement we saw today an overall positive sign or just something temporary?

It is a good idea to have someone with you when discussing these issues with medical staff. Having someone take notes or remember details can be very useful during this emotional time. If you are unclear about something you are told, don't be afraid to ask the doctor or nurse to repeat it or to say it another way that does make sense to you. Do not be reluctant to keep asking questions until you have all the information you need to make decisions. Make sure you know how to contact a member of the medical team if you have a question or if the dying person needs something. You may want to get pager numbers, email, or cell phone numbers.

Sometimes the whole family wants to be involved in every decision. Maybe that is the family's cultural tradition. Or, maybe the person dying did not pick one person to make health care choices before becoming unable to do so. That is not unusual, but it is probably a good idea to choose one person to be the spokesperson and the contact person when dealing with medical staff. The doctor and nurses will appreciate answering questions from only one person. Even if one family member is named as the decision-maker, it is a good idea, as much as possible, to have family agreement about the care plan. If you can't agree on a care plan, a decision-maker, or even a spokesperson, the family might need to hire a mediator, someone trained to bring people with different opinions to a common decision. In any case, as soon as possible after the doctor says the patient is dying, the family should try to discuss with the medical team what approach to end-of-life care they want for their family member. That way, decision making for crucial situations can be planned and does not have to be done quickly.

Chapter 52

Making Decisions about Resuscitation and Tube Feeding

Issues You May Face

Maybe you are now faced with making end-of-life choices for someone close to you. You've thought about that person's values and opinions, and you've asked the health care team to explain the treatment plan and what you can expect to happen. But there are other issues that you need to understand in case they arise. What if the dying person starts to have trouble breathing and a doctor says a ventilator might be needed? Maybe one family member wants the health care team to "do everything" to keep this relative alive. What does that involve? Or, what if family members can't agree on end-of-life care, or they disagree with the doctor? What happens then?

Here are some common end-of-life issues like those—they will give you a general understanding and may help in your conversations with the doctors.

If we say "do everything," what does that mean?

This means that if someone is dying, all measures that might keep vital organs working will be tried—for example, using a machine to

---

Text in this chapter is excerpted from "End of Life, Helping with Comfort and Care," National Institute on Aging (NIA), September 2012. Reviewed February 2016 help with breathing (ventilator) or starting dialysis for failing kidneys. Such life support can sometimes be a temporary measure that allows the body to heal itself and begin to work normally again. It is not intended to be used indefinitely in someone who is dying. "Doing everything" does not include medical treatments intended to cure a medical condition, such as surgery or chemotherapy.

What can be done if someone's heart stops beating (cardiac arrest)?

CPR (cardiopulmonary resuscitation) can sometimes restart a stopped heart. It is most effective in people who were generally healthy before their heart stopped. In CPR, the doctor repeatedly pushes on the chest with great force and periodically puts air into the lungs. Electric shocks (called defibrillation) may also be used to restart the heart, and some medicines might also be given. Although not usually shown on television, the force required for CPR can cause broken ribs or a collapsed lung. Often, CPR does not succeed, especially in an elderly person who is already failing.

What if someone needs help breathing or completely stops breathing (respiratory arrest)?

Sometimes doctors suggest using a ventilator (a respirator or breathing machine)—the machine forces the lungs to work. Initially, this involves intubation, putting a tube attached to a ventilator down the throat into the trachea or windpipe. Because this tube can be quite uncomfortable, people are often sedated. If the person needs ventilator support for more than a few days, the doctor will probably suggest a tracheotomy, sometimes called a "trach" (rhymes with "make"). This tube is then attached to the ventilator. This is more comfortable than a tube down the throat and may not require sedation. Inserting the tube into the trachea is a bedside surgery. A tracheotomy can carry risks, including collapsed lung, plugged tracheotomy tube, or bleeding.

How can I be sure the medical staff knows that we don't want efforts to restore a heart beat or breathing?

As soon as the decision that medical staff should not do CPR or other life-support procedures is made by the patient or the person making health care decisions, the doctor-in-charge should be told of this choice. The doctor will then write this on the patient's chart using terms such as DNR (Do Not Resuscitate), DNAR (Do Not Attempt to Resuscitate), or DNI (Do Not Intubate). If end-of-life care is given at home, a special "non-hospital DNR," signed by a doctor, is needed. This ensures that if emergency medical technicians (EMTs) are called to the house, they will respect your wishes. Without a non-hospital DNR, in many places EMTs are required to perform CPR and similar techniques when called to a home. Hospice staff can help determine whether a medical condition is part of the normal dying process or something that needs the attention of EMTs. DNR orders do not stop all treatment. They only mean that CPR and a ventilator will not be used. These orders are not permanent—they can be changed if the situation changes.

What about pacemakers (or similar devices)—should they be turned off?

A pacemaker is a device implanted under the skin on the chest that keeps a heartbeat regular. It will not keep a dying person alive. Some people have an implantable cardioverter defibrillator (ICD) under the skin. This is a pacemaker that also shocks the heart back into regular beats when needed. The ICD should be turned off at the point when life support is no longer wanted. This can be done without surgery.

What if the doctor suggests a feeding tube?

If a patient can't or won't eat or drink, even when spoon fed, the doctor might suggest a feeding tube. While recovering from an illness, a feeding tube can be helpful. But at the end of life, a feeding tube might cause more discomfort than not eating. As death approaches, loss of appetite is common. Body systems start shutting down, and fluids and food are not needed as before. Some experts believe that at this point few nutrients are absorbed from any type of nutrition, including that received through a feeding tube.

If tube feeding is going to be tried, there are two methods that can be used. In the first, a feeding tube, known as a nasogastric or NG tube, is threaded through the nose down to the stomach to give nutrition for a short time. Sometimes the tube is uncomfortable. If so, the doctor might try a smaller, child-sized tube. Someone with an NG tube might try to remove it. This usually means the person has to be restrained, which could mean binding his or her hands to the bed. If tube feeding is required for an extended time, then a gastric or G tube is put directly into the stomach through an opening made in the side or abdomen. This second method is also called a PEG tube for percutaneous endoscopic gastrostomy tube. These carry risks of infection, pneumonia, and nausea.

Some people try tube feeding for a short time to see if it makes a difference, while keeping open the option of removing the tube if there is no improvement. Talk to the doctor about how the feeding tube could help and how long it makes sense to try it.

Refusing food might be a conscious decision—a part of the dying person's understanding that death is near. The decision-maker should think carefully about doing something that might be against the dying person's wishes.

Should someone dying be sedated?

Sometimes very near the end of life, the doctor might suggest sedation to manage symptoms that are not responding to treatment and still make the patient uncomfortable. This means using medicines to put the patient in a sleep-like state. Sedation doesn't cause a person to die more quickly. Many doctors suggest continuing to use comfort care measures like pain medicine even if the dying person is sedated. Sedatives can be stopped at any time. A person who is sedated may still be able to hear what you are saying—so try to keep speaking directly to, not about, him or her. Do not say things you would not want the patient to hear.

What about antibiotics?

Antibiotics are medicines that fight infections caused by bacteria. Lower respiratory infections, such as pneumonia, are often caused by bacteria and are common in older people who are dying. If someone is already dying when the infection began, giving antibiotics is probably not going to prevent death but might make the person feel more comfortable. Tom was eighty-three and had lived in a nursing home for several years with advanced Parkinson disease when he choked on some food causing him to inhale a small amount into his lungs. As a result, Tom developed aspiration pneumonia. The doctors assured his wife that they could keep Tom comfortable without antibiotics, but she wanted them to try treating his pneumonia. He died a few days later despite their efforts.

Is refusing treatment legal?

Choosing to stop treatment that is not curing or controlling an illness or deciding not to start a new treatment is completely legal—whether the choice is made by someone who is dying or by the one making health care decisions. Some people think this is like allowing death to happen. The law does not consider refusing such treatment to be either suicide or euthanasia, sometimes called "mercy killing."

Chapter 53

Caring for Someone Near the End of Life

End-of-Life Care

Caring for someone in the final stage of life is always hard. It may be even harder when the person has Alzheimer disease (AD). Planning for the end of a person's life and knowing what to expect can make this time easier.

Treatment Decisions

Quality of life is an important issue when making end-of-life health care decisions for a person with Alzheimer disease. For example, it is important to consider how a treatment will benefit the person and what the side effects and risks might be. You might decide to try a treatment for a short time, or you might decide that the best choice is to do nothing.

In more advanced Alzheimer disease, some caregivers might not want certain medicines prescribed. The person's quality of life may be so diminished that the medicine is unlikely to make a difference.

This chapter includes excerpts from "Alzheimer's Caregiving Tips," National Institute on Aging (NIA), November 2012. Reviewed February 2016; and text from "End of Life: Helping With Comfort and Care," National Institute on Aging (NIA), September 2012. Reviewed February 2016.

Comfort at the End of Life

Alzheimer disease and similar conditions often progress slowly and unpredictably. Signs of the final stage of Alzheimer disease may include:

- Being unable to move around on one's own

- Being unable to speak or make oneself understood

- Needing help with most, if not all, daily activities

- Eating problems such as difficulty swallowing or no appetite

As a caregiver, you want to make the person as comfortable as possible, but he or she can't tell you how. You may become frustrated because you don't know what to do.

Making connections through senses like hearing, touch, or sight can bring comfort to people with Alzheimer disease. Being touched or massaged and listening to music, "white" noise, or sounds from nature seem to soothe some people and lessen their agitation.

Sources of Help

Geriatric care managers, grief counselors, and palliative care and hospice staff are trained to help make the person with Alzheimer disease more comfortable and to help their families through this time. Geriatric care managers can make home visits and suggest needed services. Counselors can help you understand and deal with your feelings.

Palliative care and hospice services provide care for a very ill person to keep him or her as comfortable and as pain-free as possible. Palliative care provides comfort care, along with any medical treatments a person might be receiving for a life-threatening illness. When a person is near the end of life, hospice care gives family members needed support and help with their grief, both before and after the person with Alzheimer disease dies.

Dealing with Emotions

Someone with severe memory loss might not take spiritual comfort from sharing family memories or understand when others express what an important part of their life the person has been. Even so, it's really important to say the things in your heart, whatever helps you to say goodbye.

When the person with Alzheimer disease dies, you may have lots of feelings. You may feel sad, depressed, or angry. You also may feel relieved that the person is no longer suffering and that you don't have to care for the person any longer. Relief sometimes may lead to feelings of guilt. All of these feelings are normal.

Closing Thoughts

Many Americans have little experience with someone who is dying. But, when the time comes, unless the death is unexpected and quick, there are choices to be made. These may not be easy. But planning ahead and working with the health care team can help you provide needed comfort.

You will probably remember for a long time what you do for someone who is dying. Realize that this is a difficult time for you too. Caring for someone at the end of life can be physically and emotionally exhausting. In the end, accept that there may be no perfect death, just the best you can do for the one you love. And the pain of losing someone close to you may be softened a little because, when they needed you, you did what you could.

Part Seven

Additional Help and Information

Chapter 54

Glossary of Terms Related to Alzheimer Disease

acetylcholine: A neurotransmitter that plays an important role in many neurological functions, including learning and memory.

amygdala: An almond-shaped structure involved in processing and remembering strong emotions such as fear. It is part of the limbic system and located deep inside the brain.

amyloid plaques: A largely insoluble deposit found in the space between nerve cells in the brain. Plaques are made of beta-amyloid, other molecules, and different kinds of nerve and non-nerve cells.

apolipoprotein E: A gene that has been linked to an increased risk of Alzheimer disease. People with a variant form of the gene, called APOE epsilon 4, have about 10 times the risk of developing Alzheimer disease.

ataxia: A loss of muscle control.

atherosclerosis: A blood vessel disease characterized by the buildup of plaque, or deposits of fatty substances and other matter in the inner lining of an artery.

axon: The long extension from a neuron that transmits outgoing signals to other cells.

beta-amyloid: A part of the amyloid precursor protein found in plaques, the insoluble deposits outside neurons.

This glossary contains terms excerpted from documents produced by several sources deemed reliable.

Binswanger disease: A rare form of dementia characterized by damage to small blood vessels in the white matter of the brain. This damage leads to brain lesions, loss of memory, disordered cognition, and mood changes.

brain stem: The portion of the brain that connects to the spinal cord and controls automatic body functions, such as breathing, heart rate, and blood pressure.

cerebral cortex: The outer layer of nerve cells surrounding the cerebral hemispheres.

cerebral hemispheres: The largest portion of the brain, composed of billions of nerve cells in two structures connected by the corpus callosum. The cerebral hemispheres control conscious thought, language, decision making, emotions, movement, and sensory functions.

cerebrospinal fluid: The fluid found in and around the brain and spinal cord. It protects these organs by acting like a liquid cushion and by providing nutrients.

cholinesterase inhibitors: Drugs that slow the breakdown of the neurotransmitter acetylcholine.

chromosomes: A threadlike structure in the nucleus of a cell that contains DNA. DNA sequences make up genes. Most human cells have 23 pairs of chromosomes containing approximately 30,000 genes.

chronic traumatic encephalopathy: A form of dementia caused by repeated traumatic brain injury.

clinical trial: A research study involving humans that rigorously tests safety, side effects, and how well a medication or behavioral treatment works.

closed head injury: An injury that occurs when the head suddenly and violently hits an object but the object does not break through the skull.

cognitive functions: All aspects of conscious thought and mental activity, including learning, perceiving, making decisions, and remembering.

cognitive training: A type of training in which patients practice tasks designed to improve mental performance. Examples include memory aids, such as mnemonics, and computerized recall devices.

computed tomography (CT) scan: A diagnostic procedure that uses special X-ray equipment and computers to create cross-sectional pictures of the body.

concussion: injury to the brain caused by a hard blow or violent shaking, causing a sudden and temporary impairment of brain function, such as a short loss of consciousness or disturbance of vision and equilibrium.

corticobasal degeneration: A progressive disorder characterized by nerve cell loss and atrophy in multiple areas of the brain.

Creutzfeldt-Jakob disease: A rare, degenerative, fatal brain disorder believed to be linked to an abnormal form of a protein called a prion.

dementia pugilistica: Brain damage caused by cumulative and repetitive head trauma; common in career boxers.

dementia with Lewy bodies: A type of Lewy body dementia that is a common form of progressive dementia.

dementia: A broad term referring to a decline in cognitive function to the extent that it interferes with daily life and activities.

dendrite: Branch-like extension of a neuron that receives messages from other neurons.

Do Not Resuscitate (DNR) Form: Document that tells health care staff that the person with AD does not want them to try to return the heart to a normal rhythm if it stops or is beating unevenly.

dopamine: A chemical messenger, deficient in the brains of people with Parkinson disease, that transmits impulses from one nerve cell to another.

Down syndrome: Many people with Down syndrome develop early-onset AD, with signs of dementia by the time they reach middle age.

dyskinesias: Abnormal involuntary twisting and writhing movements that can result from long-term use of high doses of levodopa.

dystonia: Involuntary muscle contractions that cause slow repetitive movements or abnormal postures.

early-onset Alzheimer disease: A rare form of AD that usually affects people between ages 30 and 60. It is called familial AD (FAD) if it runs in the family.

electroencephalogram (EEG): A medical procedure that records patterns of electrical activity in the brain.

entorhinal cortex: An area deep within the brain where damage from AD often begins.

free radical: A highly reactive molecule (typically oxygen or nitrogen) that combines easily with other molecules because it contains an unpaired electron. The combination with other molecules sometimes damages cells.

frontotemporal disorders: A group of dementias characterized by degeneration of nerve cells, especially those in the frontal and temporal lobes of the brain.

gene: The biologic unit of heredity passed from parent to child. Genes are segments of DNA and contain instructions that tell a cell how to make specific proteins.

genetic mutation: A permanent change in a gene that can be passed on to children. The rare, early-onset familial form of Alzheimer disease is associated with mutations in genes on chromosomes 21, 14, and 1.

genetic risk factor: A variant in a cell's DNA that does not cause a disease by itself but may increase the chance that a person will develop a disease.

genetic variant: A difference in a gene that may increase or decrease a person's risk of developing a disease or condition.

genome: An organism's complete set of DNA, including all of its genes. Each genome contains all of the information needed to build and maintain that organism.

genome-wide association study (GWAS): A study approach that involves rapidly scanning the genomes of many individuals to find genetic variations associated with a particular disease.

Gerstmann-Straussler-Scheinker disease: Symptoms include a loss of coordination (ataxia) and dementia that begin when people are 50 to 60 years old.

glial cell: A specialized cell that supports, protects or nourishes nerve cells.

hippocampus: A structure in the brain that plays a major role in learning and memory and is involved in converting short-term to long-term memory.

HIV-associated dementia: A dementia that results from infection with the human immunodeficiency virus that causes AIDS.

Huntington disease: A degenerative hereditary disorder caused by a faulty gene for a protein called huntingtin. The disease causes degeneration in many regions of the brain and spinal cord and patients eventually develop severe dementia.

hypersexuality: Condition in which people with AD become overly interested in sex.

hypertension: High blood pressure has been linked to cognitive decline, stroke, and types of dementia that affect the white matter regions of the brain.

hypothalamus: A structure in the brain under the thalamus that monitors activities such as body temperature and food intake.

late-onset Alzheimer disease: The most common form of AD. It occurs in people aged 60 and older.

Lewy body dementia: one of the most common types of progressive dementia, characterized by the presence of abnormal structures called Lewy bodies in the brain.

magnetic resonance imaging (MRI): A diagnostic and research technique that uses magnetic fields to generate a computer image of internal structures in the body. MRIs are very clear and are particularly good for imaging the brain and soft tissues.

meningitis: inflammation of the three membranes that envelop the brain and spinal cord, collectively known as the meninges; the meninges include the dura, pia mater, and arachnoid.

microtubule: An internal support structure for a neuron that guides nutrients and molecules from the body of the cell to the end of the axon.

mild cognitive impairment (MCI): A condition in which a person has memory problems greater than those expected for his or her age, but not the personality or cognitive problems that characterize AD.

mixed dementia: dementia in which one form of dementia and another condition or dementia cause damage to the brain, for example, Alzheimer disease and small vessel disease or vascular dementia.

multi-infarct dementia: a type of vascular dementia caused by numerous small strokes in the brain.

mutation: A permanent change in a cell's DNA that can cause a disease.

myelin: A whitish, fatty layer surrounding an axon that helps the axon rapidly transmit electrical messages from the cell body to the synapse.

myoclonus: Condition that sometimes happens with AD, in which a person's arms, legs, or whole body may jerk. It can look like a seizure, but the person doesn't pass out.

nerve growth factor (NGF): A substance that maintains the health of nerve cells. NGF also promotes the growth of axons and dendrites, the parts of the nerve cell that are essential to its ability to communicate with other nerve cells.

neural stem cells: Cells found only in adult neural tissue that can develop into several different cell types in the central nervous system.

neurodegenerative disease: A disease characterized by a progressive decline in the structure, activity, and function of brain tissue. These diseases include AD, Parkinson disease, frontotemporal lobar degeneration, and dementia with Lewy bodies. They are usually more common in older people.

neurofibrillary tangles: Bundles of twisted filaments found in nerve cells in the brains of people with Alzheimer disease. These tangles are largely made up of a protein called tau.

neuron: A nerve cell that is one of the main functional cells of the brain and nervous system.

neurotransmitter: A chemical messenger between neurons. These substances are released by the axon on one neuron and excite or inhibit activity in a neighboring neuron.

nucleus: The structure within a cell that contains the chromosomes and controls many of its activities.

oxidative damage: damage that can occur to cells when they are exposed to too many free radicals.

Parkinson disease dementia: a secondary dementia that sometimes occurs in people with advanced Parkinson disease. Many people with Parkinson disease have the amyloid plaques and neurofibrillary tangles found in Alzheimer disease, but it is not clear if the diseases are linked.

plaques: Unusual clumps of material found between the tissues of the brain in Alzheimer disease.

plasticity: Ability of the brain to adapt to deficits and injury.

positron emission tomography (PET): An imaging technique using radioisotopes that allows researchers to observe and measure activity in different parts of the brain by monitoring blood flow and concentrations of substances such as oxygen and glucose, as well as other specific constituents of brain tissues.

post-traumatic dementia: A condition marked by mental deterioration and emotional apathy following trauma.

progressive dementia: A dementia that gets worse over time, gradually interfering with more and more cognitive abilities.

putamen: An area of the brain that decreases in size as a result of the damage produced by HD.

receptor: proteins that serve as recognition sites on cells and cause a response in the body when stimulated by chemicals called neurotransmitters. They act as on-and-off switches for the next nerve cell.

recessive: A trait that is apparent only when the gene or genes for it are inherited from both parents.

rigidity: A symptom of the disease in which muscles feel stiff and display resistance to movement even when another person tries to move the affected part of the body, such as an arm.

secondary dementia: A dementia that occurs as a consequence of another disease or an injury.

seizures: Abnormal activity of nerve cells in the brain causing strange sensations, emotions, and behavior, or sometimes convulsions, muscle spasms, and loss of consciousness.

senile chorea: A relatively mild and rare disorder found in elderly adults and characterized by choreic movements. It is believed by some scientists to be caused by a different gene mutation than that causing HD.

single photon emission computed tomography (SPECT): An imaging technique that allows researchers to monitor blood flow to different parts of the brain.

striatum: Part of the basal ganglia of the brain. The striatum is composed of the caudate nucleus, putamen, and ventral striatum.

subdural hematoma: Bleeding confined to the area between the dura and the arachnoid membranes.

substantia nigra: Movement-control center in the brain where loss of dopamine-producing nerve cells triggers the symptoms of Parkinson disease; substantia nigra means "black substance," so called because the cells in this area are dark.

synapse: The tiny gap between nerve cells across which neurotransmitters pass

tau: a protein that helps the functioning of microtubules, which are part of the cell's structural support and help deliver substances throughout the cell. In Alzheimer disease, tau twists into filaments that become tangles. Disorders associated with an accumulation of tau, such as frontotemporal dementia, are called tauopathies.

thalamus: A small structure in the front of the cerebral hemispheres that serves as a way station that receives sensory information of all kinds and relays it to the cortex; it also receives information from the cortex.

trait: Any genetically determined characteristic.

transgenic: An animal that has had a gene (like human APP) inserted into its chromosomes. Mice carrying the mutated human APP gene often develop plaques in their brains as they age.

tremor: shakiness or trembling, often in a hand, which in Parkinson disease is usually most apparent when the affected part is at rest.

vascular dementia: A medical condition caused by strokes or changes in the brain's blood supply. Signs can appear suddenly. These signs include changes in memory, language, thinking skills, and mood.

ventricle: A cavity within the brain that is filled with cerebrospinal fluid.

ventriculostomy: A surgical procedure that drains cerebrospinal fluid from the brain by creating an opening in one of the small cavities called ventricles.

wearing-off effect: The tendency, following long-term levodopa treatment, for each dose of the drug to be effective for shorter and shorter periods.

Chapter 55

Directory of Resources for People with Alzheimer Disease

Government Organizations

Administration on Aging (AOA)
One Massachusetts Ave. N.W.
Washington, DC 20001
Phone: 202-619-0724
Fax: 202-357-3555
Website: www.aoa.gov
E-mail: aoainfo@aoa.hhs.gov

Agency for Healthcare Research and Quality (AHRQ)
Office of Communications and Knowledge Transfer
5600 Fishers Ln.
Rockville, MD 20857
Phone: 301-427-1104
Website: www.ahrq.gov

Centers for Disease Control and Prevention (CDC)
1600 Clifton Rd.
Atlanta, GA 30329-4027
Phone: 404-639-3311
Toll-Free: 800-232-4636
TTY: 888-232-6348
Website: www.cdc.gov
E-mail: cdcinfo@cdc.gov

Eldercare Locator
Toll-Free: 800-677-1116
Website: www.eldercare.gov
E-mail: eldercarelocator@n4a.org

Information in this chapter was compiled from sources deemed accurate. All contact information was verified and updated in February 2016.

Healthfinder®
National Health Information Center
200 Independence Ave., S.W.
Washington, DC 20201
Fax: 402-471-3996
Website: www.healthfinder.gov
E-mail: healthfinder@nhic.org

National Cancer Institute (NCI)
9609 Medical Center Dr.
Bethesda, MD 20892-9760
Phone: 800-422-6237
TTY: 800-332-8615
Website: www.cancer.gov
E-mail: cancergovstaff@mail.nih.gov

National Center for Complementary and Alternative Medicine (NCCAM)
National Institutes of Health
9000 Rockville Pike
Bethesda, MD 20892
Fax: 866-464-3616
Toll-Free: 888-644-6226
TTY: 866-464-3615
E-mail: info@nccam.nih.gov

National Center for Health Statistics (NCHS)
1600 Clifton Rd.
Atlanta, GA 30329-4027
Toll-Free: 800-232-4636
TTY: 888-232-6348
Website: www.cdc.gov/nchs
E-mail: cdcinfo@cdc.gov

National Institute on Alcohol Abuse and Alcoholism (NIAAA)
5635 Fishers Ln.
Rm. 3080
Rockville, MD 20852
Phone: 301-443-2857
Toll-Free: 888-696-4222
Website: www.niaaa.nih.gov
E-mail: niaaaweb-r@exchange.nih.gov

National Institute on Disability and Rehabilitation Research (NIDRR)
U.S. Department of Education
Office of Special Education and Rehabilitative Services
400 Maryland Ave., S.W.
Washington, DC 20202-7100
Phone: 800-872-5327
Website: www2.ed.gov/about/offices/list/osers/nidrr/index.html

National Center on Elder Abuse
University of Delaware
1000 S. Fremont Ave.
Unit 22 Bld. A-6
Alhambra, CA 91803
Phone: 302-831-3525
Fax: 626-457-4090
Website: www.ncea.aoa.gov
E-mail: ncea-info@aoa.hhs.gov

National Institute of Mental Health (NIMH)
Science Writing, Press, and Dissemination Branch
MSC 9663
Bethesda, MD 20892-9663
Phone: 301-443-4513
Fax: 301-443-4279
Toll-Free: 866-615-6464
TTY: 866-415-8051
Website: www.nimh.nih.gov
E-mail: nimhinfo@nih.gov

National Institute of Neurological Disorders and Stroke (NINDS)
NIH Neurological Institute
P.O. Box 5801
Bethesda, MD 20824
Phone: 301-496-5751
Toll-Free: 800-352-9424
TTY: 301-468-5981
Website: www.ninds.nih.gov
E-mail: braininfo@ninds.nih.gov

National Institutes of Health (NIH)
9000 Rockville Pike
Bethesda, MD 20892
Phone: 301-496-4000
TTY: 301-402-9612
Website: www.nih.gov
E-mail: NIHinfo@od.nih.gov

National Women's Health Information Center (NWHIC)
Office on Women's Health
200 Independence Ave. S.W. 712 E
Washington, DC 20201
Phone: 202-690-7650
Fax: 202-205-2631
Toll-Free: 800-994-9662
TTY: 888-220-5446
Website: www.womenshealth.gov

U.S. Food and Drug Administration (FDA)
10903 New Hampshire Ave.
Silver Spring, MD 20993
Toll-Free: 888-463-6332
Website: www.fda.gov

U.S. National Library of Medicine (NLM)
8600 Rockville Pike
Bethesda, MD 20894
Phone: 301-594-5983
Fax: 301-402-1384
Toll-Free: 888-346-3656
TDD: 800-735-2258
Website: www.nlm.nih.gov
E-mail: custserv@nlm.nih.gov

Private Organizations

AARP
601 E. St. N.W.
Washington, DC 20049
Toll-Free: 888-687-2277
Website: www.aarp.org
E-mail: member@aarp.org

Alzheimer Society of Canada
20 Eglinton Ave. W.
Ste. 1600
Toronto, ON M4R 1K8
Canada
Phone: 416-488-8772
Fax: 416-322-6656
Toll-Free: 800-616-8816 (Canada only)
E-mail: info@alzheimer.ca

Alzheimer's Association
225 N. Michigan Ave., Fl. 17
Chicago, IL 60601-7633
Phone: 312-335-8700
Fax: 866-699-1246
Toll-Free: 800-272-3900
TDD: 312-335-5886
Website: www.alz.org
E-mail: info@alz.org

Alzheimer's Australia
P.O. Box 4194
Kingston, ACT
Australia
Phone: 026-278-8900
Fax: 039-816-5733
Website: fightdementia.org.au
E-mail: nat.admin@alzheimers.org.au

Alzheimer's Disease International
64 Great Suffolk St.
London, SE1 0BL
United Kingdom
Website: www.alz.co.uk
E-mail: info@alz.co.uk

Alzheimer's Drug Discovery Foundation
57 W. 57th St.
Ste. 904
New York, NY 10019
Phone: 212-901-8000
Website: www.alzdiscovery.org
E-mail: info@alzdiscovery.org

Alzheimer's Foundation of America
322 Eighth Ave.
7th Fl.
New York, NY 10001
Phone: 646-638-1542
Fax: 646-638-1546
Toll-Free: 866-232-8484
Website: www.alzfdn.org
E-mail: info@alzfdn.org

Alzheimer's Society (UK)
Devon House
58 St. Katherine's Way
London, E1W 1LB
Phone: 207-423-3500
Fax: 207-423-3501
Website: alzheimers.org.uk
E-mail: enquiries@alzheimers.org.uk

American Academy of Neurology
201 Chicago Ave.
Minneapolis, MN 55415
Phone: 612-928-6000
Fax: 612-454-2746
Toll-Free: 800-879-1960
Website: www.aan.com
E-mail: memberservices@aan.com

American Association for Clinical Chemistry
900 Seventh St., N.W.
Ste. 400
Washington, DC 20001
Phone: 202-857-0717
Fax: 202-887-5093
Toll-Free: 800-892-1400
Website: www.aacc.org
E-mail: custserv@aacc.org

American Association for Geriatric Psychiatry
Toll-Free: 888-280-0638
Website: www.aagpgpa.org
E-mail: main@aagponline.org

American Health Assistance Foundation
22512 Gateway Center Dr.
Clarksburg, MD 20871
Phone: 301-948-3244
Fax: 301-258-9454
Toll-Free: 800-437-2423
E-mail: info@ahaf.org

American Heart Association
7272 Greenville Ave.
Dallas, TX 75231
Toll-Free: 800-242-8721
Website: www.heart.org

American Medical Association
330 N. Wabash Ave.
Chicago, IL 60611-588
Phone: 312-464-4430
Toll-Free: 800-621-8335
Website: www.ama-assn.org

American Pain Society
8735 W. Higgins Rd.
Ste. 300
Chicago, IL 60631
Phone: 847-375-4715
Fax: 866-574-2654
Website: www.ampainsoc.org
E-mail: info@ampainsoc.org

American Parkinson Disease Association
135 Parkinson Ave.
Staten Island, NY 10305-1425
Phone: 718-981-8001
Fax: 718-981-4399
Toll-Free: 800-223-2732
Website: www.apdaparkinson.org
E-mail: apda@apdaparkinson.org

American Psychiatric Association
1000 Wilson Blvd.
Ste. 1825
Arlington, VA 22209
Phone: 703-907-7300
Toll-Free: 888-357-7924
Website: www.psych.org
E-mail: apa@psych.org

American Psychological Association
750 First St. N.E.
Washington, DC 20002-4242
Phone: 202-336-5500
Toll-Free: 800-374-2721
TDD/TTY: 202-336-6123
Website: www.apa.org

American Society on Aging
575 Market St.
Ste. 2100
San Francisco, CA 94105-2869
Phone: 415-974-9600
Fax: 415-974-0300
Toll-Free: 800-537-9728
Website: www.asaging.org
E-mail: info@asaging.org

Assisted Living Federation of America
1650 King St.
Ste. 602
Alexandria, VA 22314
Website: www.alfa.org

Association for Frontotemporal Degeneration
Radnor Stn Bldg. #2
Ste. 320
Radnor, PA 19087
Phone: 267-514-7221
Toll-Free: 866-507-7222
E-mail: info@FTD-Picks.org

Bachmann-Strauss Dystonia and Parkinson Foundation
551 Fifth Ave.
Ste. 520
New York, NY 10176
Phone: 212-682-9900
Fax: 212-682-6156
Website: www.dystonia-parkinsons.org

Brain Injury Association of America, Inc.
1608 Spring Hill Rd.
Ste. 110
Vienna, VA 22182
Phone: 703-761-0750
Fax: 703-761-0755
Toll-Free: 800-444-6443
Website: www.biausa.org
E-mail: braininjuryinfo@biausa.org

Brain Trauma Foundation
1 Broadway
6th Fl.
New York, NY 10004
Phone: 212-772-0608
Fax: 212-772-0357
Website: www.braintrauma.org

Caregiving, Palliative Care, and Hospice Information Caring Connections
Toll-Free: 800-658-8898
Website: www.caringinfo.org
E-mail: caringinfo@nhpco.org

Caring.com
2600 S. El Camino Real
Ste. 300
San Mateo, CA 94403
Toll-Free: 800-973-1540
Website: www.caring.com

CJD Aware!
2527 S. Carrollton Ave.
New Orleans, LA 70118-3013
Website: www.cjdaware.com
E-mail: info@cjdaware.com

Cleveland Clinic
9500 Euclid Ave.
Cleveland,OH 44195
Toll-Free: 800-223-2273
TTY: 216-444-0261
Website: my.clevelandclinic.org

Creutzfeldt-Jakob Disease Foundation Inc.
P.O. Box 5312
Akron, OH 44334
Fax: 330-668-2474
Toll-Free: 800-659-1991
Website: www.cjdfoundation.org
E-mail: help@cjdfoundation.org

CurePSP: Foundation for Progressive Supranuclear Palsy, Corticobasal Degeneration, and Related Brain Diseases
30 E. Padonia Rd.
Ste. 201
Timonium, MD 21093
Phone: 410-785-7004
Fax: 410-785-7009
Toll-Free: 800-457-4777
Website: www.curepsp.org
E-mail: info@curepsp.org

Dana Alliance for Brain Initiatives
505 Fifth Ave.
6th Fl.
New York, NY 10017
Phone: 212-223-4040
Fax: 212-317-8721
Website: www.dana.org
E-mail: dabiinfo@dana.org

Davis Phinney Foundation
4730 Table Mesa Dr.
Boulder, CO 80305
Phone: 303-733-3340
Fax: 303-733-3350
Toll-Free: 866-358-0285
Website: www.
davisphinneyfoundation.org
E-mail: info@
davisphinneyfoundation.org

Family Caregiver Alliance
180 Montgomery St.
Ste. 900
San Francisco, CA 94104
Phone: 415-434-3388
Toll-Free: 800-445-8106
Website: www.caregiver.org
E-mail: info@caregiver.org

Fisher Center for Alzheimer's Research Foundation
110 E. 42nd St.
16th Fl.
New York, NY 10017
Fax: 212-915-1319
Toll-Free: 800-259-4636
Website: www.alzinfo.org
E-mail: info@alzinfo.org

Hospice Foundation of America
1710 Rhode Island Ave N.W.
Ste. 400
Washington, DC 20036
Phone: 202-457-5811
Fax: 202-457-5815
Toll-Free: 800-854-3402
Website: www.
hospicefoundation.org
E-mail: hfaoffice@
hospicefoundation.org

Huntington's Disease Society of America
505 Eighth Ave.
Ste. 902
New York, NY 10018
Phone: 212-242-1968
Fax: 212-239-3430
Toll-Free: 800-345-4372
Website: www.hdsa.org
E-mail: hdsainfo@hdsa.org

Lewy Body Dementia Association
912 Killian Hill Rd. S.W.
Lilburn, GA 30047
Phone: 404-935-6444
Fax: 480-422-5434
Toll-Free: 800-539-9767
Website: www.lbda.org
E-mail: lbda@lbda.org

Meals-on-Wheels Association of America
203 S. Union St.
Alexandria, VA 22314
Phone: 703-548-5558
Fax: 703-548-8024
E-mail: mowaa@mowaa.org

Mental Health America
2000 N. Beauregard St.
6th Fl.
Alexandria, VA 22311
Phone: 703-684-7722
Fax: 703-684-5968
Toll-Free: 800-969-6642
Website: www.nmha.org

Michael J. Fox Foundation for Parkinson's Research
Church St. Stn
P.O. Box 780
New York, NY 10008-0780
Phone: 212-509-0995
Website: www.michaeljfox.org

National Academy of Elder Law Attorneys
1577 Spring Hill Rd.
Ste. 220
Vienna, VA 22182
Phone: 703-942-5711
Fax: 703-563-9504
Toll-Free: 800-677-1116
Website: www.naela.org

National Adult Day Services Association
1421 E. Broad St.
Ste. 425
Fuquay Varina, NC 27526
Phone: 877-745-1440
Fax: 919-825-3945
Website: www.nadsa.org
E-mail: info@NADSA.org

National Alliance for Caregiving
4720 Montgomery Ln.
Ste. 205
Bethesda, MD 20814
Phone: 301-718-8444
Fax: 301-951-9067
Website: www.caregiving.org
E-mail: info@caregiving.org

National Association for Continence
P.O. Box 1019
Charleston, SC 29402-1019
Phone: 843-377-0900
Fax: 843-377-0905
Website: www.nafc.org
E-mail: memberservices@nafc.org

National Association of Professional Geriatric Care Managers
3275 W. Ina Rd.
Ste. 130
Tucson, AZ 85741-2198
Phone: 520-881-8008
Fax: 520-325-7925

National Down Syndrome Society
666 Broadway, 8th Fl.
New York, NY 10012
Fax: 212-979-2873
Toll-Free: 800-221-4602
Website: www.ndss.org
E-mail: info@ndss.org

National Gerontological Nursing Association
446 E. High St.
Ste. 10
Lexington, KY 40507
Phone: 859-977-7453
Fax: 859-271-0607
Toll-Free: 800-723-0560
Website: www.ngna.org

National Hospice and Palliative Care Organization / National Hospice Foundation
1731 King St.
Alexandria, VA 22314
Phone: 703-837-1500
Fax: 703-837-1233
Toll-Free: 800-658-8898
Website: www.nhpco.org
E-mail: nhpco_info@nhpco.org

National Organization for Rare Disorders
55 Kenosia Ave.
Danbury, CT 06810-1968
Phone: 203-744-0100
Fax: 203-798-2291
Toll-Free: 800-999-6673
Website: www.rarediseases.org
E-mail: orphan@rarediseases.org

National Palliative Care Research Center Brookdale Department of Geriatrics & Adult Development
Box 1070
Mt. Sinai School of Medicine
One Gustave L. Levy Place
New York, NY 10029
Phone: 212-241-7447
Fax: 212-241-5977
Website: www.npcrc.org
E-mail: npcrc@mssm.edu

National Parkinson Foundation
1501 N.W. 9th Ave.
Bob Hope Rd.
Miami, FL 33136-1494
Phone: 305-243-6666
Fax: 305-243-5595
Toll-Free: 800-327-4545
Website: www.parkinson.org
E-mail: contact@parkinson.org

National Rehabilitation Information Center
8400 Corporate Dr.
Ste. 500
Landover, MD 20785
Phone: 301-459-5900
Fax: 301-459-4263
Toll-Free: 800-346-2742
Website: www.naric.com
E-mail: naricinfo@
heitechservices.com

National Respite Network and Resource Center
Website: www.archrespite.org

National Senior Citizens Law Center
1444 Eye St. N.W.
Ste. 1100
Washington, DC 20005
Phone: 202-289-6976
Fax: 202-289-7224
Website: www.nsclc.org

National Stroke Association
9707 E. Easter Ln.
Ste. B
Centennial, CO 80112-3747
Phone: 303-649-9299
Fax: 303-649-1328
Toll-Free: 800-787-6537
Website: www.stroke.org
E-mail: info@stroke.org

Palliative Care Policy Center
2000 M St. N.W.
Ste. 400
Washington, DC 20036
Website: www.medicaring.org
E-mail: info@medicaring.org

Parkinson Alliance
P.O. Box 308
Kingston, NJ 08528-0308
Phone: 609-688-0870
Fax: 609-688-0875
Toll-Free: 800-579-8440
Website: www.
parkinsonalliance.org
E-mail: admin@
parkinsonalliance.org

Parkinson's Action Network (PAN)
1025 Vermont Ave. N.W.
Ste. 1120
Washington, DC 20005
Phone: 202-638-4101
Fax: 202-638-7257
Toll-Free: 800-850-4726
Website: www.parkinsonsaction.
org
E-mail: info@parkinsonsaction.
org

Parkinson's Disease Foundation
1359 Broadway
Ste. 1509
New York, NY 10018
Phone: 212-923-4700
Fax: 212-923-4778
Toll-Free: 800-457-6676
Website: www.pdf.org
E-mail: info@pdf.org

Parkinson's Institute and Clinical Center
675 Almanor Ave.
Sunnyvale, CA 94085
Phone: 408-734-2800
Fax: 408-734-8522
Toll-Free: 800-655-2273
Website: www.thepi.org
E-mail: info@thepi.org

PsychCentral
55 Pleasant St.
Ste. 207
Newburyport, MA 01950
Website: www.psychcentral.com
E-mail: talkback@psychcentral.com

Society Foundation for Health in Aging
The Empire State Building
40 Fulton St., 18th Fl.
New York, NY 10038
Phone: 212-308-1414
Fax: 212-832-8646
Toll-Free: 800-563-4916
Website: www.healthinaging.org

Society of Certified Senior Advisors
1325 S. Colorado Blvd.
Ste. B-300
Denver, CO 80222
Toll-Free: 800-653-1785

Visiting Nurses Associations of America
900 19th St. N.W.
Ste. 200
Washington, DC 20006
Phone: 202-384-1420
Fax: 202-384-1444
Website: www.vnaa.org
E-mail: vnaa@vnaa.org

Well Spouse Association
63 W. Main St.
Ste. H
Freehold, NJ 07728
Phone: 732-577-8899
Fax: 732-577-8644
Toll-Free: 800-838-0879
Website: www.wellspouse.org
E-mail: info@wellspouse.org

Index

Index

"Instruments to Detect Cognitive
   Impairment in Older Adults" (NIA)
   264n
insulin
   amylin 315
   diabetes 338
   memory loss treatment 88
   type 2 diabetes 96
insulin resistance
   amylin 315
   type 2 diabetes 97
insurance
   emergency bag 487
   Medicare Advantage 382
   presymptomatic test 168
   primary doctor 231
intellectual stimulation, cognitive
   health 339

J

JC virus, progressive multifocal
   leukoencephalopathy 205
Jell-O®, constipation 351
juvenile, Huntington disease 163

K

Klonopin®
   anti-anxiety drugs 290
   Lewy body dementia 155
kuru, transmissible spongiform
   encephalopathies 197

L

laboratory tests
   Creutzfeldt-Jakob disease 198
   described 244
   genealogy 164
late-onset Alzheimer disease
   defined 513
   overview 80
   tissue culture 306
LBD *see* Lewy body dementia
LDL *see* low-density lipoprotein
levodopa, pain 176
Lewy bodies
   dementia overview 145–57
   described 26
   Parkinson disease 178

"Lewy Body Dementia" (NIH) 145n
Lewy body dementia (LBD)
   alpha-synuclein 248
   defined 513
   neurodegenerative disorders 22
   overview 145–57
Lewy Body Dementia Association,
   contact 524
life insurance
   financial abuse 456
   loss of employment 168
   see also insurance coverage
lifestyle factors
   Alzheimer disease 54
   late-onset Alzheimer 308
life-threatening illness, hospice
   services 504
light therapy, overview 297–8
living will
   legal documents 399
   tabulated *408*
lithium, tranquilizers 169
lobes
   frontotemporal disorders 24
   overview 5–6
   short-term memory 159
"Long-Distance Caregiving-a Family
   Affair" (NIA) 419n
"Long-Distance Caregiving-Getting
   Started" (NIA) 419n
long-term care insurance, nursing
   homes 477
lorazepam
   anti-anxiety drugs 290
   delirium 214
Lou Gehrig disease *see* amyotrophic
   lateral sclerosis
low-density lipoprotein (LDL),
   atherosclerosis 33
Lunesta® (eszopiclone), sleep aids 290

M

mad cow disease *see* bovine
   spongiform encephalopathy
"Magnetic Resonance Imaging (MRI)"
   (NIBIB) 271n
magnetic resonance imaging (MRI)
   daydreaming 312